東京喰種 TOKYO GHOUL

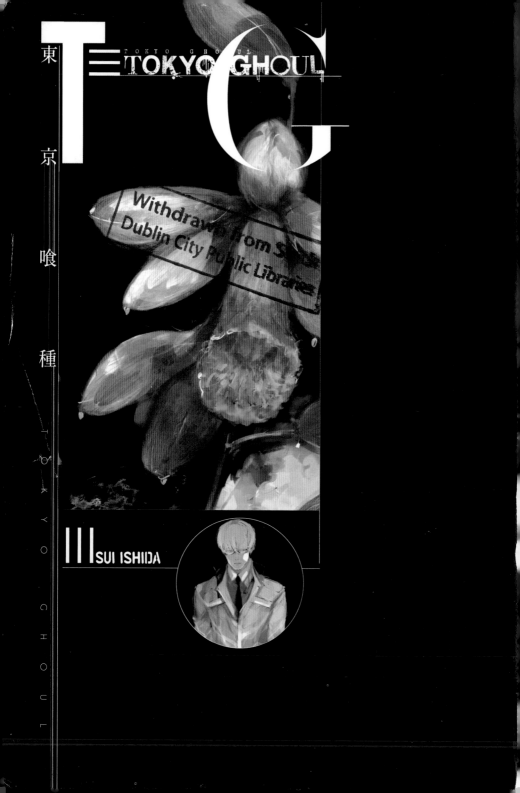

東京喰種 TOKYO GHOUL

III SUI ISHIDA

TOKYO GHOUL

SEN TAKA-TSUKI/ ETO

高槻泉 / エト（タカツキセン）

Novelist

(Aogiri Tree) One-Eyed Owl

Size: 151 cm 44 kg   FEET 22.5 CM

EYE-PATCH GHOUL/ CENTI-PEDE

眼帯の喰種（ガンタイノグール）/ ムカデ

BLOOD-TYPE: AB
Size: 169.5 cm 58 kg   FEET 25.5 CM

Rc Type: **Rinkaku**

Unique States: **Kakuja (incomplete)**

Presumed to have cannibalized numerous Ghouls, judging from the condition of his Kagune.

According to the **CCG:**
During the **20th Ward/One-Eyed Owl Eradication Operation,** he wounded **Senior Investigator Amon** and caused great damage.

Eradicated by **Special Investigator Arima** at underground V14 route during said operation.

SUI ISHIDA was born in Fukuoka, Japan. He is the author of *Tokyo Ghoul* and several *Tokyo Ghoul* one-shots, including one that won him second place in the *Weekly Young Jump* 113th Grand Prix award in 2010. *Tokyo Ghoul* began serialization in *Weekly Young Jump* in 2011 and was adapted into an anime series in 2014.

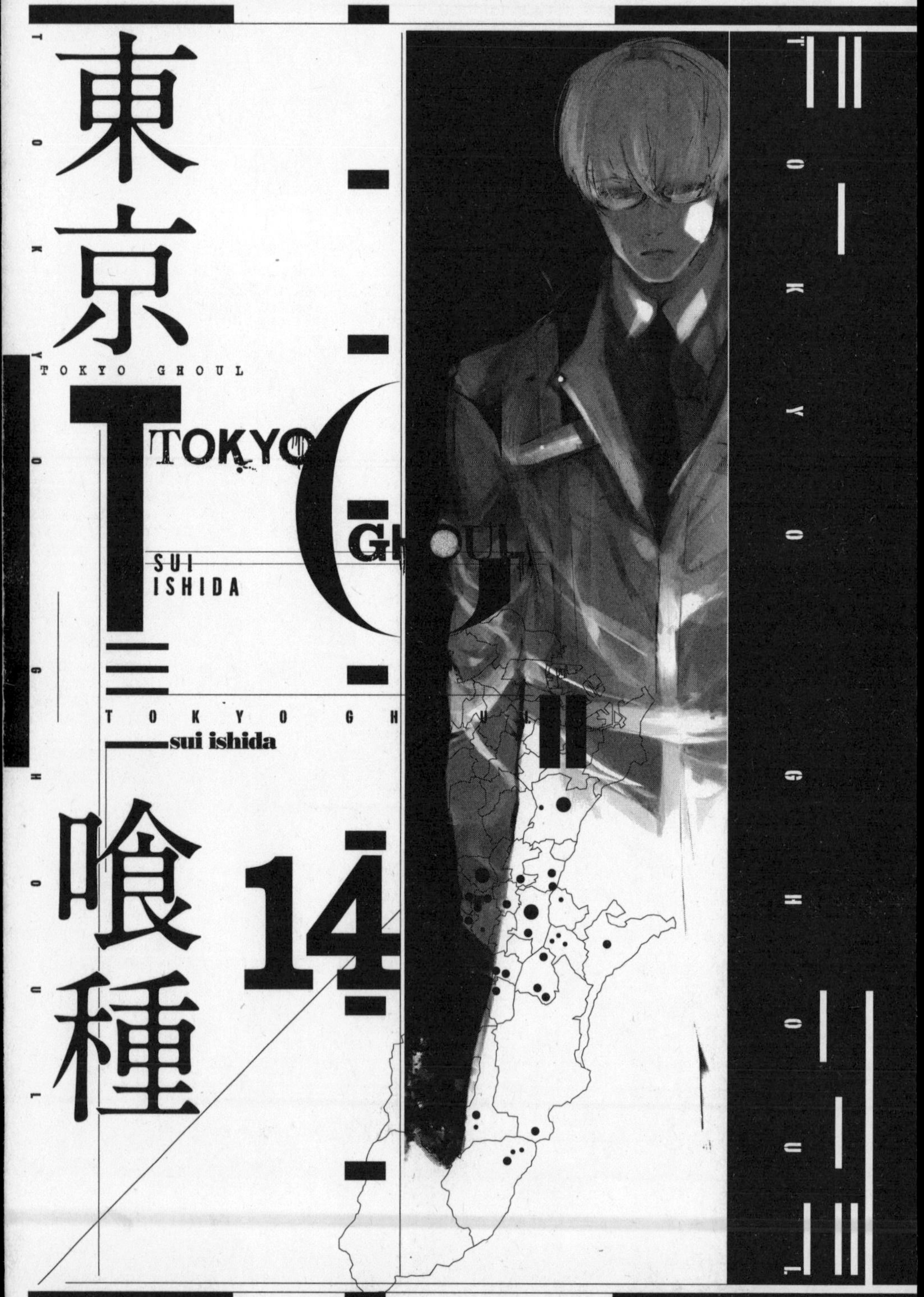
東京喰種
TOKYO GHOUL
TOKYO GHOUL
SUI ISHIDA
TOKYO GHOUL
sui ishida
14
TOKYO GHOUL
TOKYO GHOUL

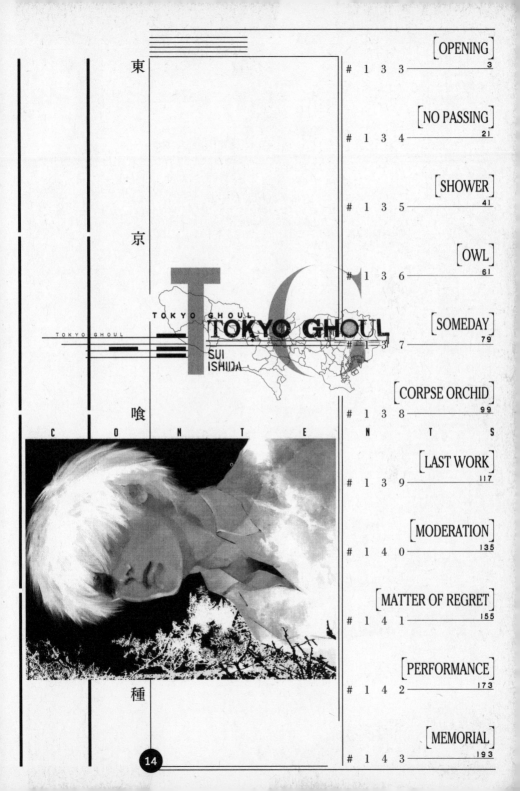

東
京
喰
種

TOKYO GHOUL
TOKYO GHOUL
SUI ISHIDA

C O N T E N T S

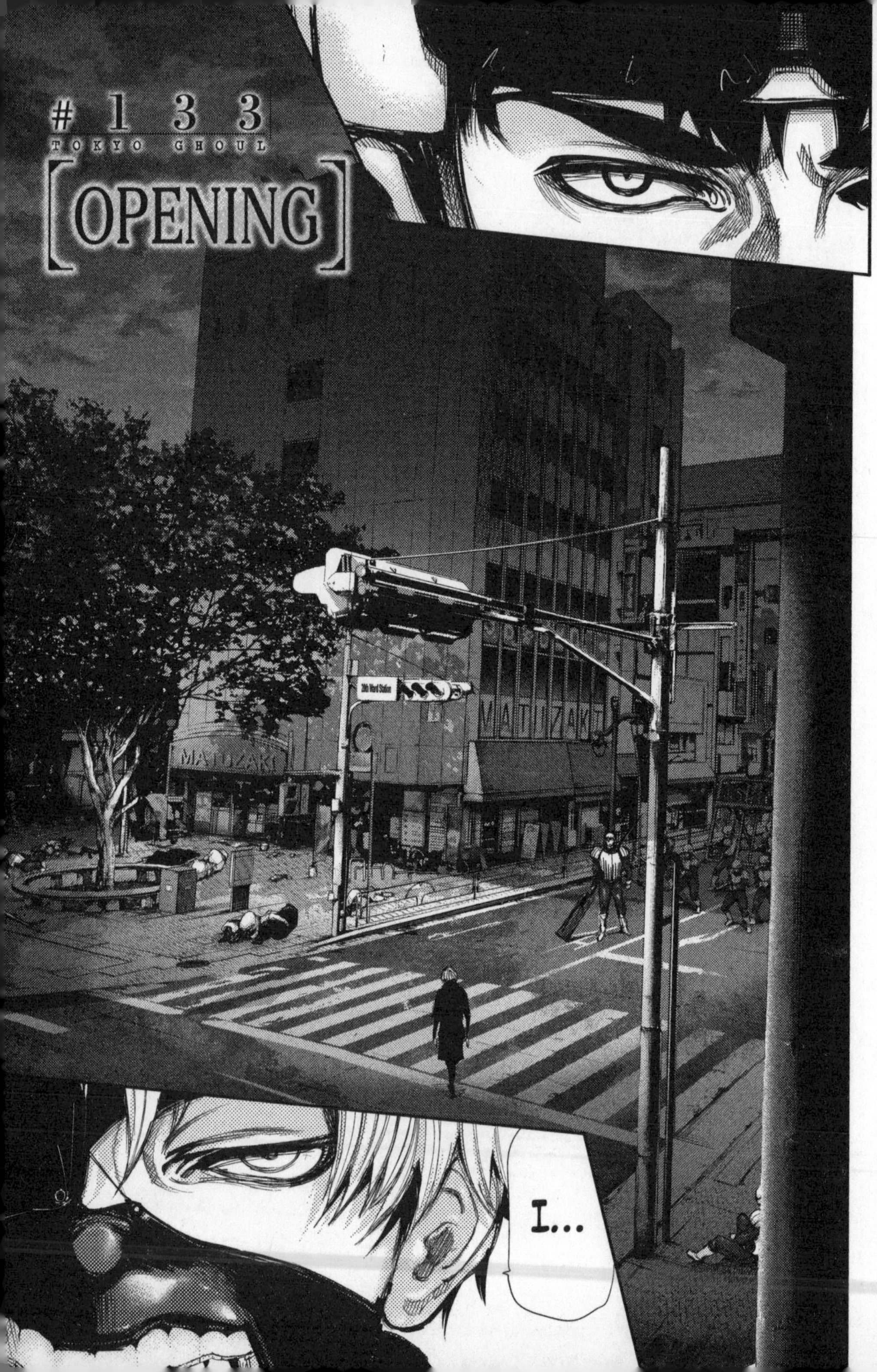
#133
TOKYO GHOUL
[OPENING]
20th Ward Station
MATUZAKI
I...

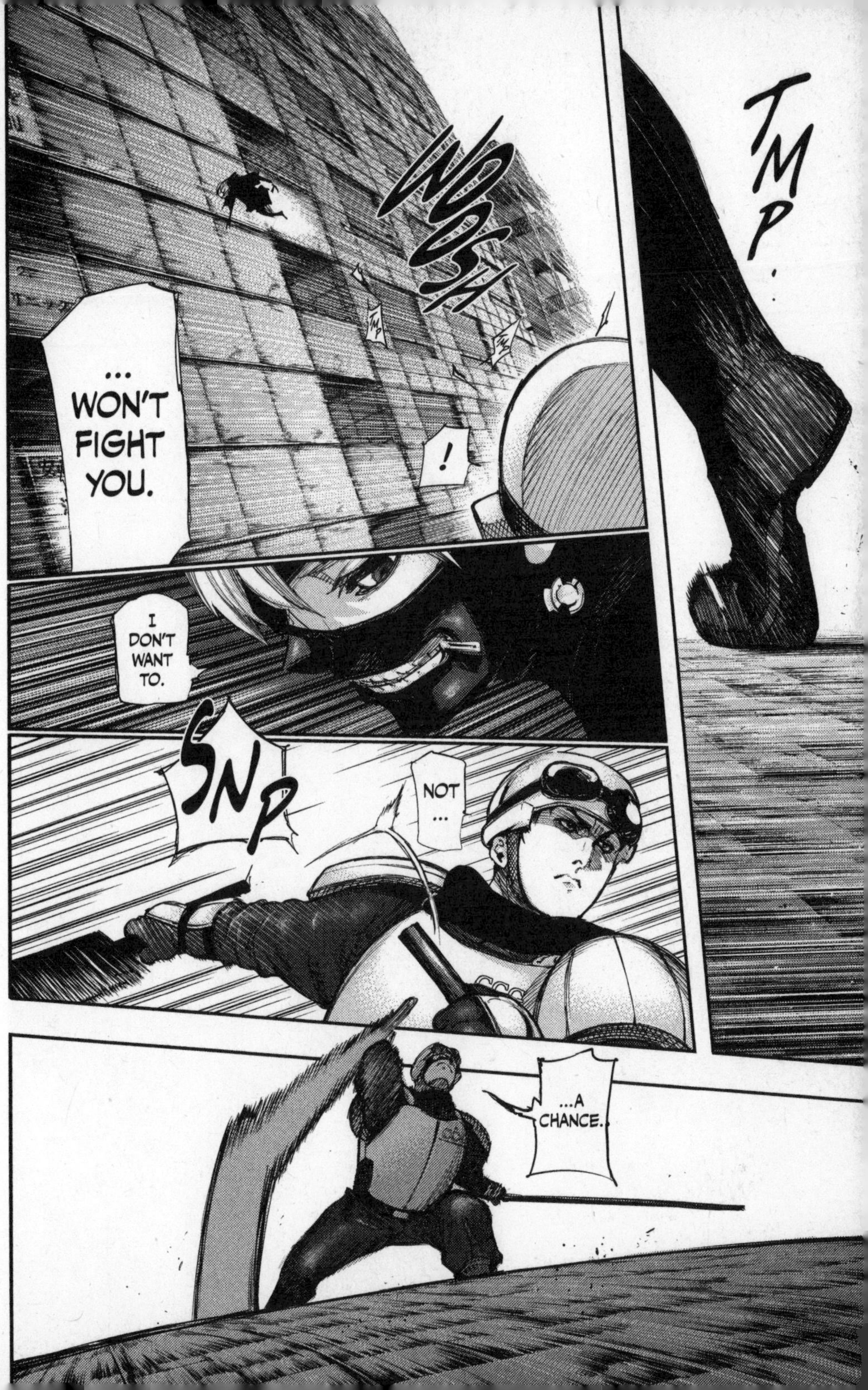
TMP.
WOOSH
TMP
TMP
!
... WON'T FIGHT YOU.
I DON'T WANT TO.
NOT ...
SNP
...A CHANCE.

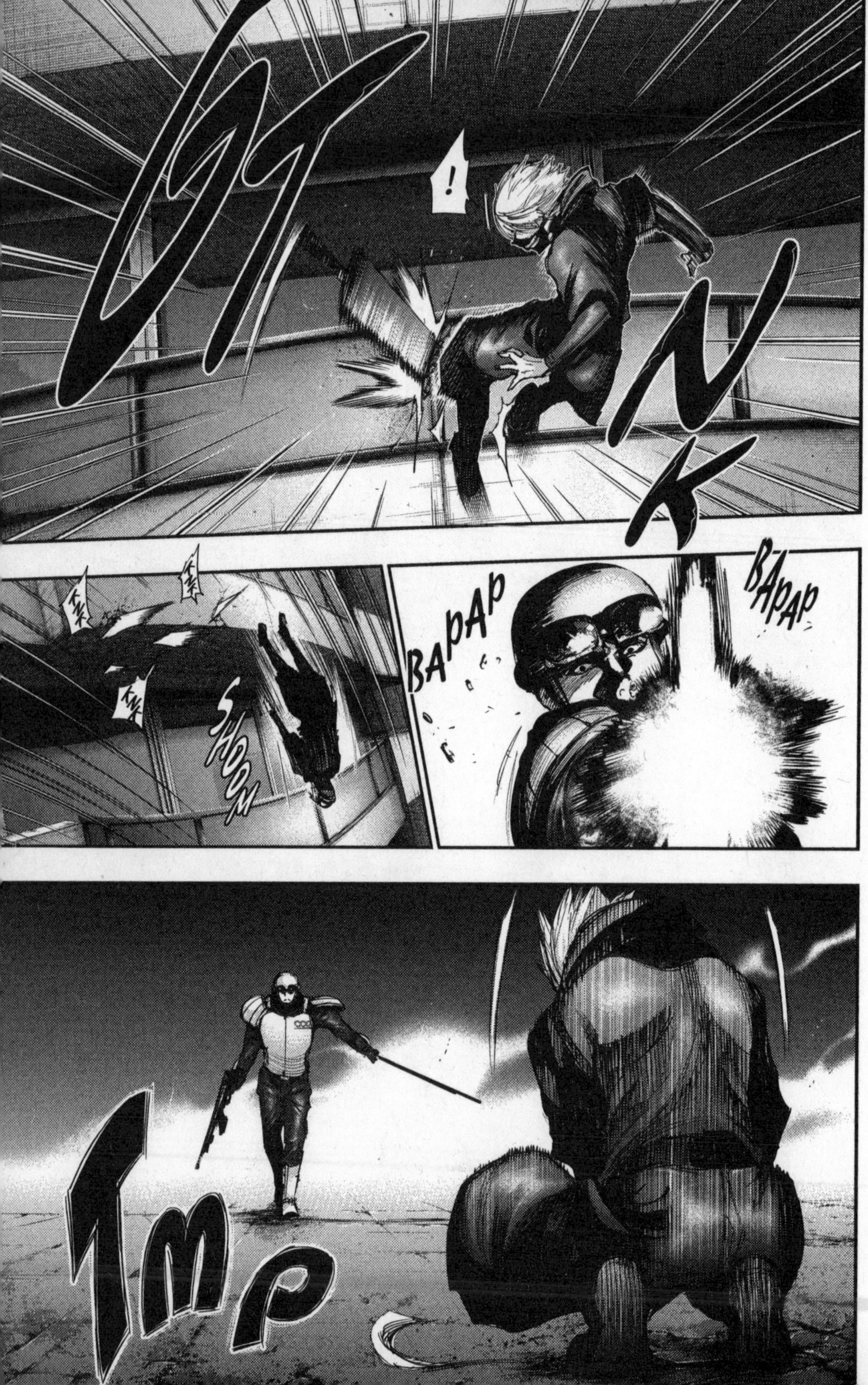
!
BAPAP
BAPAP
KNK
KNK
KNK
SHOOM
TMP

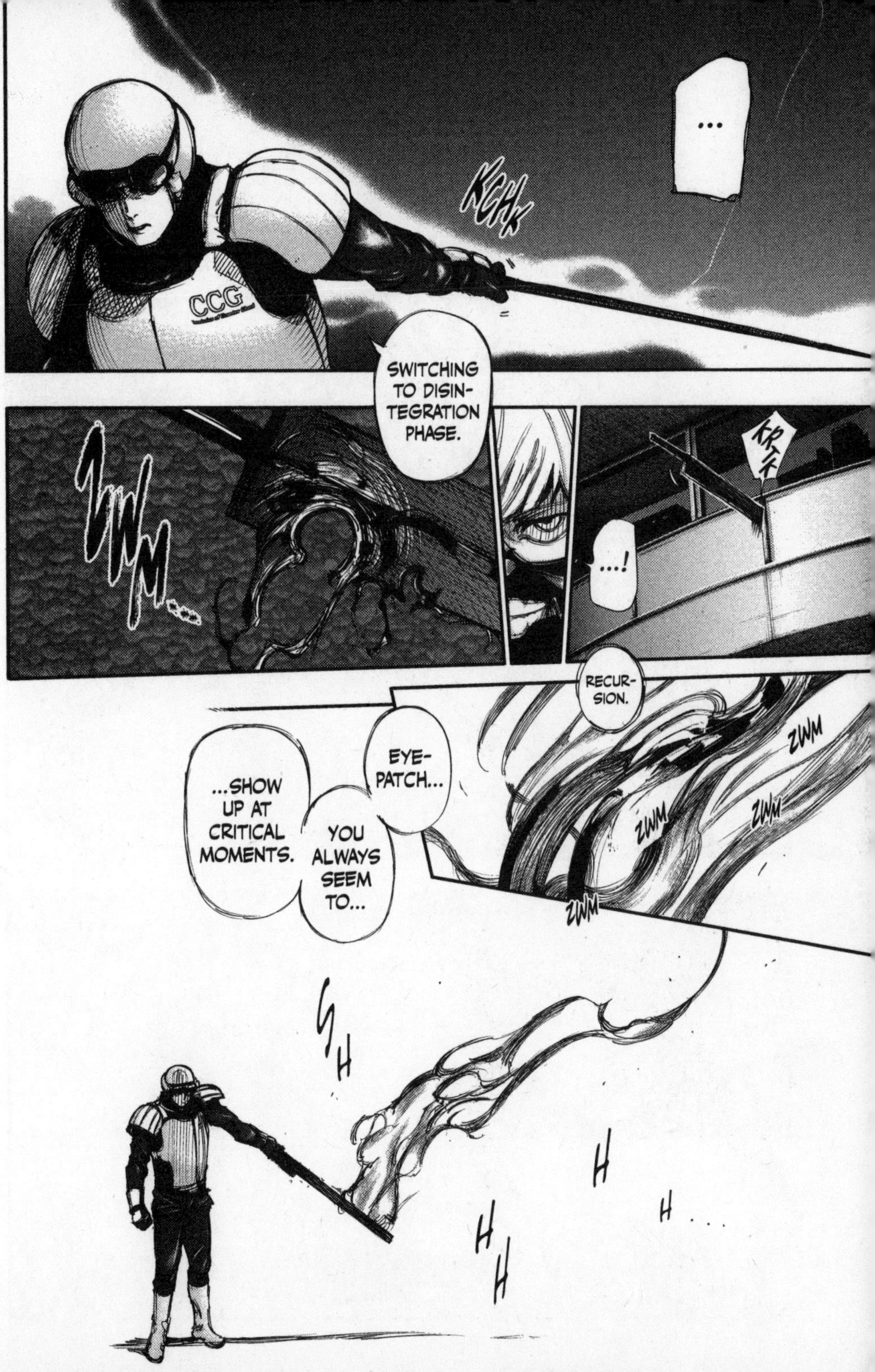
...
KCHK
SWITCHING TO DISIN-TEGRATION PHASE.
KRTK
...!
ZWM...
RECUR-SION.
ZWM
ZWM
ZWM
ZWM
EYE-PATCH...
YOU ALWAYS SEEM TO...
...SHOW UP AT CRITICAL MOMENTS.
SHHHHH...

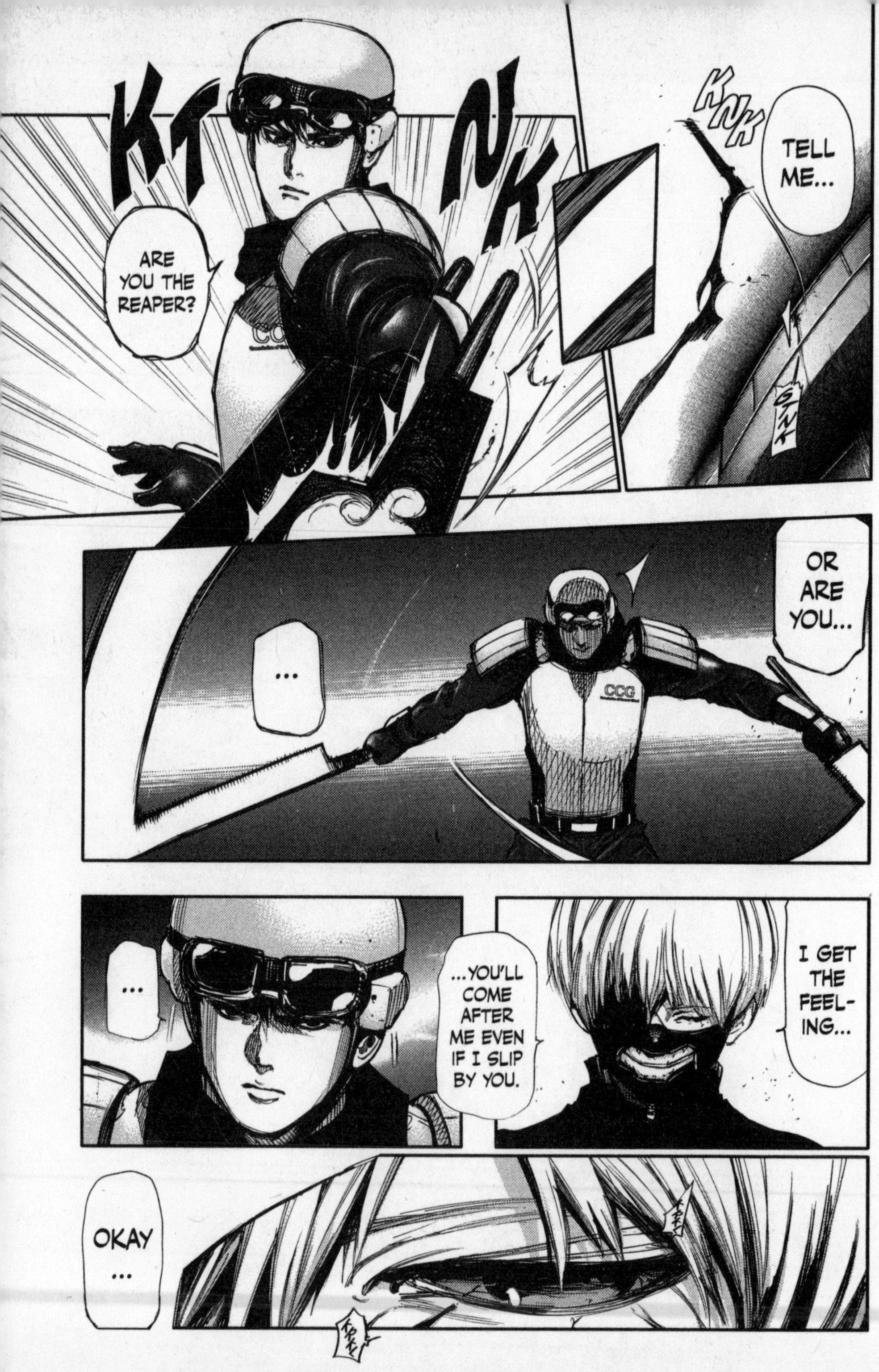
KNK
TELL ME...
ARE YOU THE REAPER?
OR ARE YOU...
...
I GET THE FEEL-ING...
...YOU'LL COME AFTER ME EVEN IF I SLIP BY YOU.
...
OKAY ...

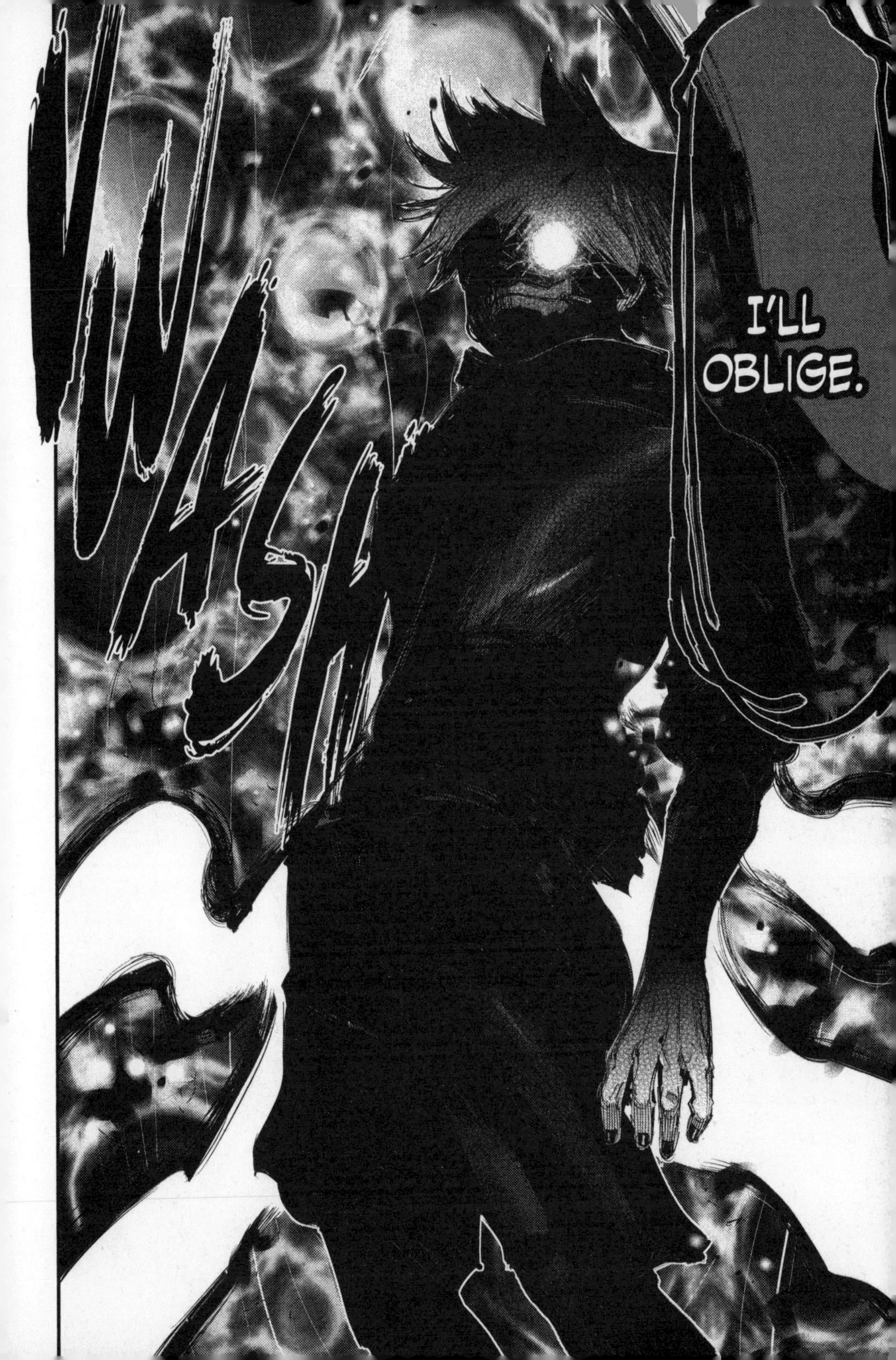
I'LL OBLIGE.

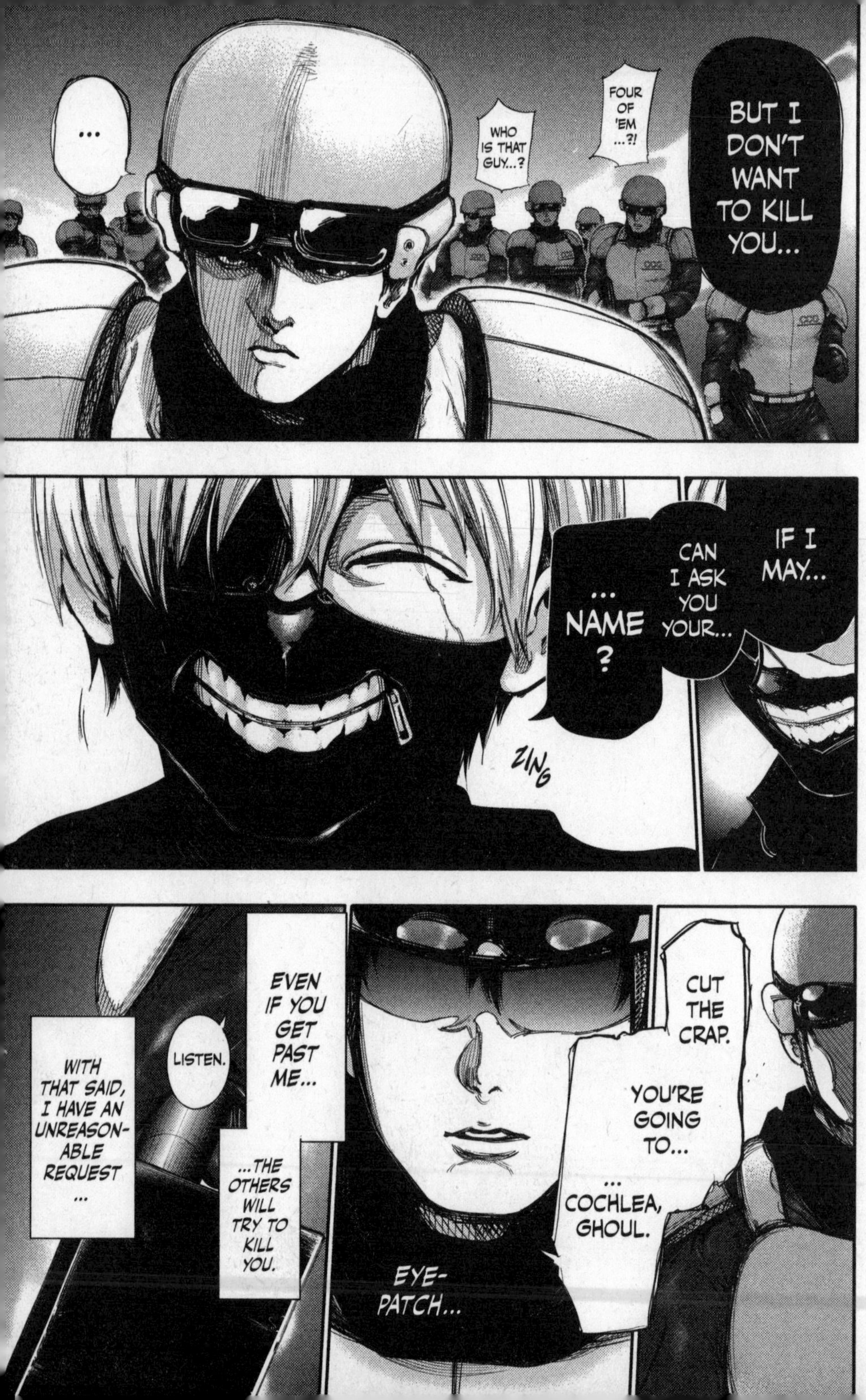

BUT I DON'T WANT TO KILL YOU...
FOUR OF 'EM ...?!
WHO IS THAT GUY...?
...
IF I MAY...
CAN I ASK YOU YOUR...
... NAME ?
ZING
CUT THE CRAP.
YOU'RE GOING TO...
... COCHLEA, GHOUL.
EYE-PATCH...
EVEN IF YOU GET PAST ME...
...THE OTHERS WILL TRY TO KILL YOU.
LISTEN.
WITH THAT SAID, I HAVE AN UNREASON-ABLE REQUEST ...

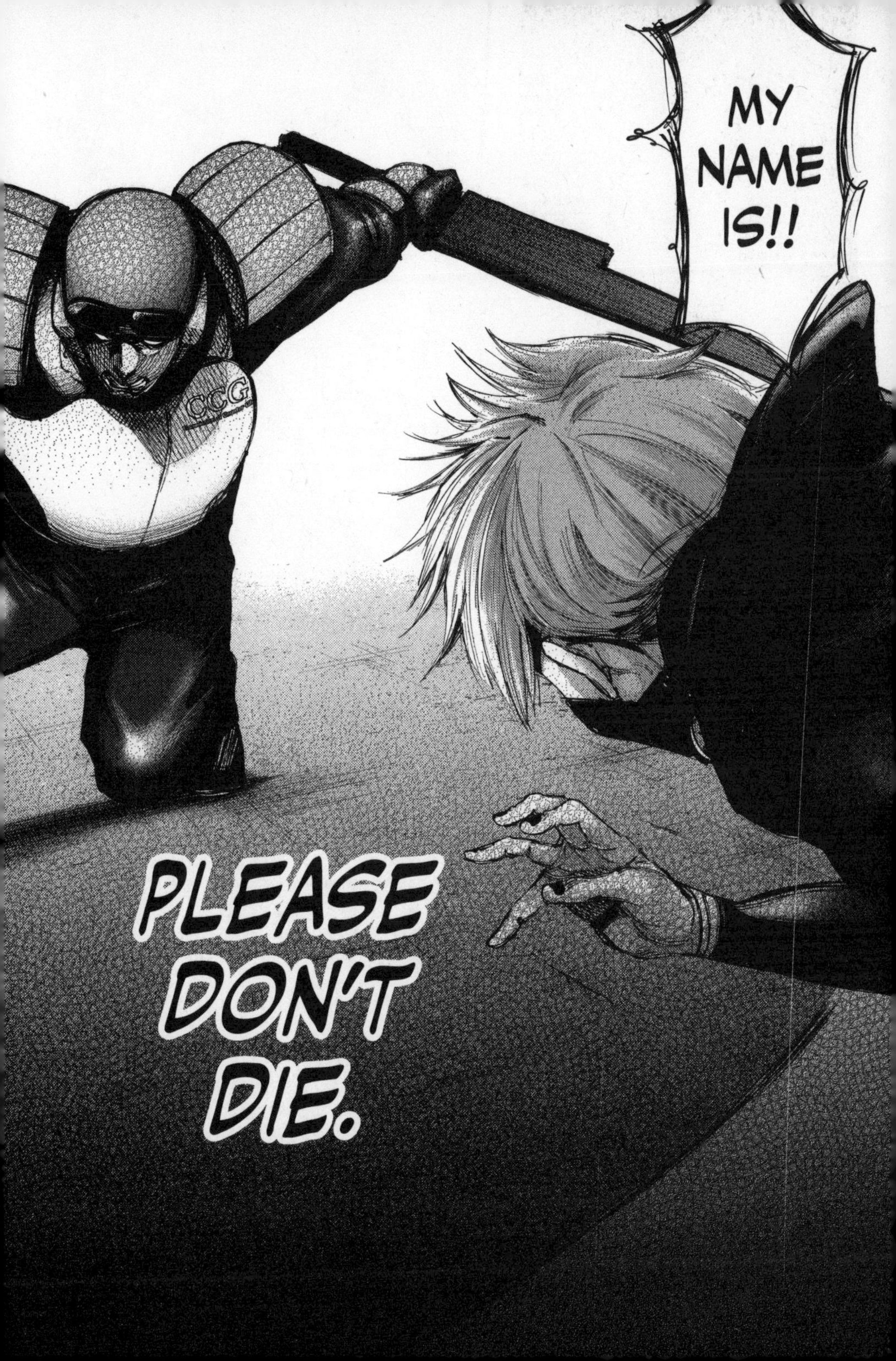
MY NAME IS!!
CCG
PLEASE DON'T DIE.

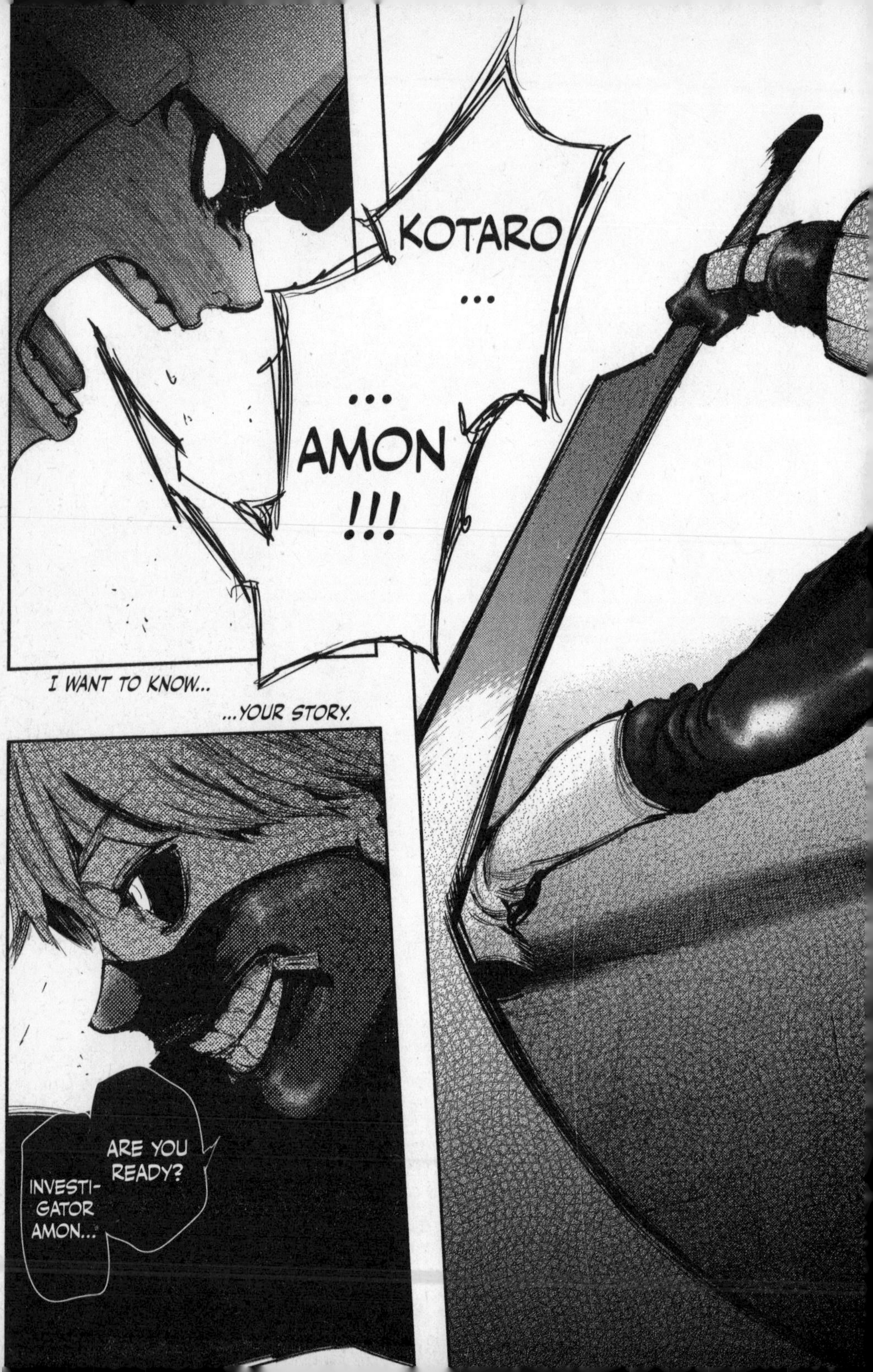
KOTARO ... ... AMON !!!
I WANT TO KNOW...
...YOUR STORY.
ARE YOU READY?
INVESTI-GATOR AMON...

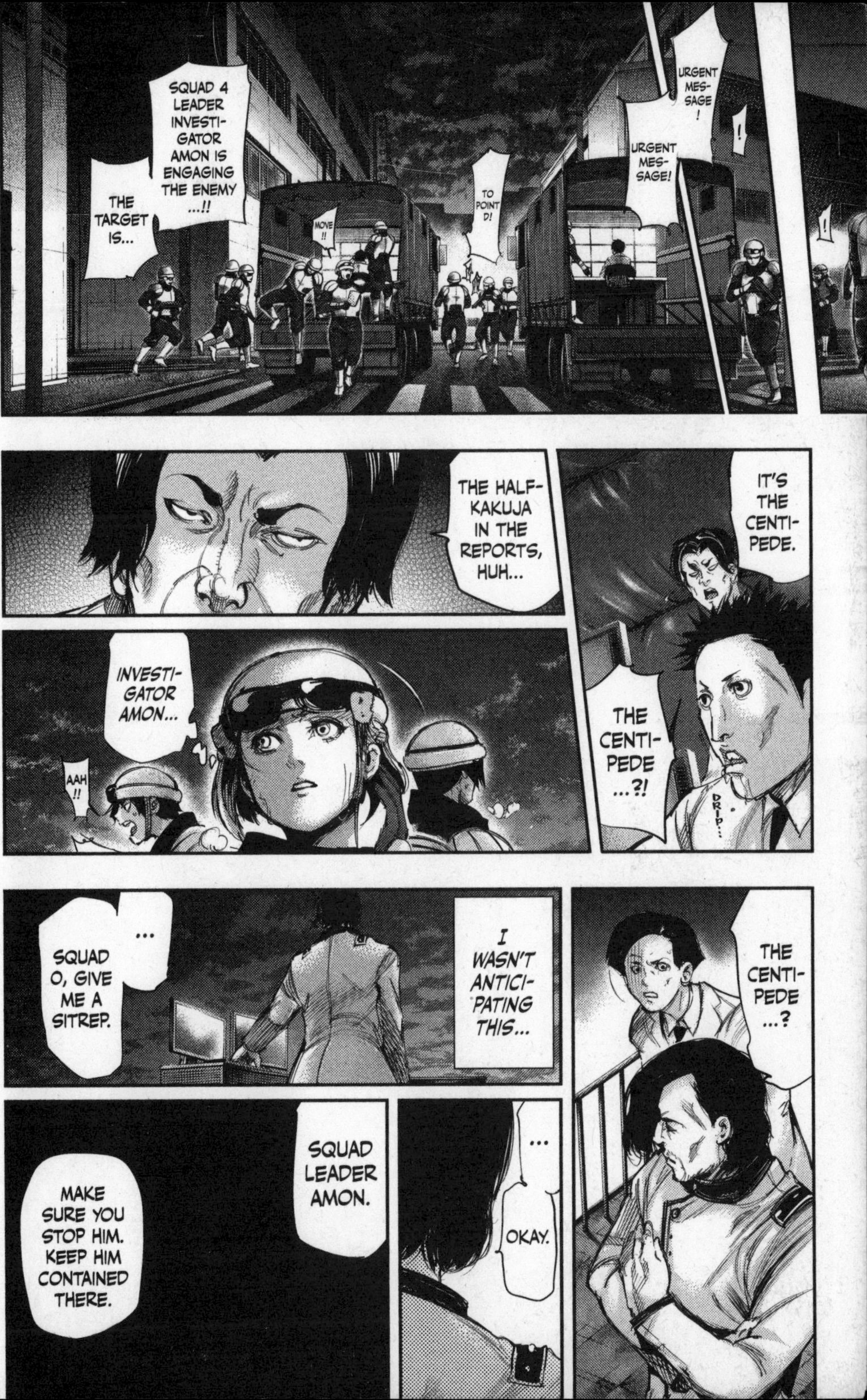
URGENT MES-SAGE!
!
URGENT MES-SAGE!
!
TO POINT D!
SQUAD 4 LEADER INVESTI-GATOR AMON IS ENGAGING THE ENEMY ...!!
MOVE !!
THE TARGET IS...
IT'S THE CENTI-PEDE.
THE CENTI-PEDE ...?!
DRIP...
THE HALF-KAKUJA IN THE REPORTS, HUH...
INVESTI-GATOR AMON...
AAH !!
THE CENTI-PEDE ...?
I WASN'T ANTICI-PATING THIS...
...
SQUAD 0, GIVE ME A SITREP.
...
OKAY.
SQUAD LEADER AMON.
MAKE SURE YOU STOP HIM. KEEP HIM CONTAINED THERE.

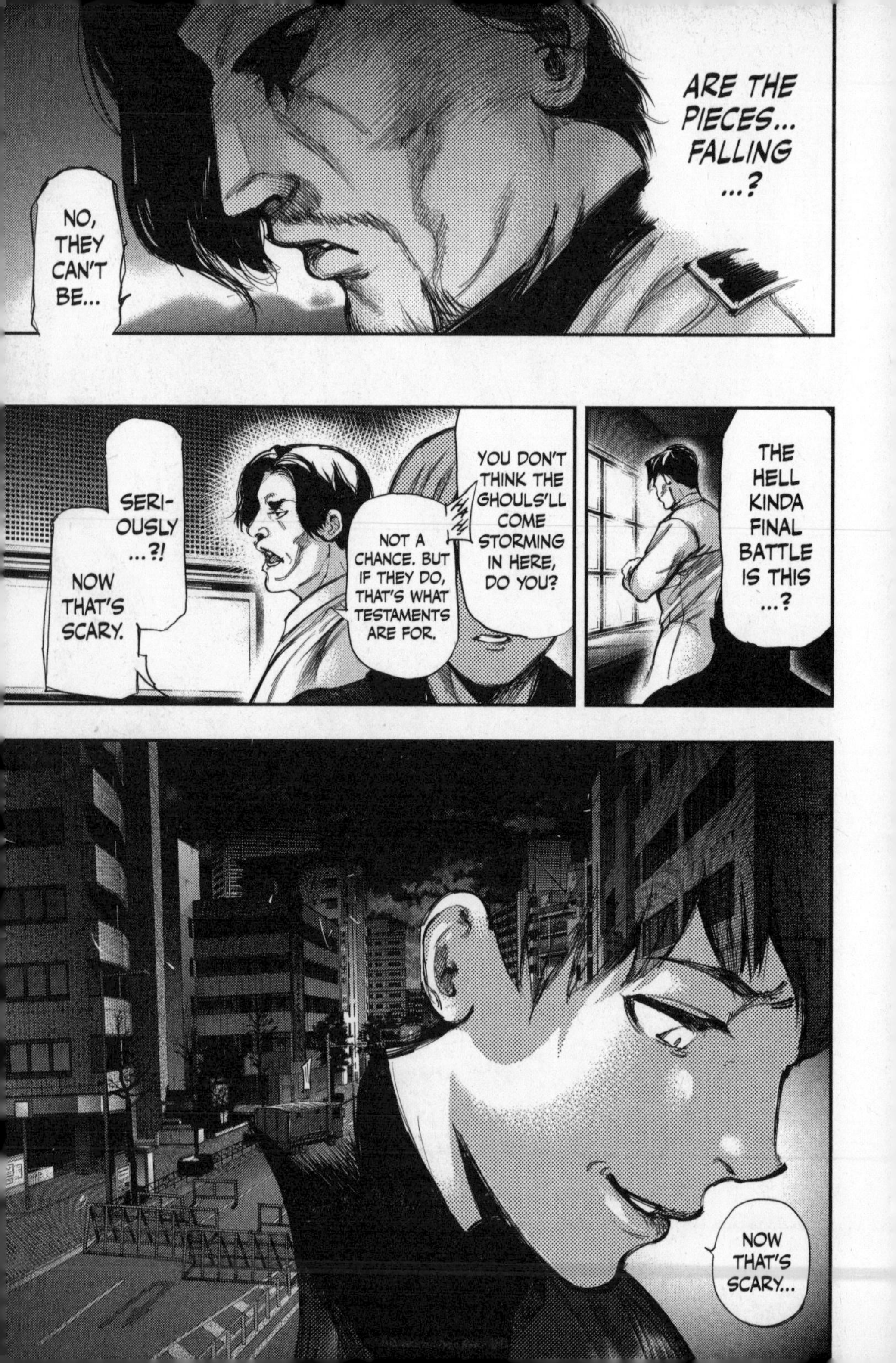
ARE THE PIECES... FALLING ...?
NO, THEY CAN'T BE...
THE HELL KINDA FINAL BATTLE IS THIS ...?
YOU DON'T THINK THE GHOULS'LL COME STORMING IN HERE, DO YOU?
NOT A CHANCE. BUT IF THEY DO, THAT'S WHAT TESTAMENTS ARE FOR.
SERIOUSLY ...?!
NOW THAT'S SCARY.
NOW THAT'S SCARY...

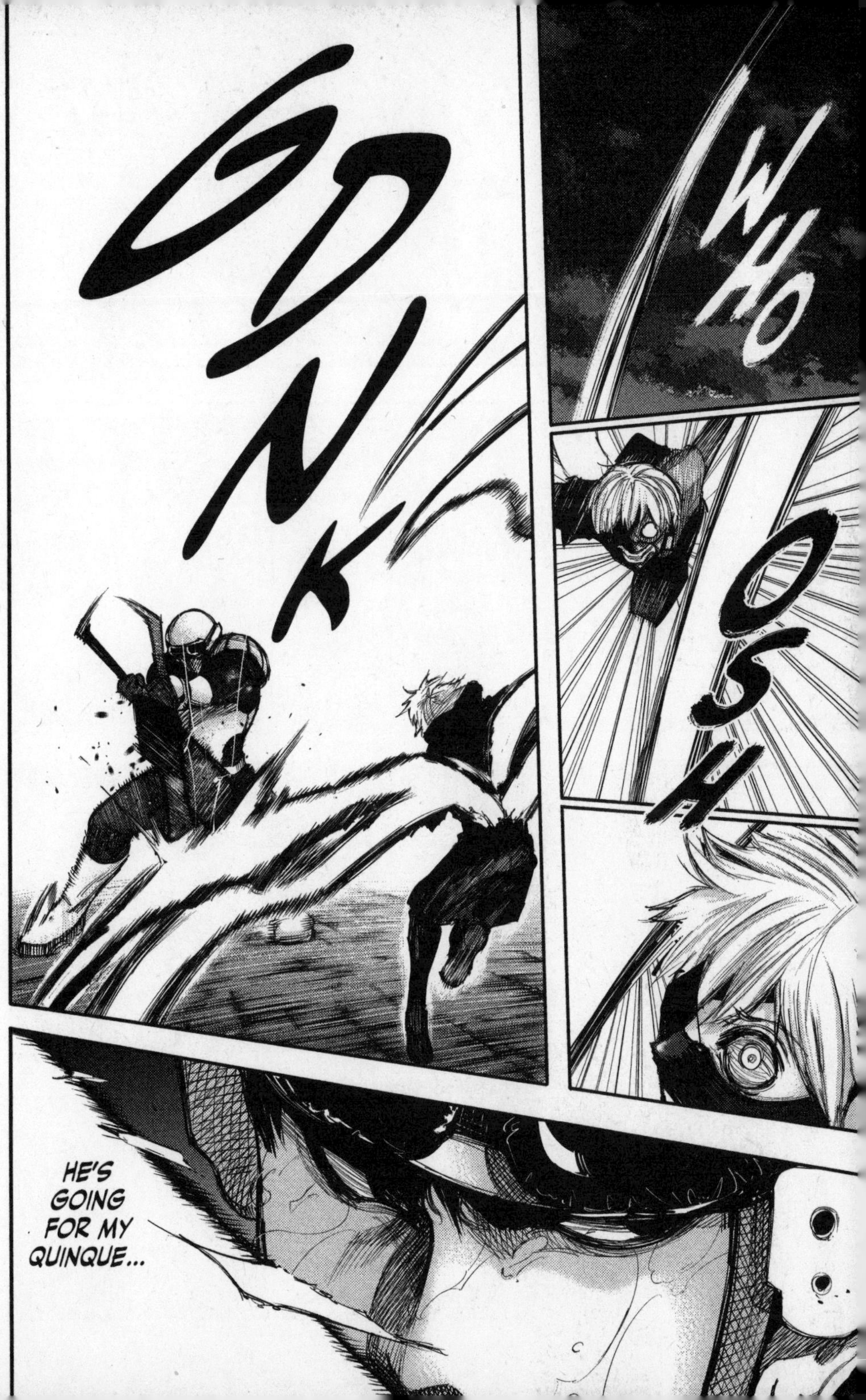
WHOOSH
GONK
HE'S GOING FOR MY QUINQUE...

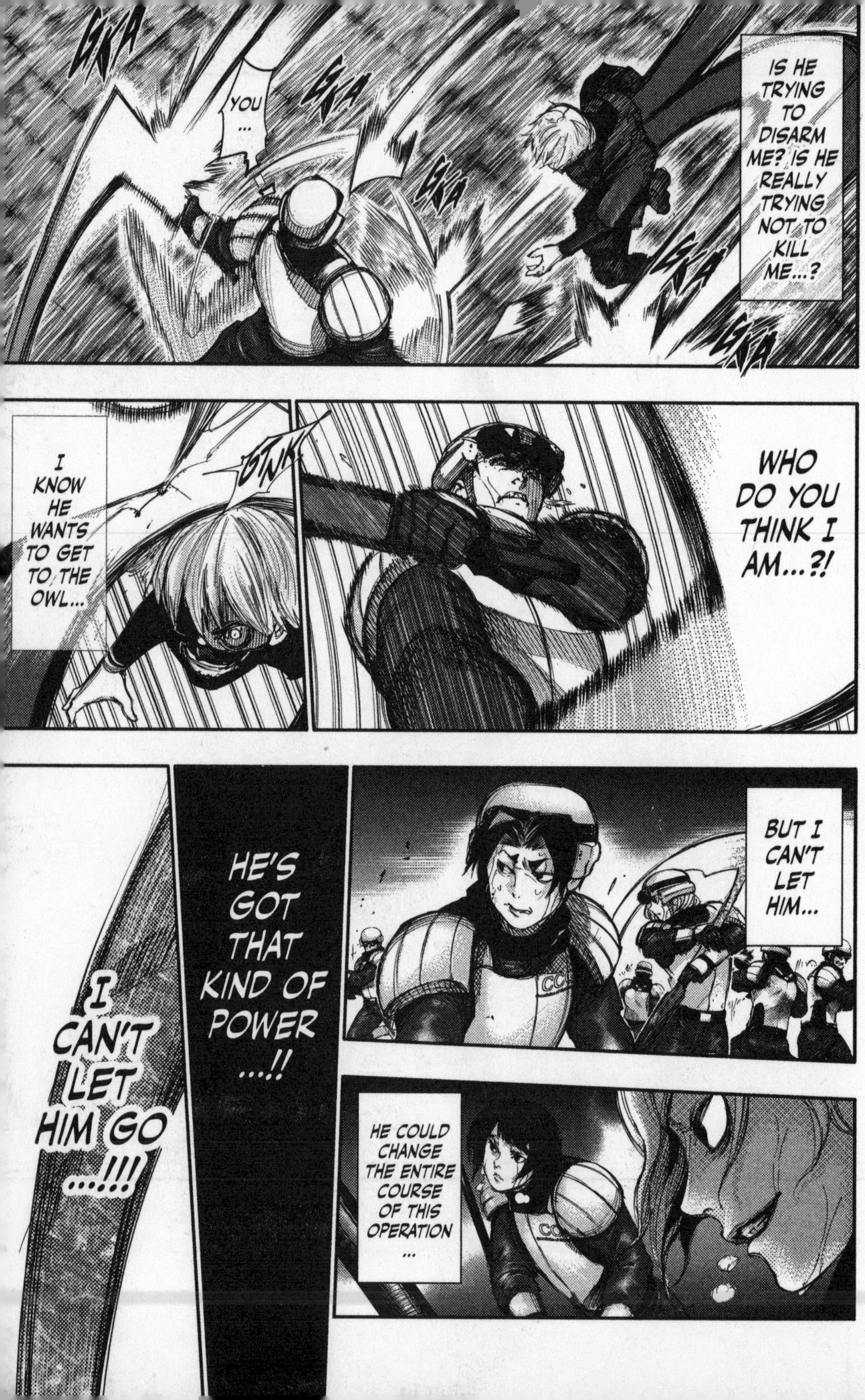
IS HE TRYING TO DISARM ME? IS HE REALLY TRYING NOT TO KILL ME...?
GKA
GKA
GKA
YOU ...
WHO DO YOU THINK I AM...?!
GINK
I KNOW HE WANTS TO GET TO THE OWL...
BUT I CAN'T LET HIM...
HE COULD CHANGE THE ENTIRE COURSE OF THIS OPERATION ...
HE'S GOT THAT KIND OF POWER ...!!
I CAN'T LET HIM GO ...!!!

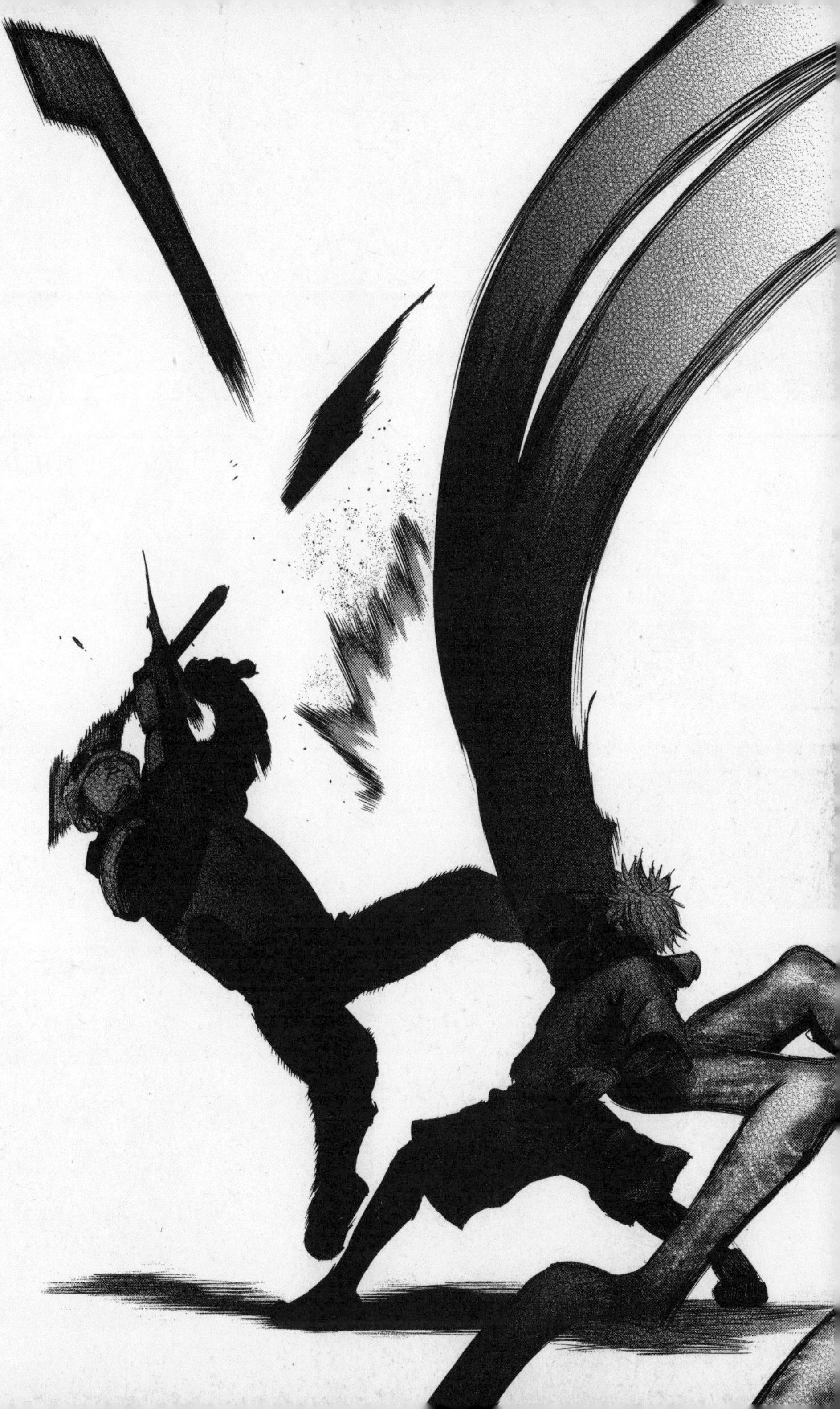

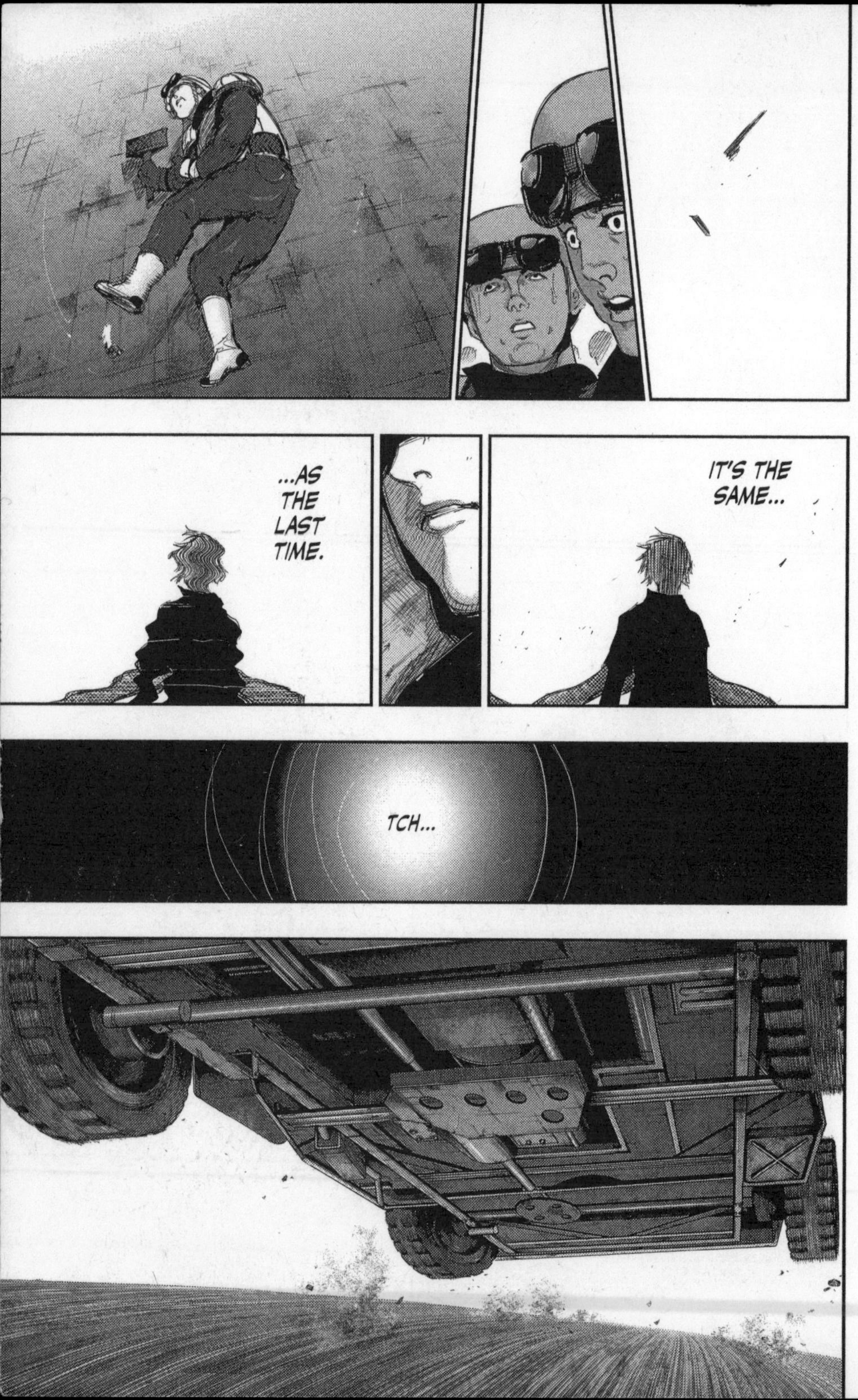
IT'S THE SAME...
...AS THE LAST TIME.
TCH...

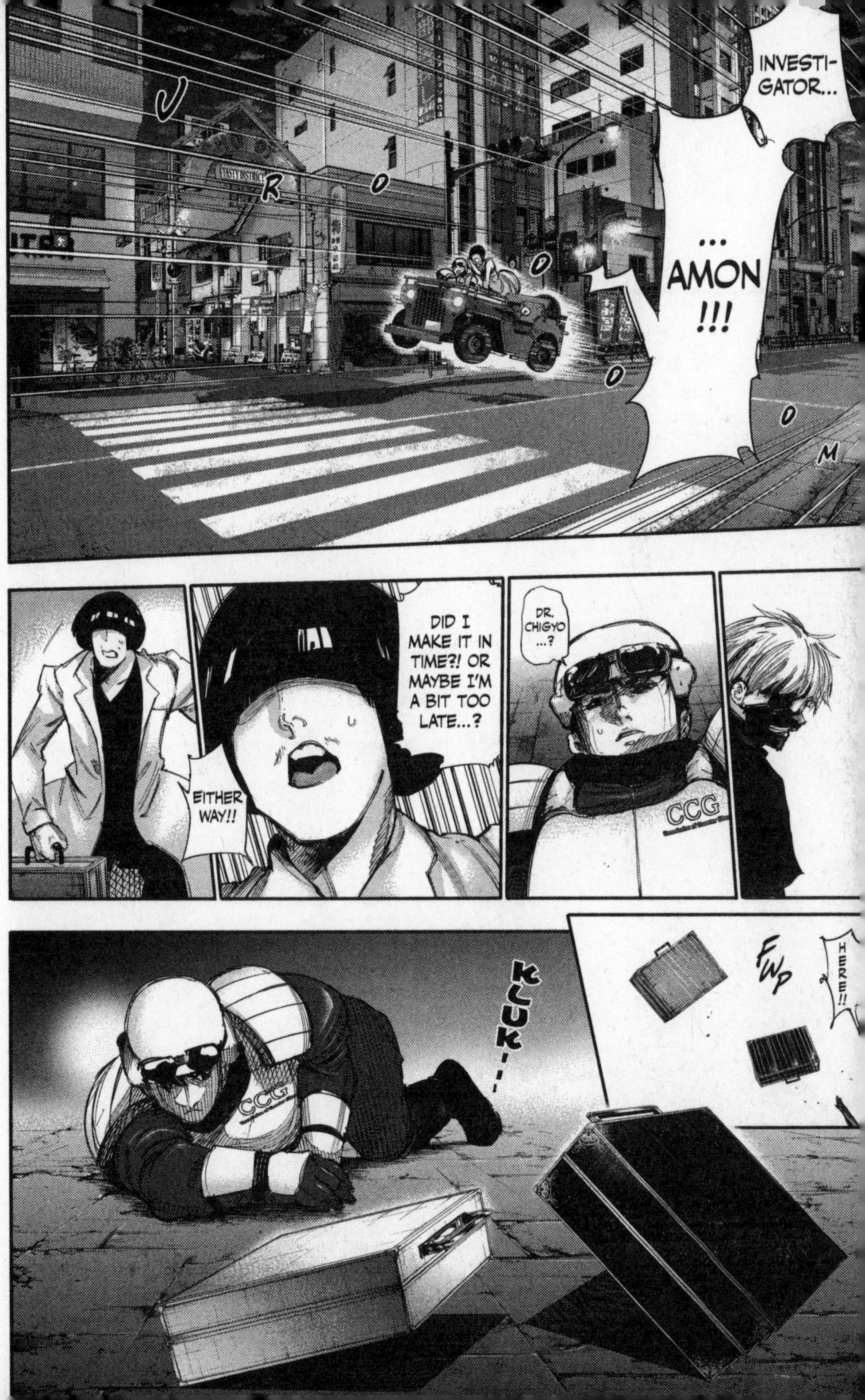
INVESTI-
GATOR...
...AMON!!!
VROOOOM
DR. CHIGYO ...?
DID I MAKE IT IN TIME?! OR MAYBE I'M A BIT TOO LATE...?
EITHER WAY!!
CCG
HERE!!
FWP
KLUK...
CCG

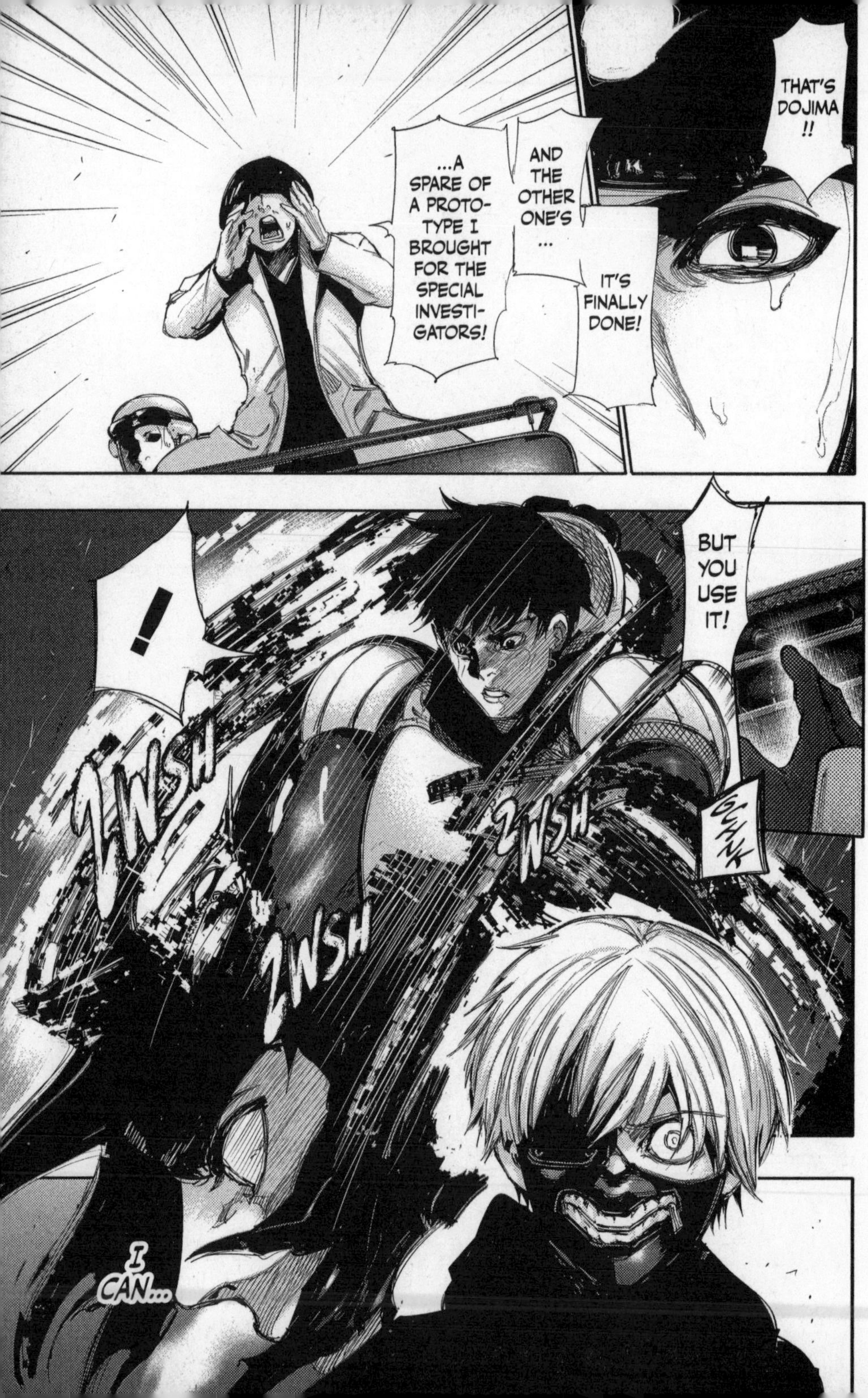
THAT'S DOJIMA!!
AND THE OTHER ONE'S...
IT'S FINALLY DONE!
...A SPARE OF A PROTOTYPE I BROUGHT FOR THE SPECIAL INVESTIGATORS!
BUT YOU USE IT!
GCHNK
!
ZWSH
ZWSH
ZWSH
I CAN...

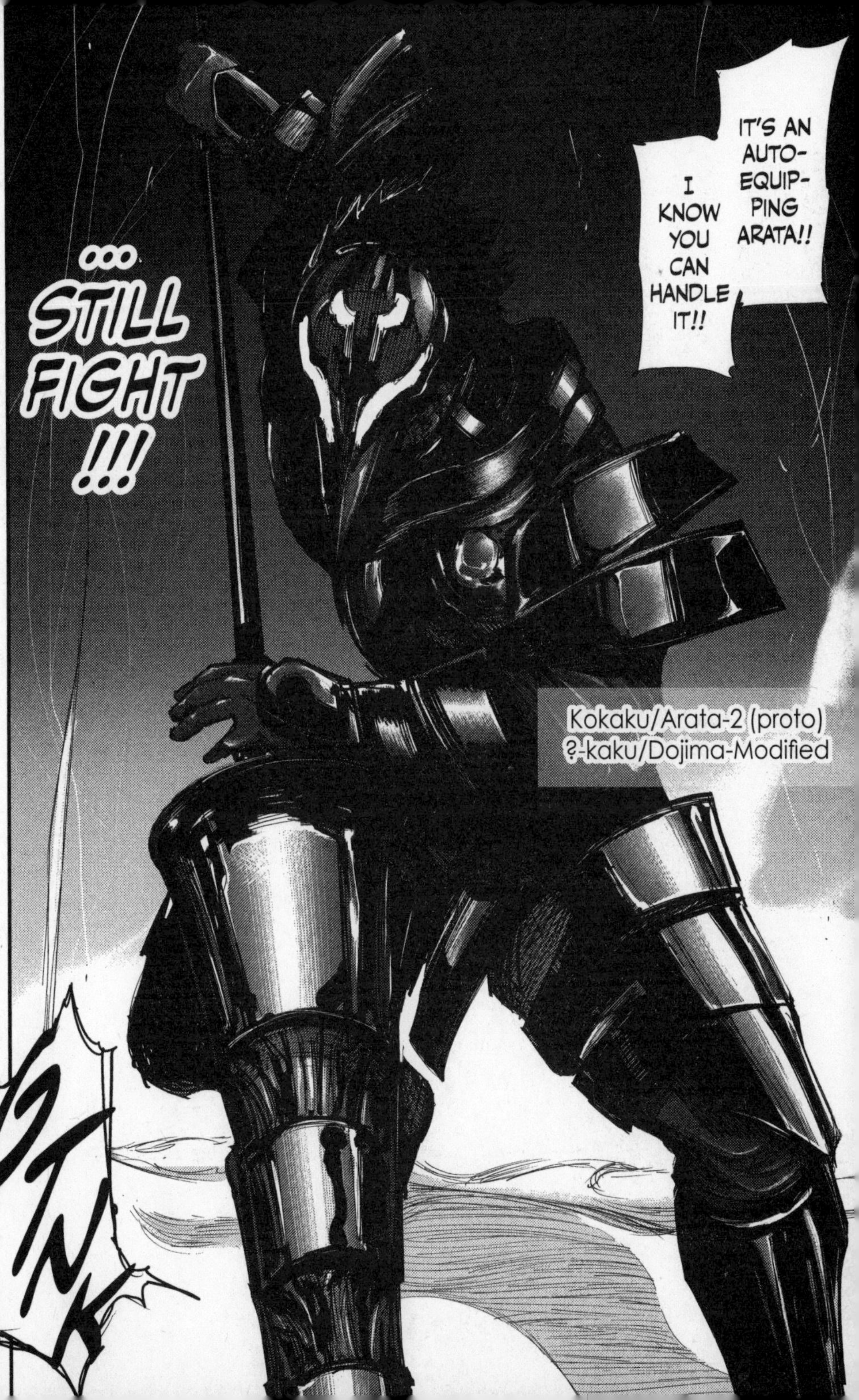
IT'S AN AUTO-EQUIPPING ARATA!!
I KNOW YOU CAN HANDLE IT!!
...STILL FIGHT!!!
Kokaku/Arata-2 (proto)
?-kaku/Dojima-Modified

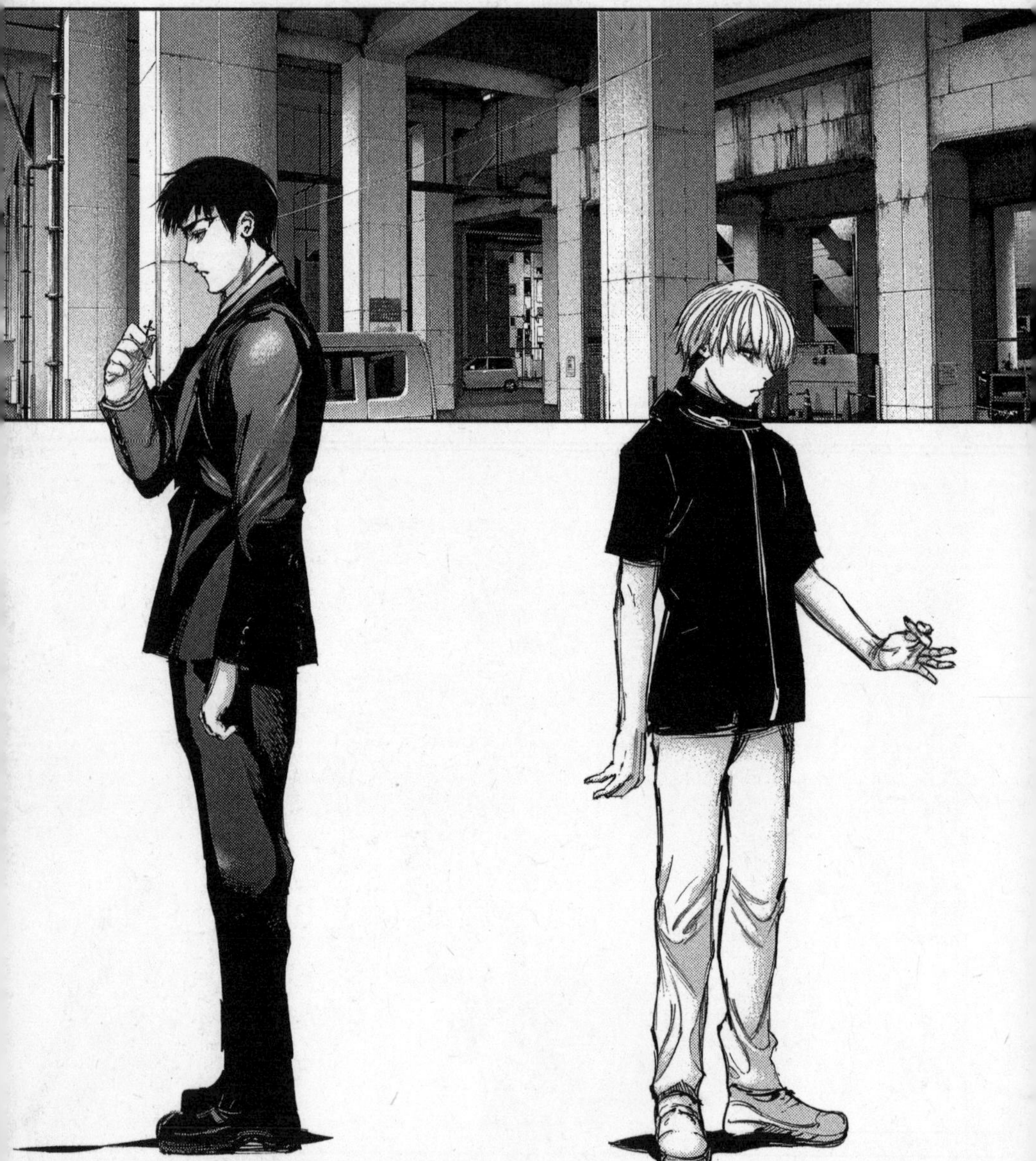

#134 [NO PASSING]

TOKYO GHOUL

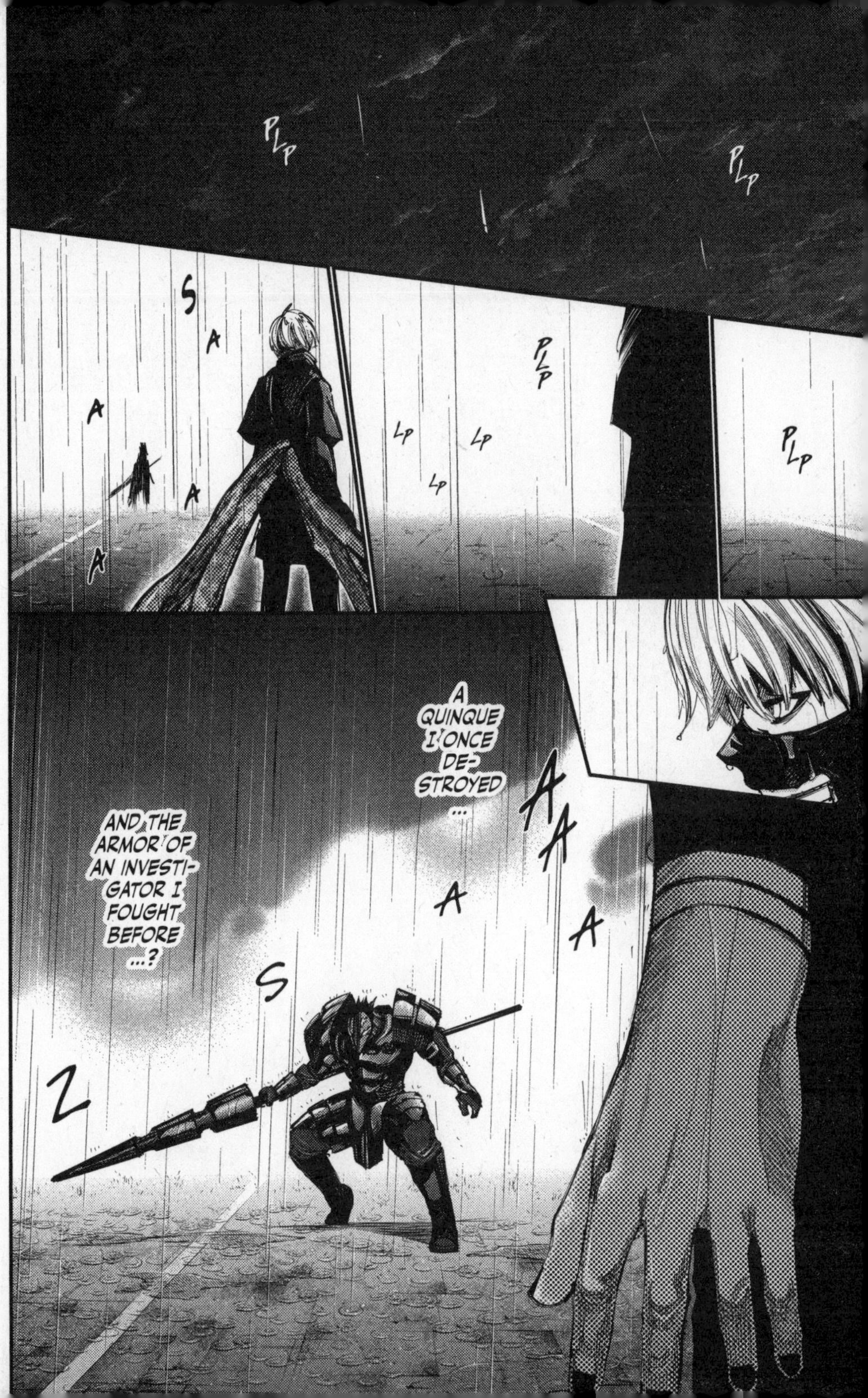
PLP
PLP
PLP
PLP
LP
LP
LP
SAAAA
AAAA
A QUINQUE I ONCE DE-STROYED...
AND THE ARMOR OF AN INVESTI-GATOR I FOUGHT BEFORE...?
ZS

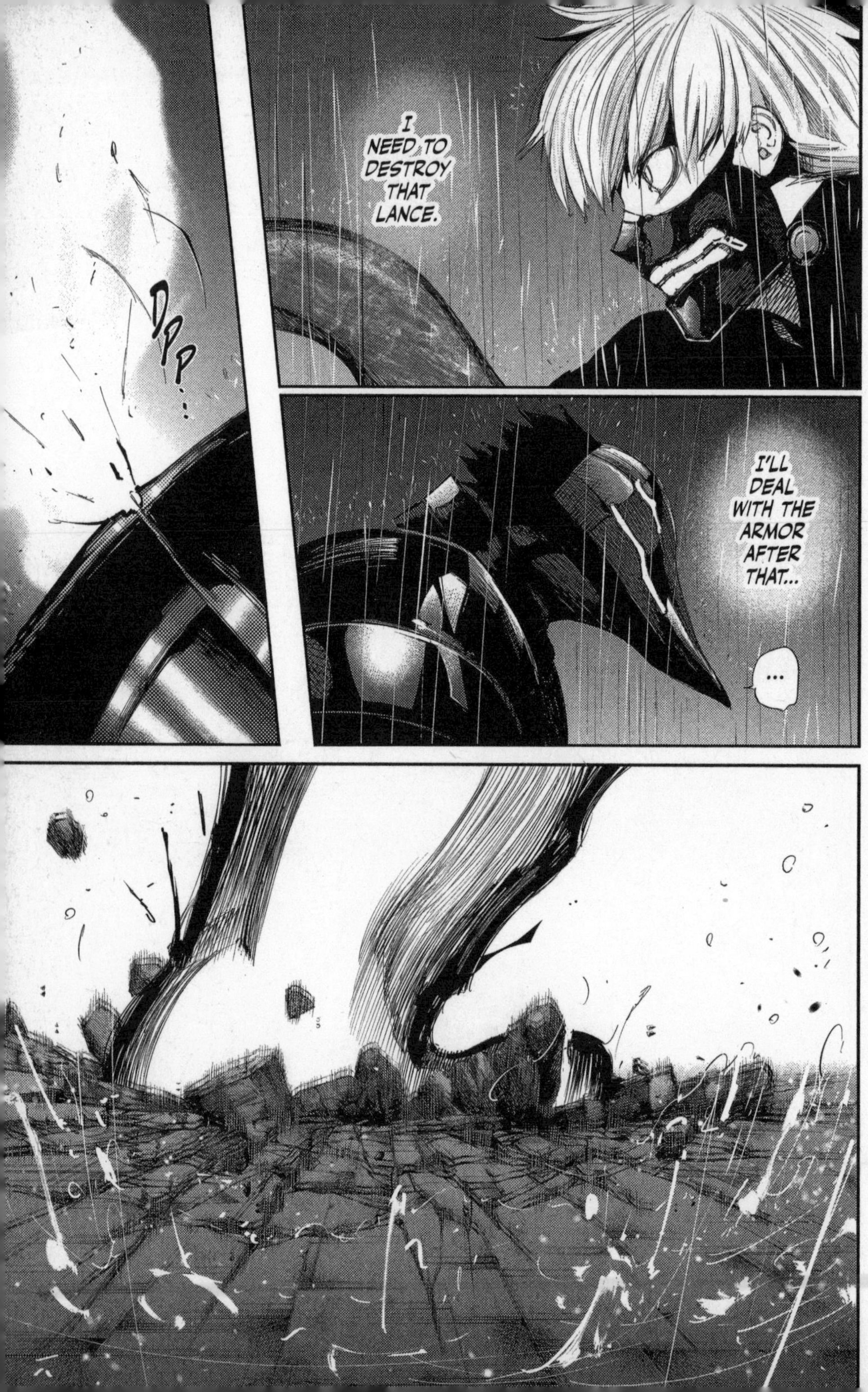
I NEED TO DESTROY THAT LANCE.
I'LL DEAL WITH THE ARMOR AFTER THAT...
...
DPP...

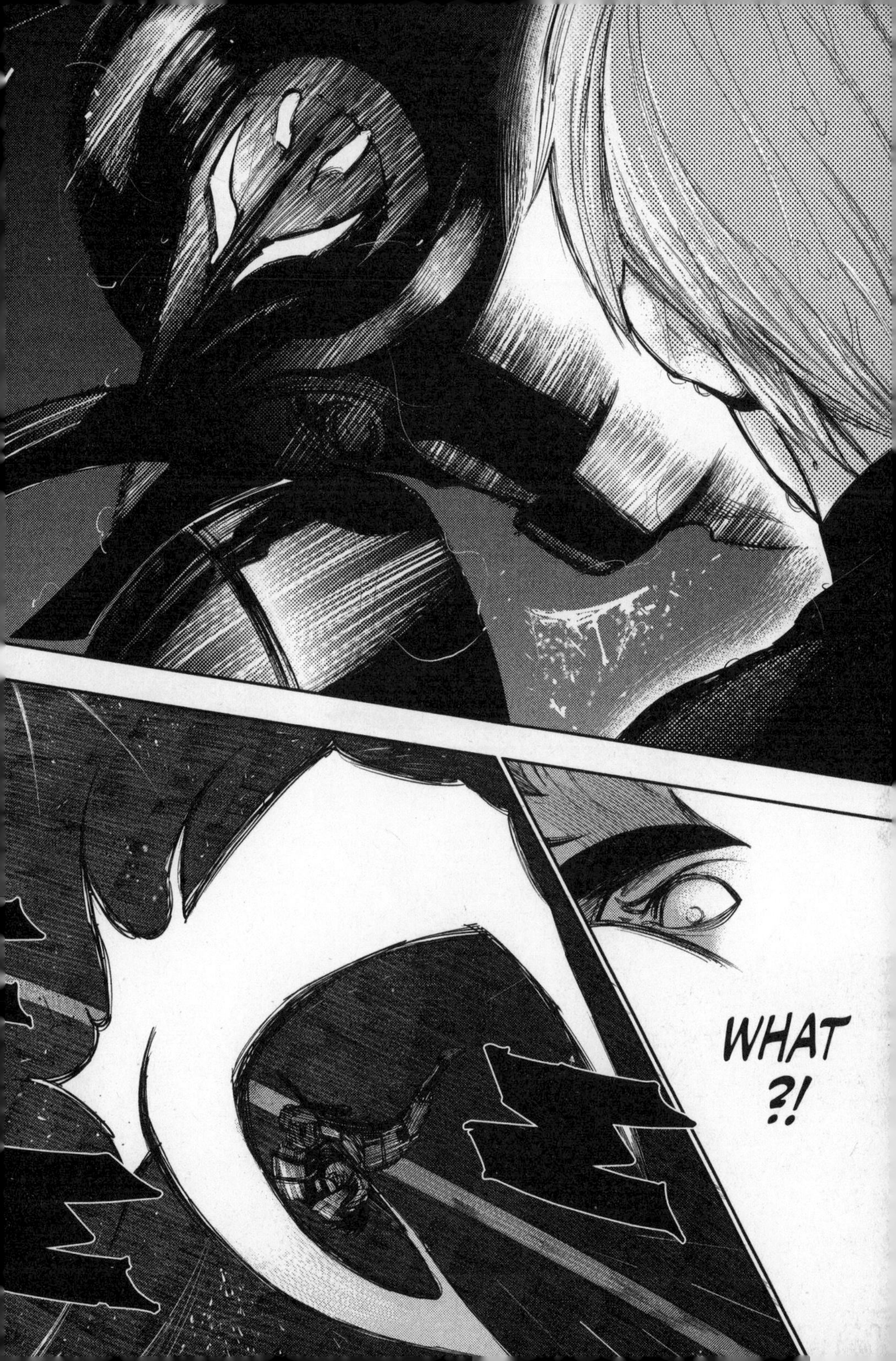
WHAT ?!

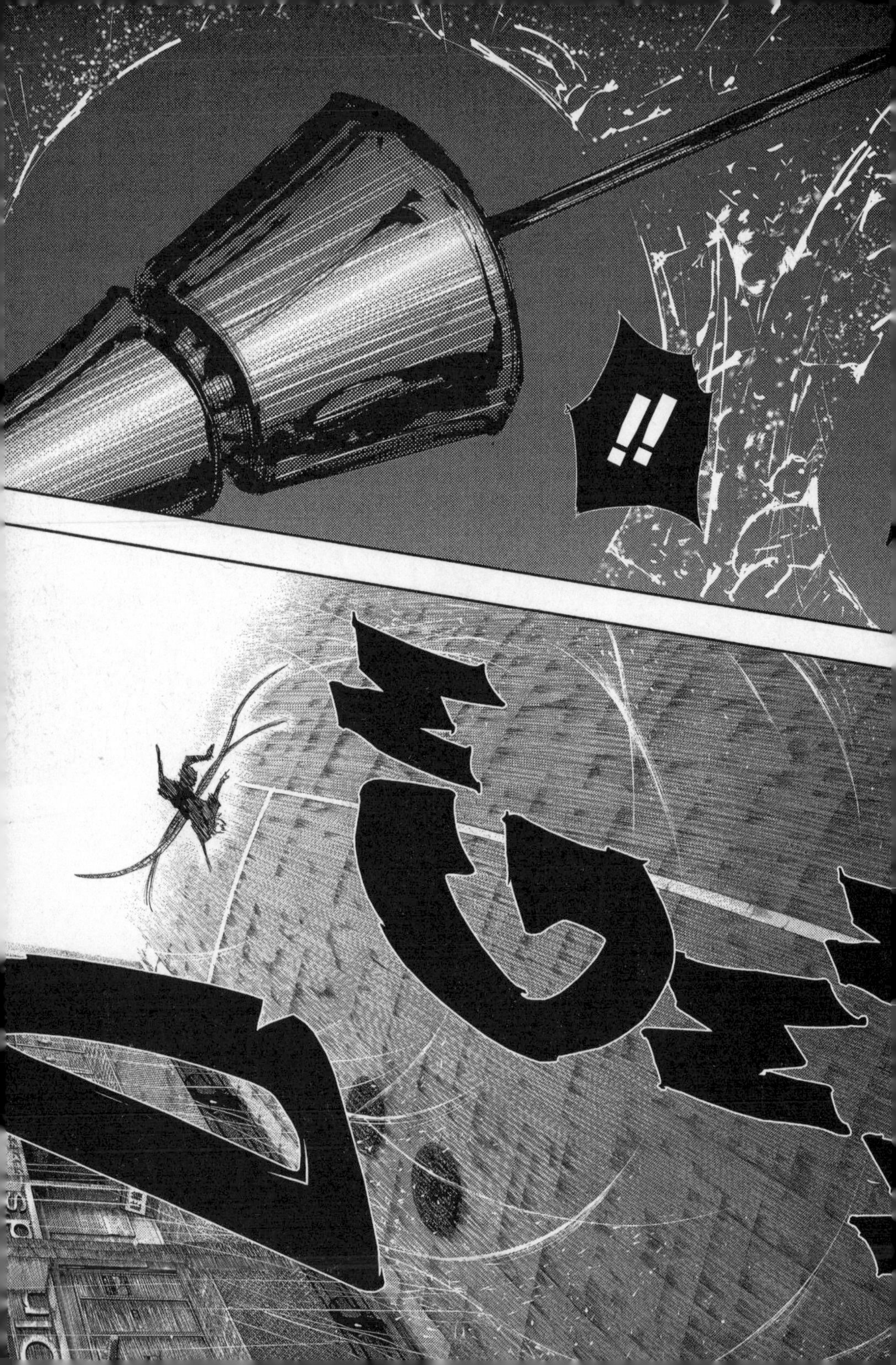
!!

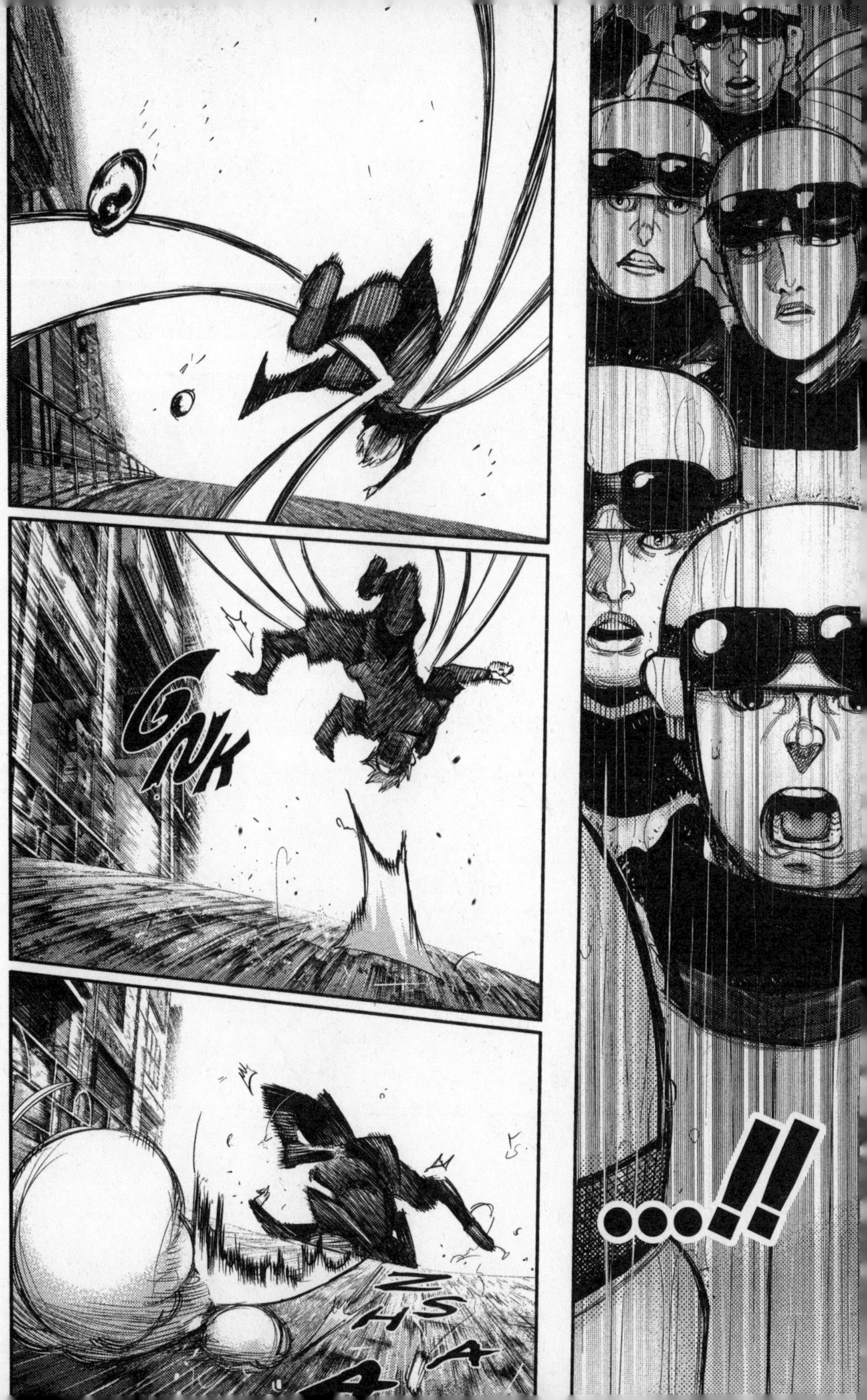
...!!
GNK
ZSHAA

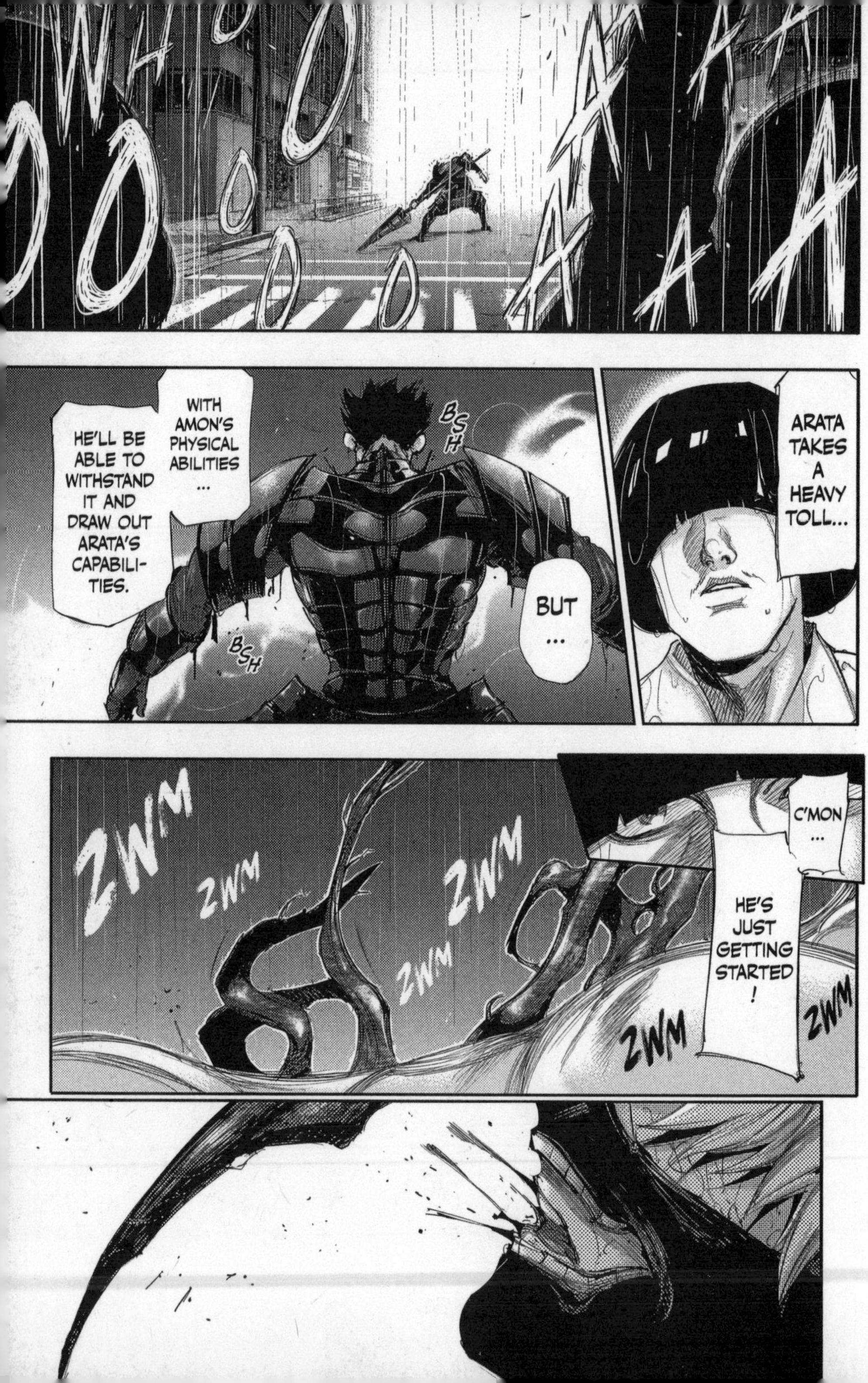
WHOOOOOOOAAAAAAAAA
ARATA TAKES A HEAVY TOLL...
BSH
WITH AMON'S PHYSICAL ABILITIES ...
HE'LL BE ABLE TO WITHSTAND IT AND DRAW OUT ARATA'S CAPABILITIES.
BUT ...
BSH
C'MON ...
HE'S JUST GETTING STARTED !
ZWM
ZWM
ZWM
ZWM
ZWM
ZWM
ZWM

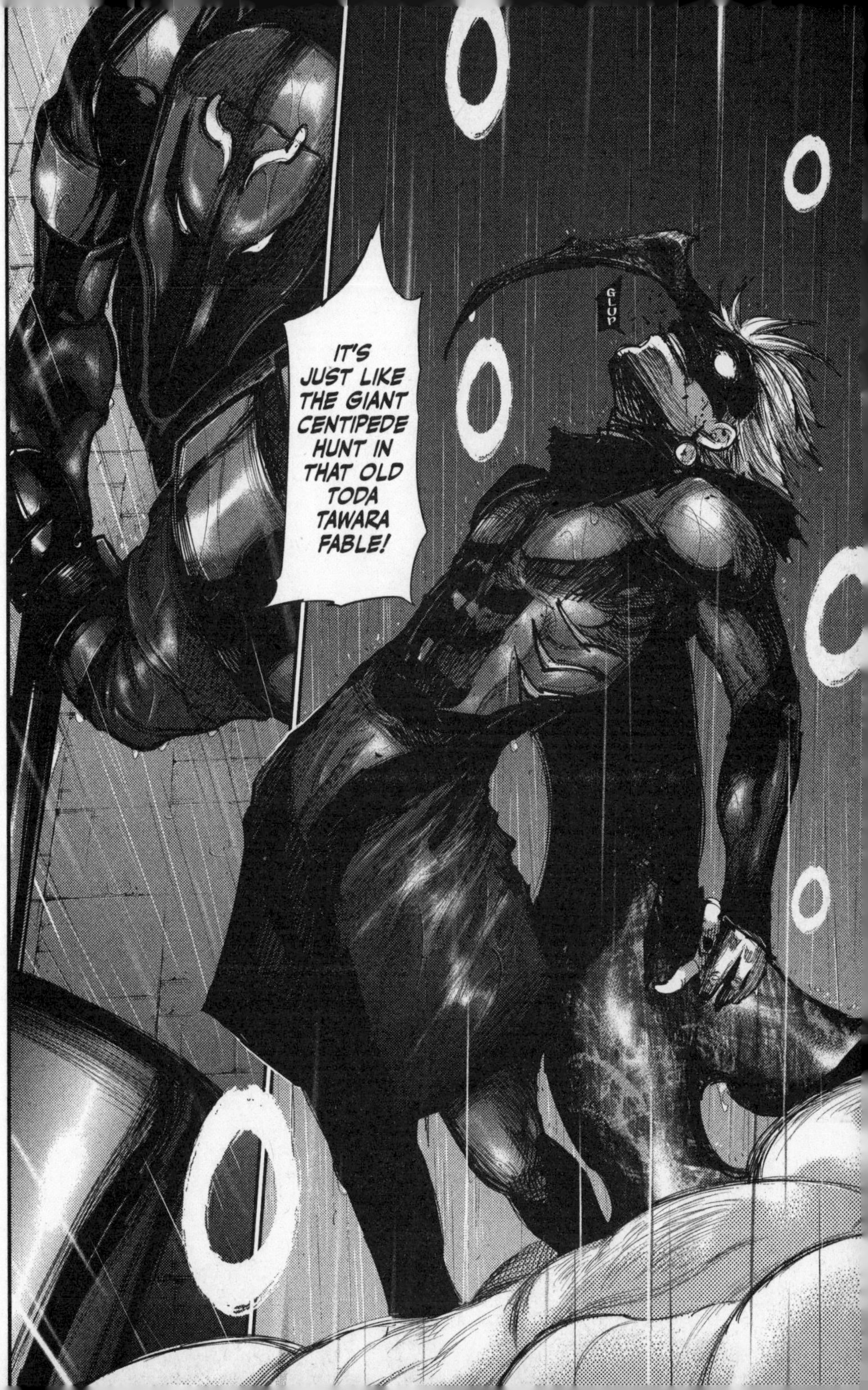

IT'S JUST LIKE THE GIANT CENTIPEDE HUNT IN THAT OLD TODA TAWARA FABLE!
GLUP

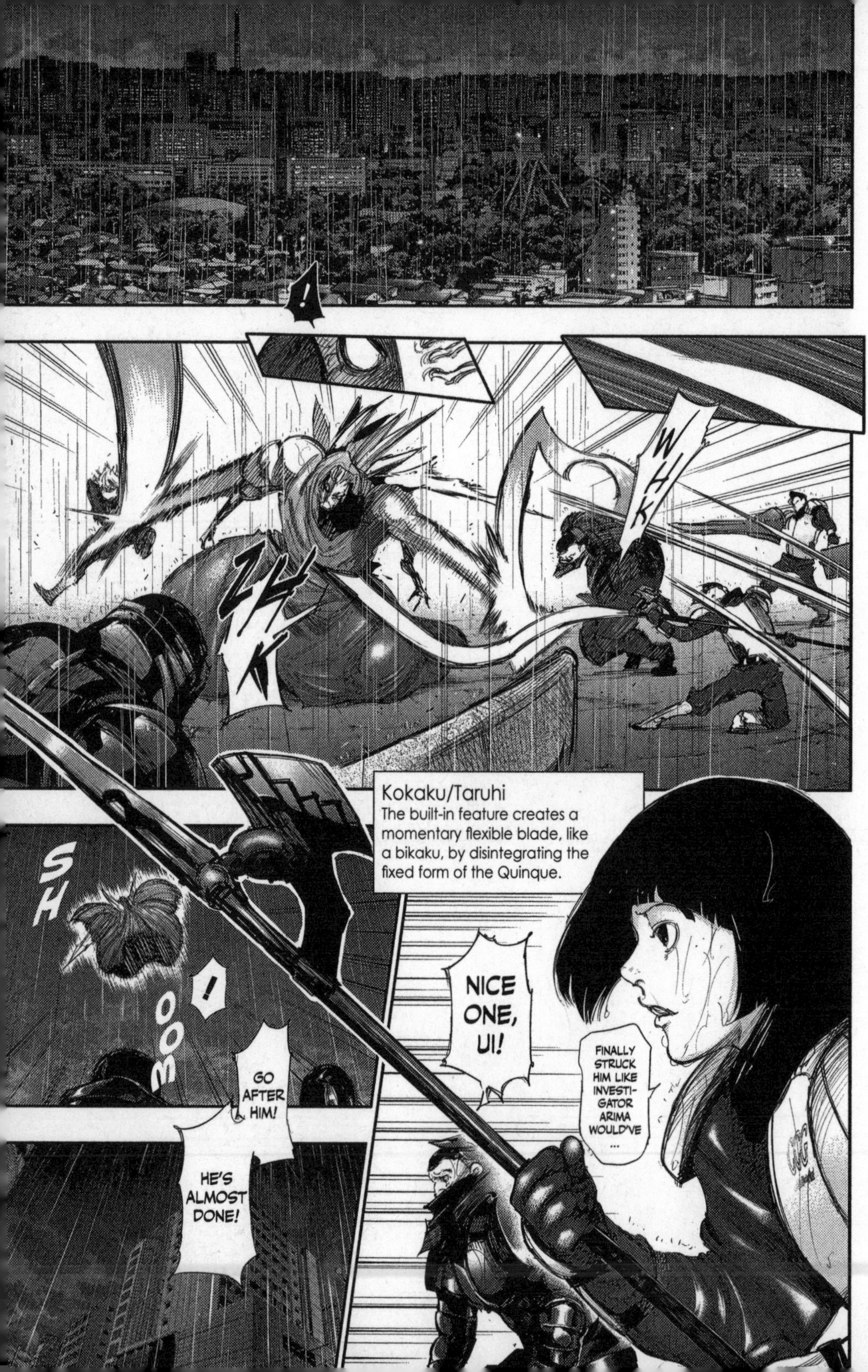
!
WHK
ZZK
Kokaku/Taruhi
The built-in feature creates a momentary flexible blade, like a bikaku, by disintegrating the fixed form of the Quinque.
NICE ONE, UI!
FINALLY STRUCK HIM LIKE INVESTI-GATOR ARIMA WOULD'VE ...
SH
!
GO AFTER HIM!
HE'S ALMOST DONE!

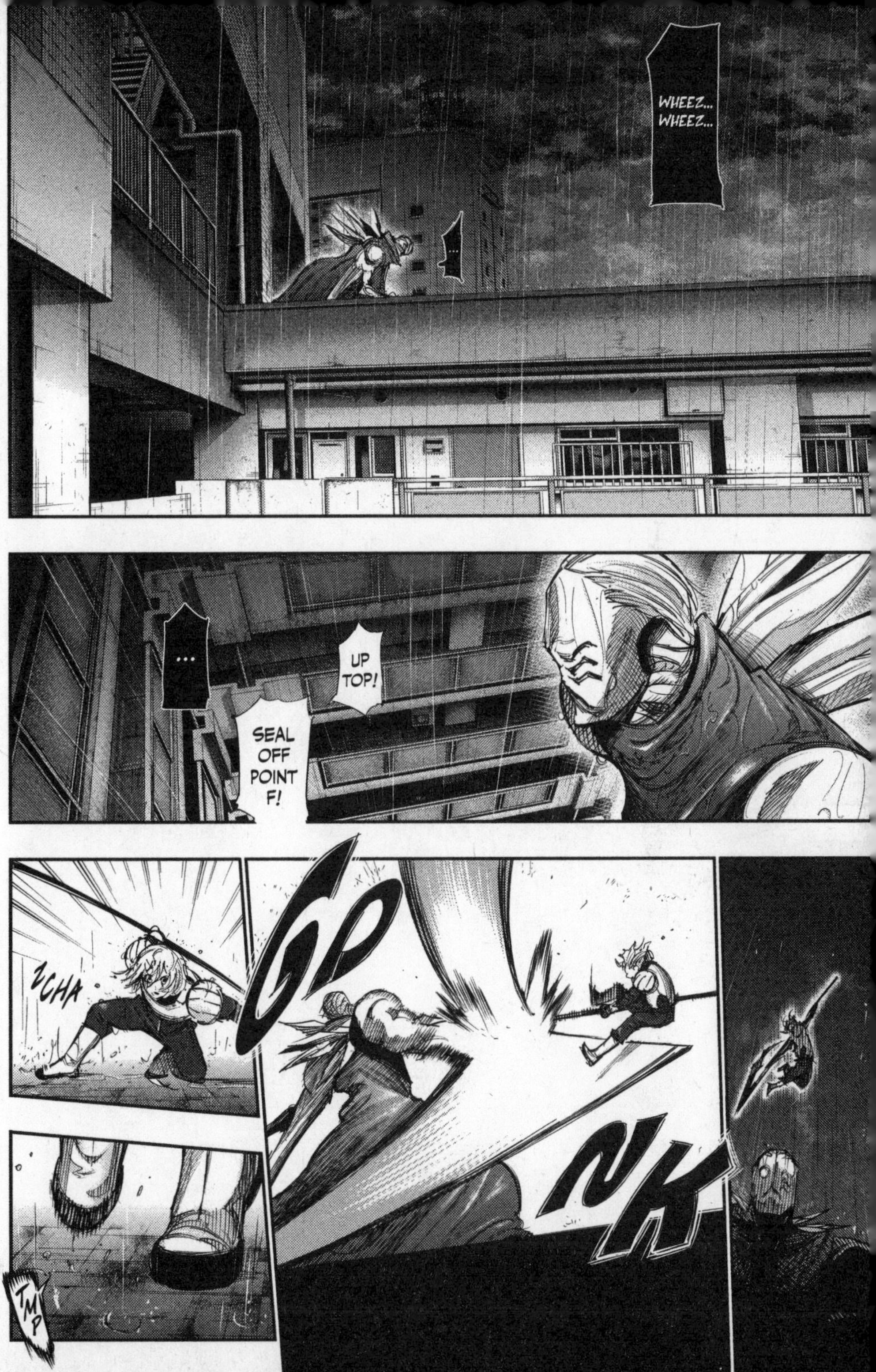
WHEEZ... WHEEZ...
...
UP TOP!
SEAL OFF POINT F!
...
GP
CK
ZCHA
TMP

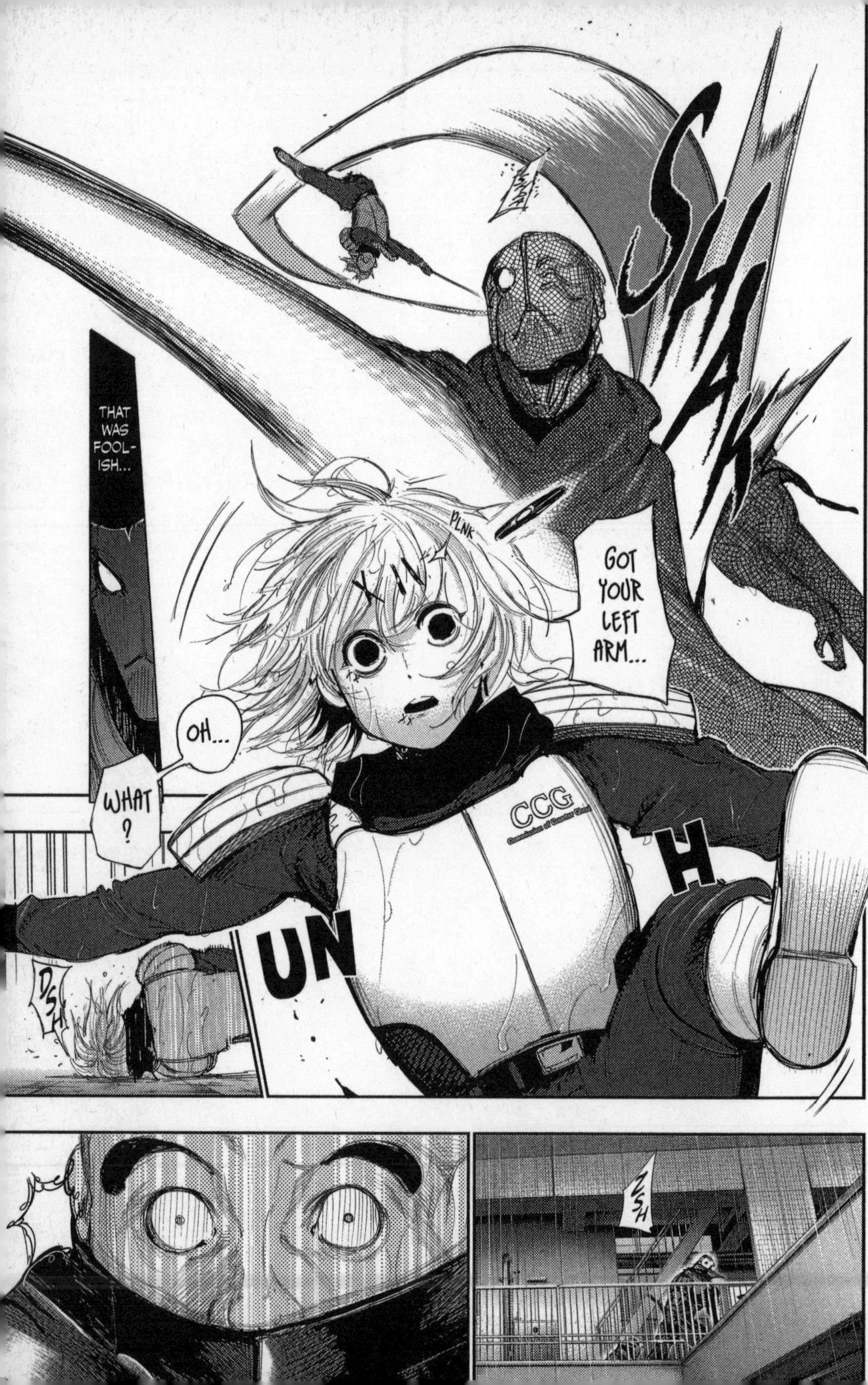
SHAK
GOT YOUR LEFT ARM...
PLNK
THAT WAS FOOL-ISH...
OH...
WHAT?
UNH
DSH
ZSH

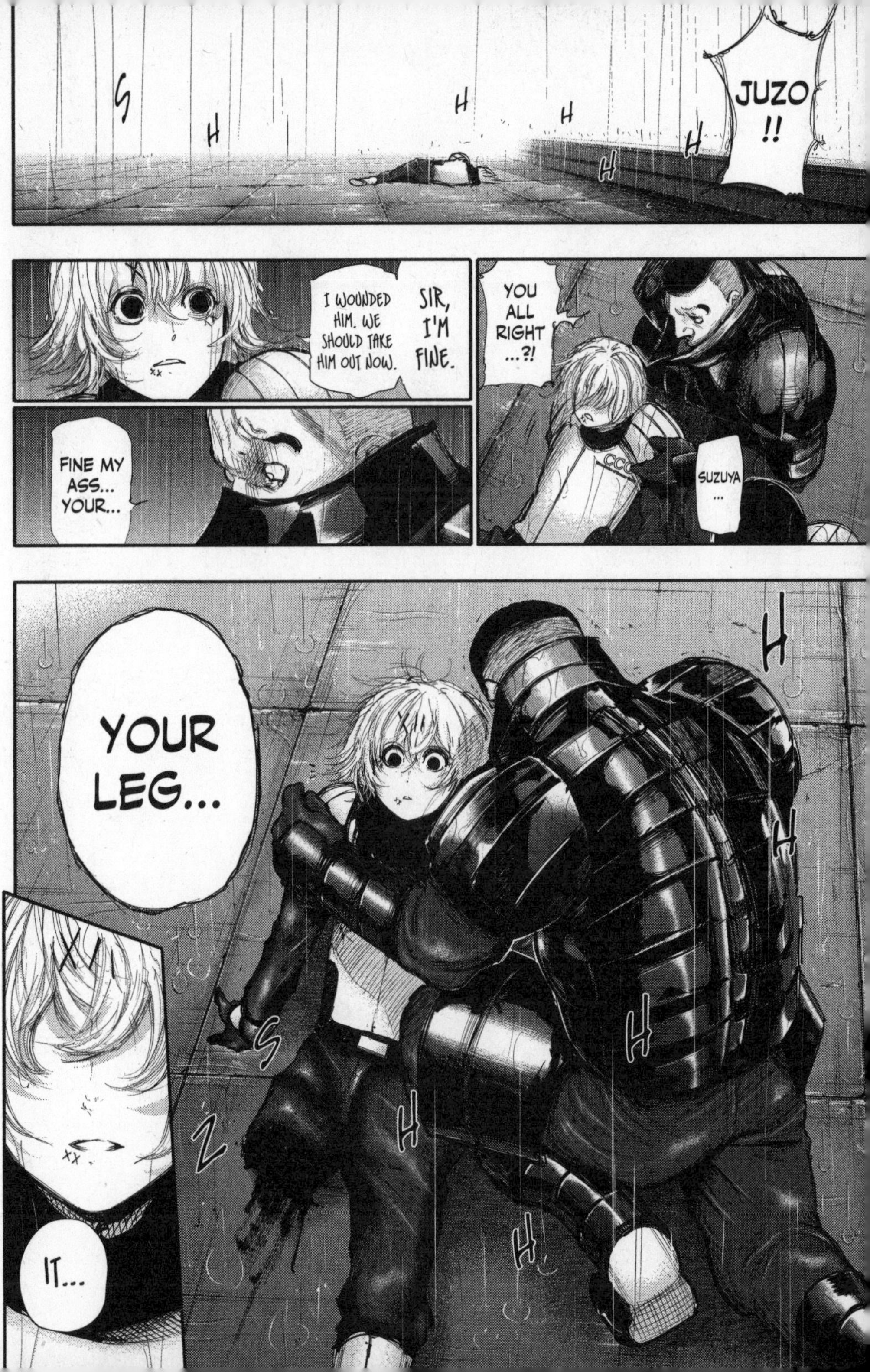
JUZO !!
S H H H H H
YOU ALL RIGHT ...?!
SUZUYA ...
SIR, I'M FINE.
I WOUNDED HIM. WE SHOULD TAKE HIM OUT NOW.
FINE MY ASS... YOUR...
YOUR LEG...
H H H S Z H H
IT...

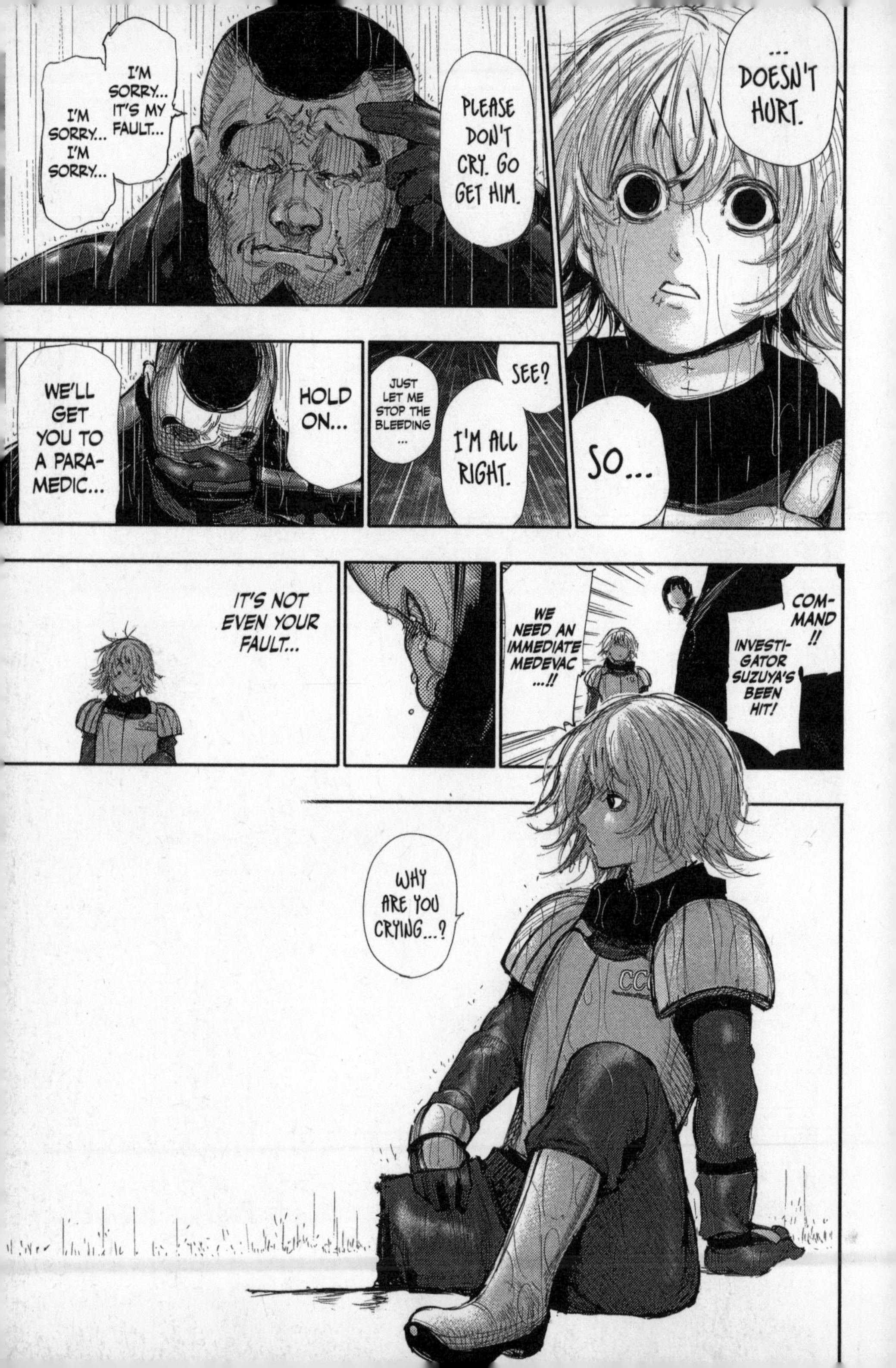
... DOESN'T HURT.
SO...
PLEASE DON'T CRY. GO GET HIM.
I'M SORRY... IT'S MY FAULT...
I'M SORRY... I'M SORRY...
SEE?
I'M ALL RIGHT.
JUST LET ME STOP THE BLEEDING ...
HOLD ON...
WE'LL GET YOU TO A PARA-MEDIC...
COM-MAND!!
INVESTI-GATOR SUZUYA'S BEEN HIT!
WE NEED AN IMMEDIATE MEDEVAC ...!!
IT'S NOT EVEN YOUR FAULT...
WHY ARE YOU CRYING...?

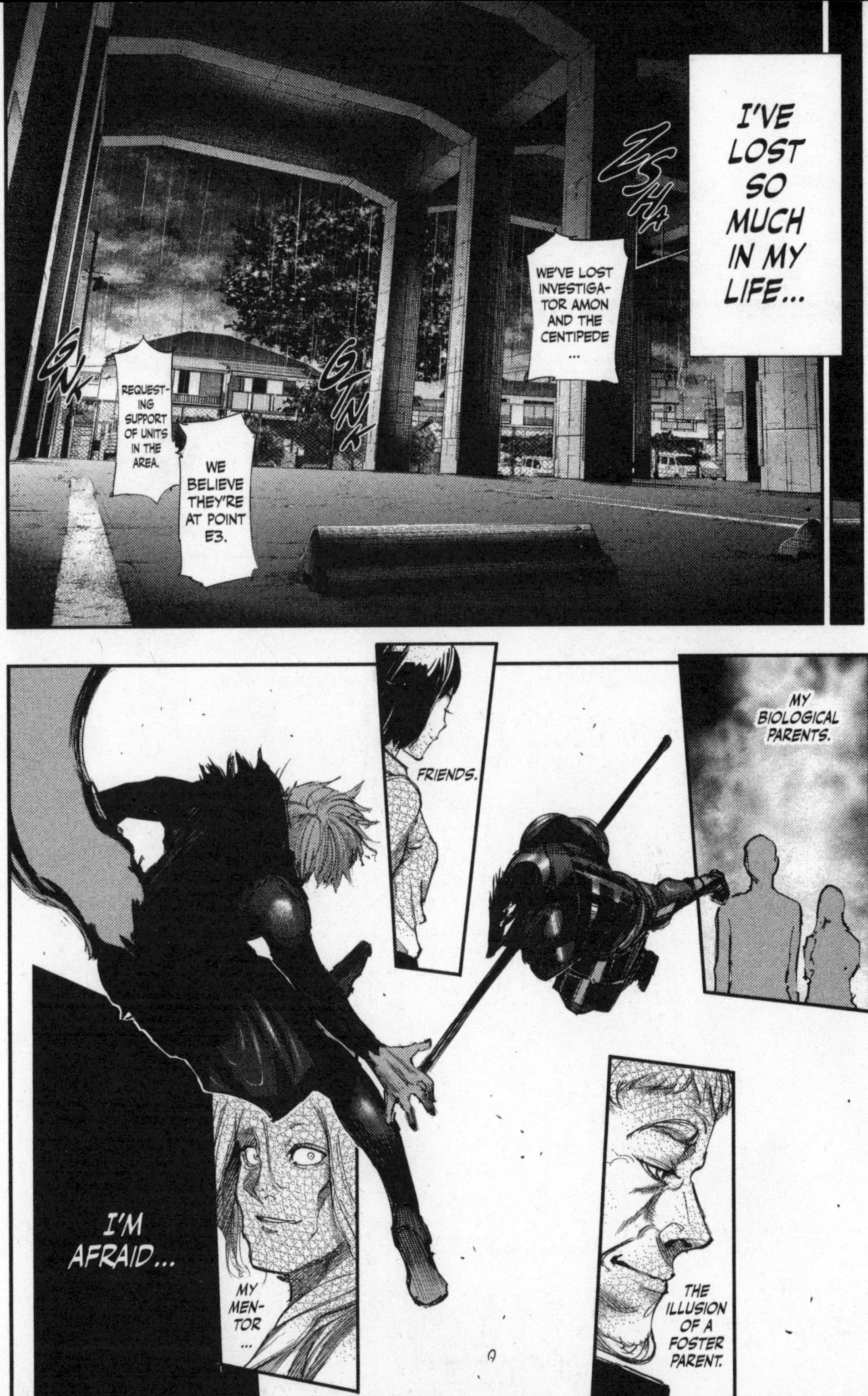
I'VE LOST SO MUCH IN MY LIFE...
ZSHA
WE'VE LOST INVESTIGATOR AMON AND THE CENTIPEDE...
GTNK
REQUESTING SUPPORT OF UNITS IN THE AREA.
WE BELIEVE THEY'RE AT POINT E3.
GNK
MY BIOLOGICAL PARENTS.
FRIENDS.
THE ILLUSION OF A FOSTER PARENT.
MY MENTOR...
I'M AFRAID...

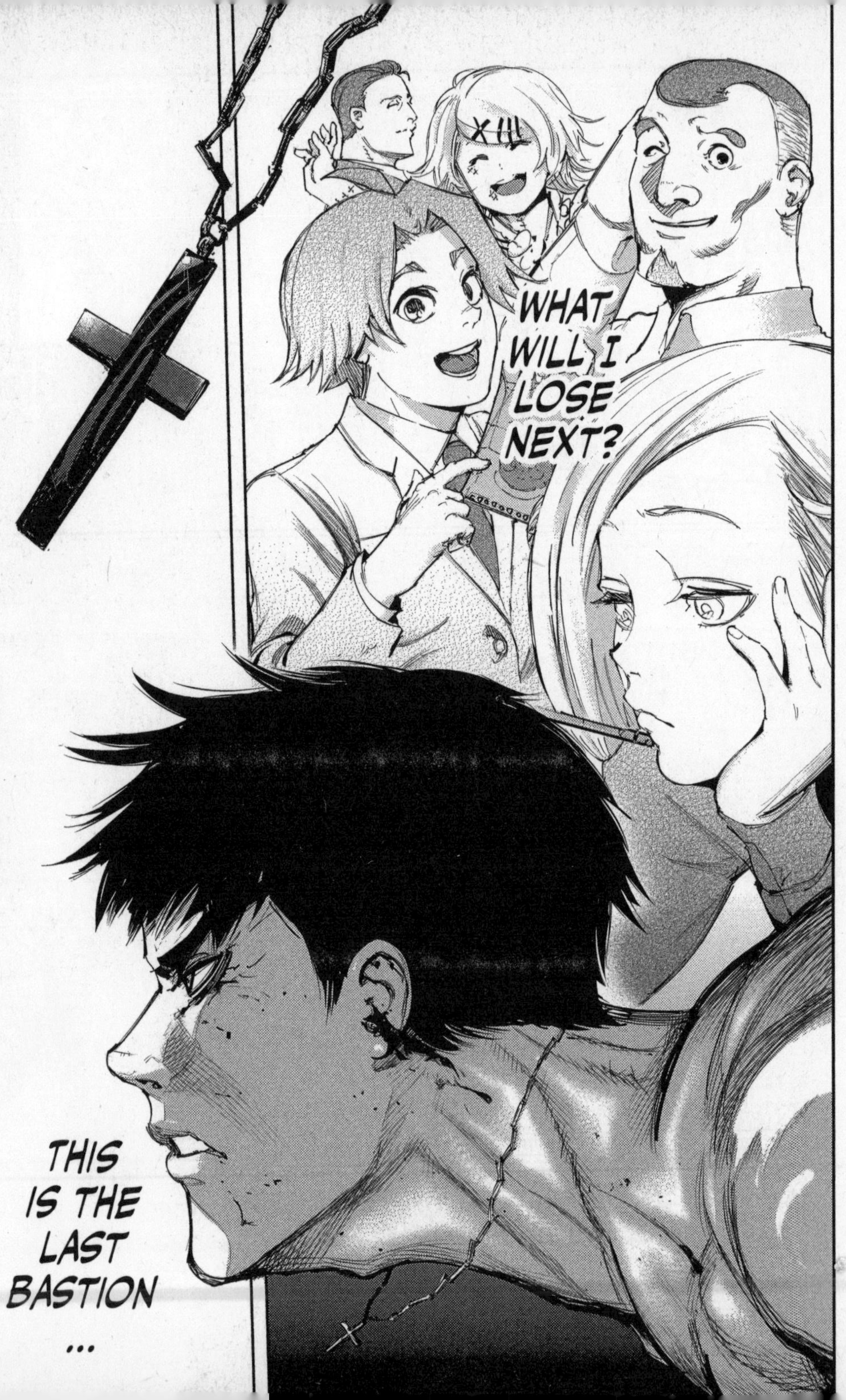
WHAT WILL I LOSE NEXT?
THIS IS THE LAST BASTION ...

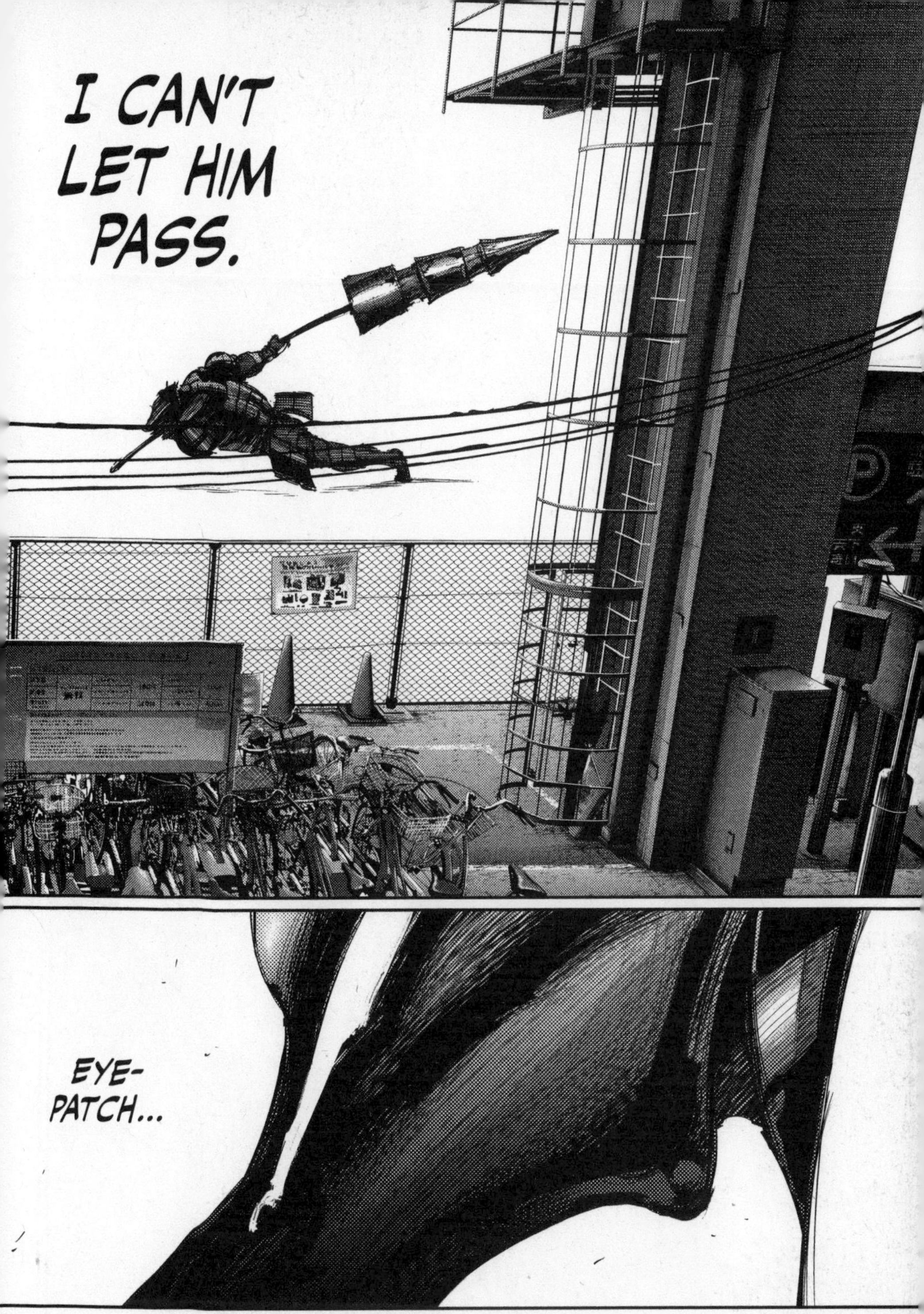
I CAN'T LET HIM PASS.
EYE-PATCH...

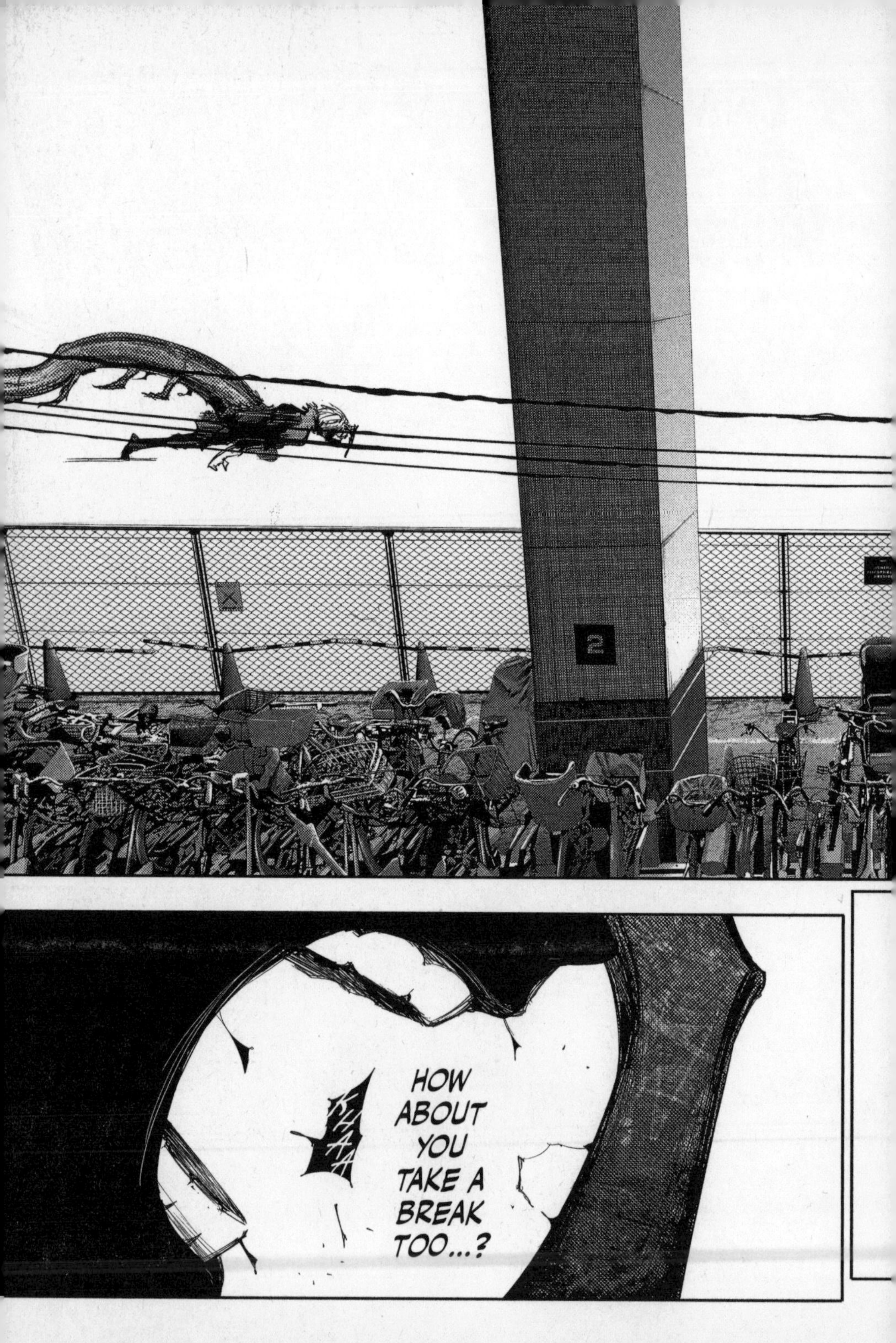
HOW ABOUT YOU TAKE A BREAK TOO...?
KHAAA

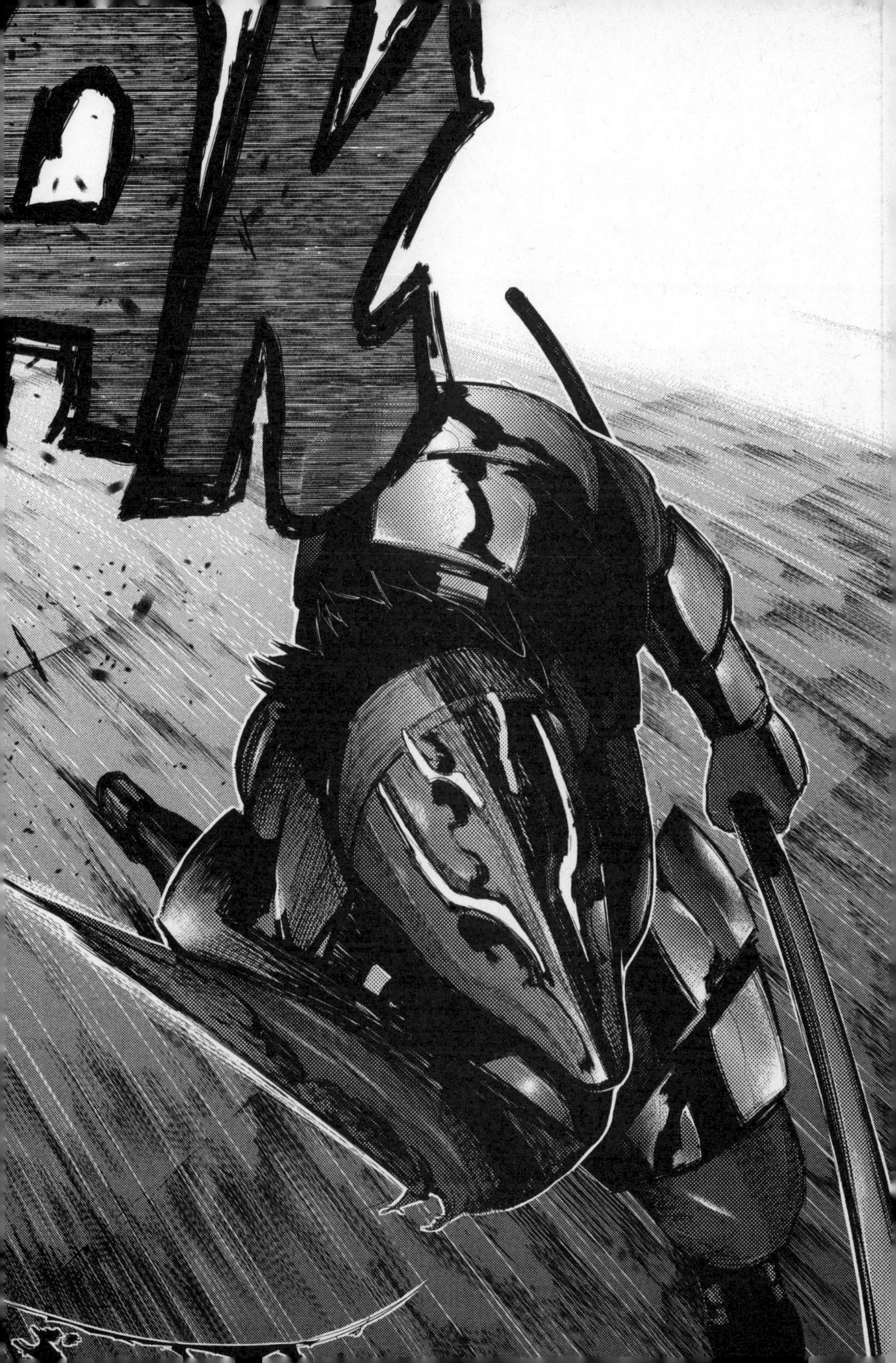

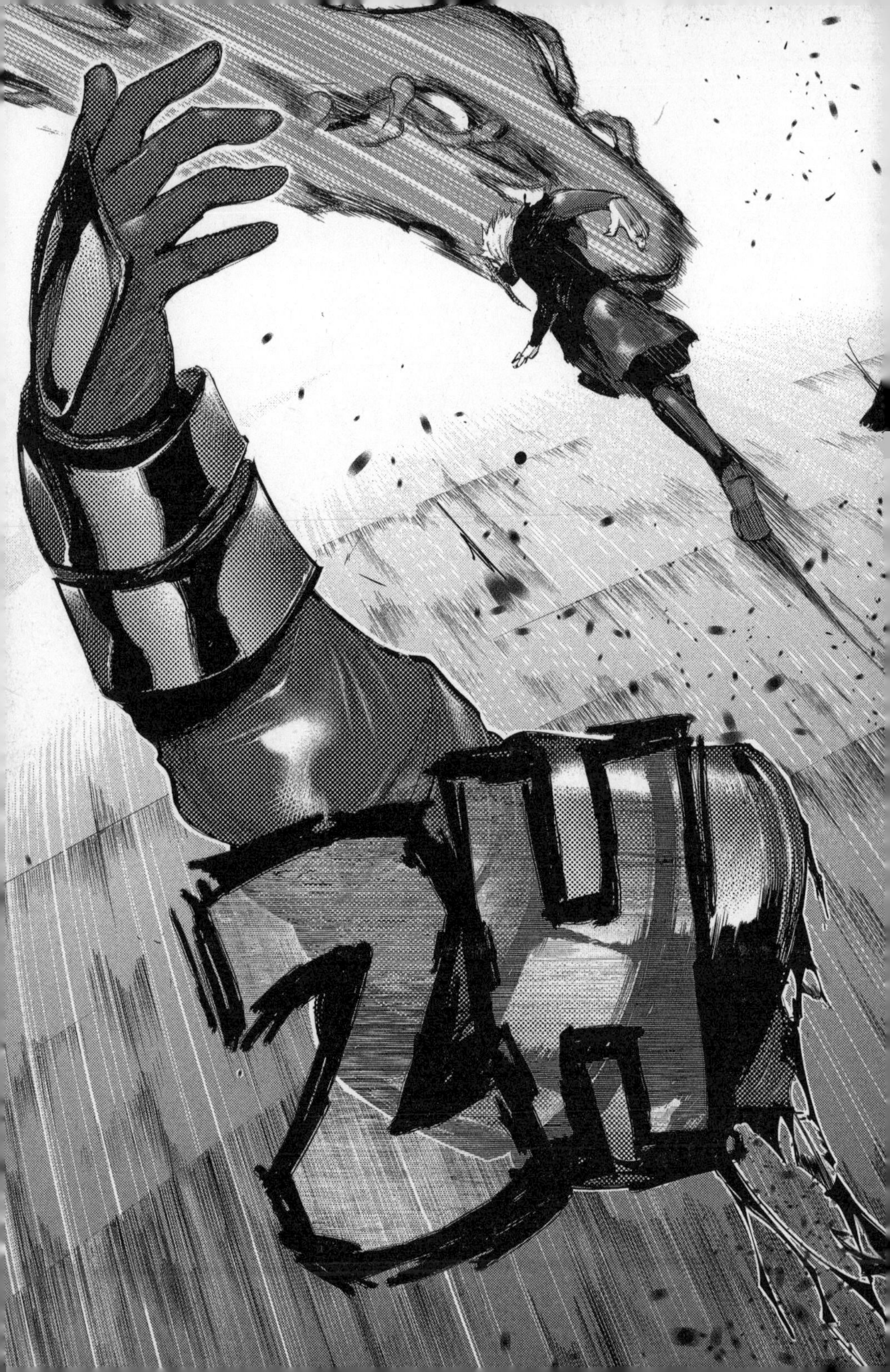

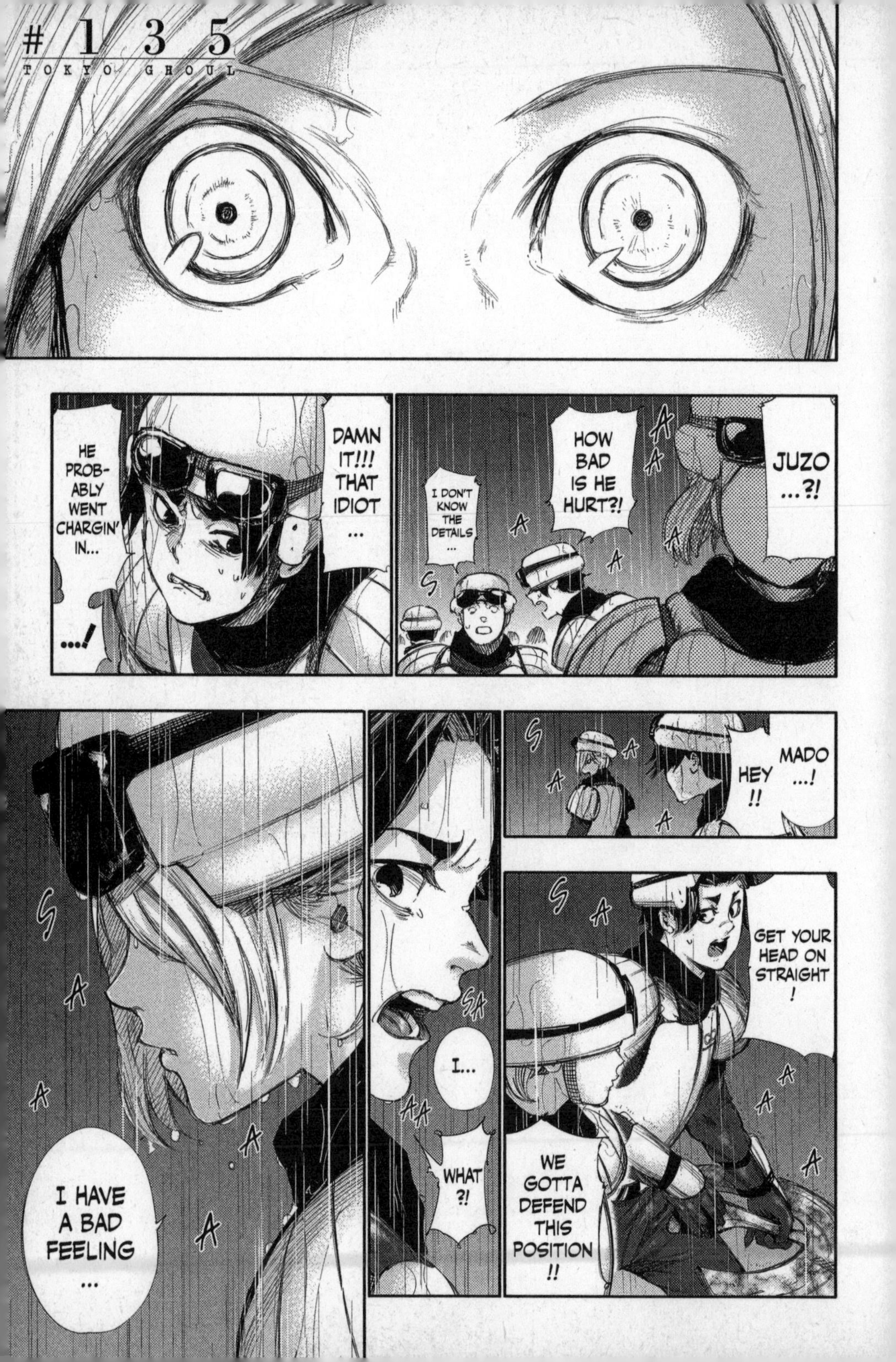
#135
TOKYO GHOUL
JUZO ...?!
HOW BAD IS HE HURT?!
I DON'T KNOW THE DETAILS ...
SAAA
DAMN IT!!! THAT IDIOT ...
HE PROBABLY WENT CHARGIN' IN...
...!
MADO ...!
HEY !!
SAAA
GET YOUR HEAD ON STRAIGHT!
WE GOTTA DEFEND THIS POSITION!!
SAAA
I...
WHAT ?!
I HAVE A BAD FEELING ...

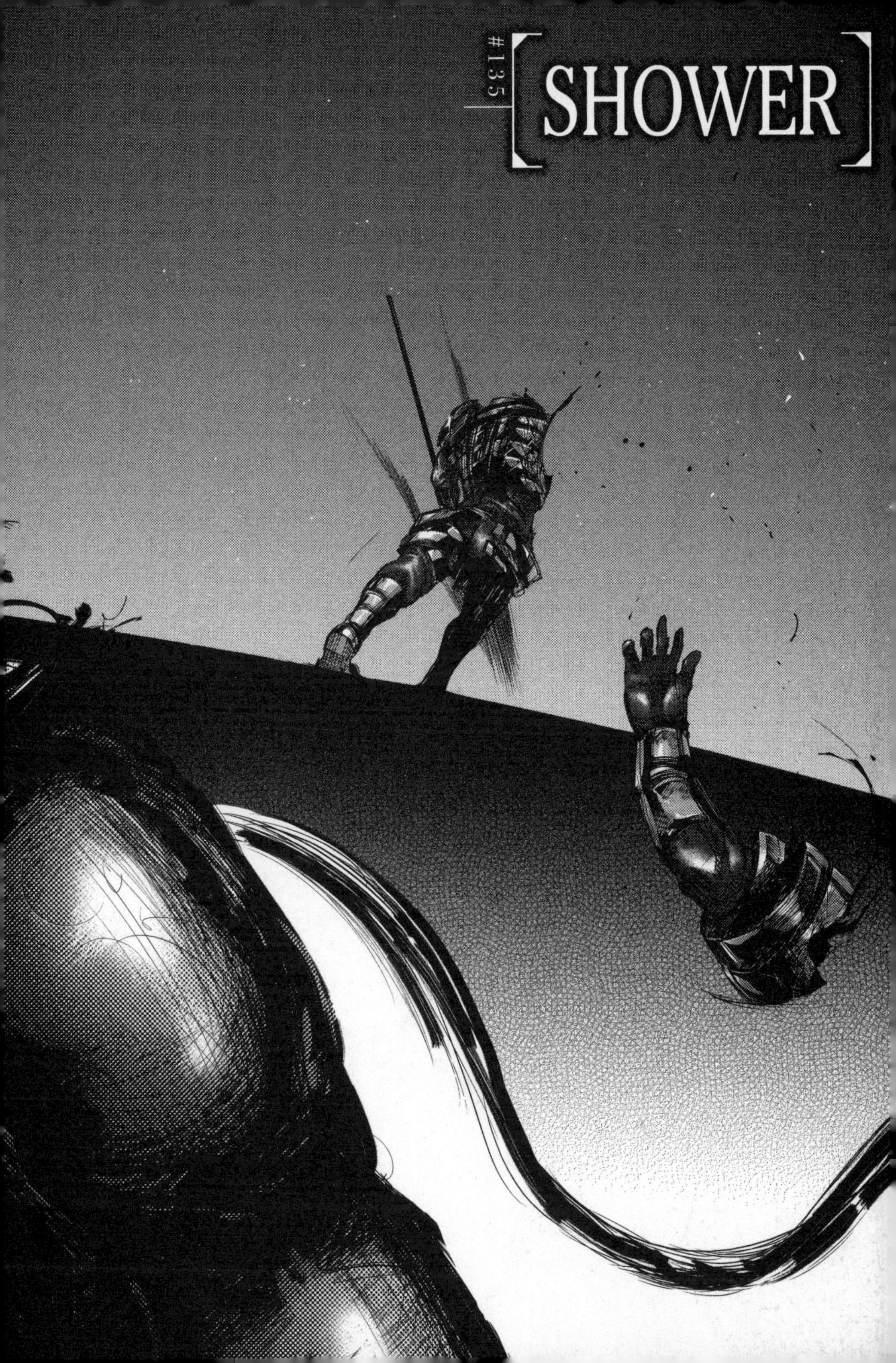
#135
SHOWER

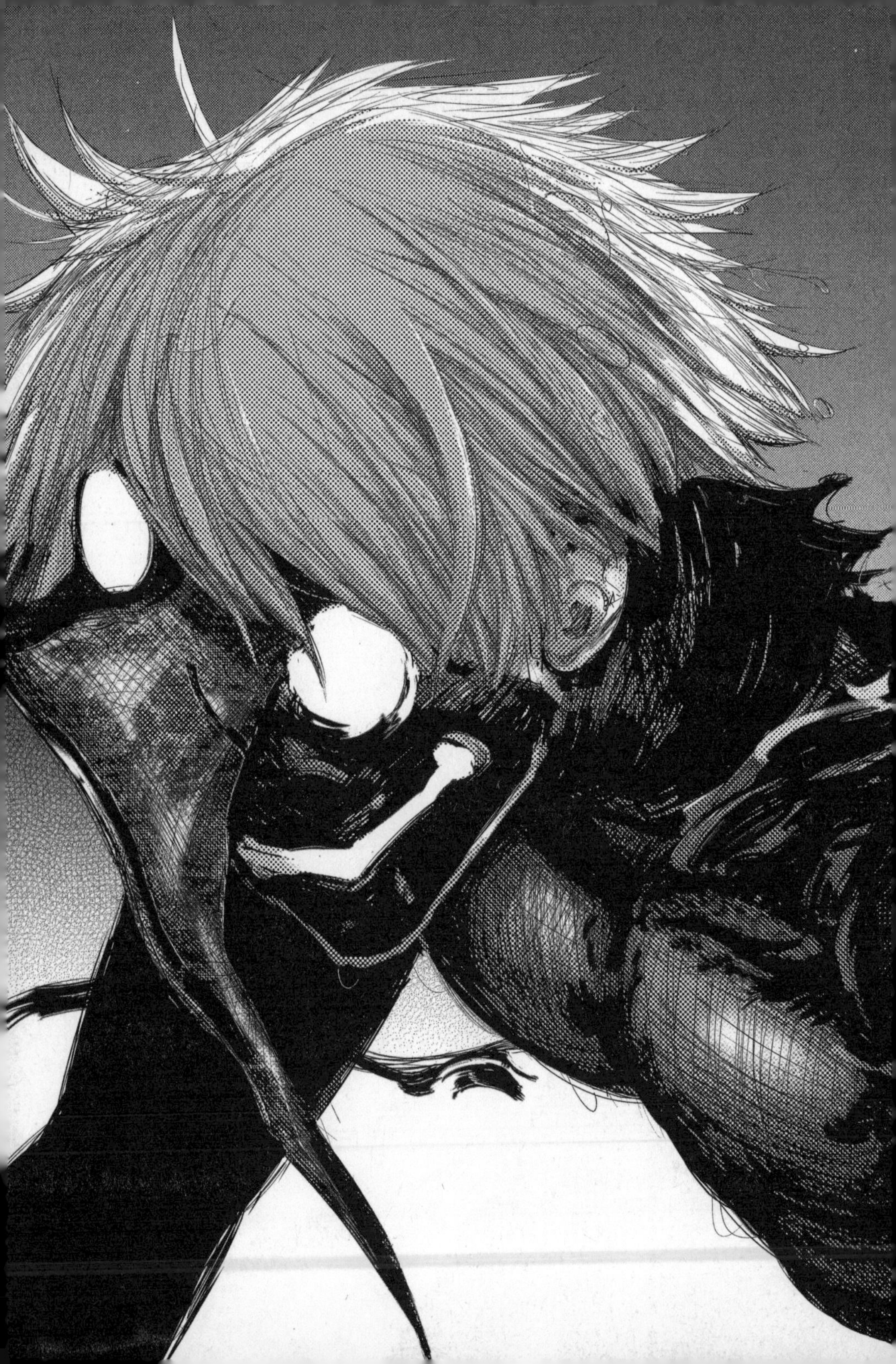

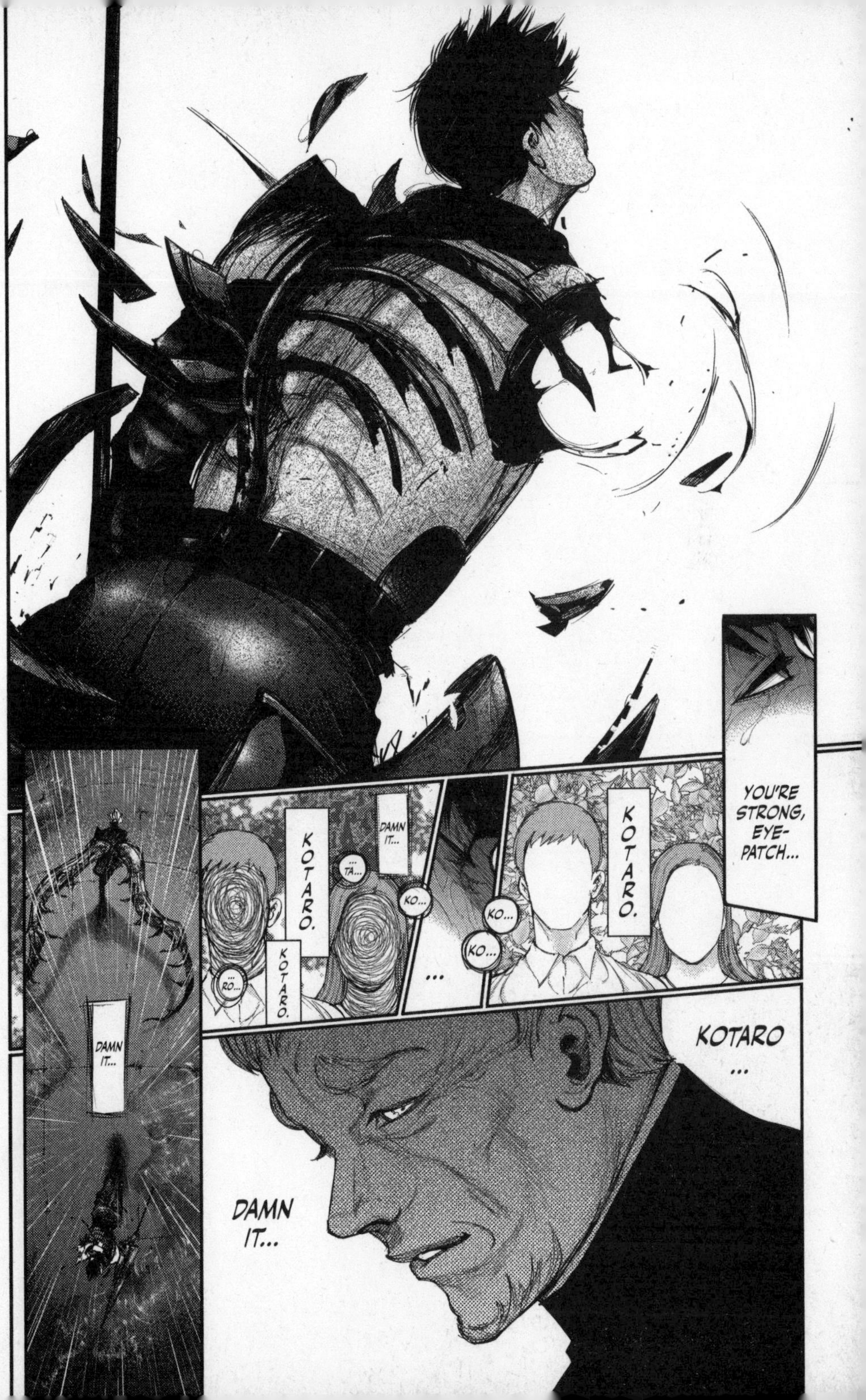
YOU'RE STRONG, EYE-PATCH...
KOTARO.
KO...
KO...
...
DAMN IT...
KOTARO.
...TA...
KO...
KOTARO.
...RO...
KOTARO ...
DAMN IT...
DAMN IT...

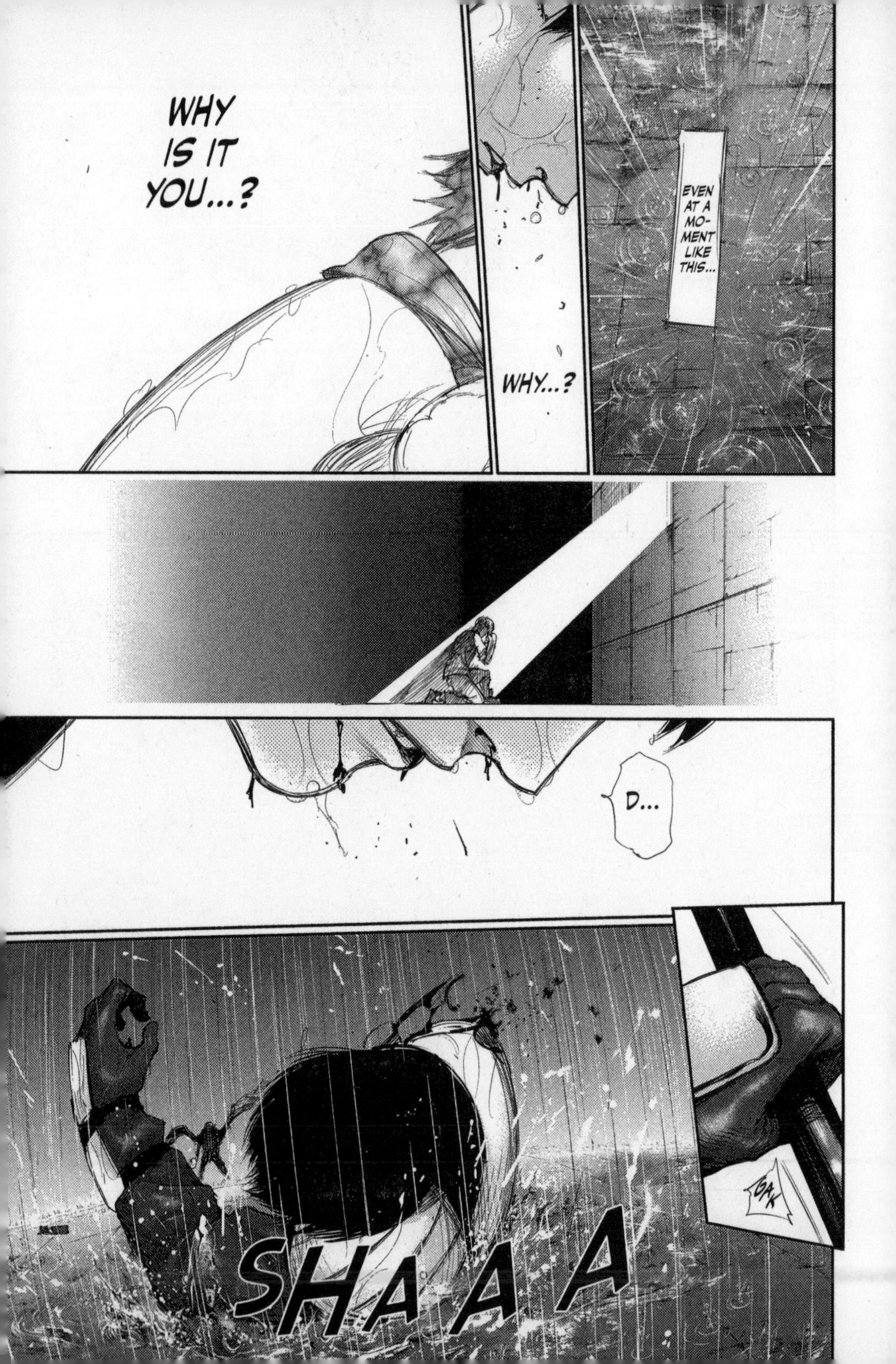
EVEN AT A MOMENT LIKE THIS...
WHY...?
WHY IS IT YOU...?
D...
GAK
SHAAA

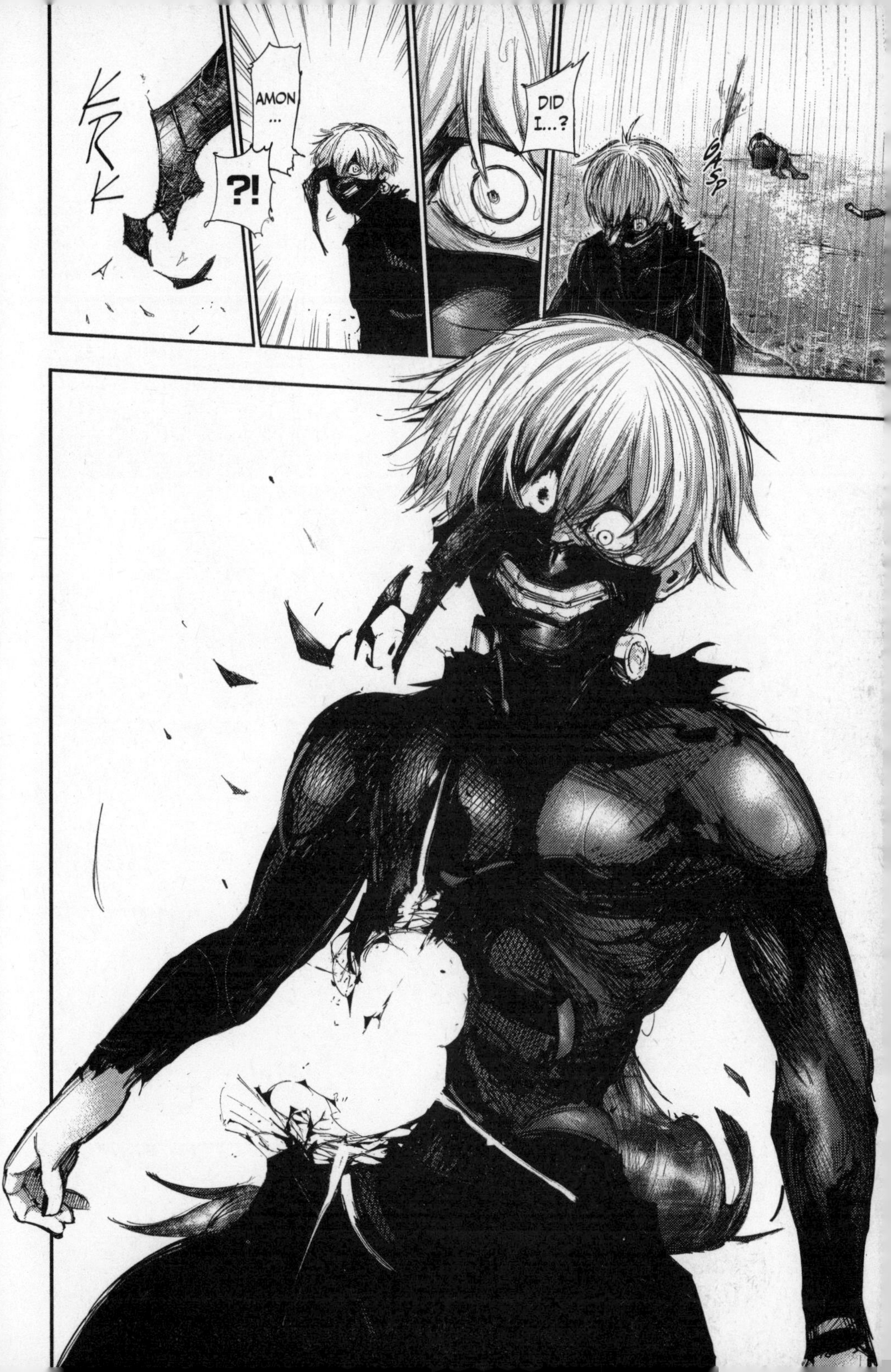
GASP
DID I...?
AMON ...
?!
KRK

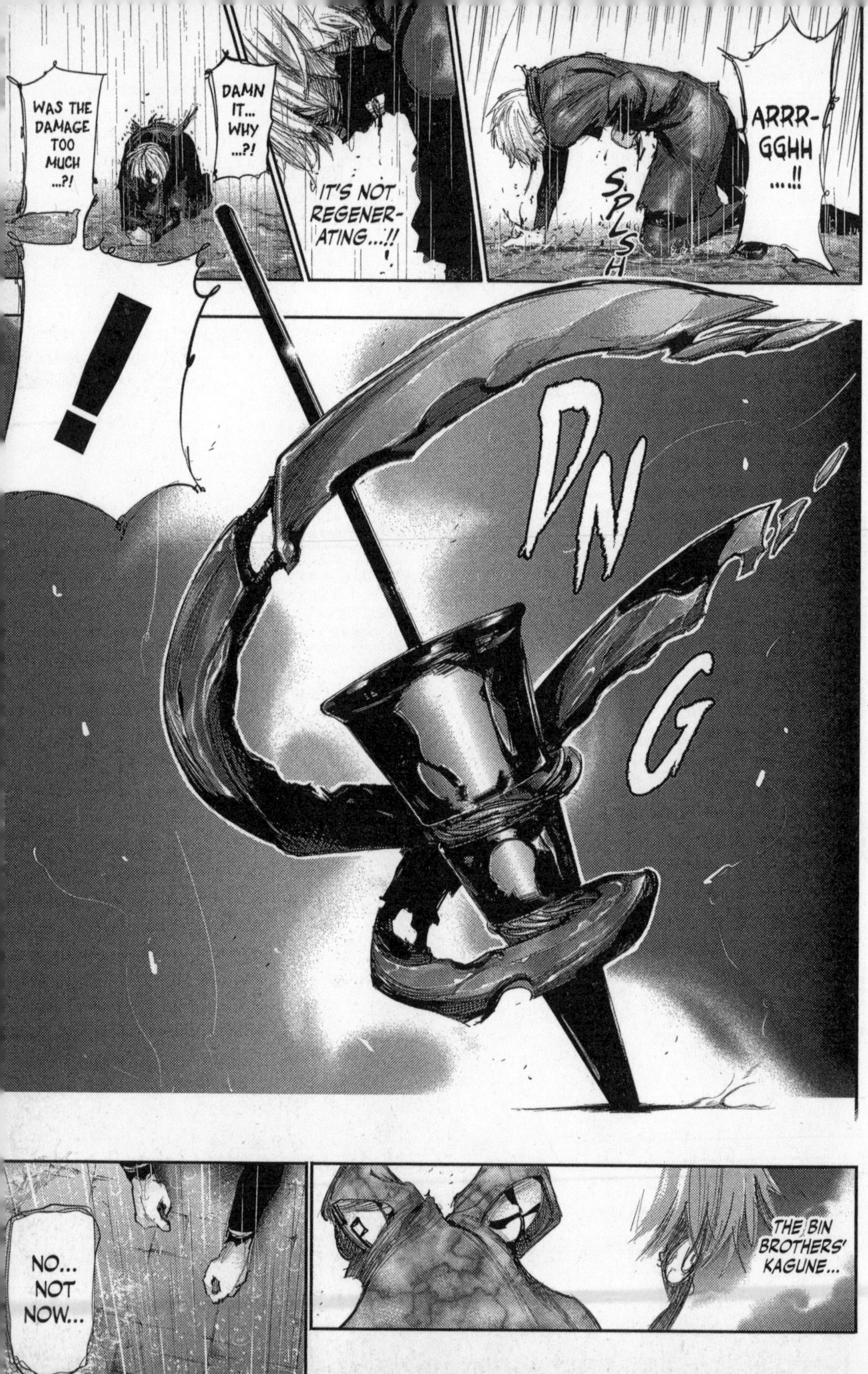
ARRR-GGHH ...!!
SPLSH
DAMN IT... WHY ...?!
IT'S NOT REGENER-ATING...!!
WAS THE DAMAGE TOO MUCH ...?!
!
DNG
THE BIN BROTHERS' KAGUNE...
NO... NOT NOW...

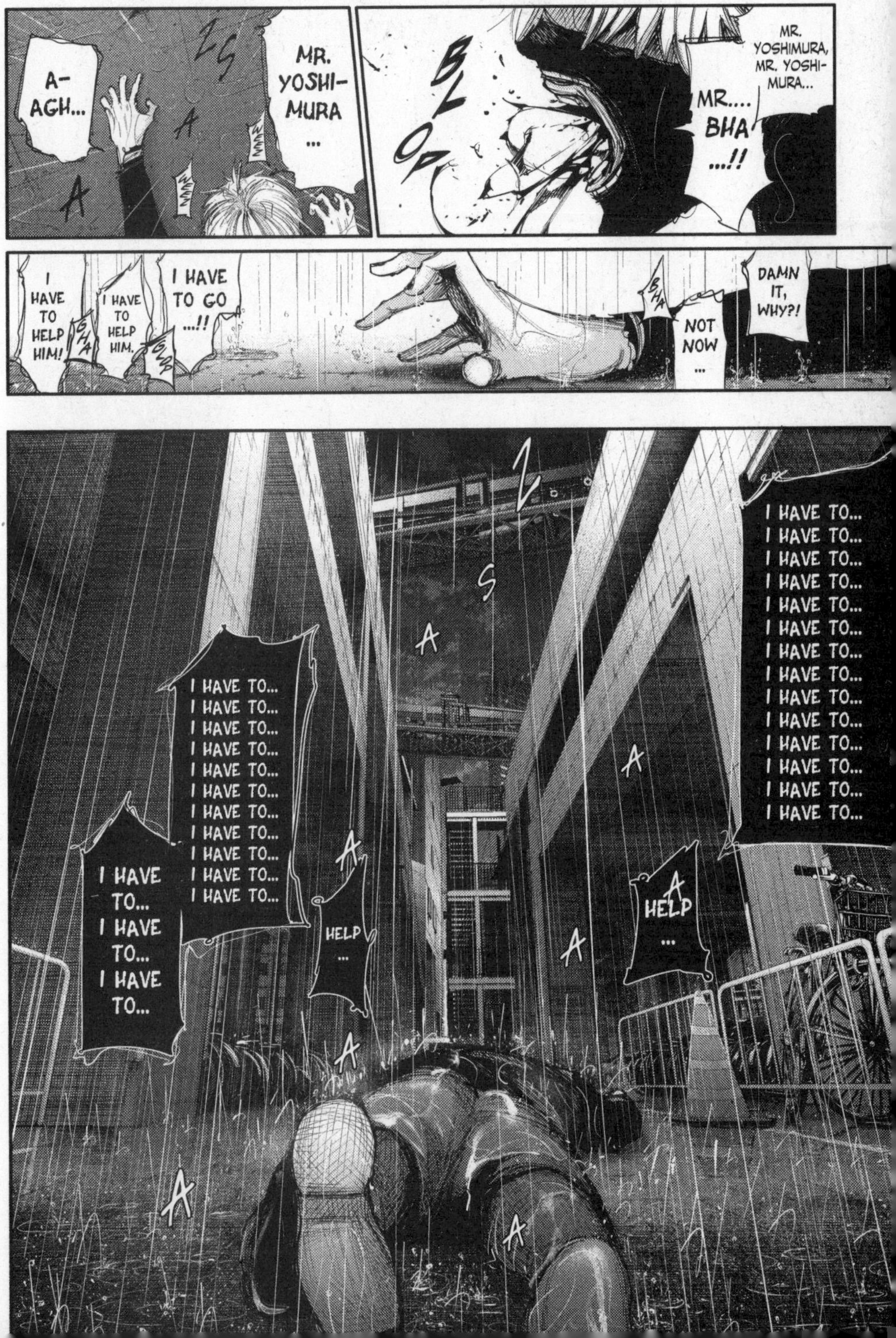
MR. YOSHIMURA, MR. YOSHIMURA...
MR.... BHA ...!!
BLOP
MR. YOSHIMURA ...
A-AGH...
ZSAA
DAMN IT, WHY?!
NOT NOW ...
BHA
I HAVE TO GO ...!!
I HAVE TO HELP HIM.
I HAVE TO HELP HIM!
SHA
I HAVE TO... I HAVE TO... I HAVE TO... I HAVE TO... I HAVE TO... I HAVE TO... I HAVE TO... I HAVE TO... I HAVE TO... I HAVE TO... I HAVE TO... I HAVE TO... I HAVE TO... I HAVE TO...
HELP ...
HELP ...
I HAVE TO... I HAVE TO... I HAVE TO... I HAVE TO... I HAVE TO... I HAVE TO... I HAVE TO... I HAVE TO... I HAVE TO... I HAVE TO... I HAVE TO...
I HAVE TO... I HAVE TO... I HAVE TO...
ZSAAAAAAAA

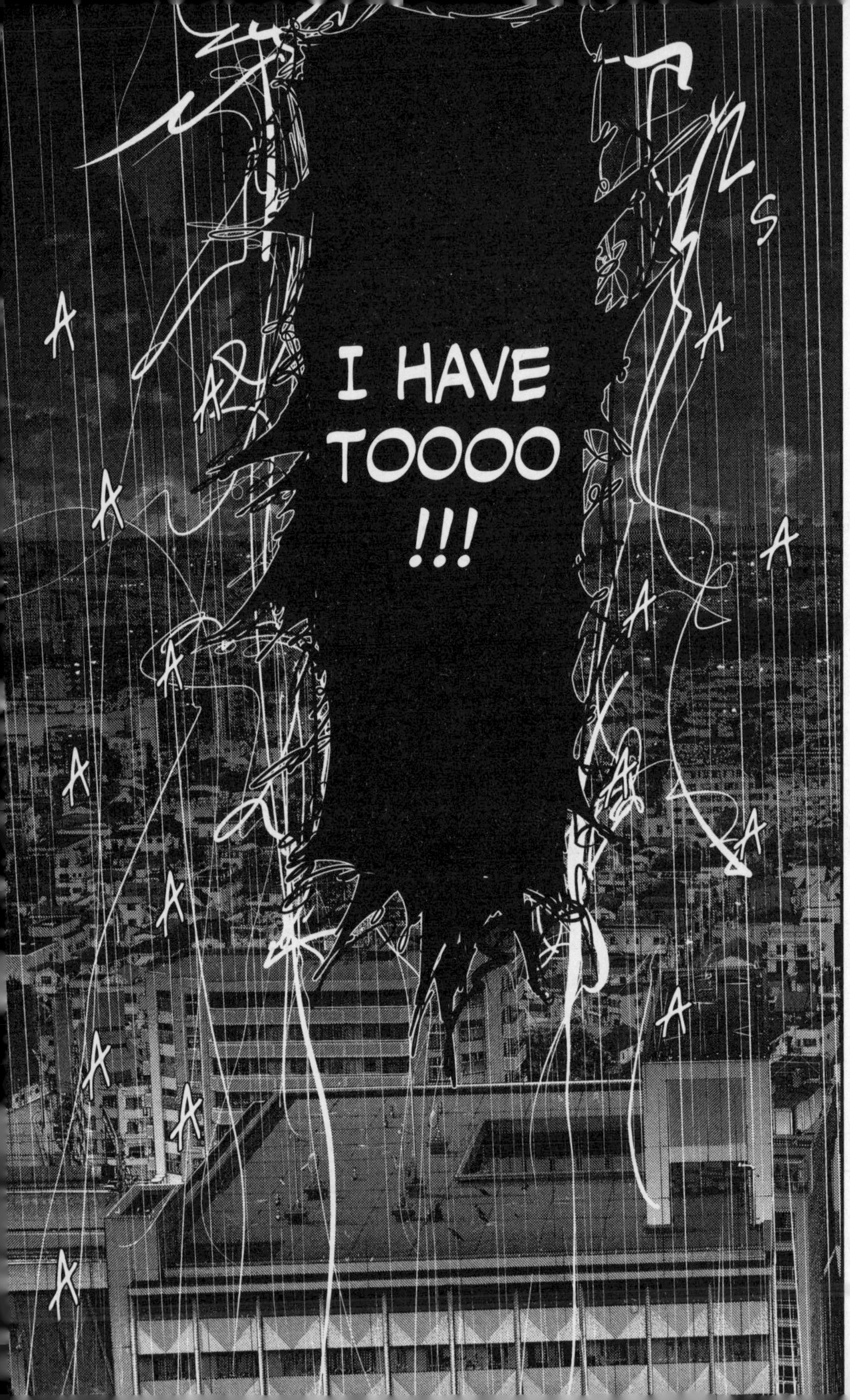
I HAVE TOOOO !!!

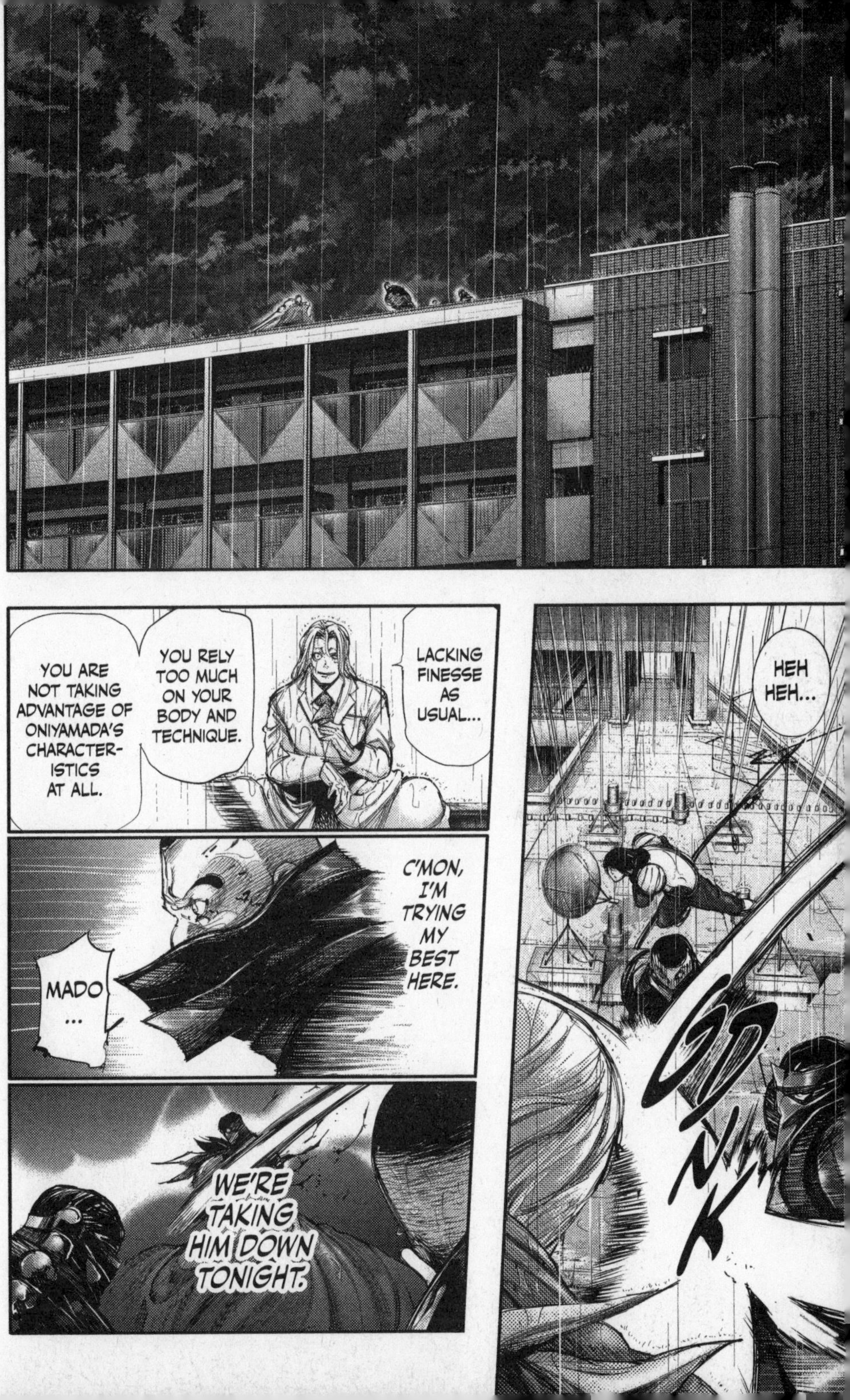
HEH HEH...
GONK
LACKING FINESSE AS USUAL...
YOU RELY TOO MUCH ON YOUR BODY AND TECHNIQUE.
YOU ARE NOT TAKING ADVANTAGE OF ONIYAMADA'S CHARACTER-ISTICS AT ALL.
C'MON, I'M TRYING MY BEST HERE.
MADO ...
WE'RE TAKING HIM DOWN TONIGHT.

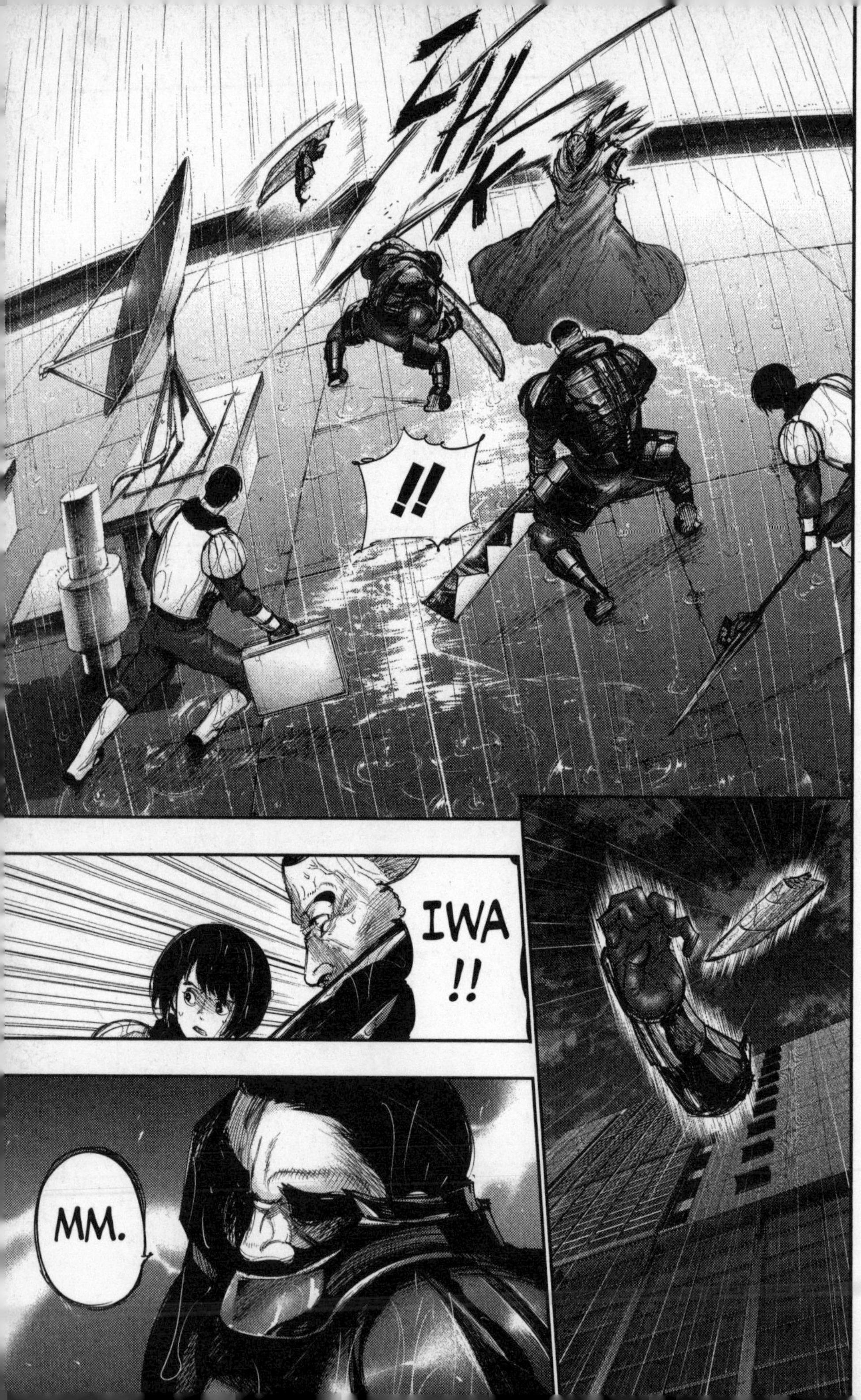
ZHK
!!
IWA!!
MM.

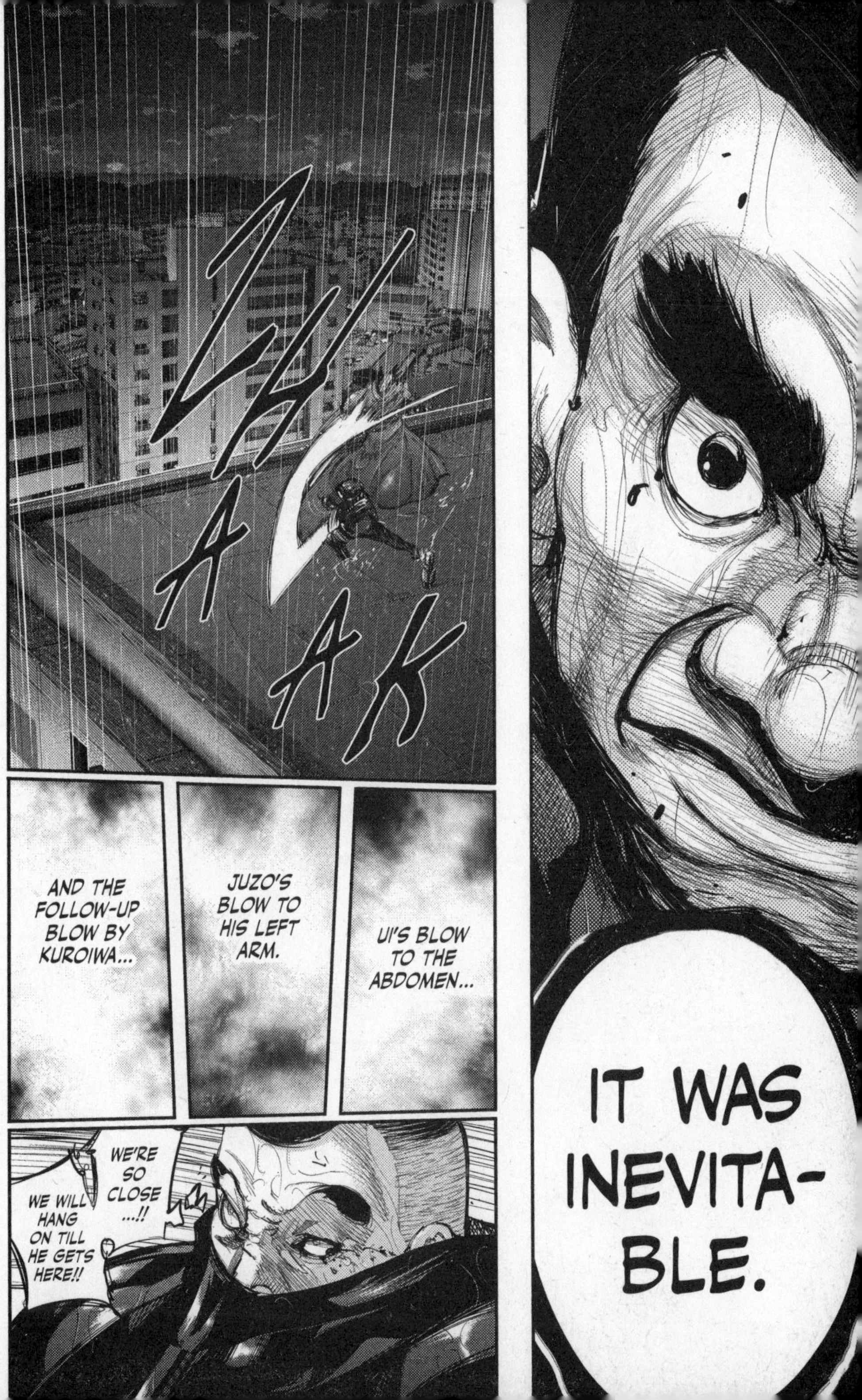
IT WAS INEVITABLE.
ZWAAK
UI'S BLOW TO THE ABDOMEN...
JUZO'S BLOW TO HIS LEFT ARM.
AND THE FOLLOW-UP BLOW BY KUROIWA...
WE'RE SO CLOSE ...!!
WE WILL HANG ON TILL HE GETS HERE!!

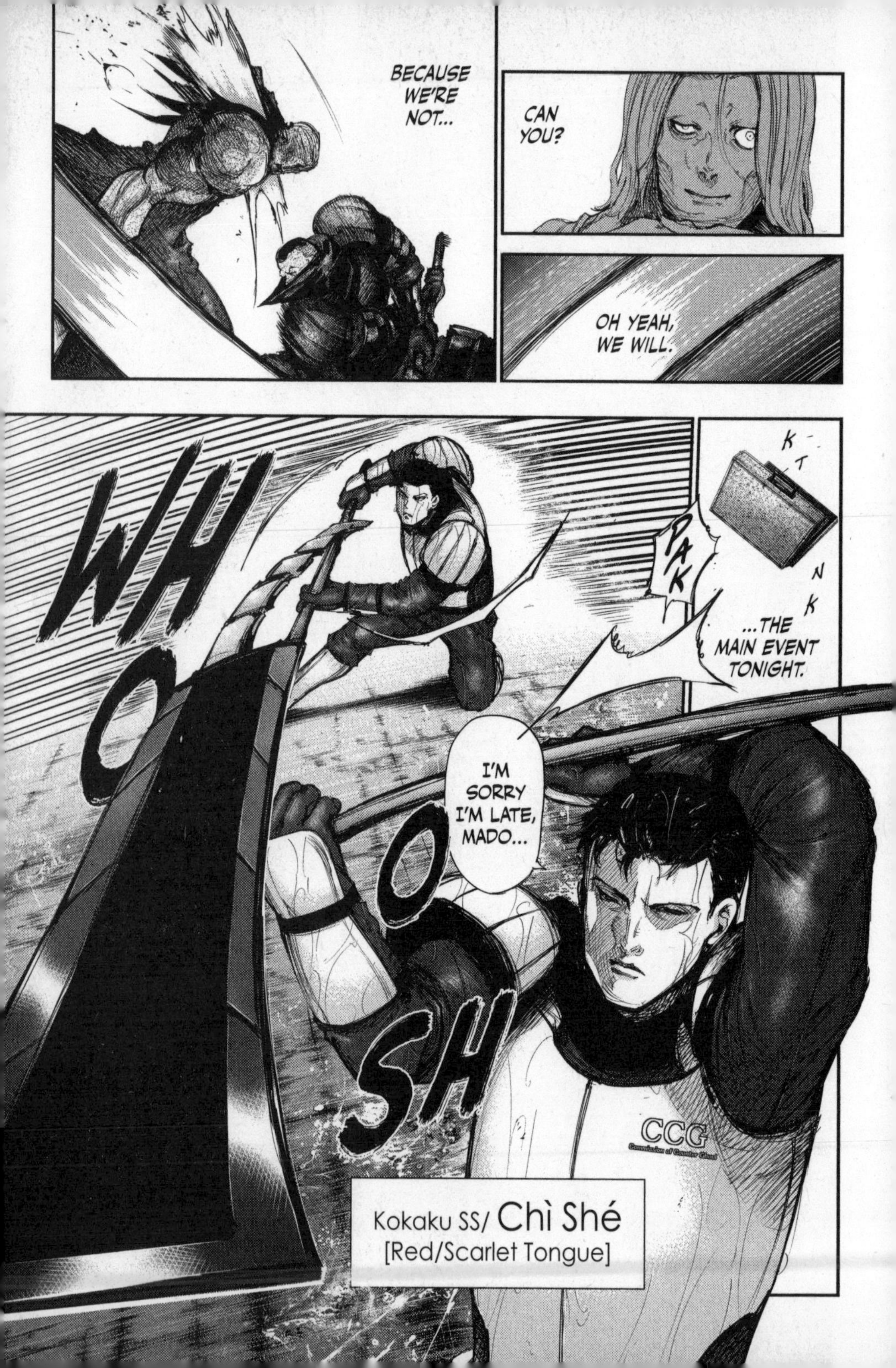
CAN YOU?
OH YEAH, WE WILL.
BECAUSE WE'RE NOT...
KTNK
DAK
...THE MAIN EVENT TONIGHT.
I'M SORRY I'M LATE, MADO...
WHOOOSH
CCG
Commission of Counter Ghoul
Kokaku SS/ Chì Shé
[Red/Scarlet Tongue]

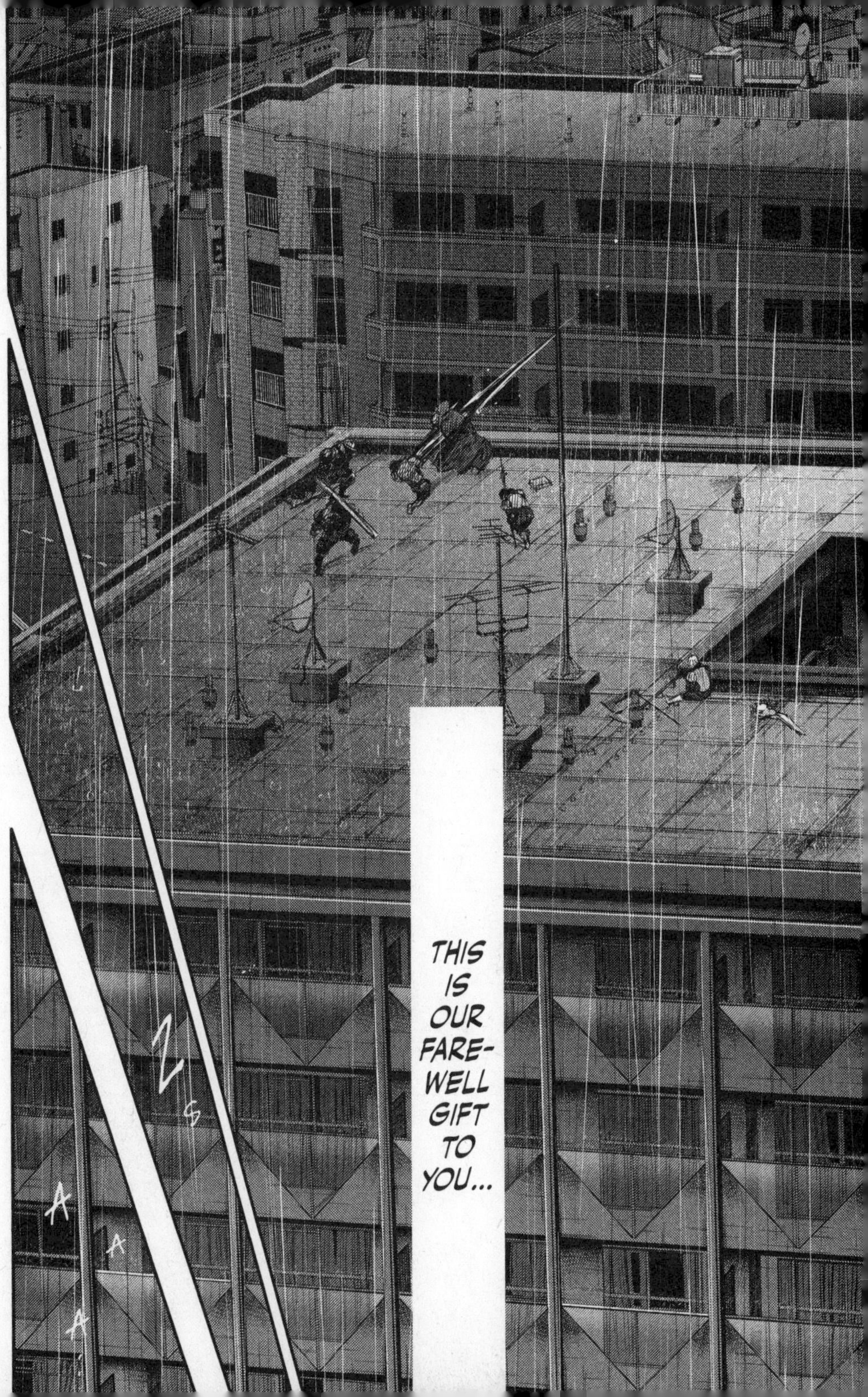
THIS IS OUR FARE-WELL GIFT TO YOU...
ZAAA

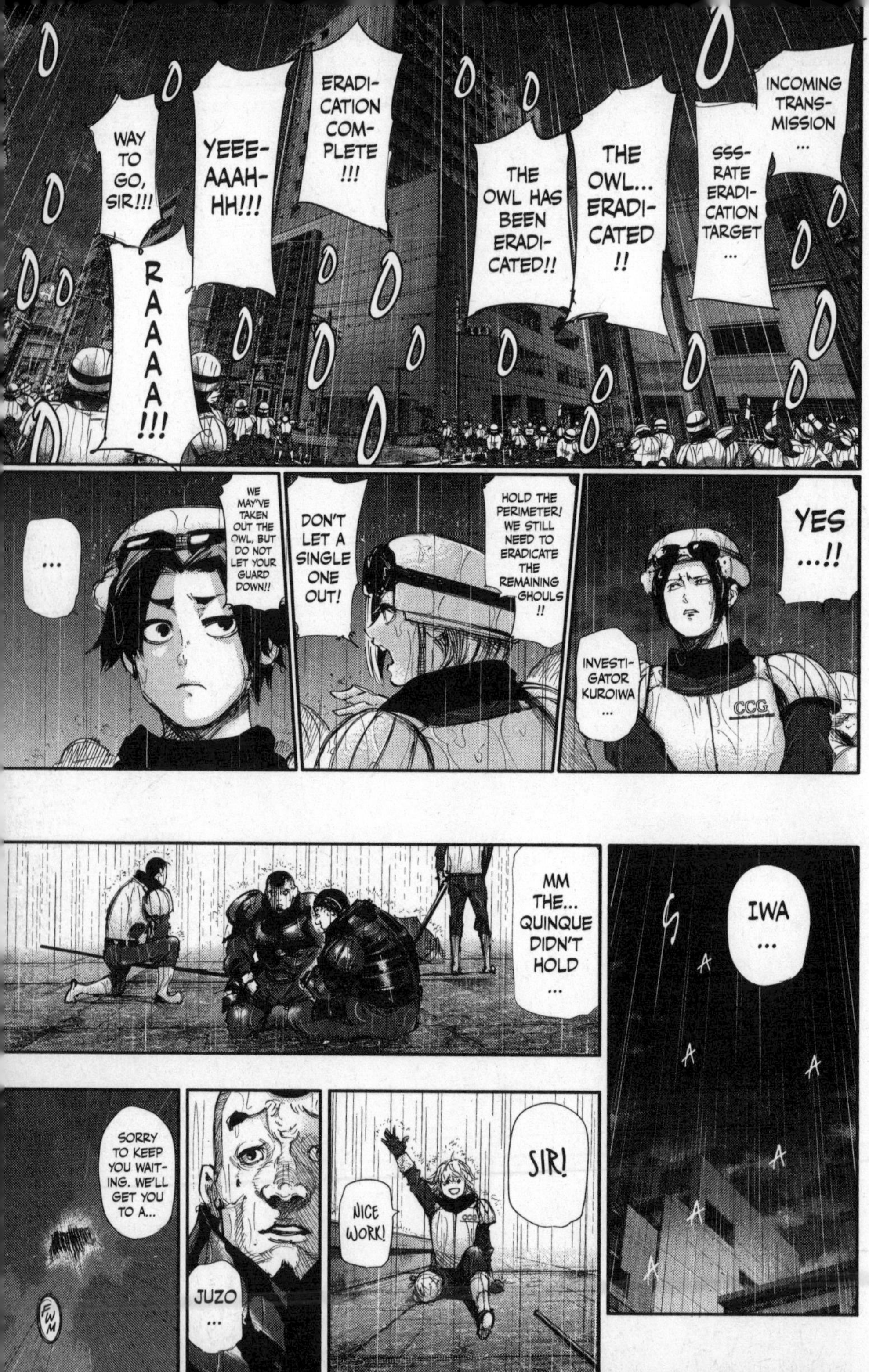
INCOMING TRANSMISSION...
SSS-RATE ERADICATION TARGET...
THE OWL... ERADICATED!!
THE OWL HAS BEEN ERADICATED!!
ERADICATION COMPLETE!!!
YEEE-AAAH-HH!!!
WAY TO GO, SIR!!!
RAAAAA!!!
YES...!!
INVESTIGATOR KUROIWA...
CCG
HOLD THE PERIMETER! WE STILL NEED TO ERADICATE THE REMAINING GHOULS!!
DON'T LET A SINGLE ONE OUT!
WE MAY'VE TAKEN OUT THE OWL, BUT DO NOT LET YOUR GUARD DOWN!!
...
IWA...
SAAAAAAA
MM THE... QUINQUE DIDN'T HOLD...
SIR!
NICE WORK!
SORRY TO KEEP YOU WAITING. WE'LL GET YOU TO A...
JUZO...
FWM

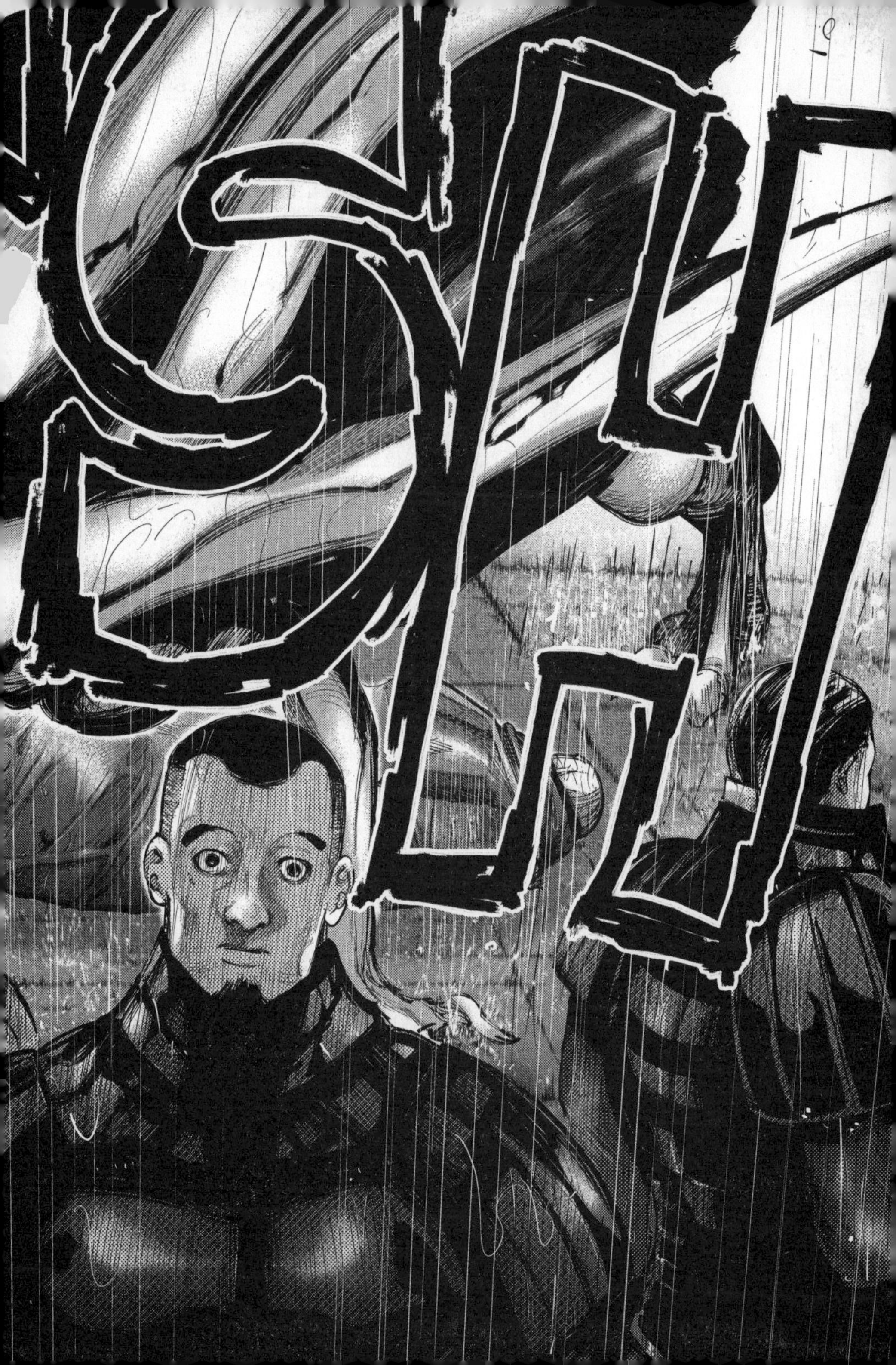
SHH

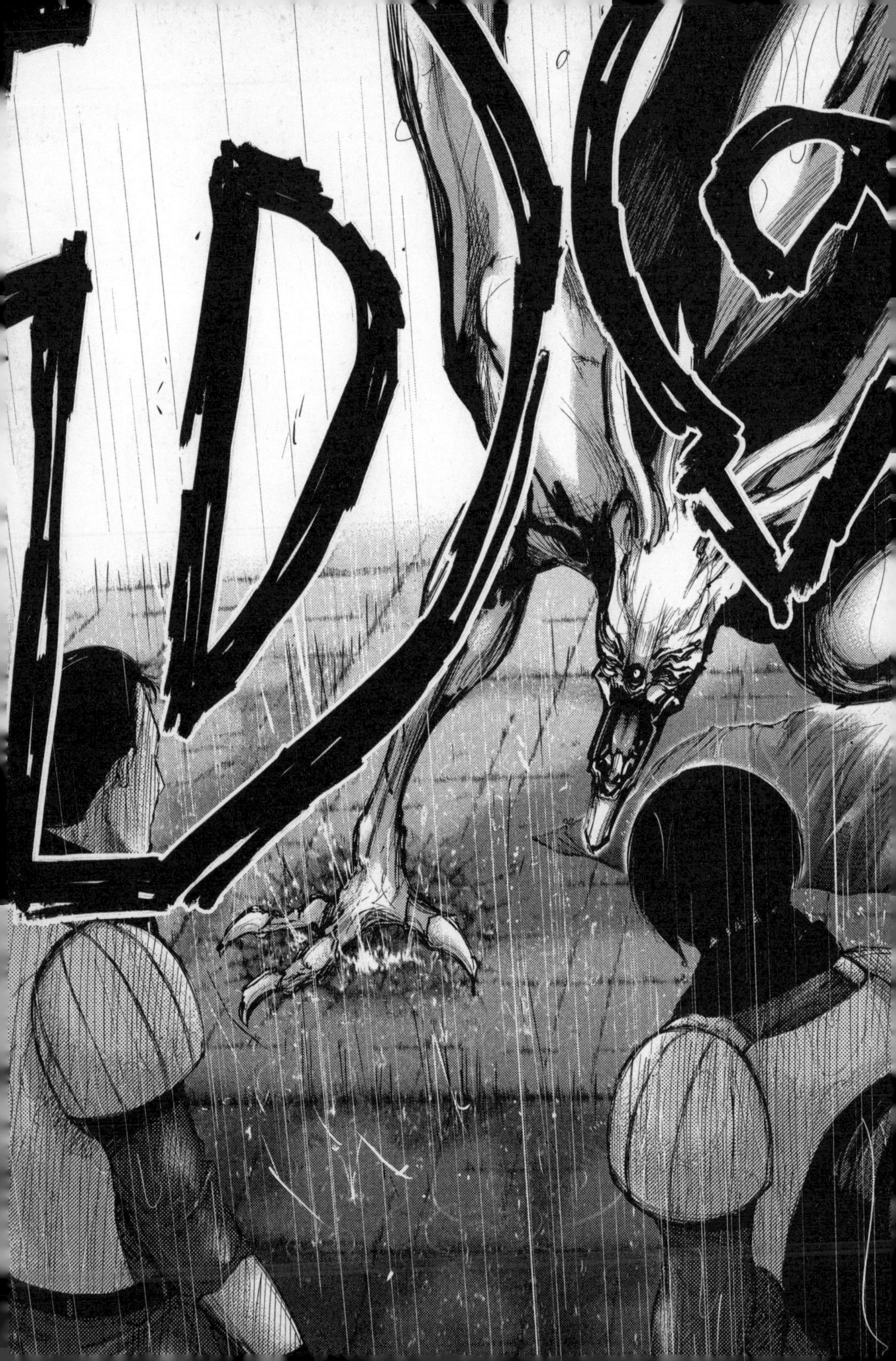

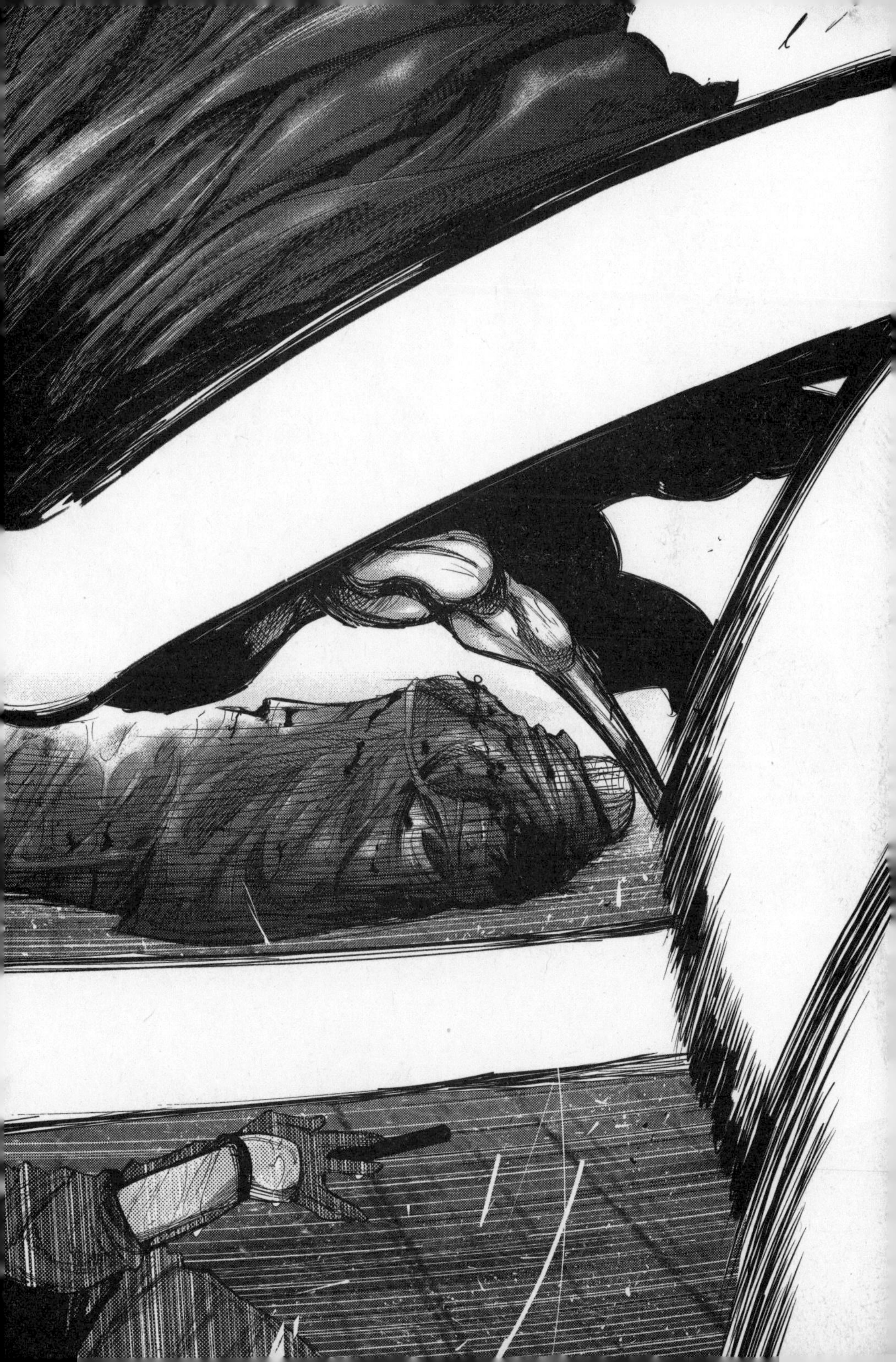

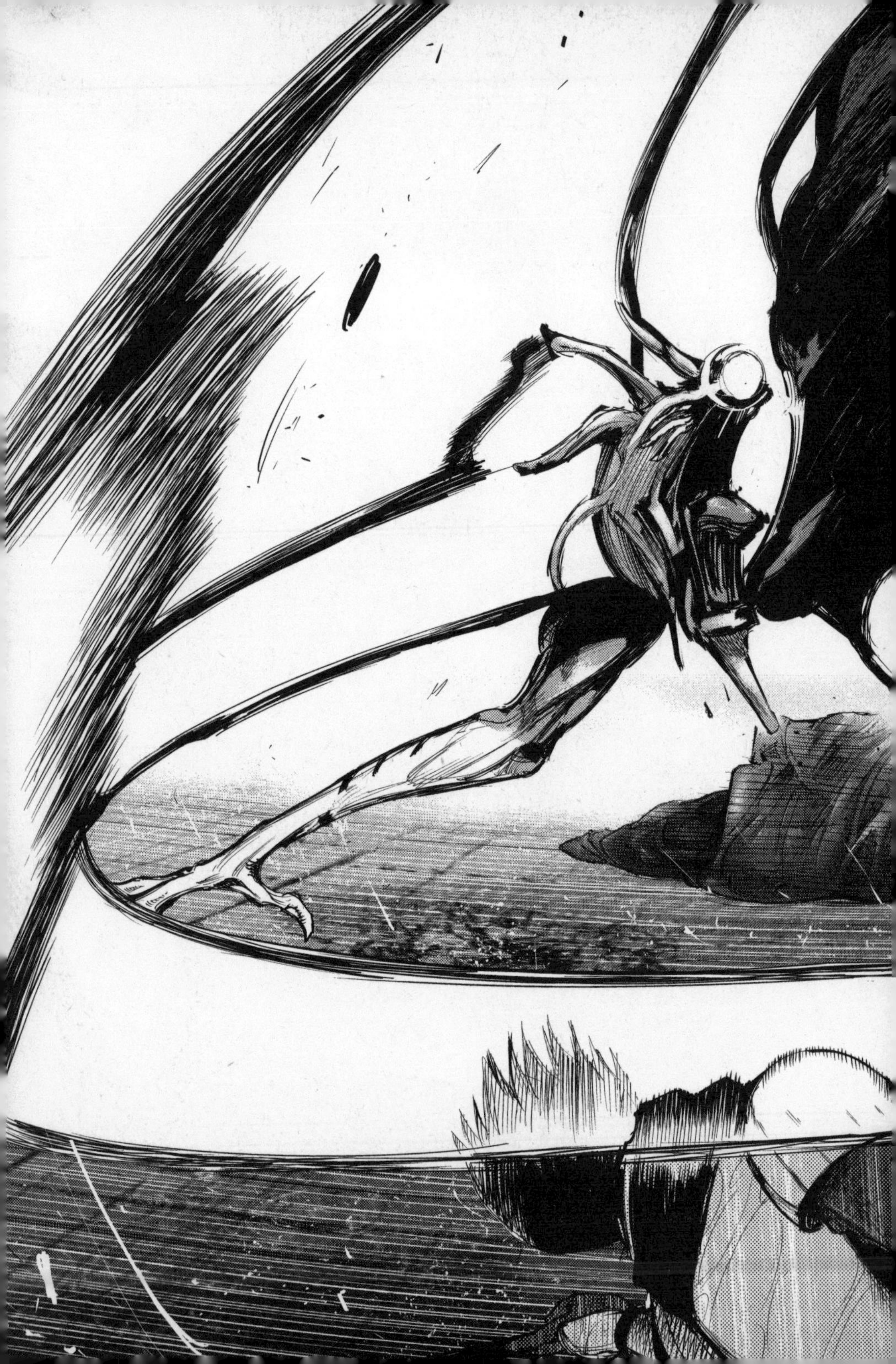

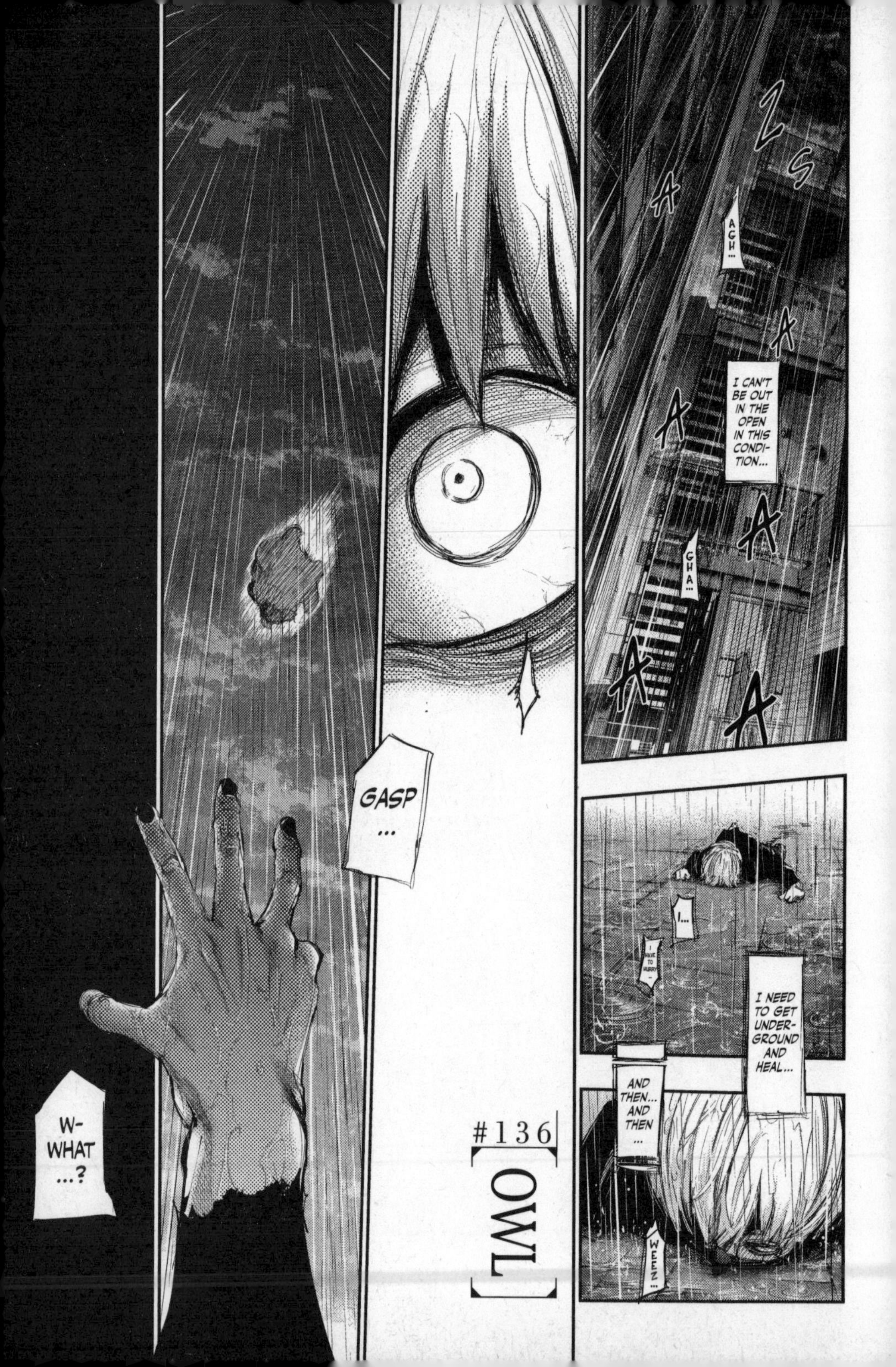
AGH...
I CAN'T BE OUT IN THE OPEN IN THIS CONDITION...
GHA...
I NEED TO GET UNDERGROUND AND HEAL...
I...
I HAVE TO HURRY...
AND THEN... AND THEN ...
WEEZ...
GASP ...
#136
OWL
W-WHAT ...?

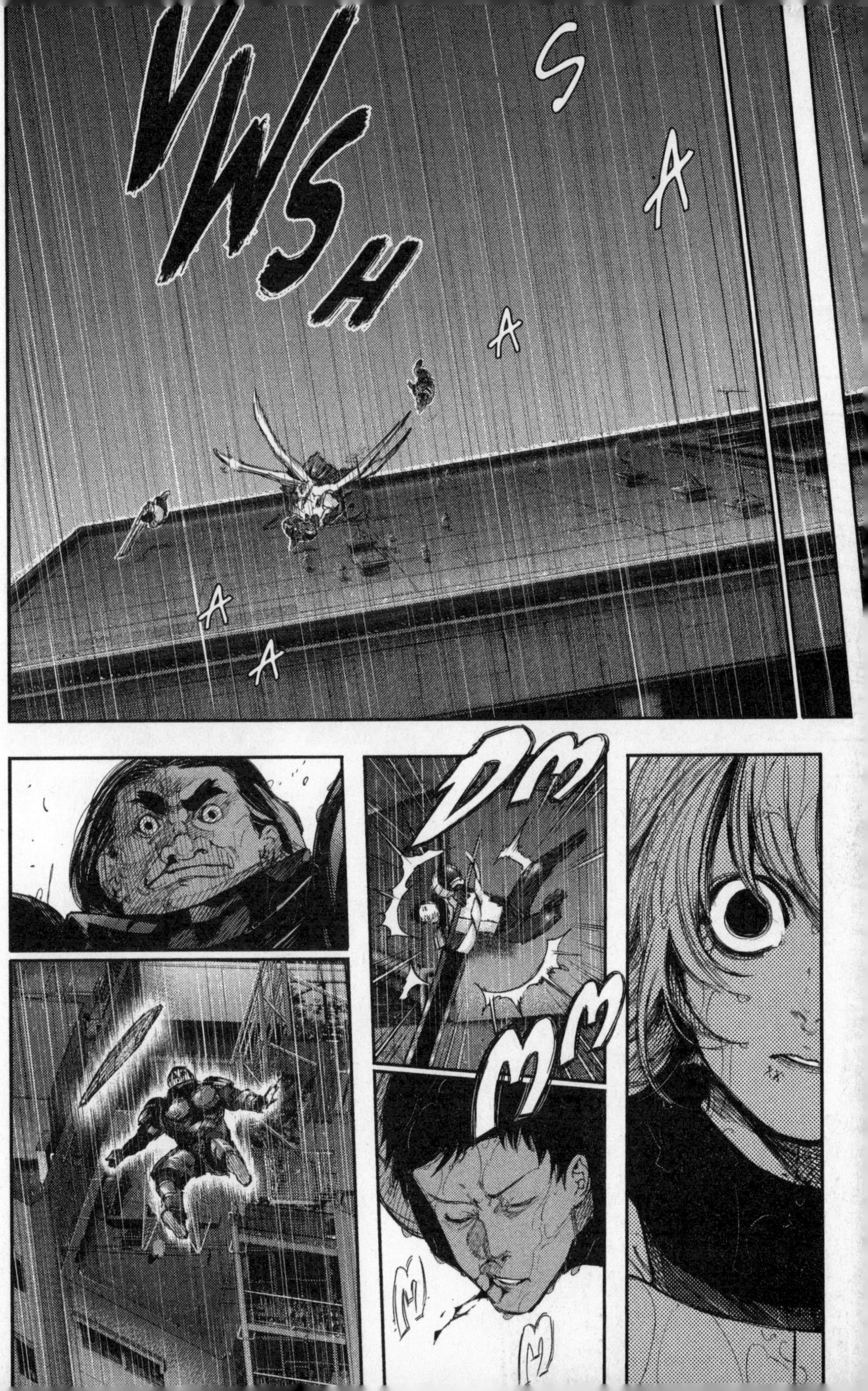
SAAAA
VWSH
DMMMM
M M M

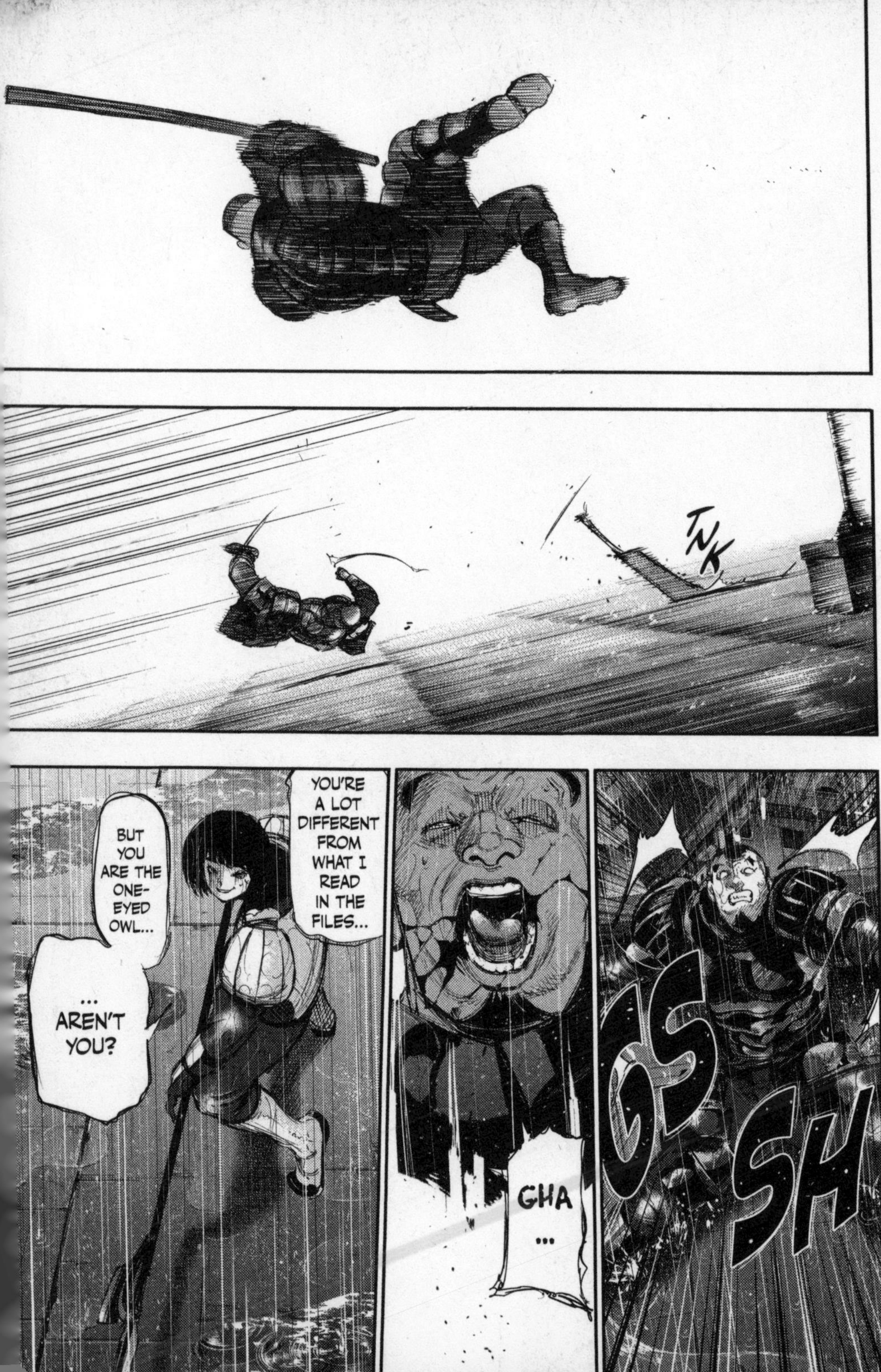
TNK
GSSH
GHA ...
YOU'RE A LOT DIFFERENT FROM WHAT I READ IN THE FILES...
BUT YOU ARE THE ONE-EYED OWL...
... AREN'T YOU?

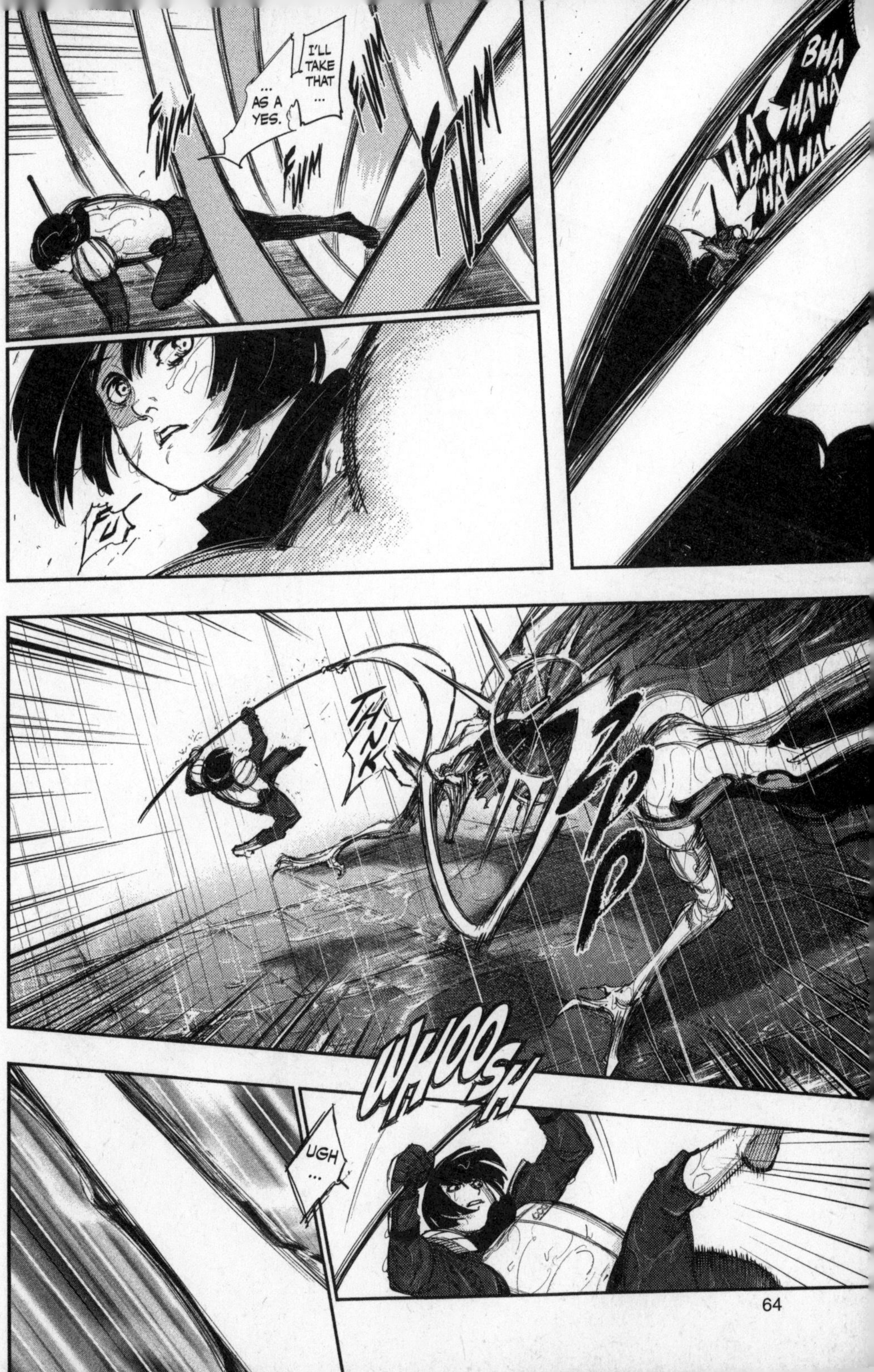

BHA HAHA HA HA HAHAHA HA
FWM
I'LL TAKE THAT ...
... AS A YES.
FWM
FWM
FWM
FWM
FU
THUNK
WHOOSH
UGH ...

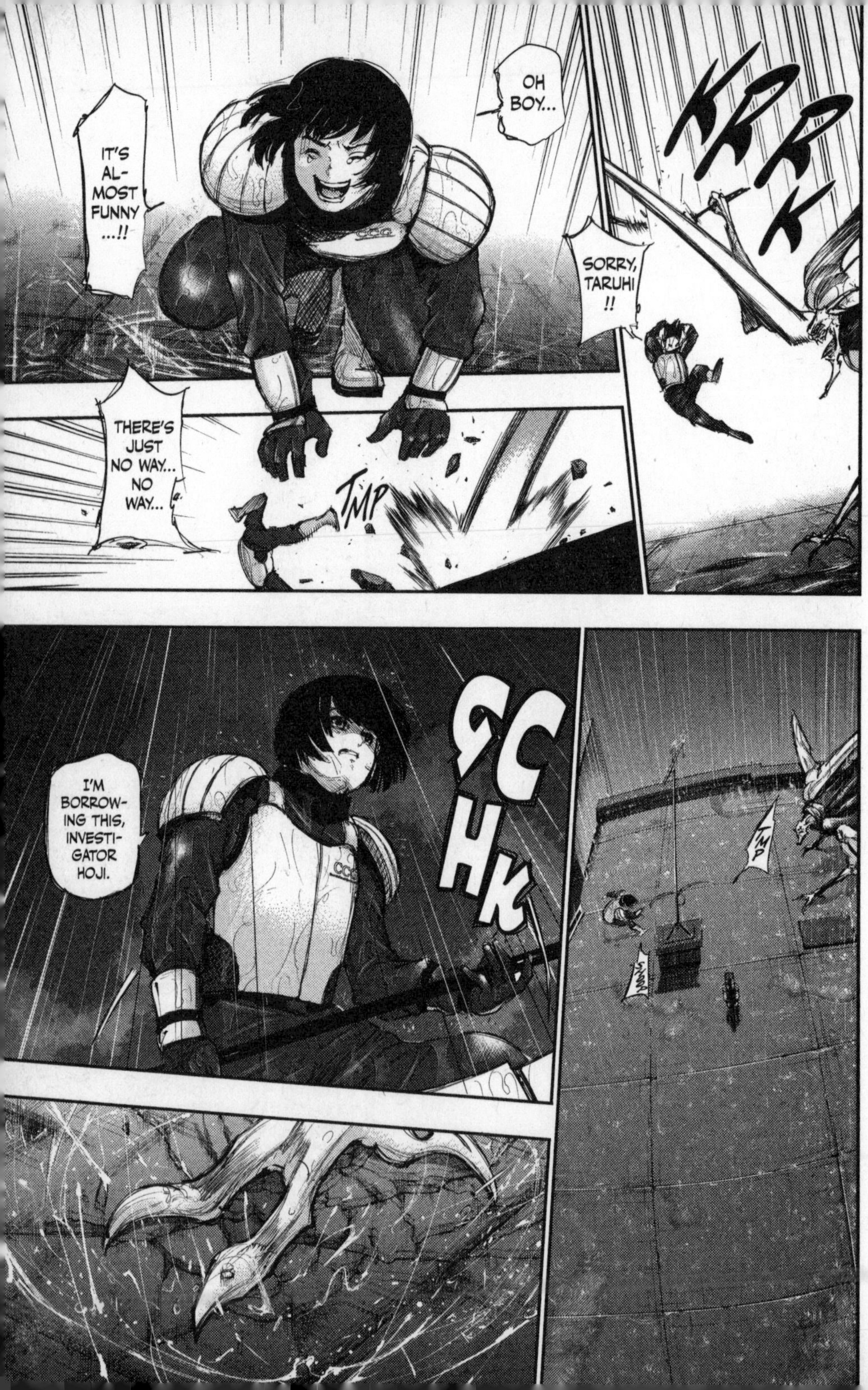
KRRK
SORRY, TARUHI!!
OH BOY...
IT'S AL-MOST FUNNY...!!
THERE'S JUST NO WAY... NO WAY...
TMP
TMP
GCHHK
I'M BORROW-ING THIS, INVESTI-GATOR HOJI.

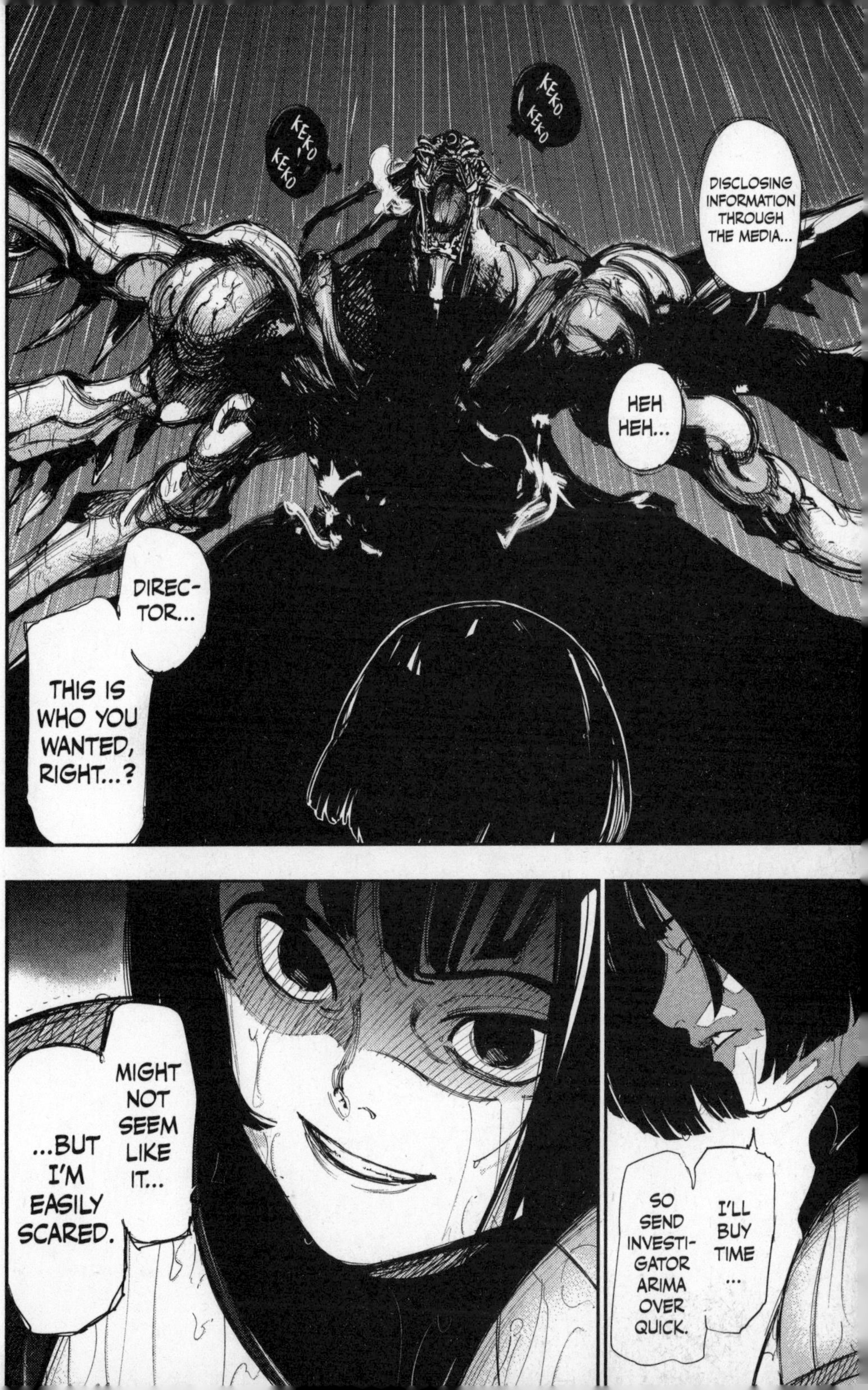
DISCLOSING INFORMATION THROUGH THE MEDIA...
KEKO KEKO
KEKO! KEKO
HEH HEH...
DIRECTOR...
THIS IS WHO YOU WANTED, RIGHT...?
I'LL BUY TIME ...
SO SEND INVESTIGATOR ARIMA OVER QUICK.
MIGHT NOT SEEM LIKE IT...
...BUT I'M EASILY SCARED.

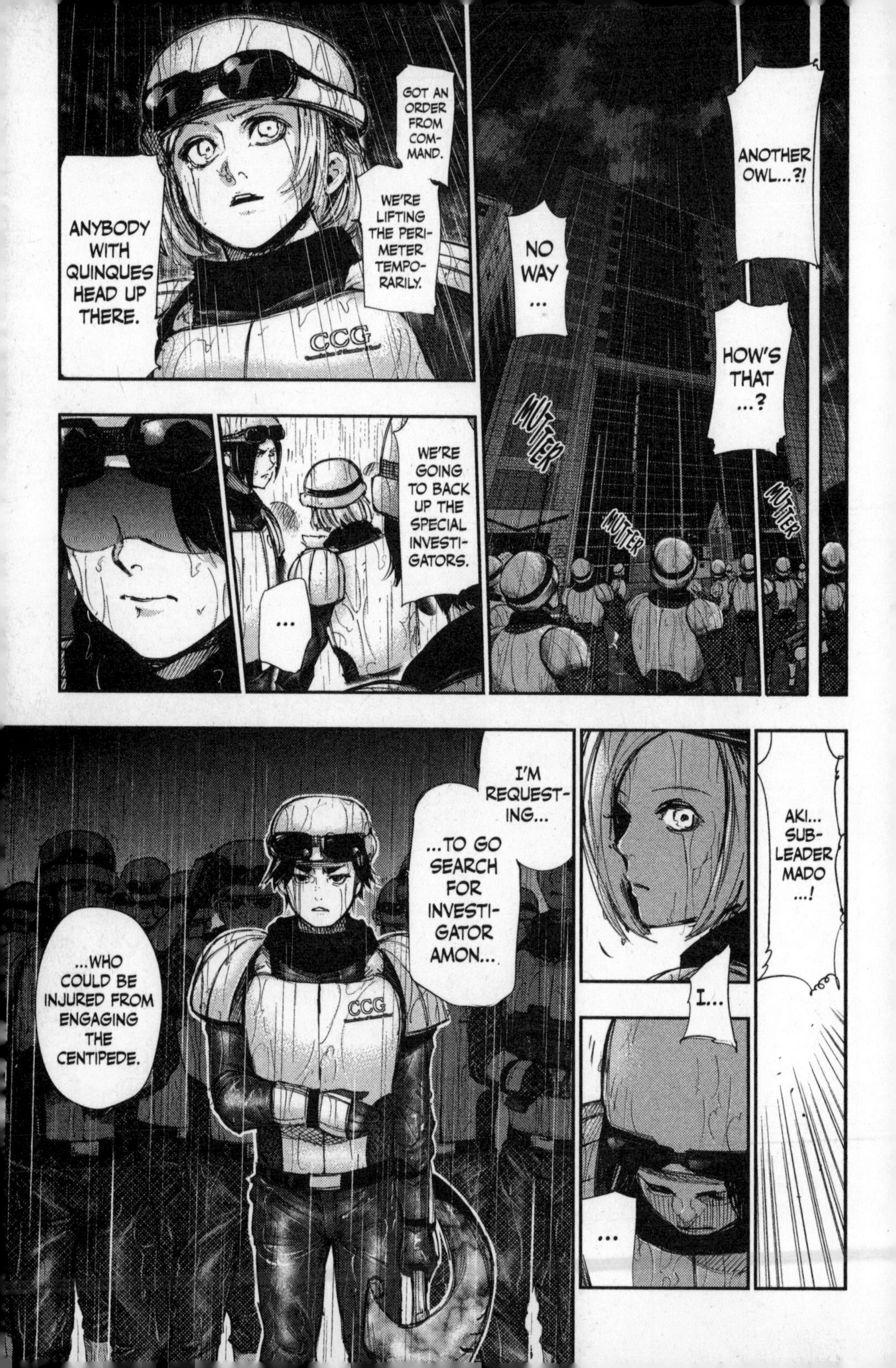
ANOTHER OWL...?!
NO WAY ...
HOW'S THAT ...?
MUTTER
MUTTER
MUTTER
GOT AN ORDER FROM COM-MAND.
WE'RE LIFTING THE PERI-METER TEMPO-RARILY.
ANYBODY WITH QUINQUES HEAD UP THERE.
WE'RE GOING TO BACK UP THE SPECIAL INVESTI-GATORS.
...
AKI... SUB-LEADER MADO ...!
I...
...
I'M REQUEST-ING...
...TO GO SEARCH FOR INVESTI-GATOR AMON...
...WHO COULD BE INJURED FROM ENGAGING THE CENTIPEDE.

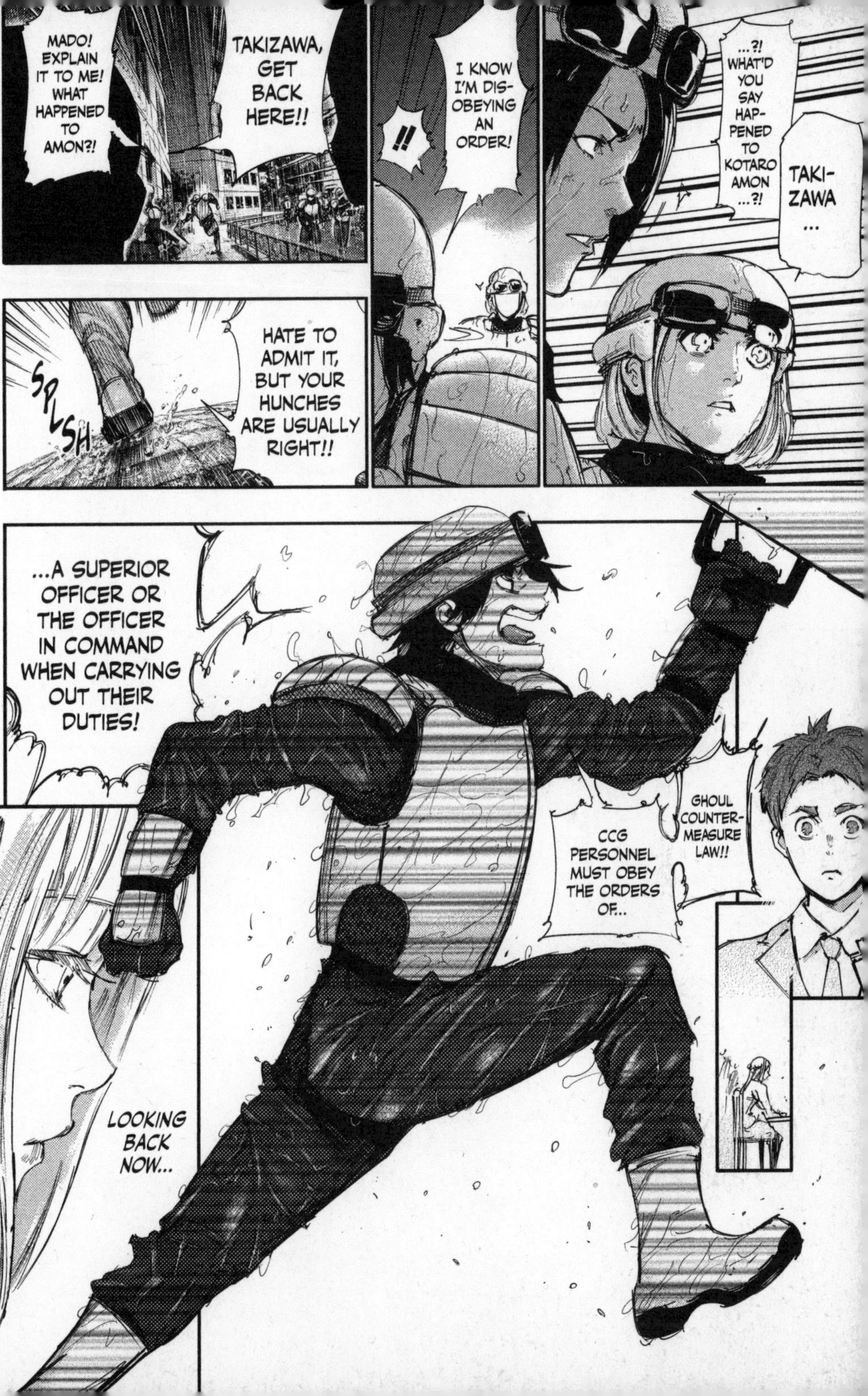
TAKI-ZAWA...
...?! WHAT'D YOU SAY HAP-PENED TO KOTARO AMON...?!
!!
I KNOW I'M DIS-OBEYING AN ORDER!
TAKIZAWA, GET BACK HERE!!
MADO! EXPLAIN IT TO ME! WHAT HAPPENED TO AMON?!
HATE TO ADMIT IT, BUT YOUR HUNCHES ARE USUALLY RIGHT!!
SPLSH
GHOUL COUNTER-MEASURE LAW!!
CCG PERSONNEL MUST OBEY THE ORDERS OF...
...A SUPERIOR OFFICER OR THE OFFICER IN COMMAND WHEN CARRYING OUT THEIR DUTIES!
LOOKING BACK NOW...

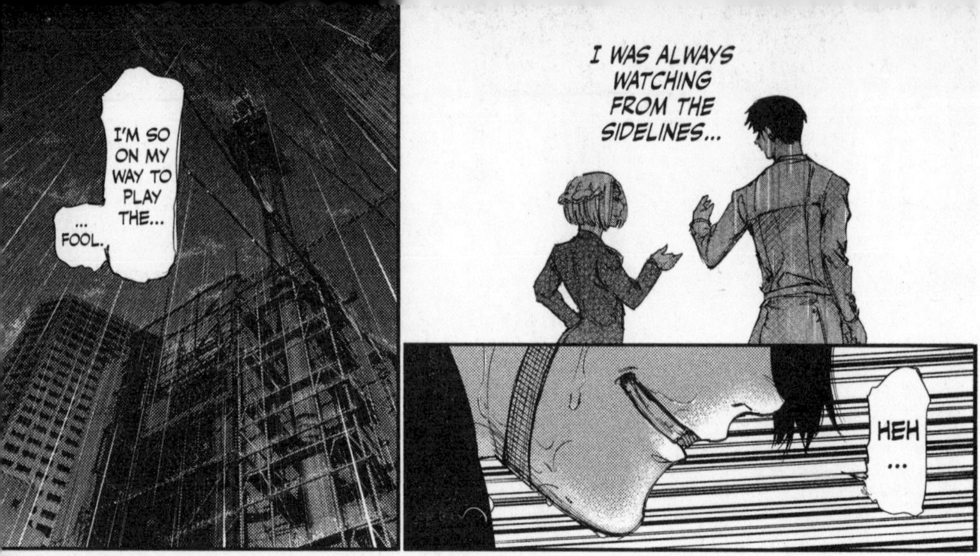
I WAS ALWAYS WATCHING FROM THE SIDELINES...
HEH...
I'M SO ON MY WAY TO PLAY THE...
...FOOL.

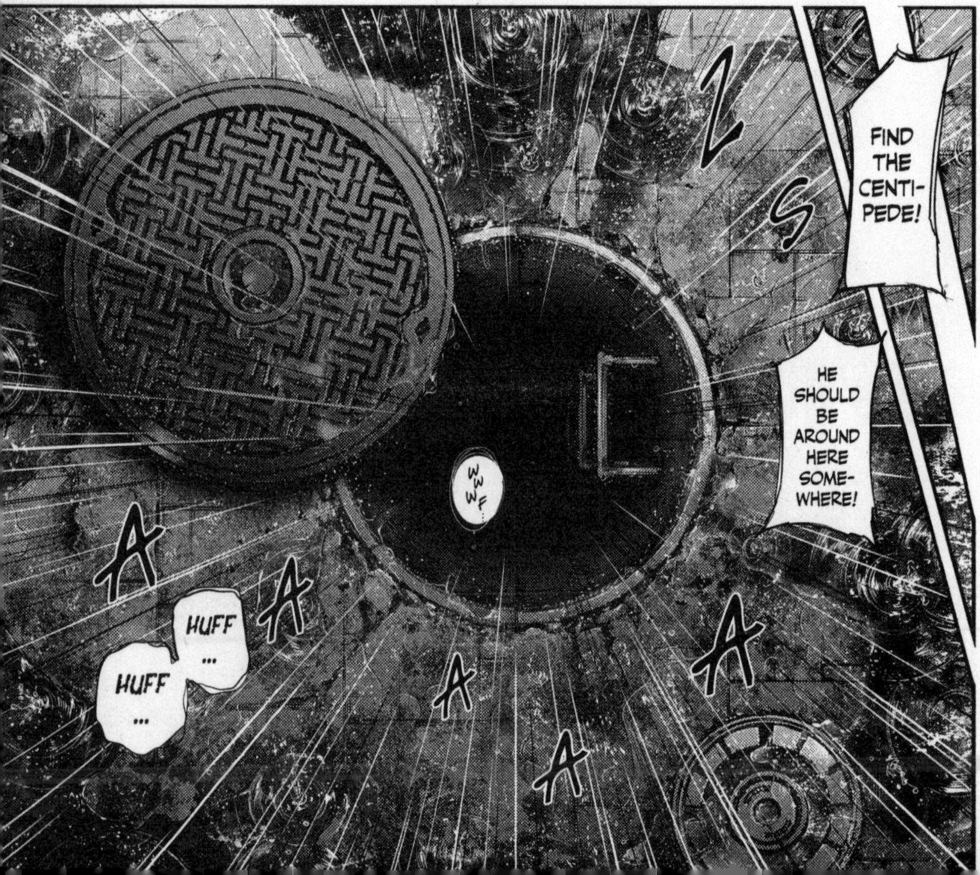
FIND THE CENTI-PEDE!
Z
S
HE SHOULD BE AROUND HERE SOME-WHERE!
WWF...
A
A
A
A
A
A
HUFF...
HUFF...

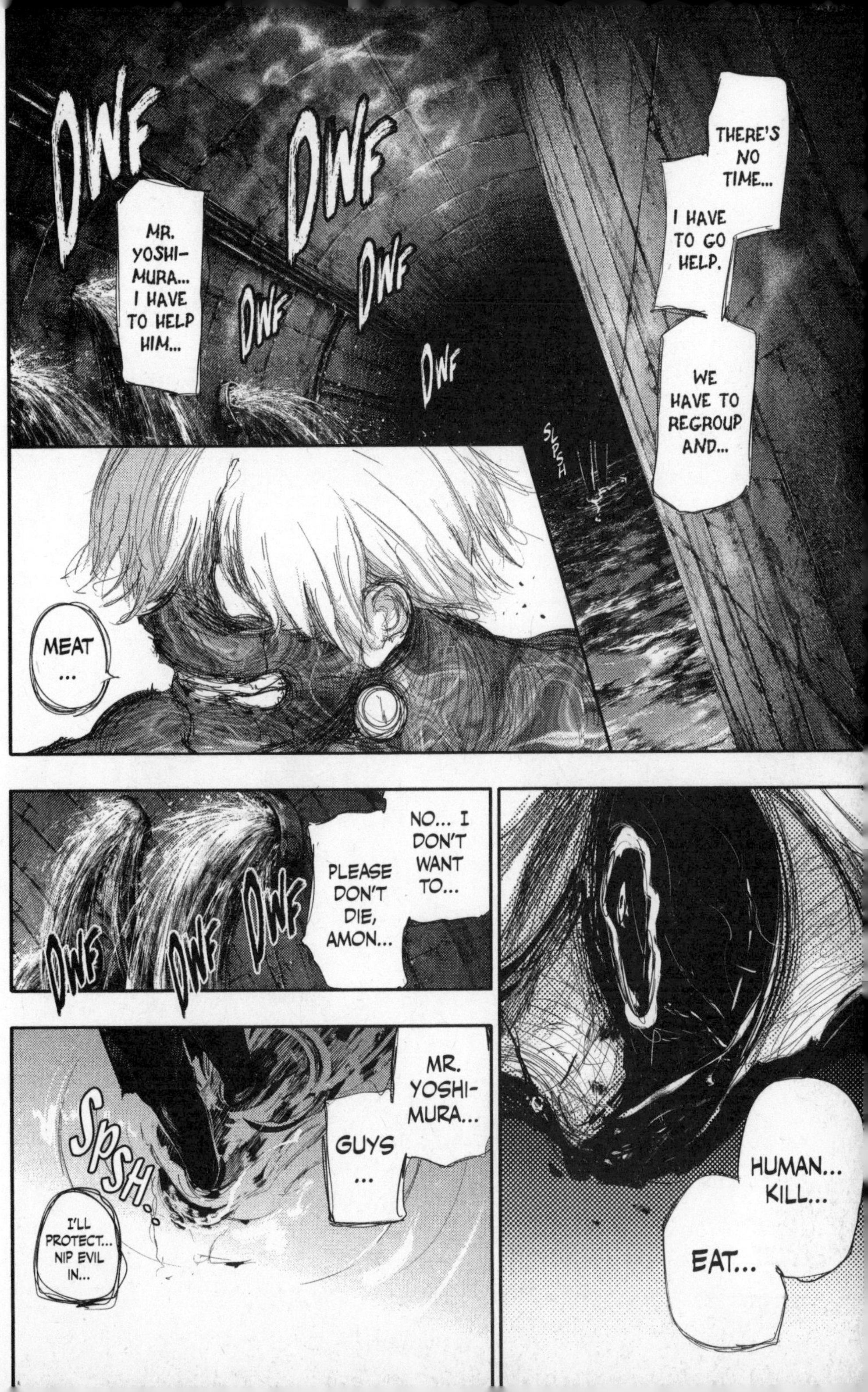
THERE'S NO TIME...
I HAVE TO GO HELP.
WE HAVE TO REGROUP AND...
DWF
DWF
DWF
DWF
DWF
MR. YOSHI-MURA... I HAVE TO HELP HIM...
SLPSH
MEAT ...
HUMAN... KILL...
EAT...
NO... I DON'T WANT TO...
PLEASE DON'T DIE, AMON...
DWF
DWF
DWF
MR. YOSHI-MURA...
GUYS ...
SPSH..
I'LL PROTECT... NIP EVIL IN...

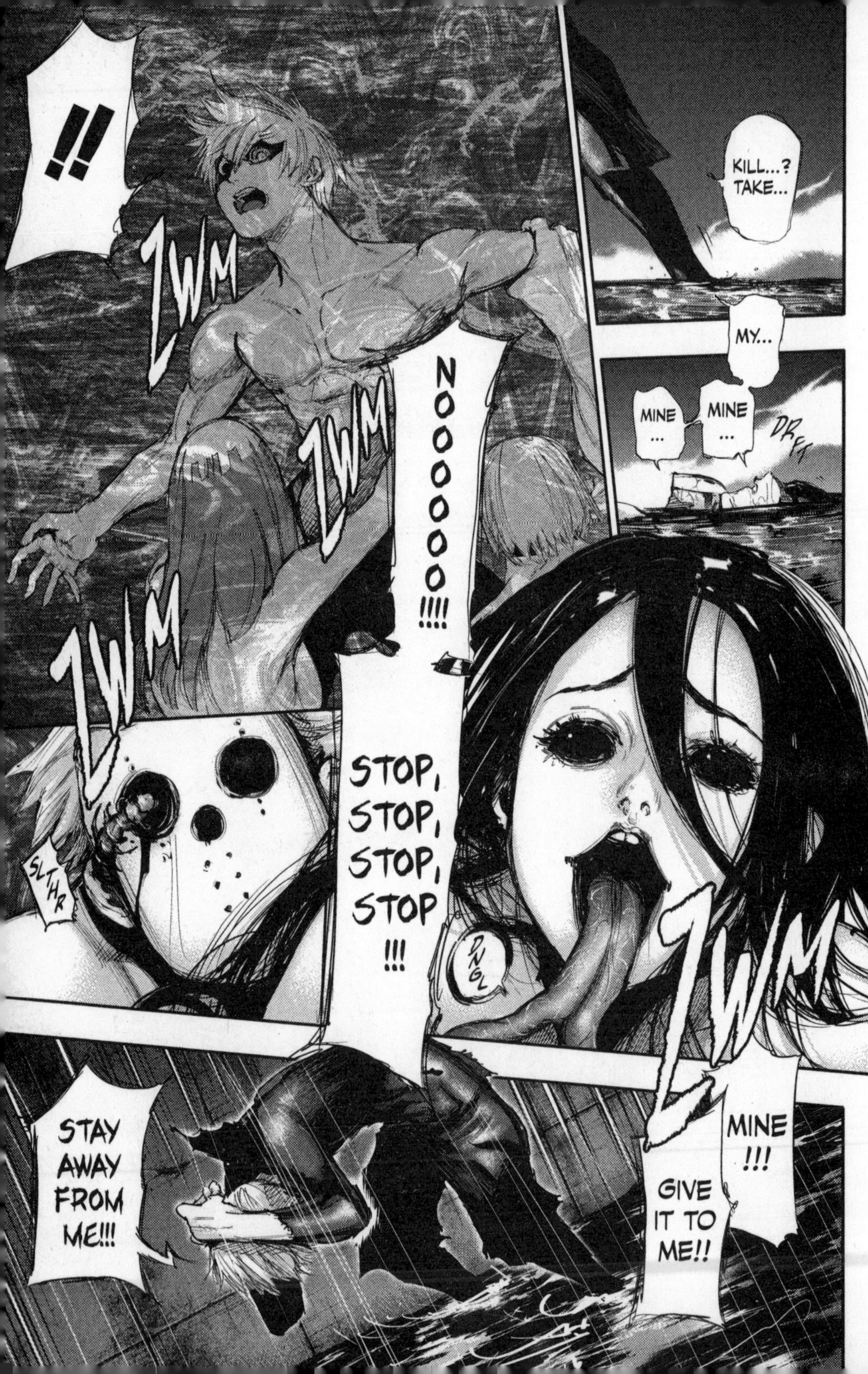
KILL...? TAKE...
MY...
MINE ...
MINE ...
!!
ZWM
ZWM
NOOOOOOO!!!!
ZWM
ZWM
DNGL
STOP, STOP, STOP, STOP!!!
SLTHR
MINE!!!
GIVE IT TO ME!!
STAY AWAY FROM ME!!!

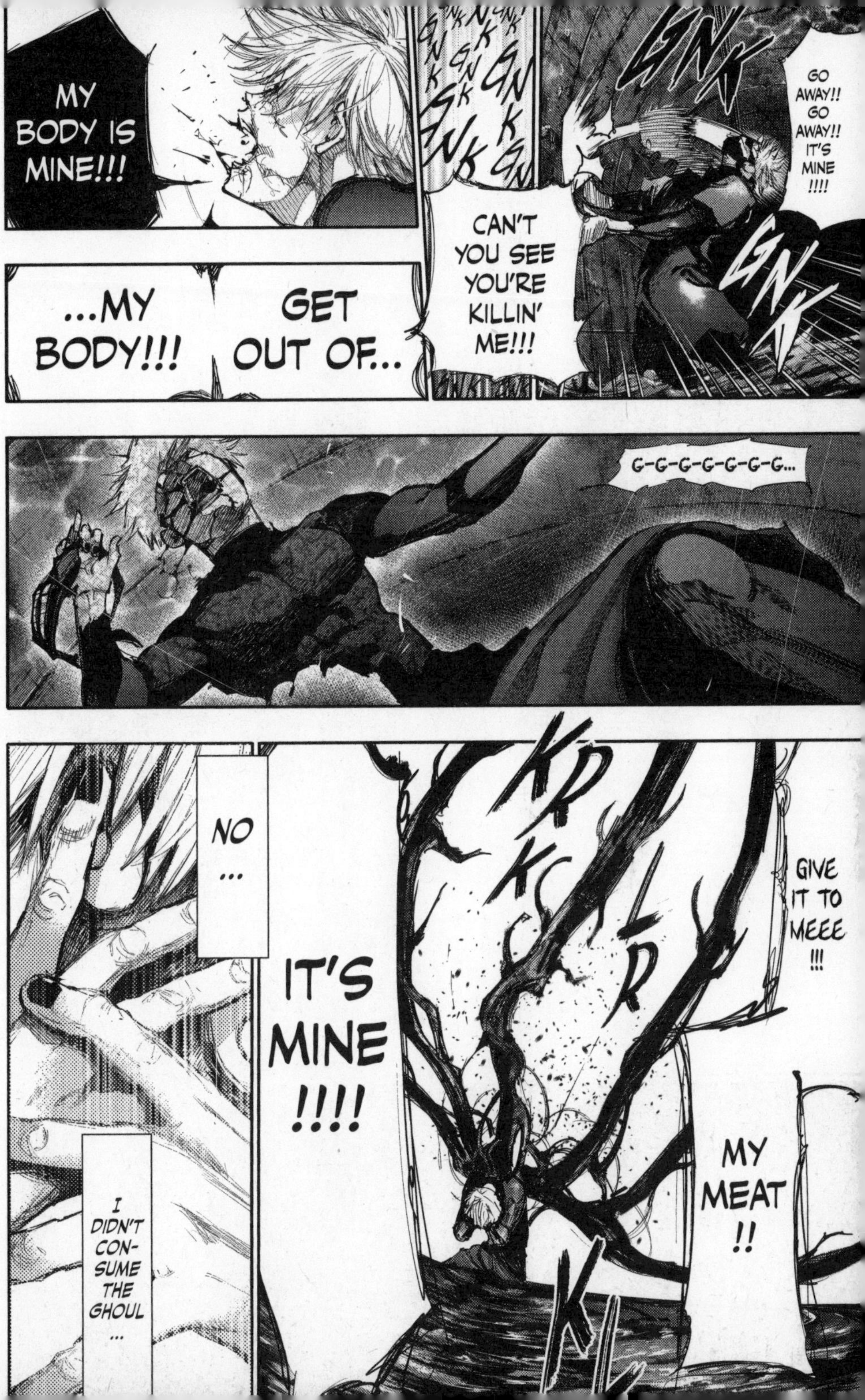
GNK
GO AWAY!! GO AWAY!! IT'S MINE!!!!
GNK
CAN'T YOU SEE YOU'RE KILLIN' ME!!!
MY BODY IS MINE!!!
GET OUT OF...
...MY BODY!!!
G-G-G-G-G-G-G...
GIVE IT TO MEEE!!!
MY MEAT!!
IT'S MINE!!!!
NO...
I DIDN'T CON-SUME THE GHOUL...

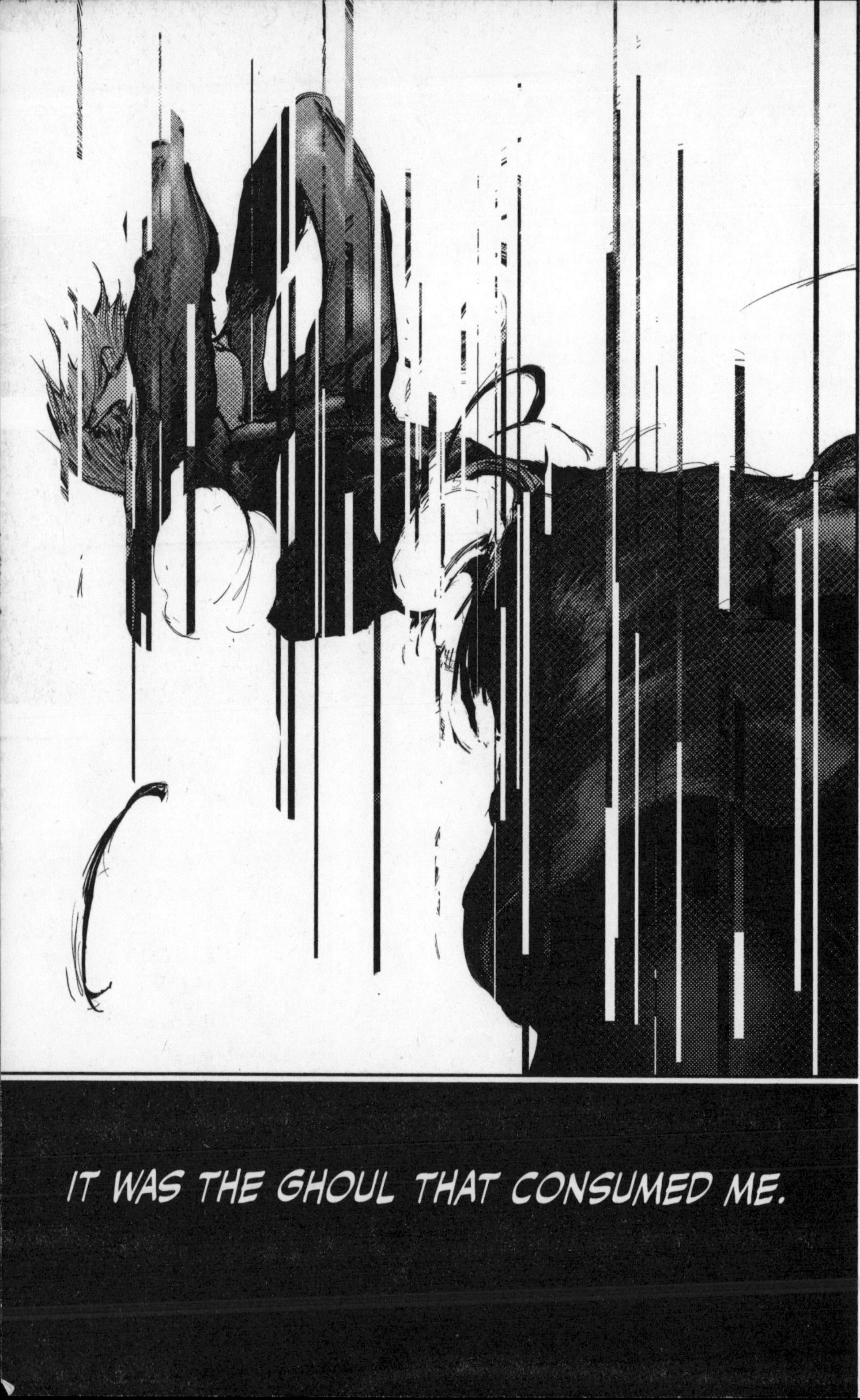
IT WAS THE GHOUL THAT CONSUMED ME.

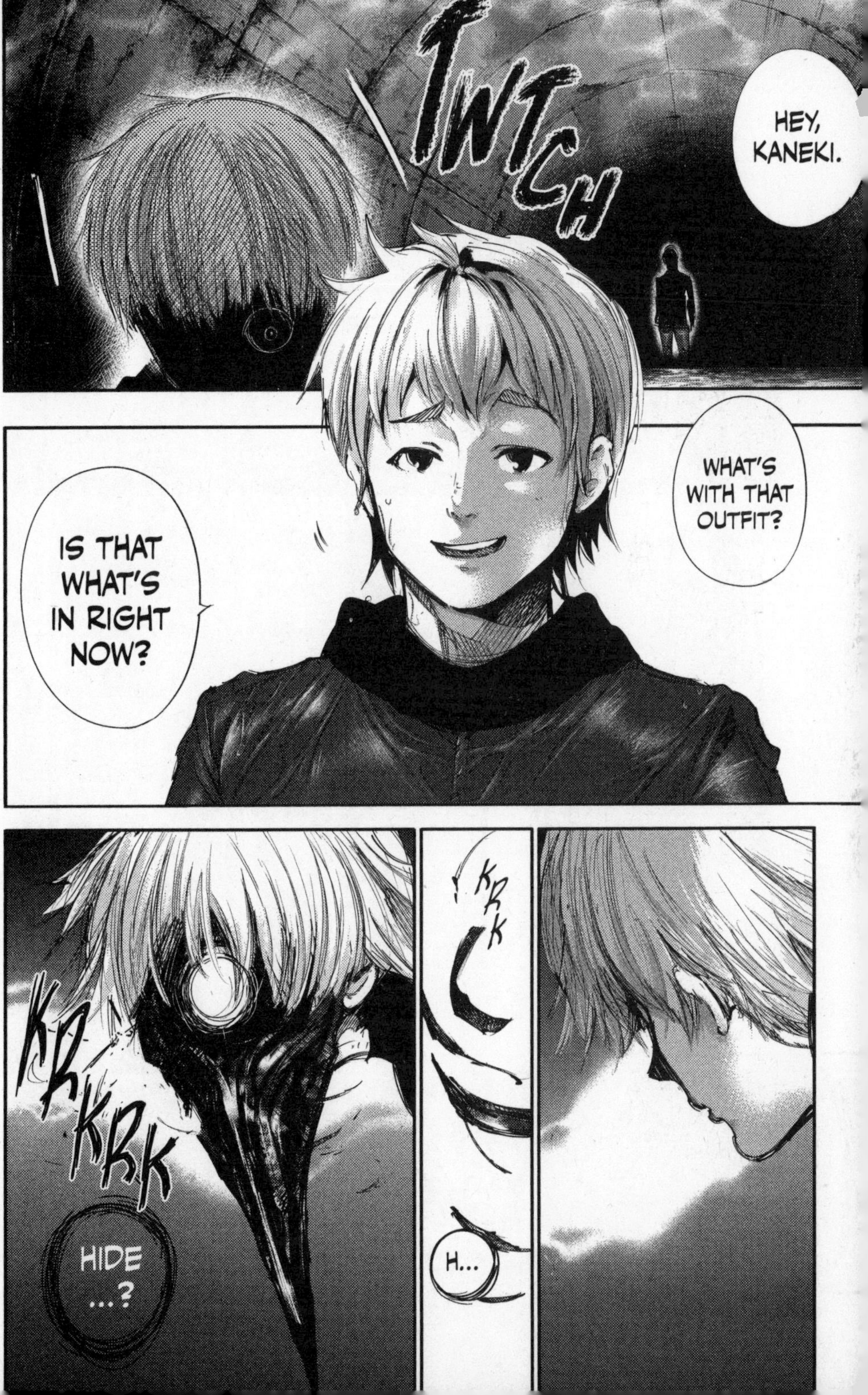
HEY, KANEKI.
TWITCH
WHAT'S WITH THAT OUTFIT?
IS THAT WHAT'S IN RIGHT NOW?
KRK
H...
KRKRKRK
HIDE ...?

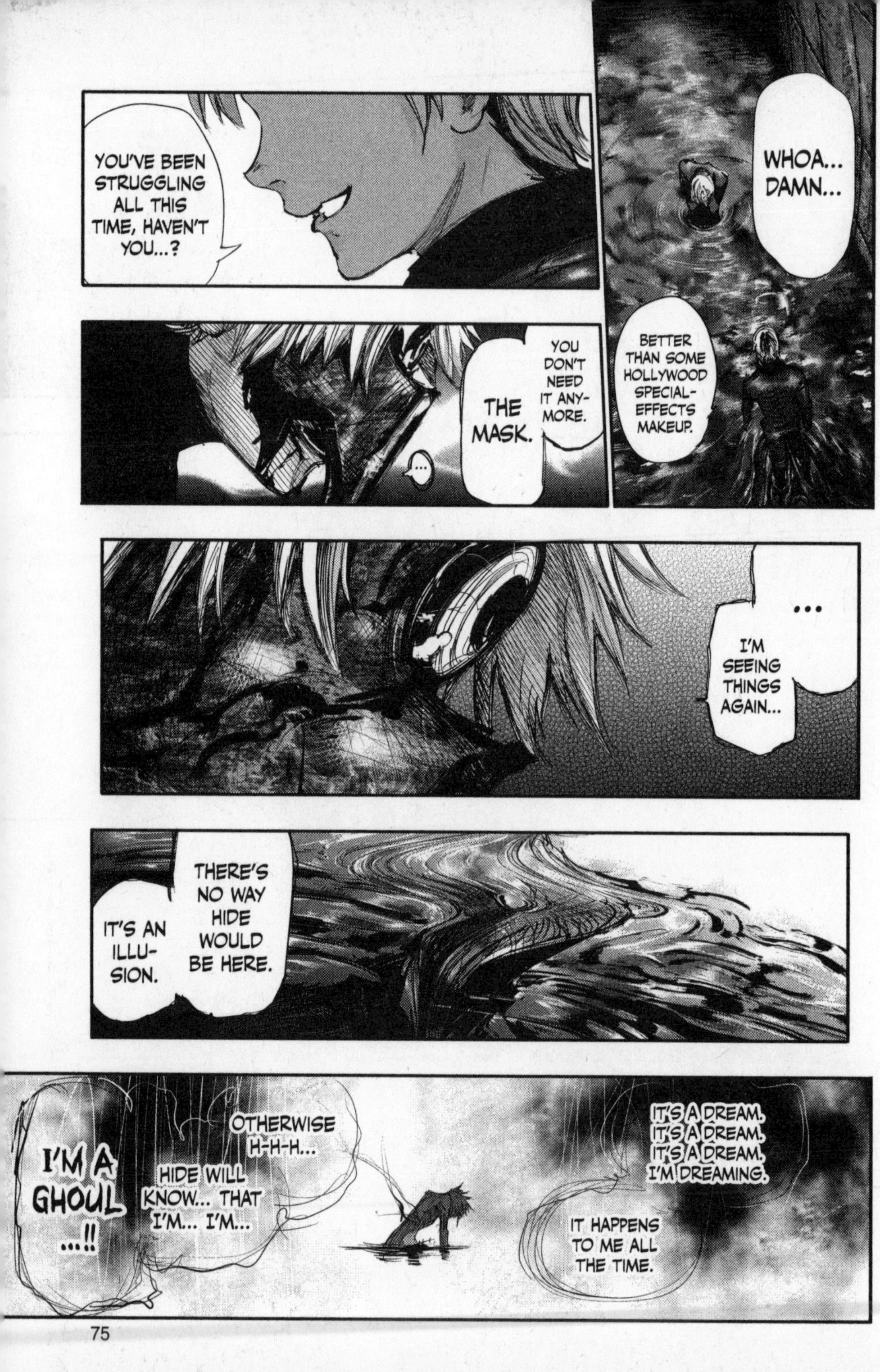

WHOA... DAMN...
YOU'VE BEEN STRUGGLING ALL THIS TIME, HAVEN'T YOU...?
BETTER THAN SOME HOLLYWOOD SPECIAL-EFFECTS MAKEUP.
YOU DON'T NEED IT ANYMORE.
THE MASK.
...
...
I'M SEEING THINGS AGAIN...
THERE'S NO WAY HIDE WOULD BE HERE.
IT'S AN ILLUSION.
IT'S A DREAM. IT'S A DREAM. IT'S A DREAM. I'M DREAMING.
IT HAPPENS TO ME ALL THE TIME.
OTHERWISE H-H-H...
HIDE WILL KNOW... THAT I'M... I'M...
I'M A GHOUL ...!!

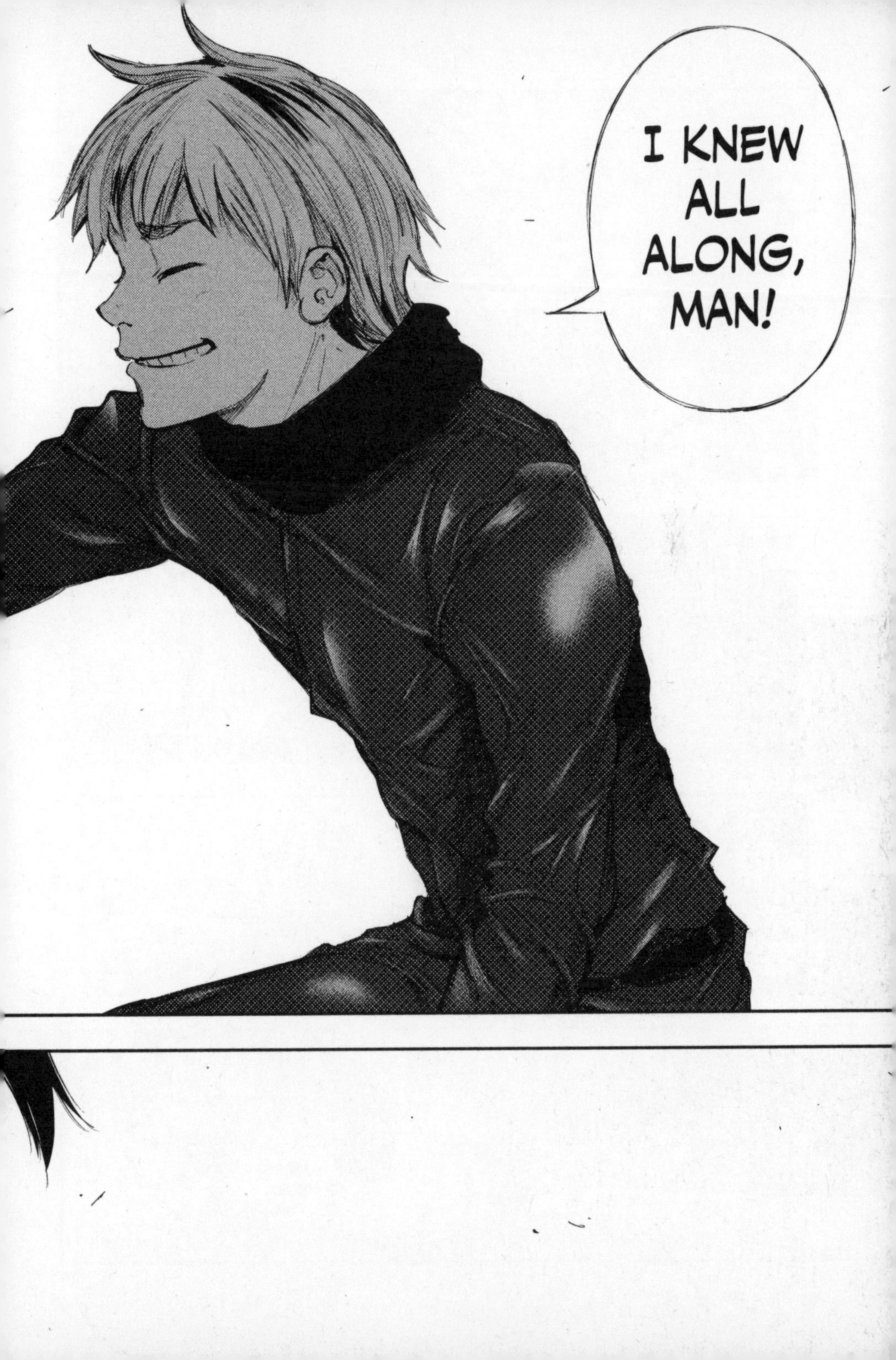
I KNEW ALL ALONG, MAN!

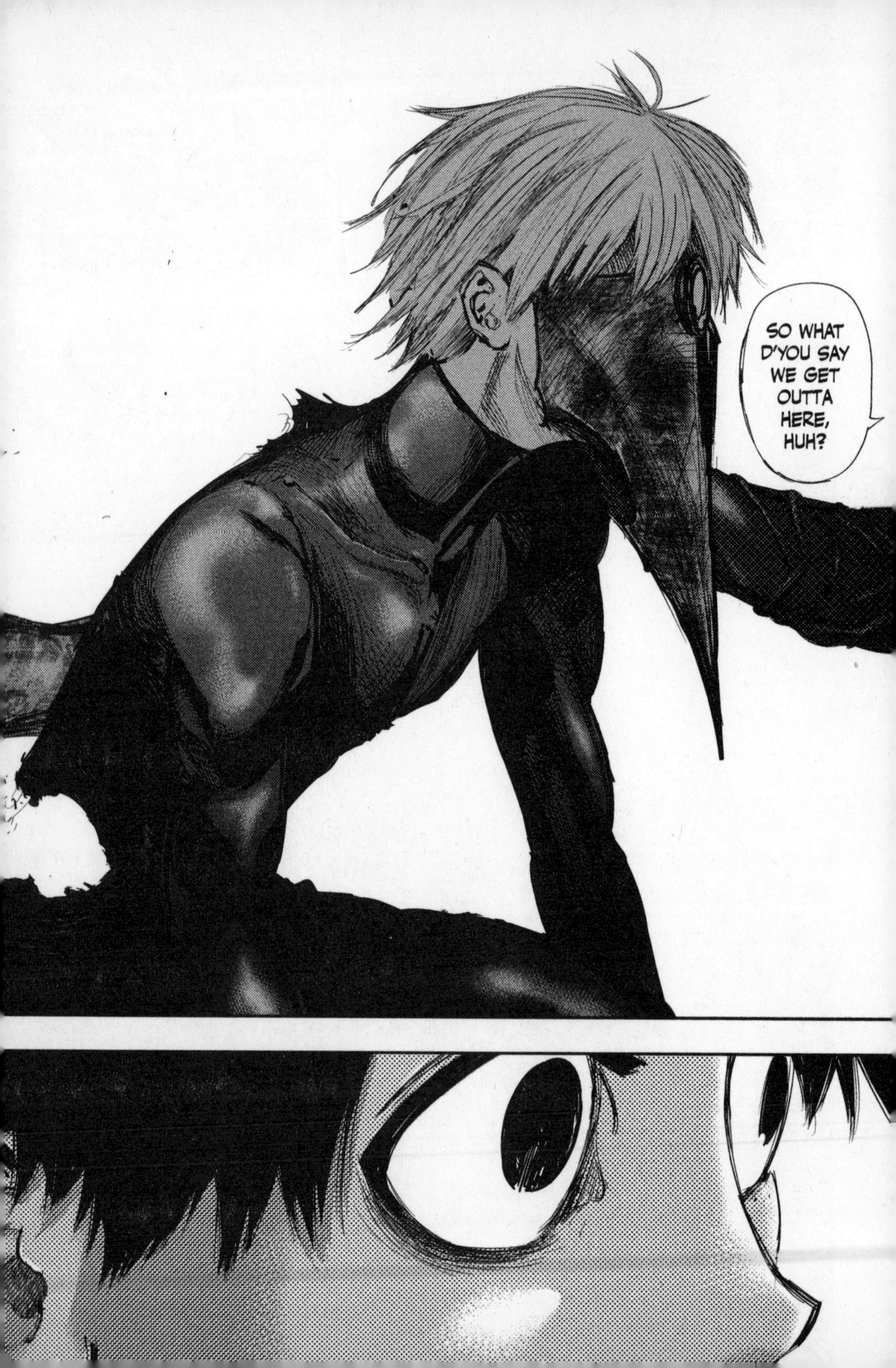
SO WHAT D'YOU SAY WE GET OUTTA HERE, HUH?

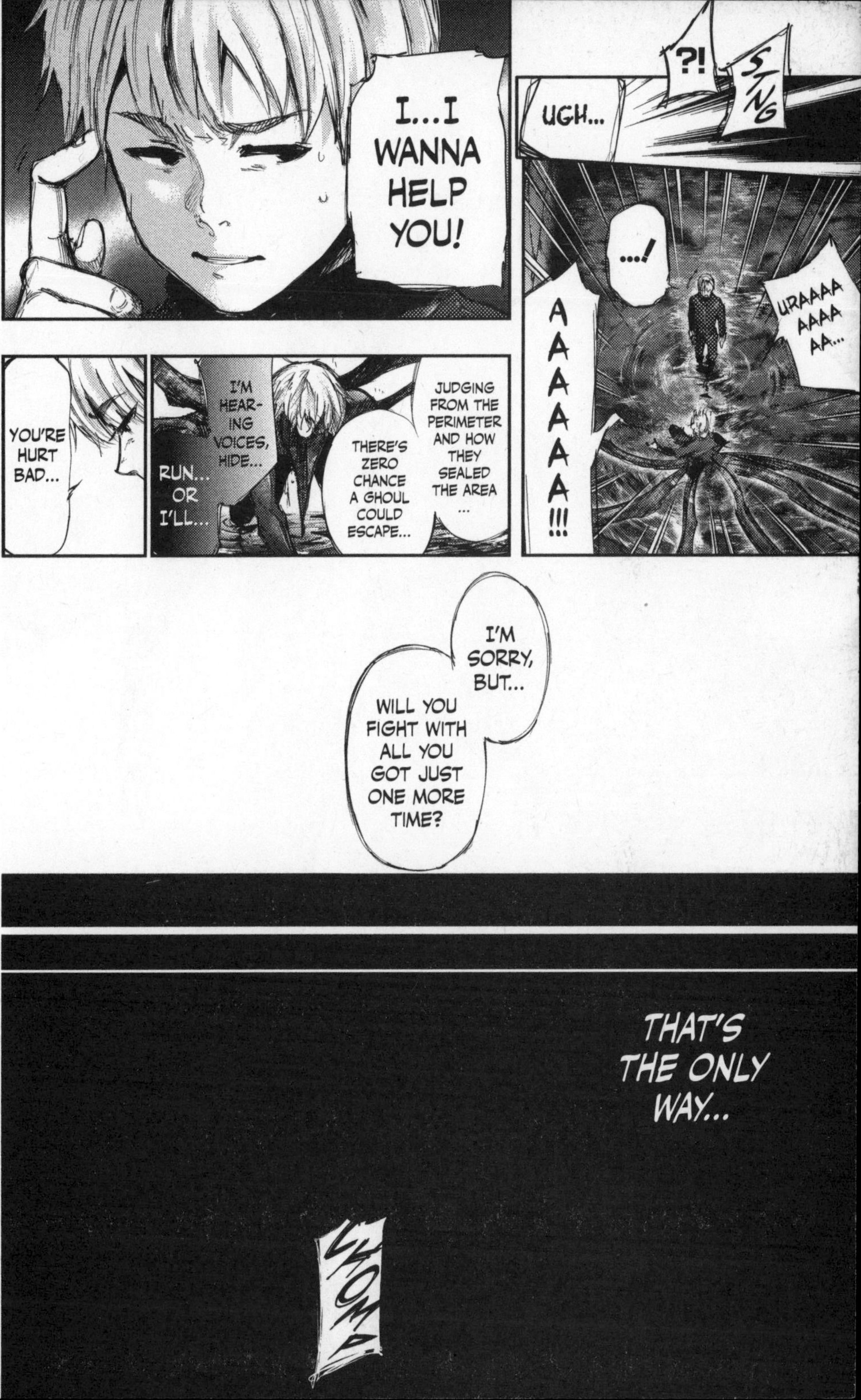
?!
STING
UGH...
...!
URAAAAAAAAAA...
AAAAAA!!!
I...I WANNA HELP YOU!
JUDGING FROM THE PERIMETER AND HOW THEY SEALED THE AREA...
THERE'S ZERO CHANCE A GHOUL COULD ESCAPE...
I'M HEARING VOICES, HIDE...
RUN... OR I'LL...
YOU'RE HURT BAD...
I'M SORRY, BUT...
WILL YOU FIGHT WITH ALL YOU GOT JUST ONE MORE TIME?
THAT'S THE ONLY WAY...
WHOMP

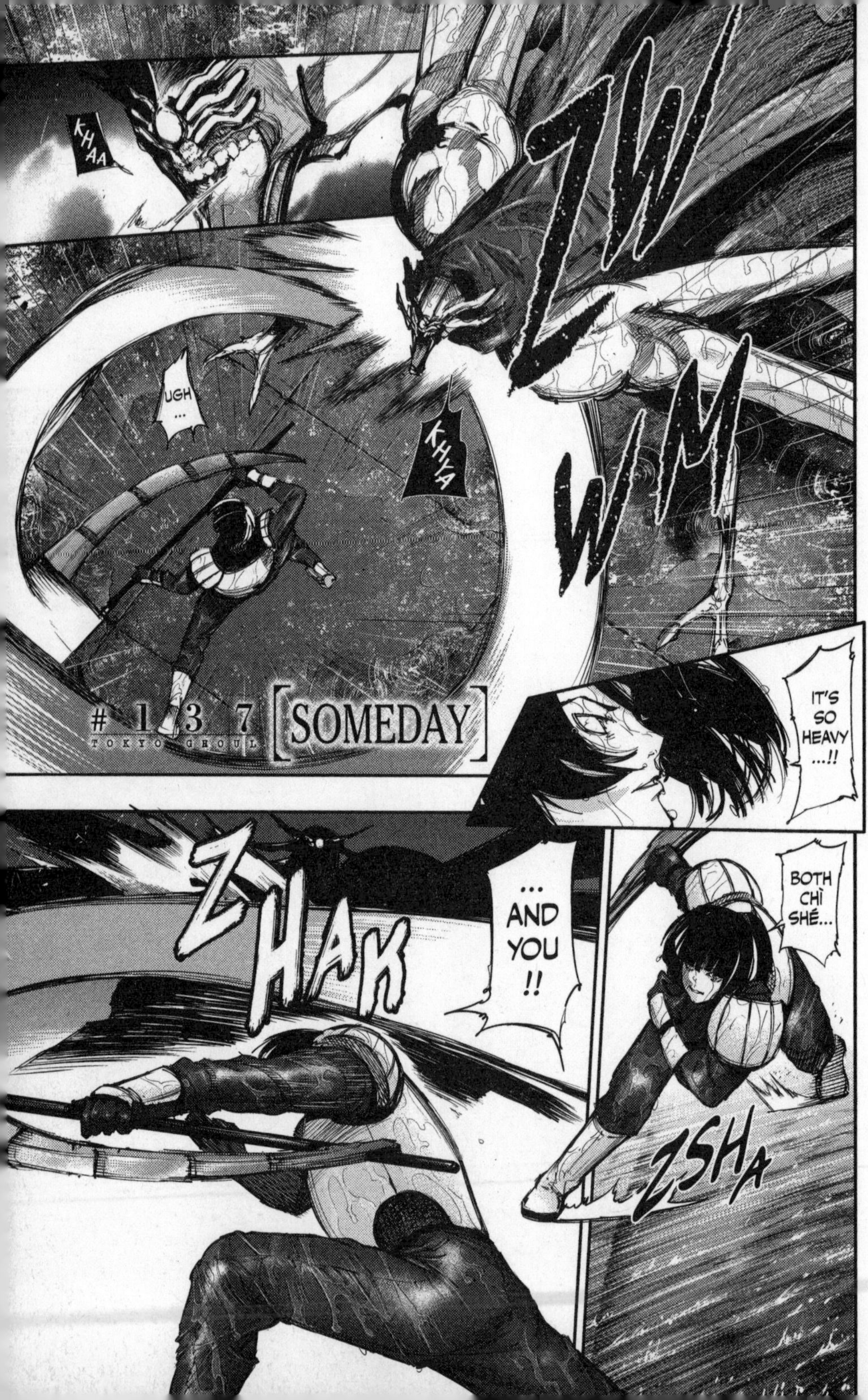
ZWWM
KHAA
KHYA
UGH...
#137 [SOMEDAY]
TOKYO GHOUL
IT'S SO HEAVY ...!!
BOTH CHÌ SHÉ...
ZSHA
... AND YOU !!
ZHAK

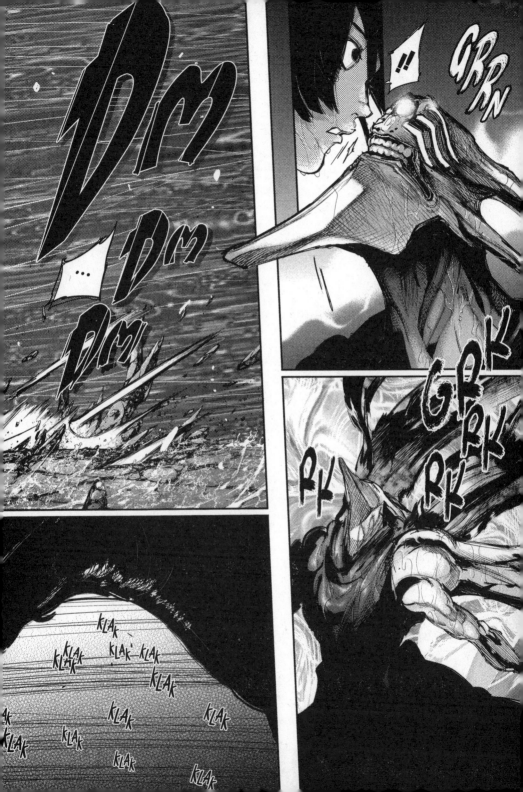

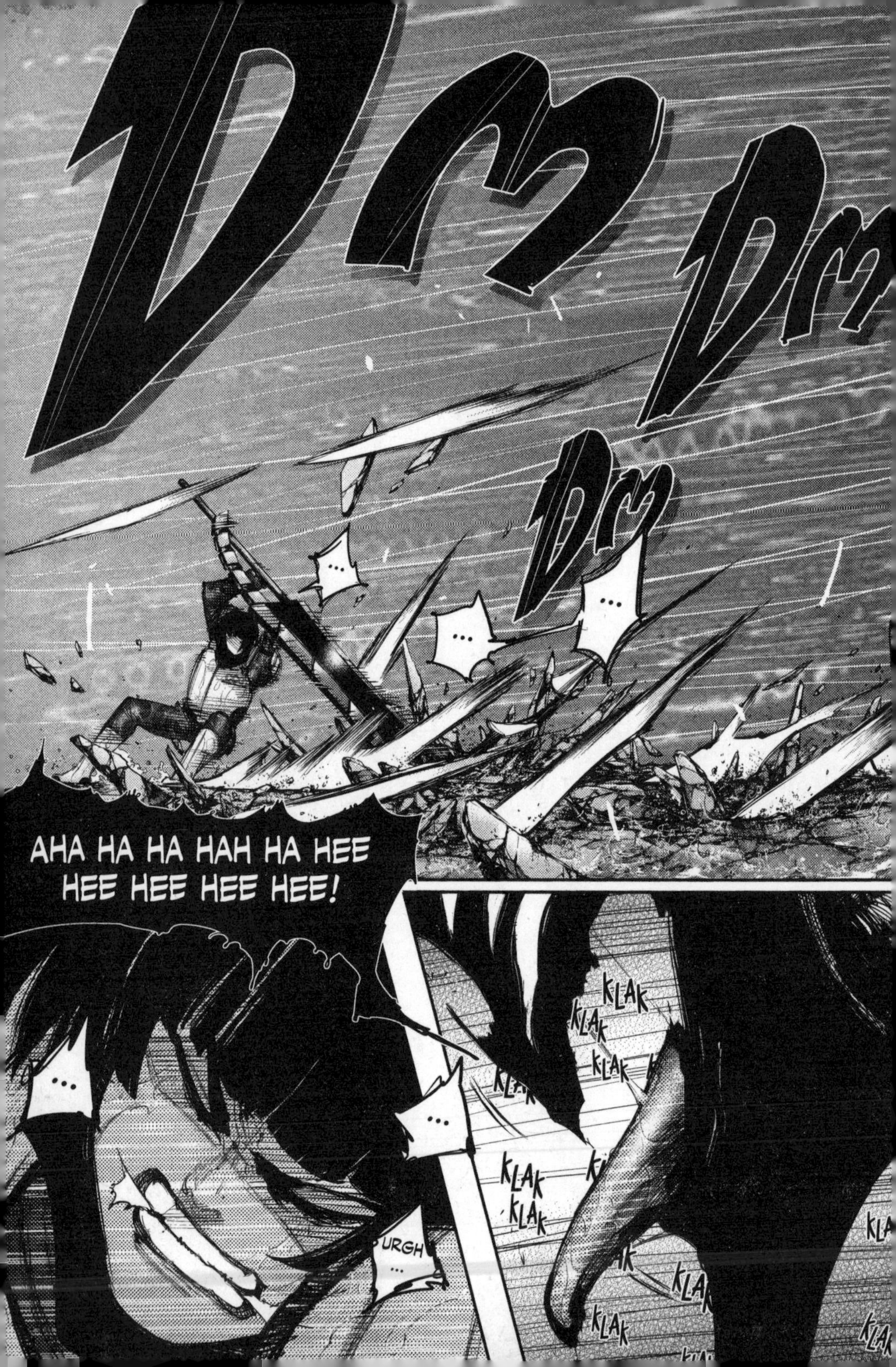
DM
DM
DM
...
...
...
AHA HA HA HAH HA HEE HEE HEE HEE HEE!
KLAK KLAK KLAK
KLAK KLAK
KLAK
KLAK
KLAK
KLAK
...
...
URGH ...

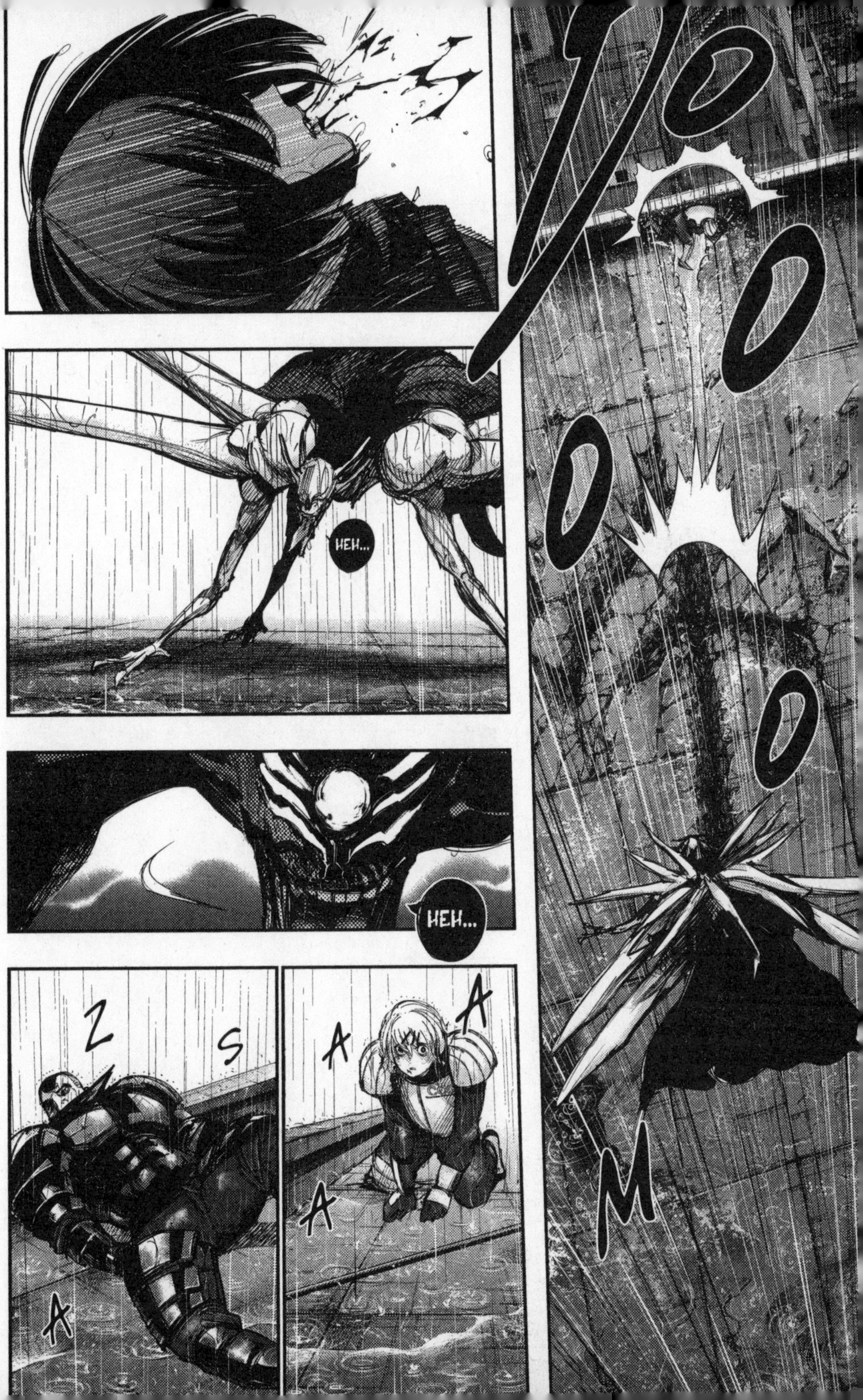
DOOOOM
HEH...
HEH...
ZSAAAA

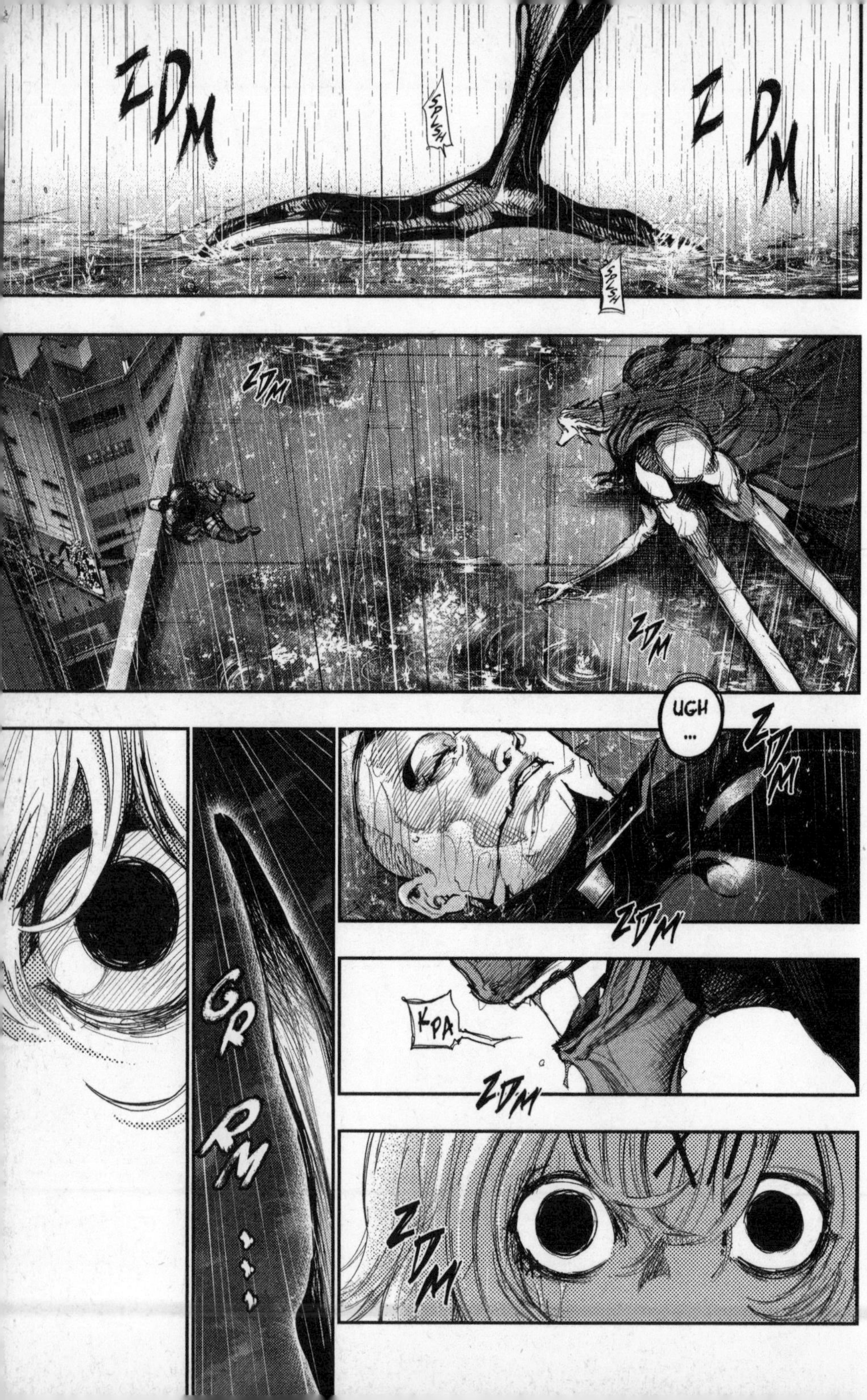
ZDM
SPLSH
ZDM
SPLSH
ZDM
ZDM
UGH ...
ZDM
ZDM
KPA
ZDM
ZDM
GR RM ...

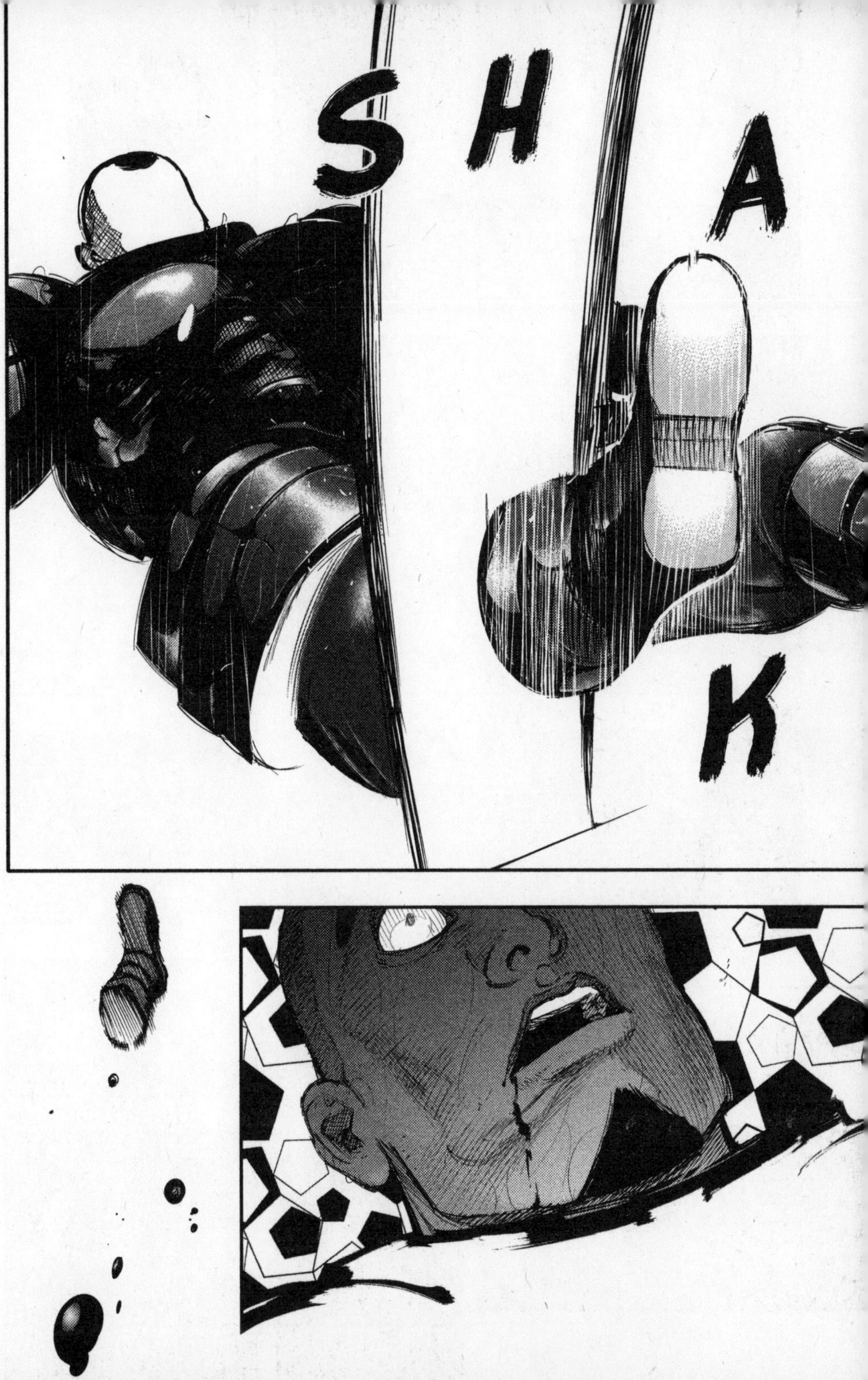
SHAK

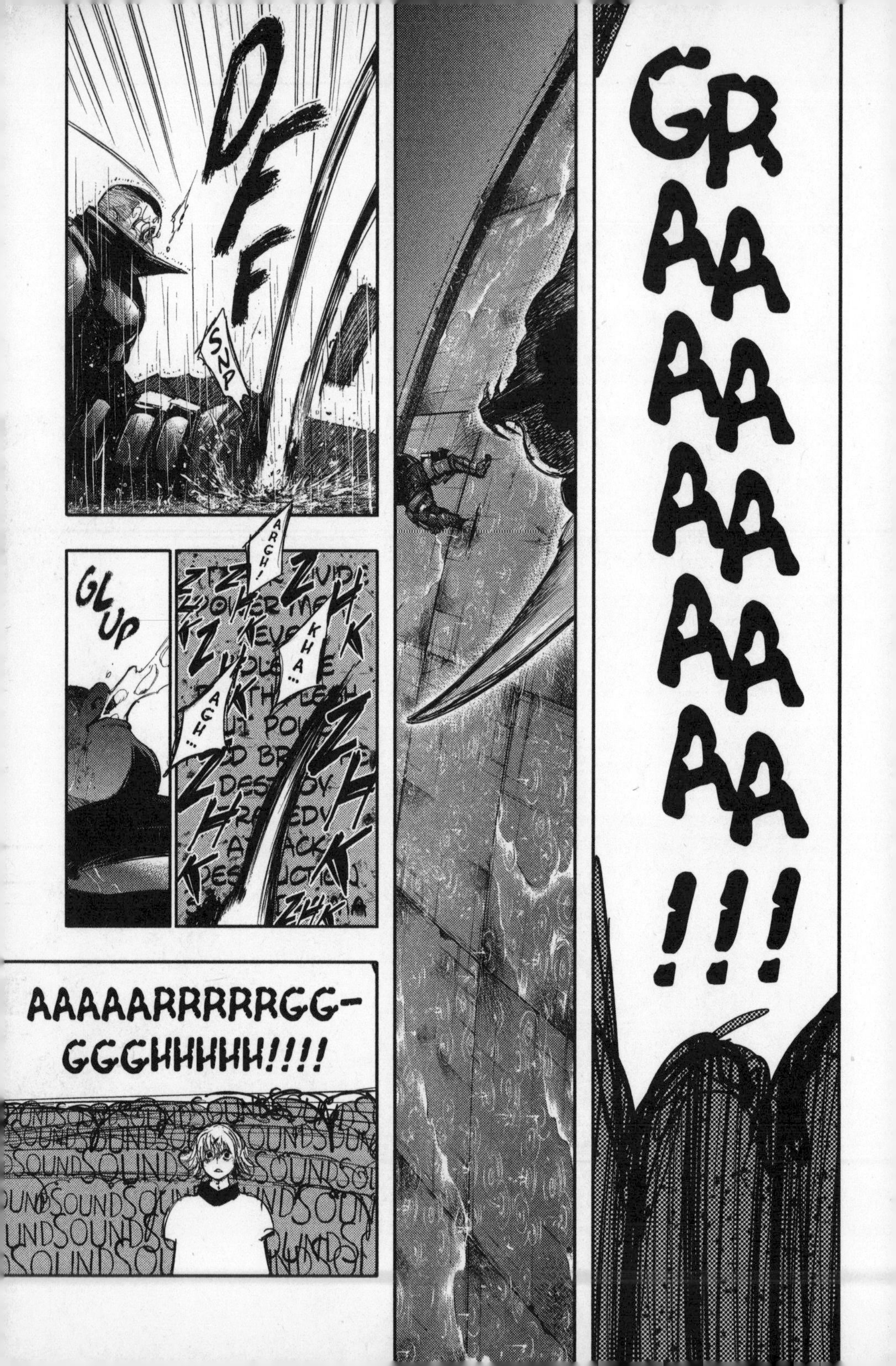
GRAAAAAAAAAAAA!!!
SNAP
ARGH!
KHA...
AGH...
GLUP
AAAAARRRRRGG-
GGGHHHHHH!!!!

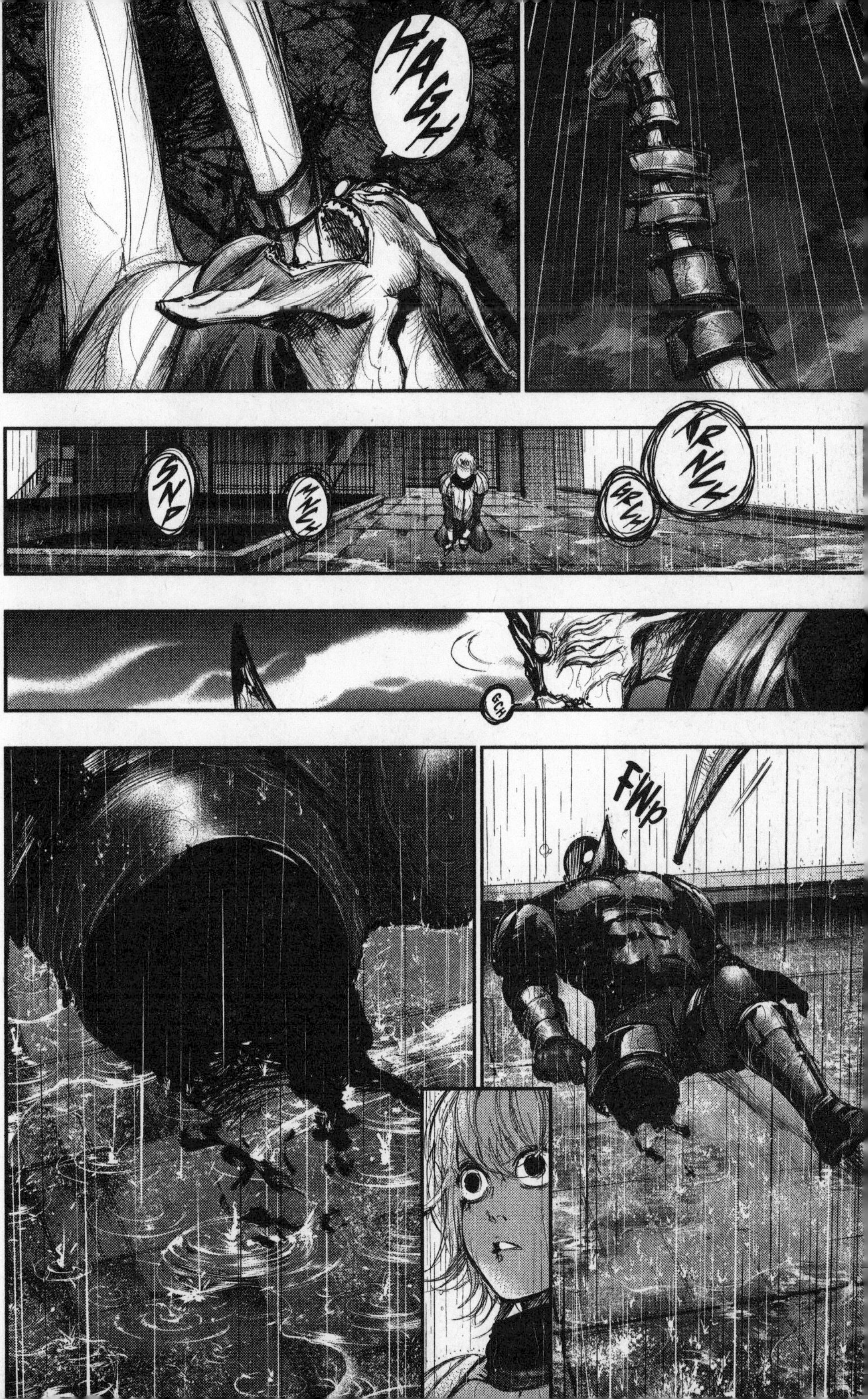
HAGK
KRNCH
CRCH
MNCH
SNP
GCH
FWP

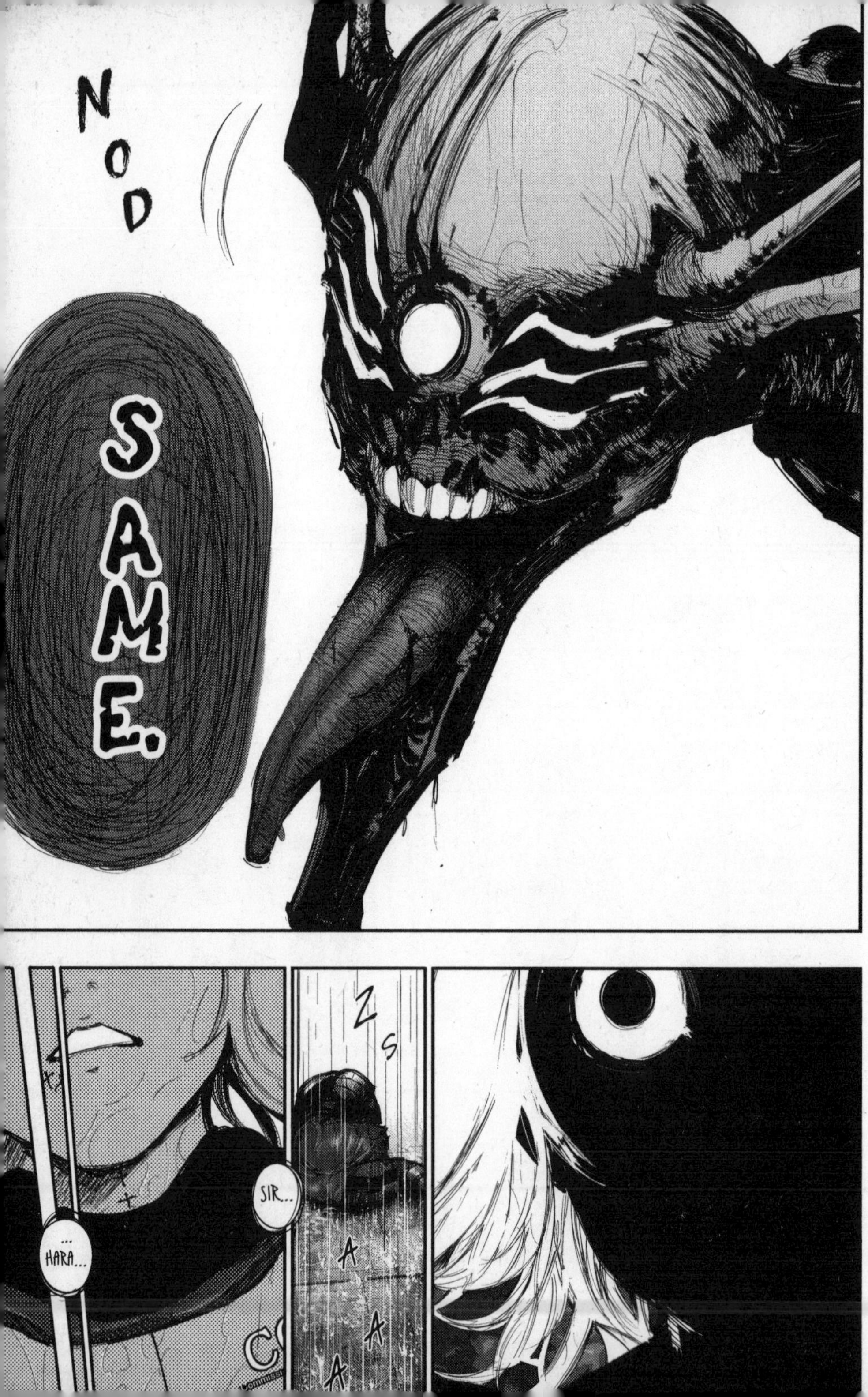
NOD
SAME.
ZS
SIR...
AAA
...HARA...

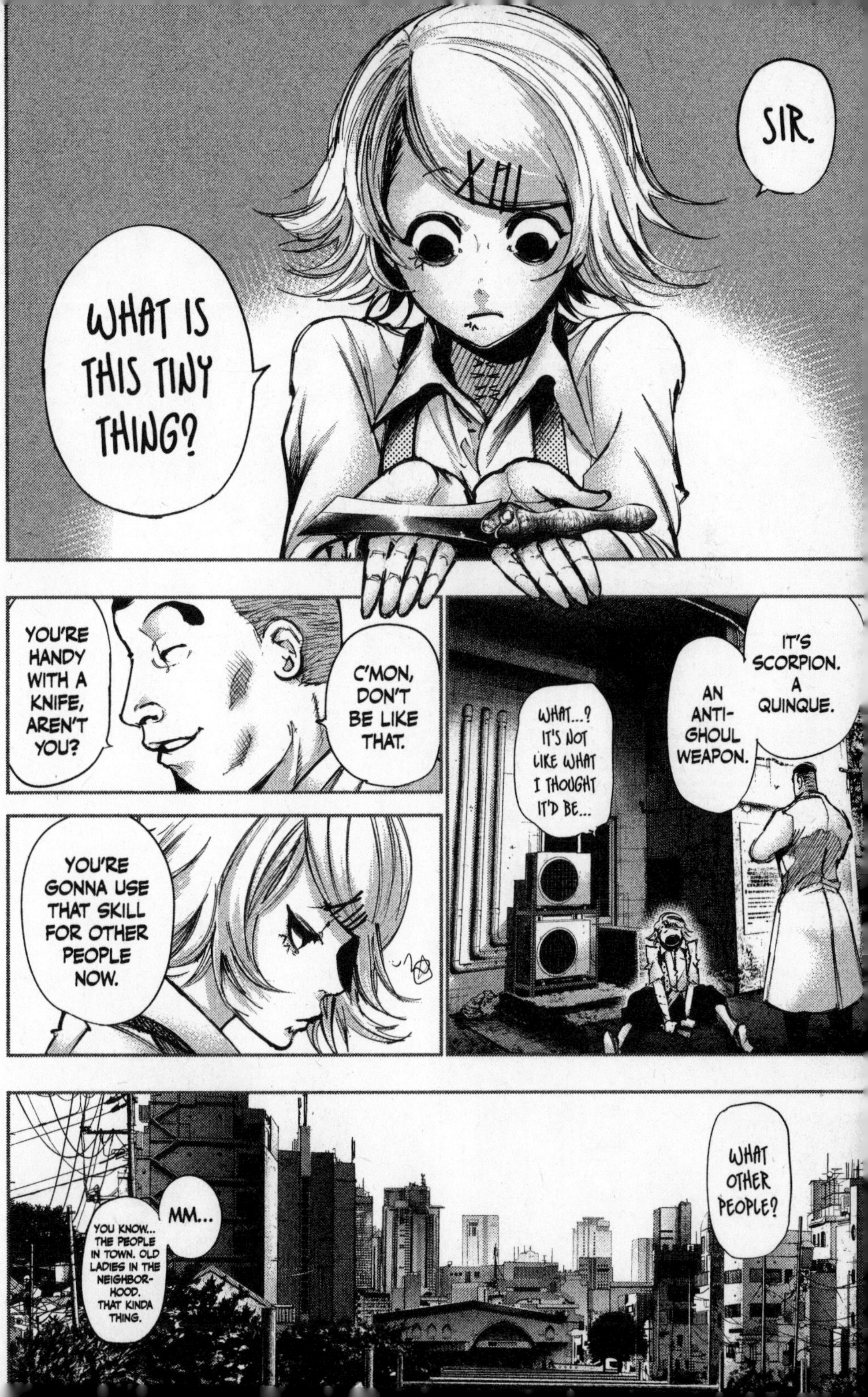
SIR.
WHAT IS THIS TINY THING?
IT'S SCORPION. A QUINQUE.
AN ANTI-GHOUL WEAPON.
WHAT...? IT'S NOT LIKE WHAT I THOUGHT IT'D BE...
C'MON, DON'T BE LIKE THAT.
YOU'RE HANDY WITH A KNIFE, AREN'T YOU?
YOU'RE GONNA USE THAT SKILL FOR OTHER PEOPLE NOW.
WHAT OTHER PEOPLE?
MM...
YOU KNOW... THE PEOPLE IN TOWN. OLD LADIES IN THE NEIGHBOR-HOOD. THAT KINDA THING.

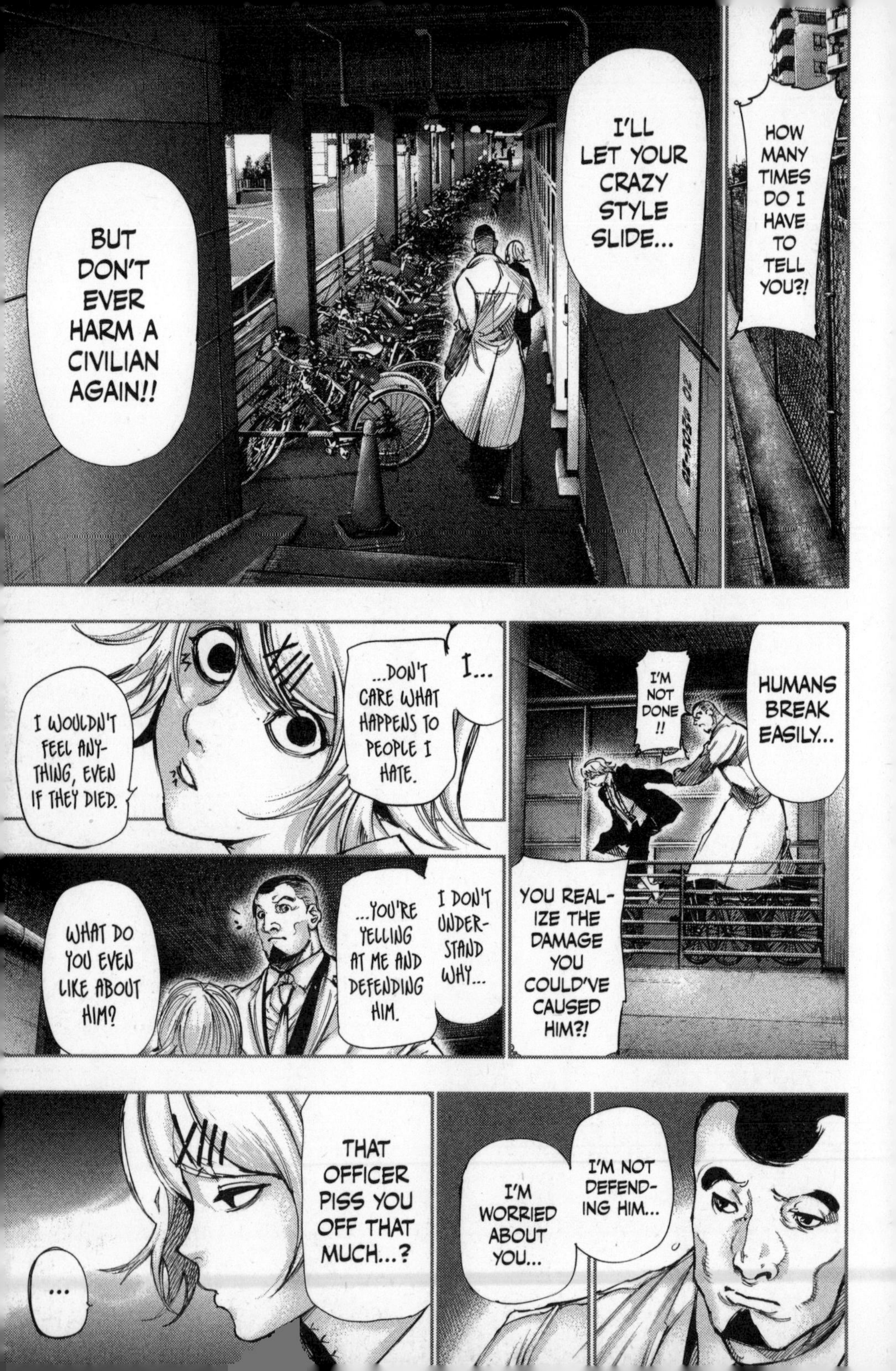

HOW MANY TIMES DO I HAVE TO TELL YOU?!
I'LL LET YOUR CRAZY STYLE SLIDE...
BUT DON'T EVER HARM A CIVILIAN AGAIN!!
HUMANS BREAK EASILY...
I'M NOT DONE!!
YOU REAL-IZE THE DAMAGE YOU COULD'VE CAUSED HIM?!
I...
...DON'T CARE WHAT HAPPENS TO PEOPLE I HATE.
I WOULDN'T FEEL ANY-THING, EVEN IF THEY DIED.
I DON'T UNDER-STAND WHY...
...YOU'RE YELLING AT ME AND DEFENDING HIM.
WHAT DO YOU EVEN LIKE ABOUT HIM?
I'M NOT DEFEND-ING HIM...
I'M WORRIED ABOUT YOU...
THAT OFFICER PISS YOU OFF THAT MUCH...?
...

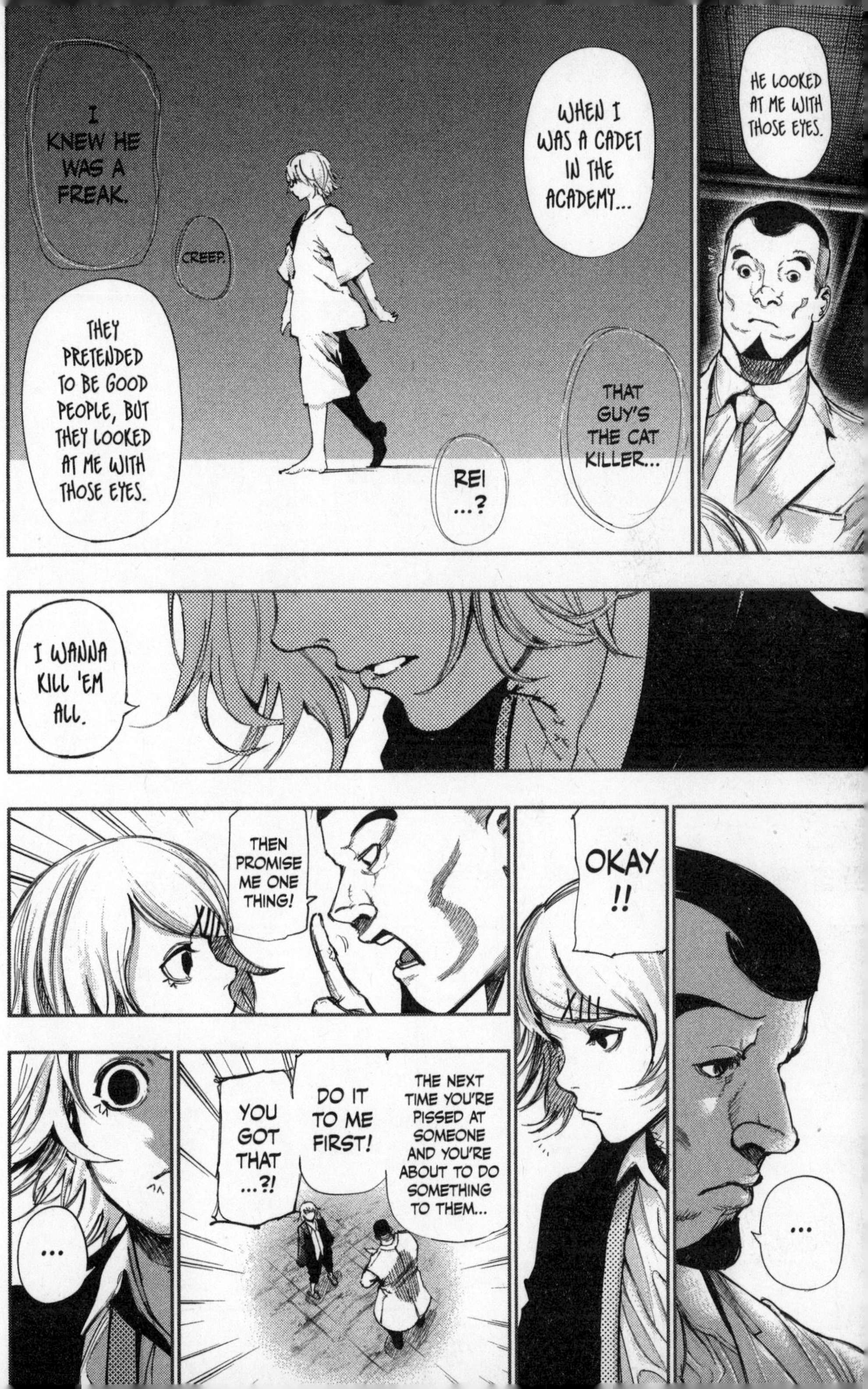
HE LOOKED AT ME WITH THOSE EYES.
WHEN I WAS A CADET IN THE ACADEMY...
THAT GUY'S THE CAT KILLER...
REI ...?
I KNEW HE WAS A FREAK.
CREEP.
THEY PRETENDED TO BE GOOD PEOPLE, BUT THEY LOOKED AT ME WITH THOSE EYES.
I WANNA KILL 'EM ALL.
OKAY !!
...
THEN PROMISE ME ONE THING!
THE NEXT TIME YOU'RE PISSED AT SOMEONE AND YOU'RE ABOUT TO DO SOMETHING TO THEM...
DO IT TO ME FIRST!
YOU GOT THAT ...?!
...

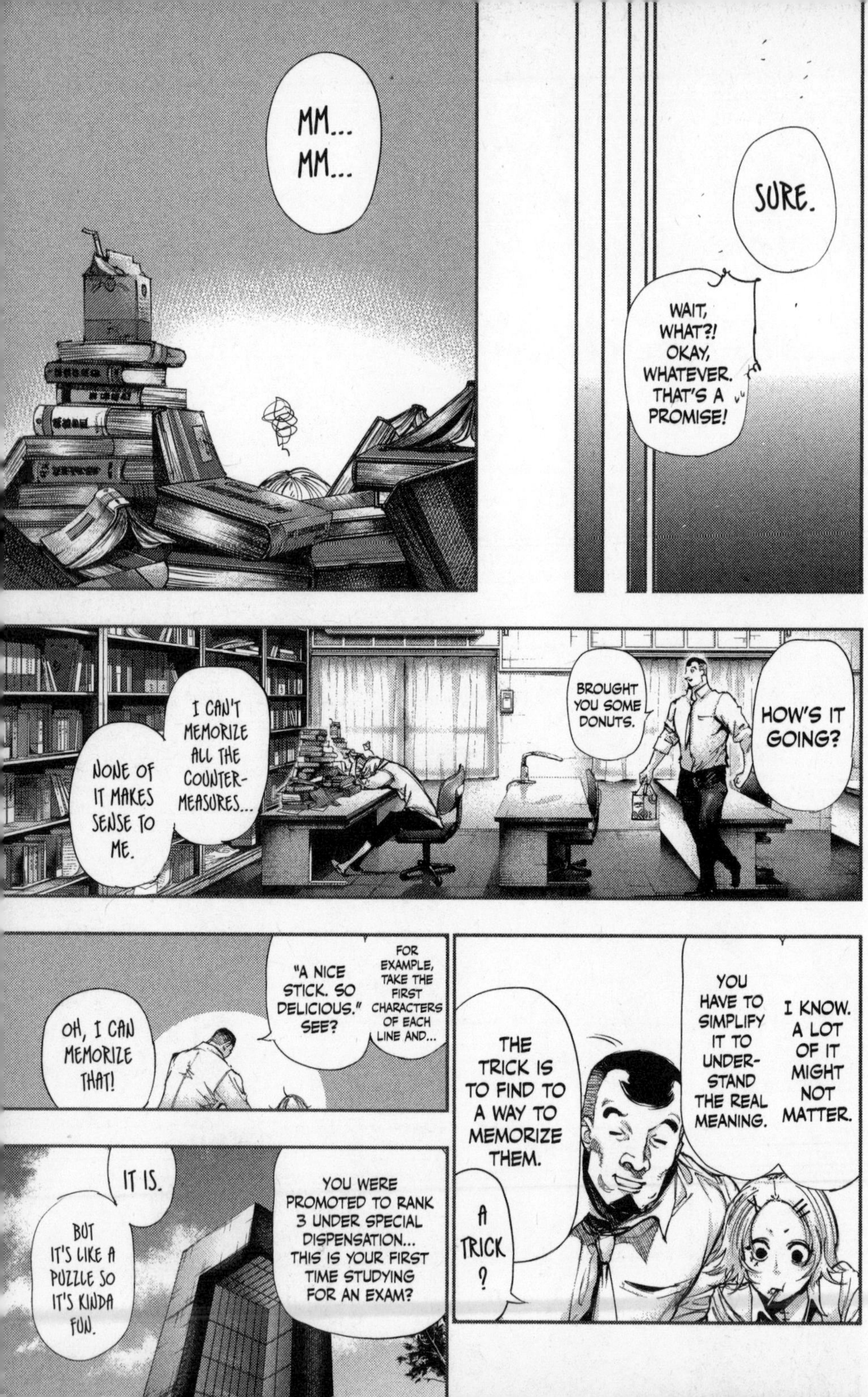
SURE.
WAIT, WHAT?! OKAY, WHATEVER. THAT'S A PROMISE!
MM... MM...
HOW'S IT GOING?
BROUGHT YOU SOME DONUTS.
I CAN'T MEMORIZE ALL THE COUNTER-MEASURES...
NONE OF IT MAKES SENSE TO ME.
I KNOW. A LOT OF IT MIGHT NOT MATTER.
YOU HAVE TO SIMPLIFY IT TO UNDER-STAND THE REAL MEANING.
THE TRICK IS TO FIND TO A WAY TO MEMORIZE THEM.
A TRICK?
FOR EXAMPLE, TAKE THE FIRST CHARACTERS OF EACH LINE AND...
"A NICE STICK. SO DELICIOUS." SEE?
OH, I CAN MEMORIZE THAT!
YOU WERE PROMOTED TO RANK 3 UNDER SPECIAL DISPENSATION... THIS IS YOUR FIRST TIME STUDYING FOR AN EXAM?
IT IS.
BUT IT'S LIKE A PUZZLE SO IT'S KINDA FUN.

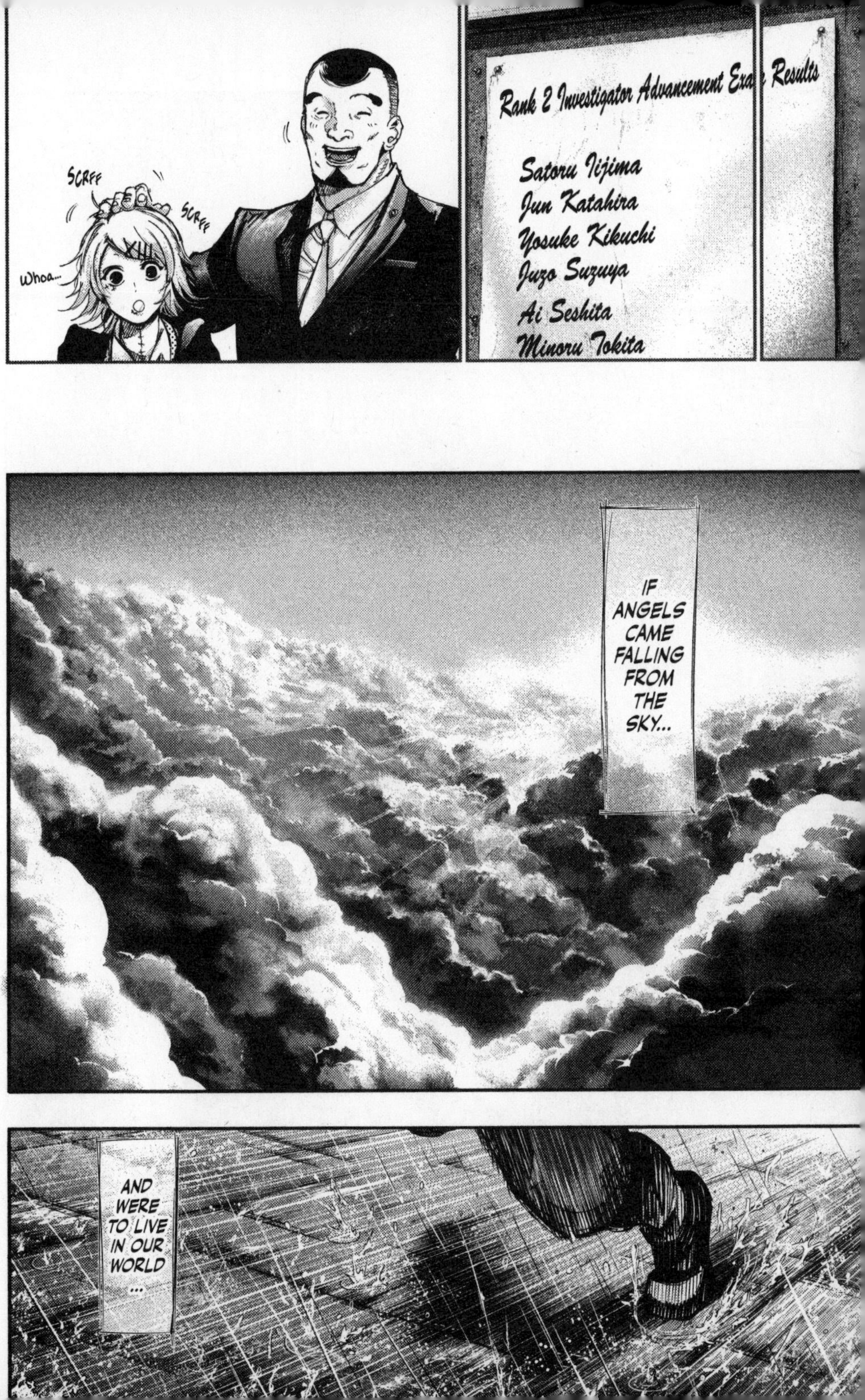
Rank 2 Investigator Advancement Exa Results
Satoru Iijima
Jun Katahira
Yosuke Kikuchi
Juzo Suzuya
Ai Seshita
Minoru Tokita
SCRFF
SCRFF
Whoa...
IF ANGELS CAME FALLING FROM THE SKY...
AND WERE TO LIVE IN OUR WORLD...

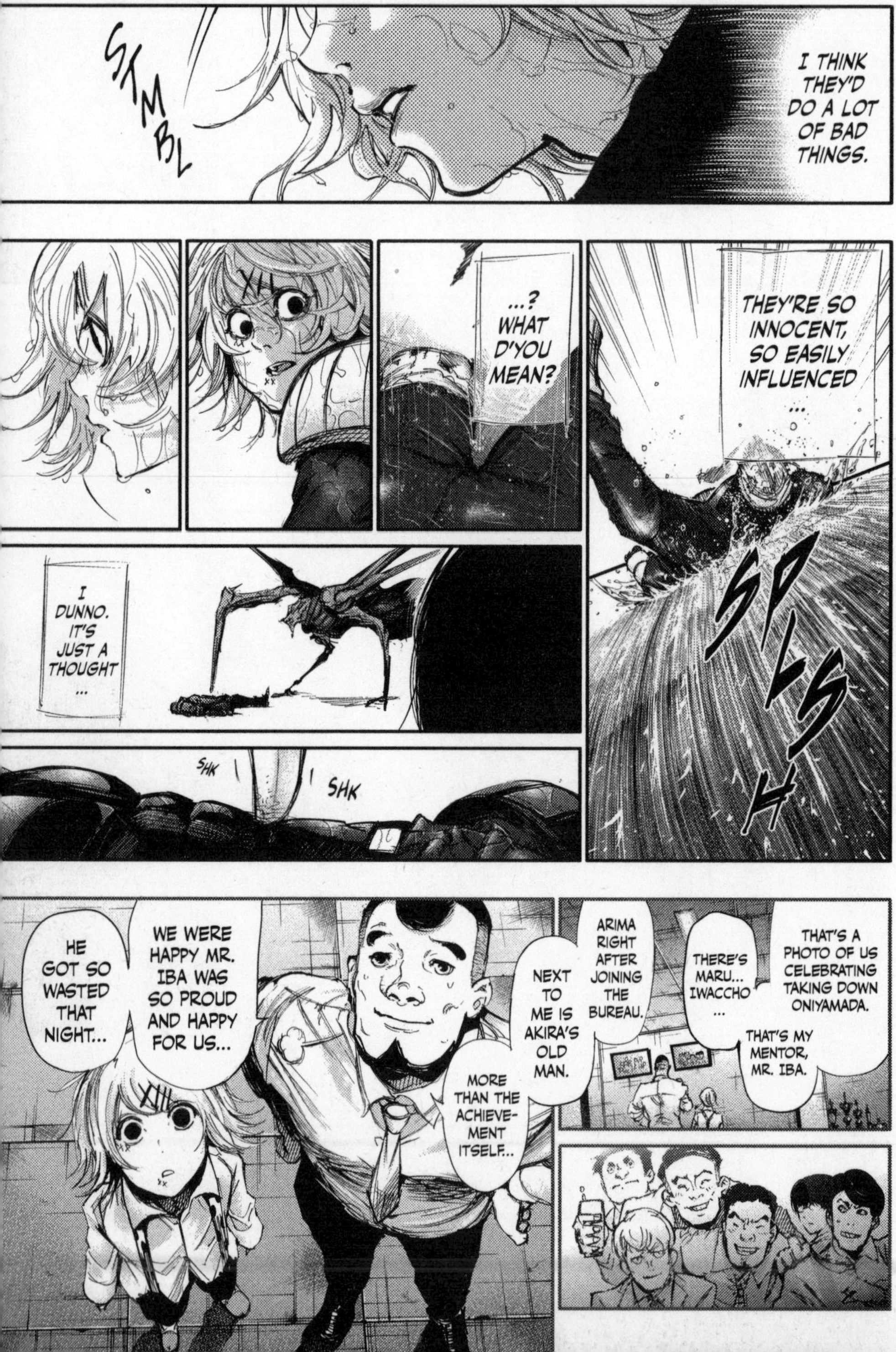
I THINK THEY'D DO A LOT OF BAD THINGS.
SKMBL
THEY'RE SO INNOCENT, SO EASILY INFLUENCED ...
SPLSSH
...? WHAT D'YOU MEAN?
I DUNNO. IT'S JUST A THOUGHT ...
SHK
SHK
THAT'S A PHOTO OF US CELEBRATING TAKING DOWN ONIYAMADA.
THAT'S MY MENTOR, MR. IBA.
THERE'S MARU... IWACCHO ...
ARIMA RIGHT AFTER JOINING THE BUREAU.
NEXT TO ME IS AKIRA'S OLD MAN.
MORE THAN THE ACHIEVEMENT ITSELF...
WE WERE HAPPY MR. IBA WAS SO PROUD AND HAPPY FOR US...
HE GOT SO WASTED THAT NIGHT...

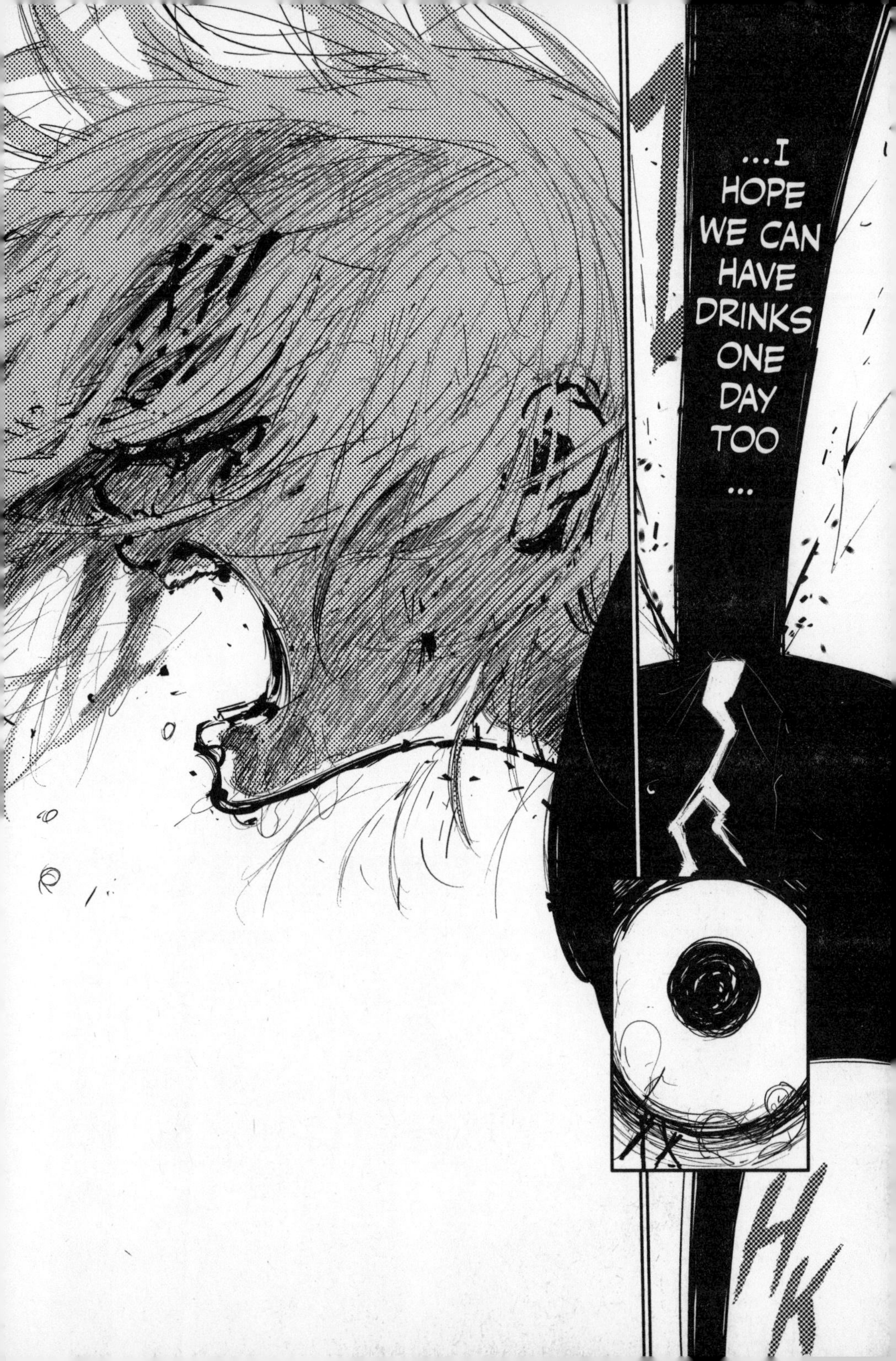
...I HOPE WE CAN HAVE DRINKS ONE DAY TOO ...
HK

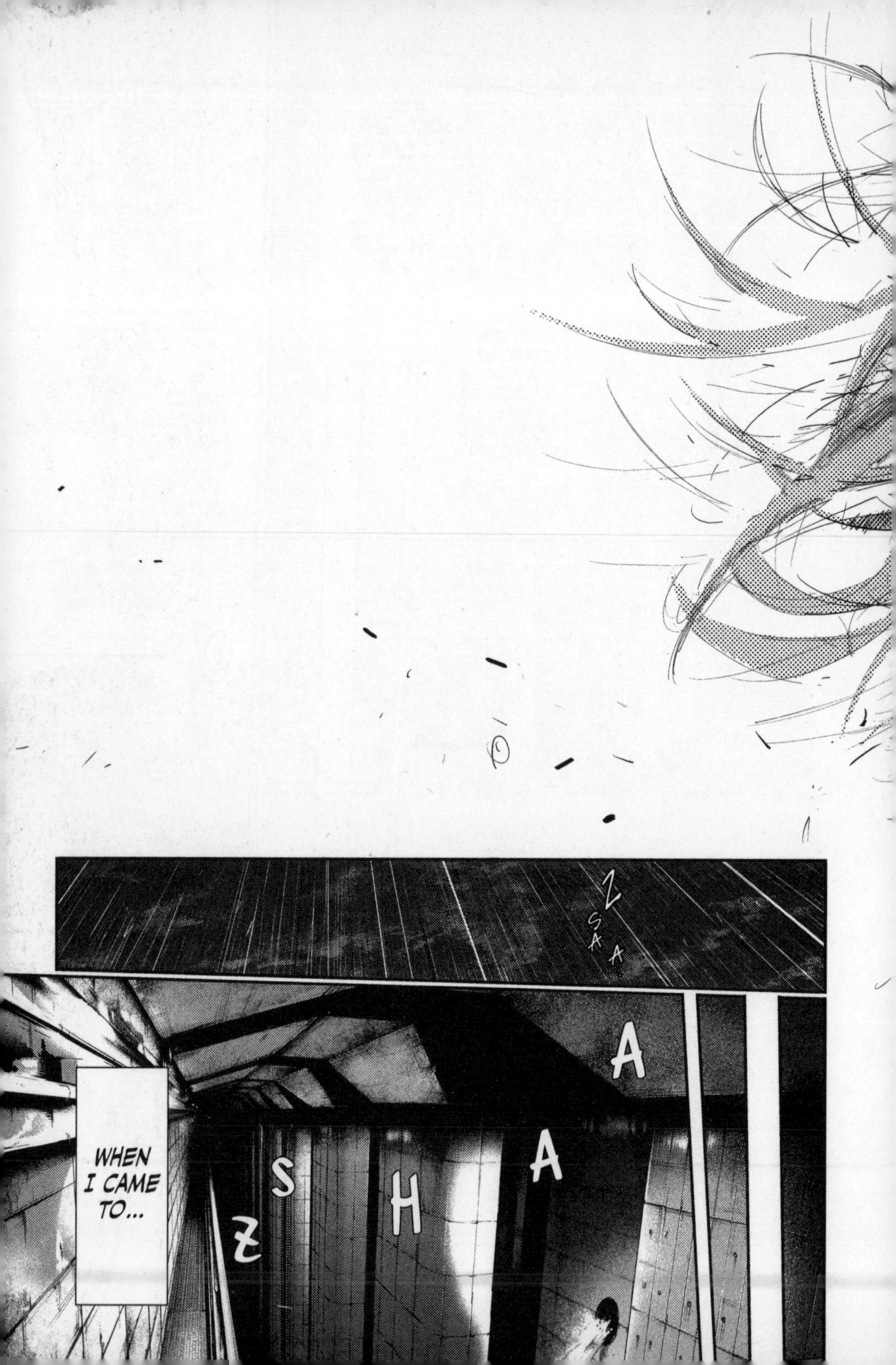
ZSAA
WHEN I CAME TO...
ZSHAA

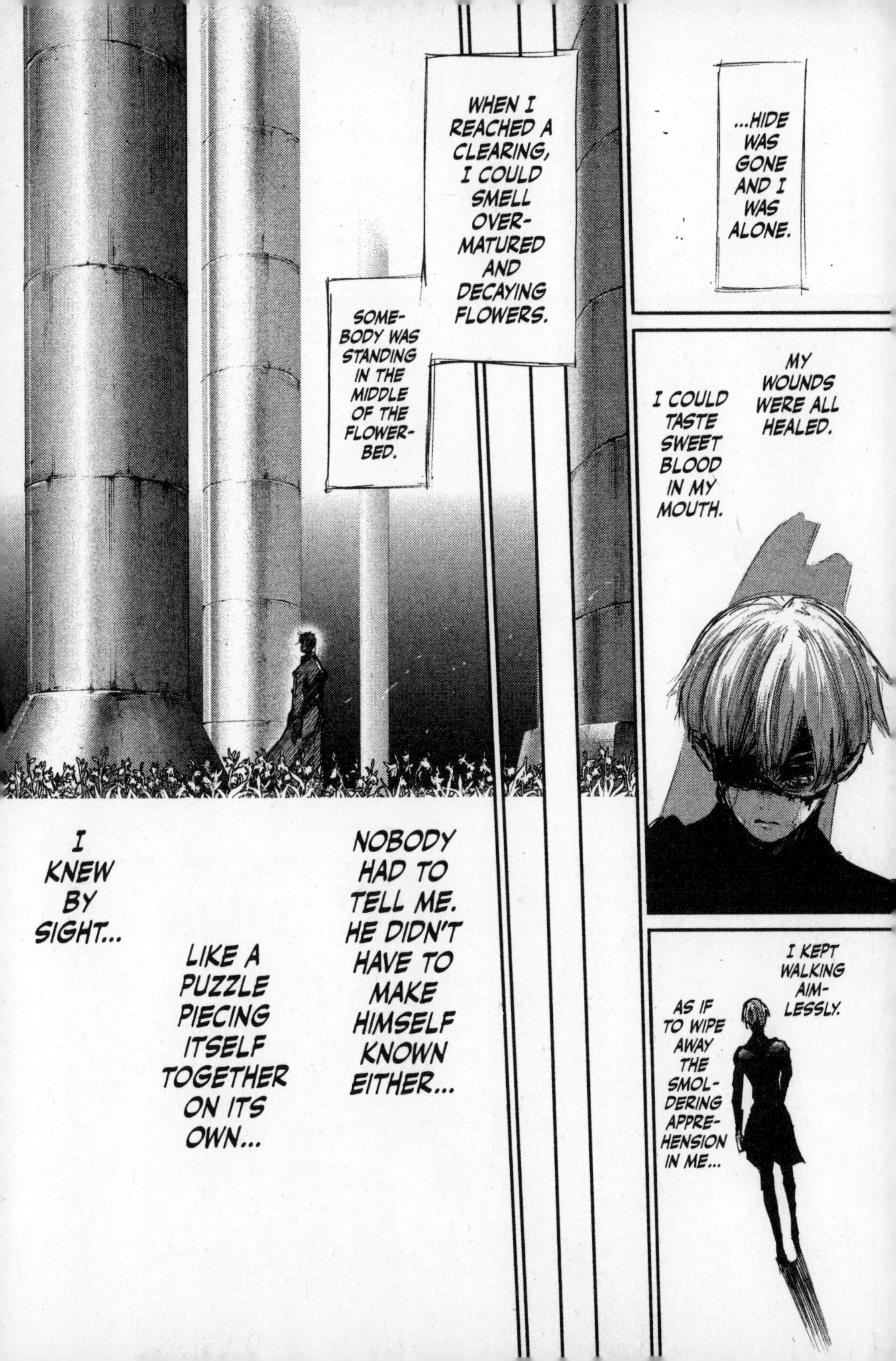
...HIDE WAS GONE AND I WAS ALONE.
MY WOUNDS WERE ALL HEALED.
I COULD TASTE SWEET BLOOD IN MY MOUTH.
I KEPT WALKING AIMLESSLY.
AS IF TO WIPE AWAY THE SMOLDERING APPREHENSION IN ME...
WHEN I REACHED A CLEARING, I COULD SMELL OVER-MATURED AND DECAYING FLOWERS.
SOMEBODY WAS STANDING IN THE MIDDLE OF THE FLOWERBED.
NOBODY HAD TO TELL ME. HE DIDN'T HAVE TO MAKE HIMSELF KNOWN EITHER...
LIKE A PUZZLE PIECING ITSELF TOGETHER ON ITS OWN...
I KNEW BY SIGHT...

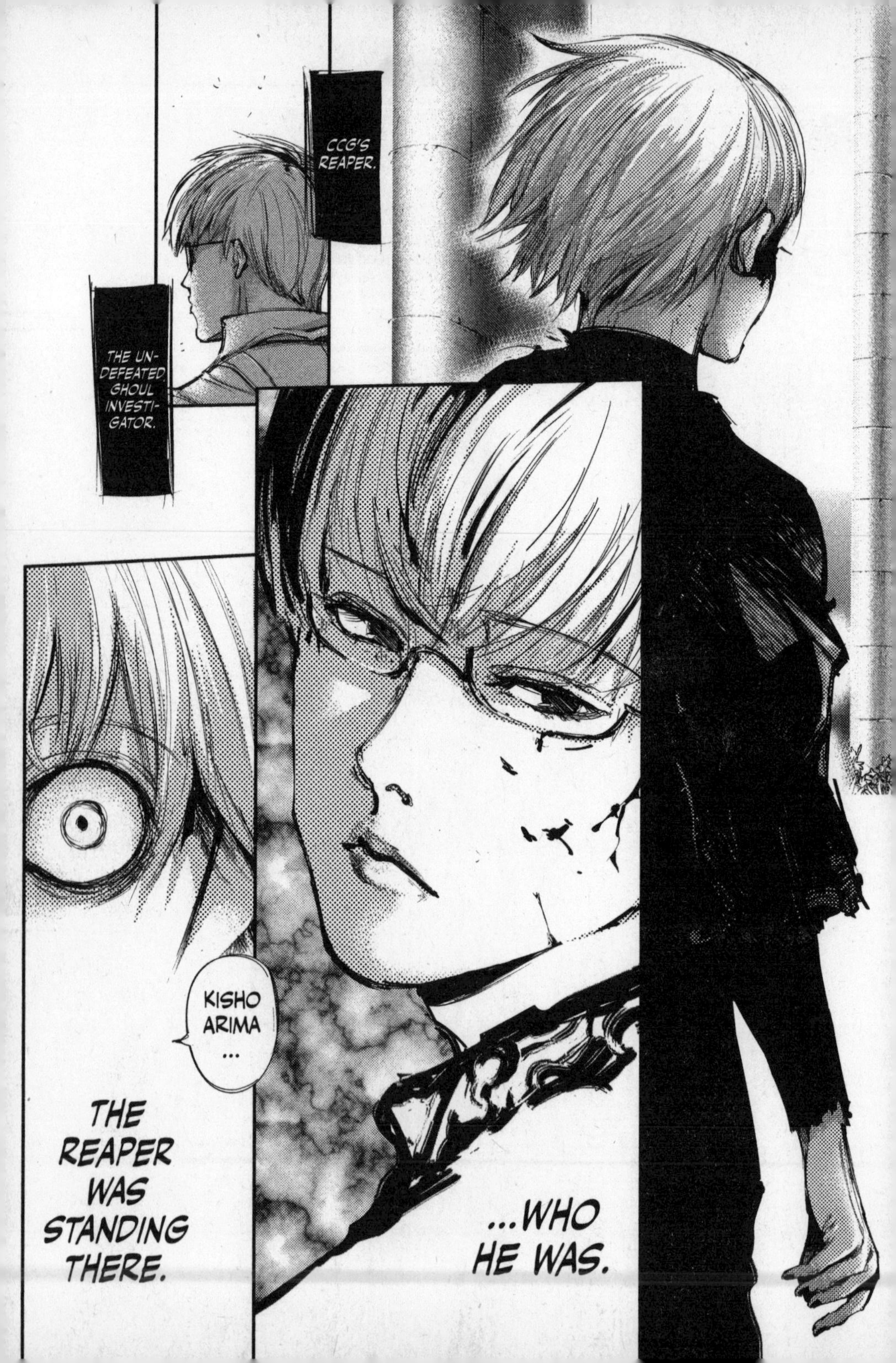
CCG'S REAPER.
THE UN-DEFEATED GHOUL INVESTIGATOR.
...WHO HE WAS.
KISHO ARIMA ...
THE REAPER WAS STANDING THERE.

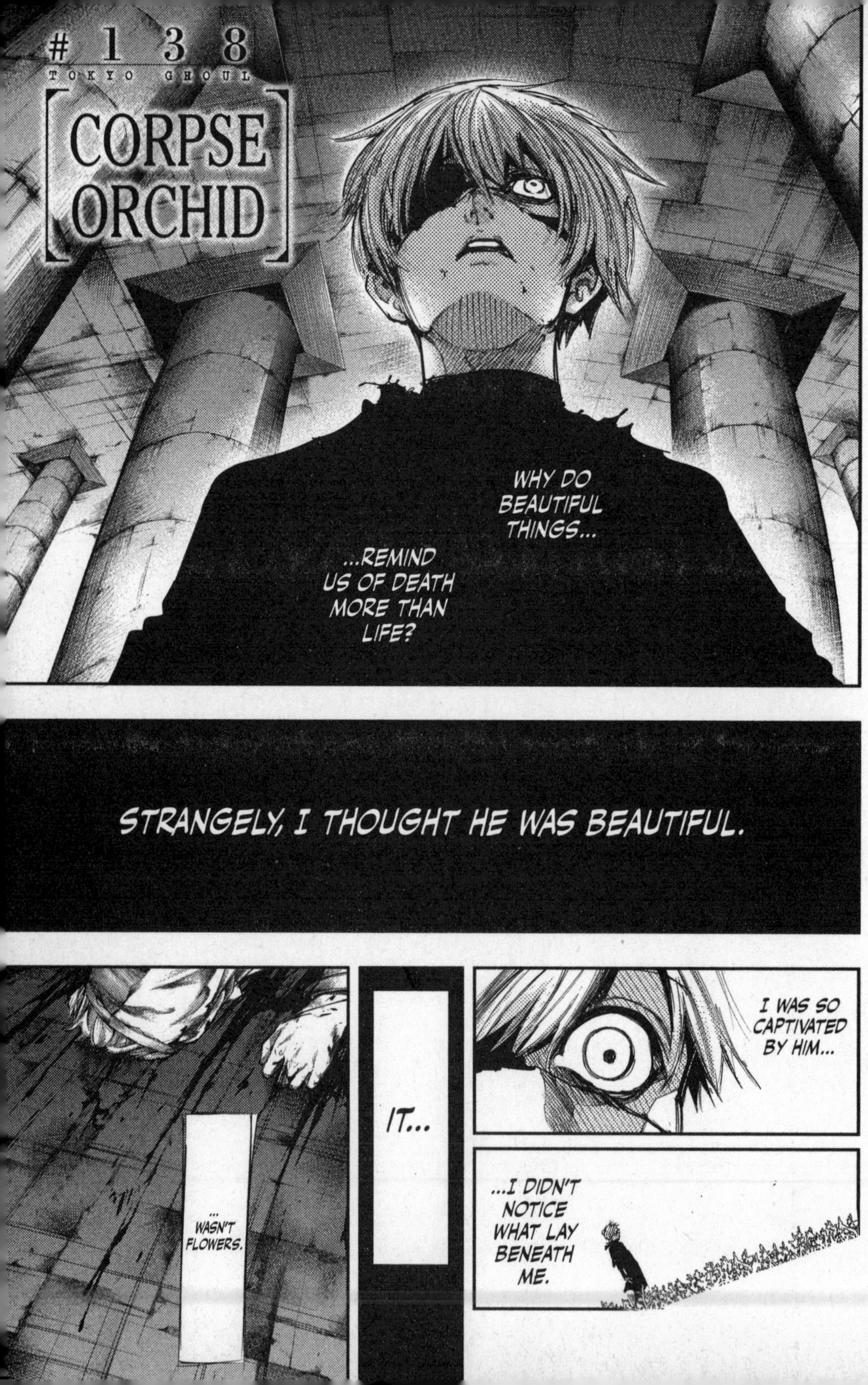
#138
TOKYO GHOUL
CORPSE ORCHID
WHY DO BEAUTIFUL THINGS...
...REMIND US OF DEATH MORE THAN LIFE?
STRANGELY, I THOUGHT HE WAS BEAUTIFUL.
I WAS SO CAPTIVATED BY HIM...
...I DIDN'T NOTICE WHAT LAY BENEATH ME.
IT...
...WASN'T FLOWERS.

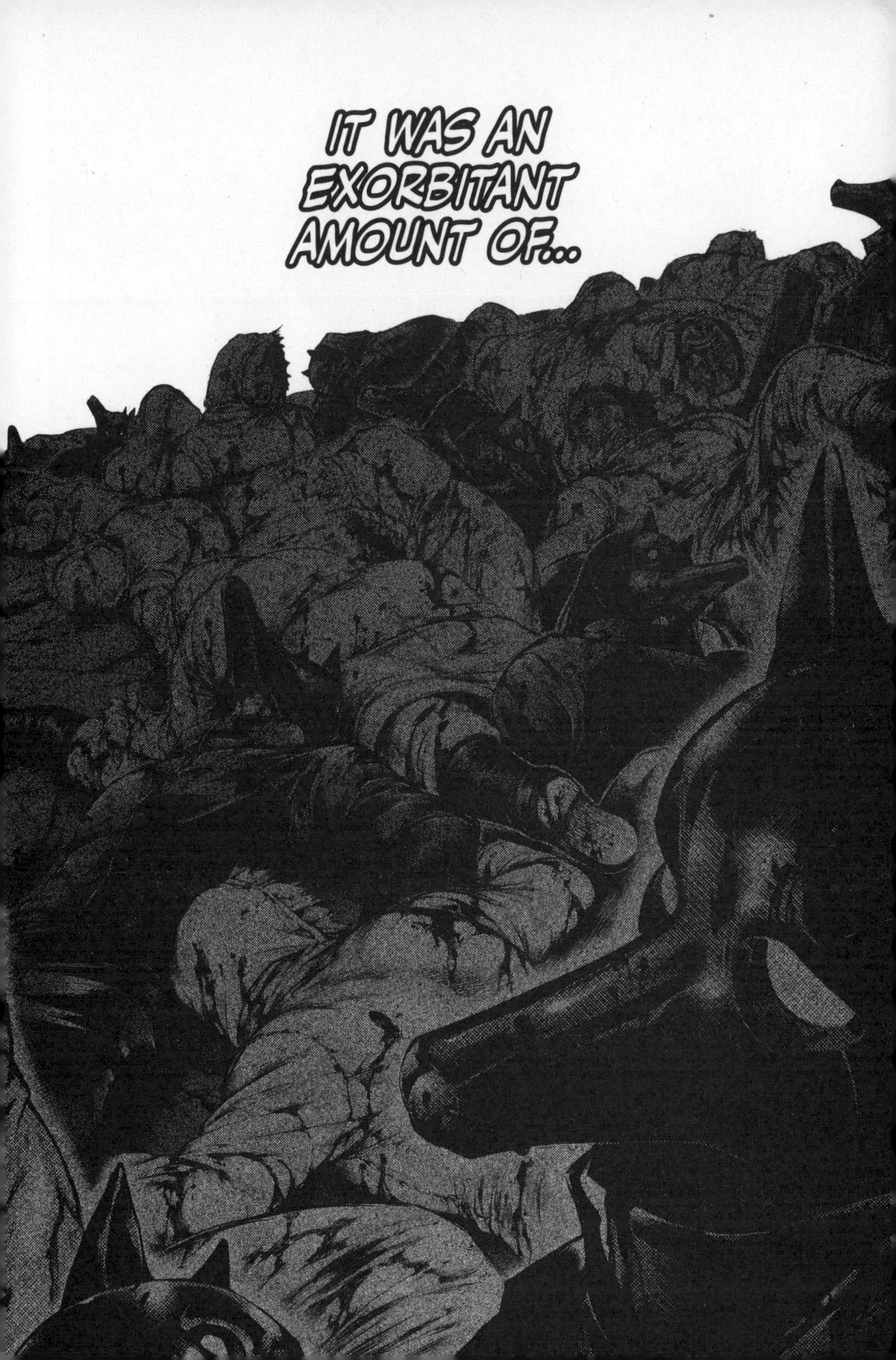
IT WAS AN EXORBITANT AMOUNT OF...

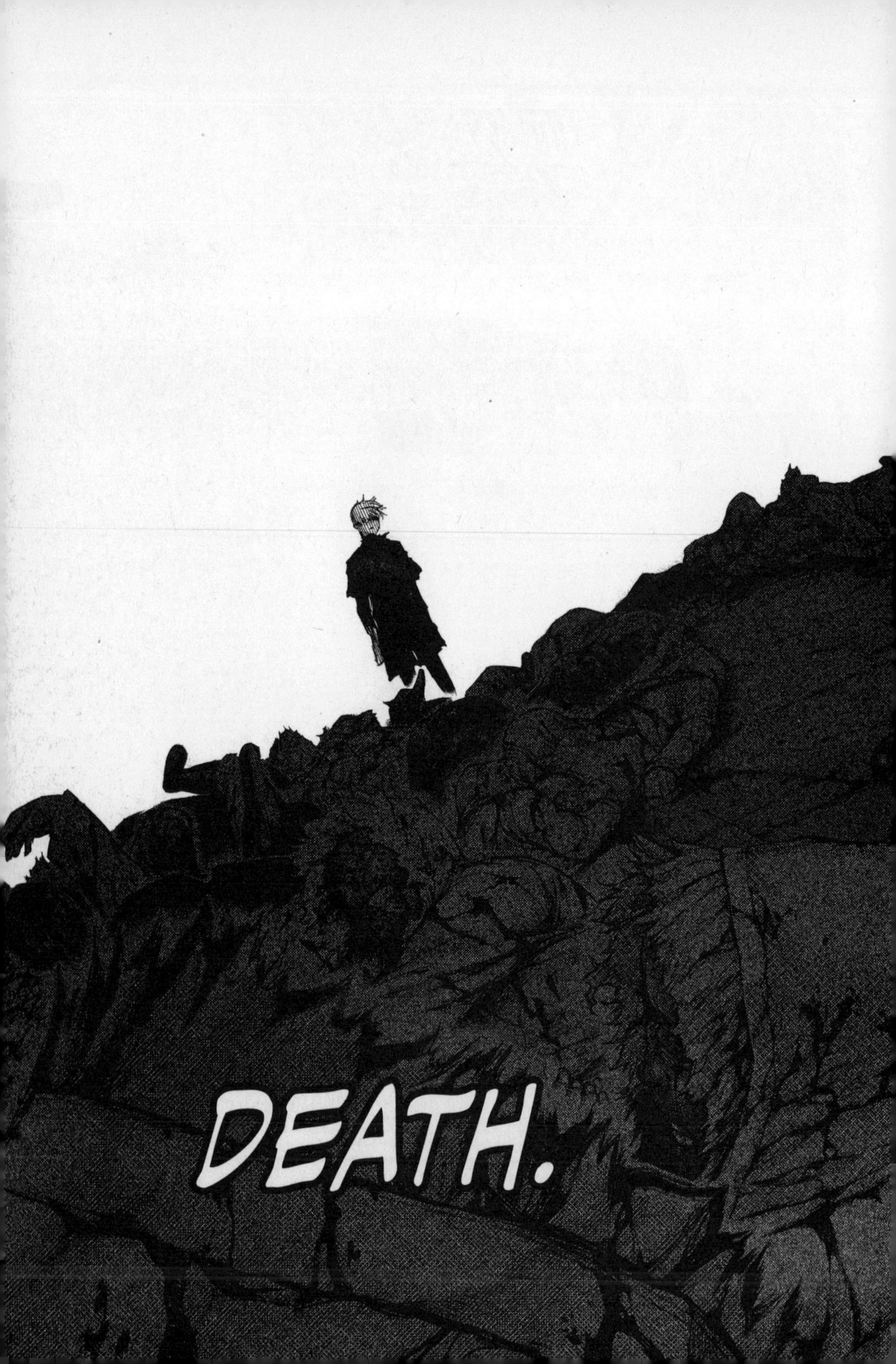
DEATH.

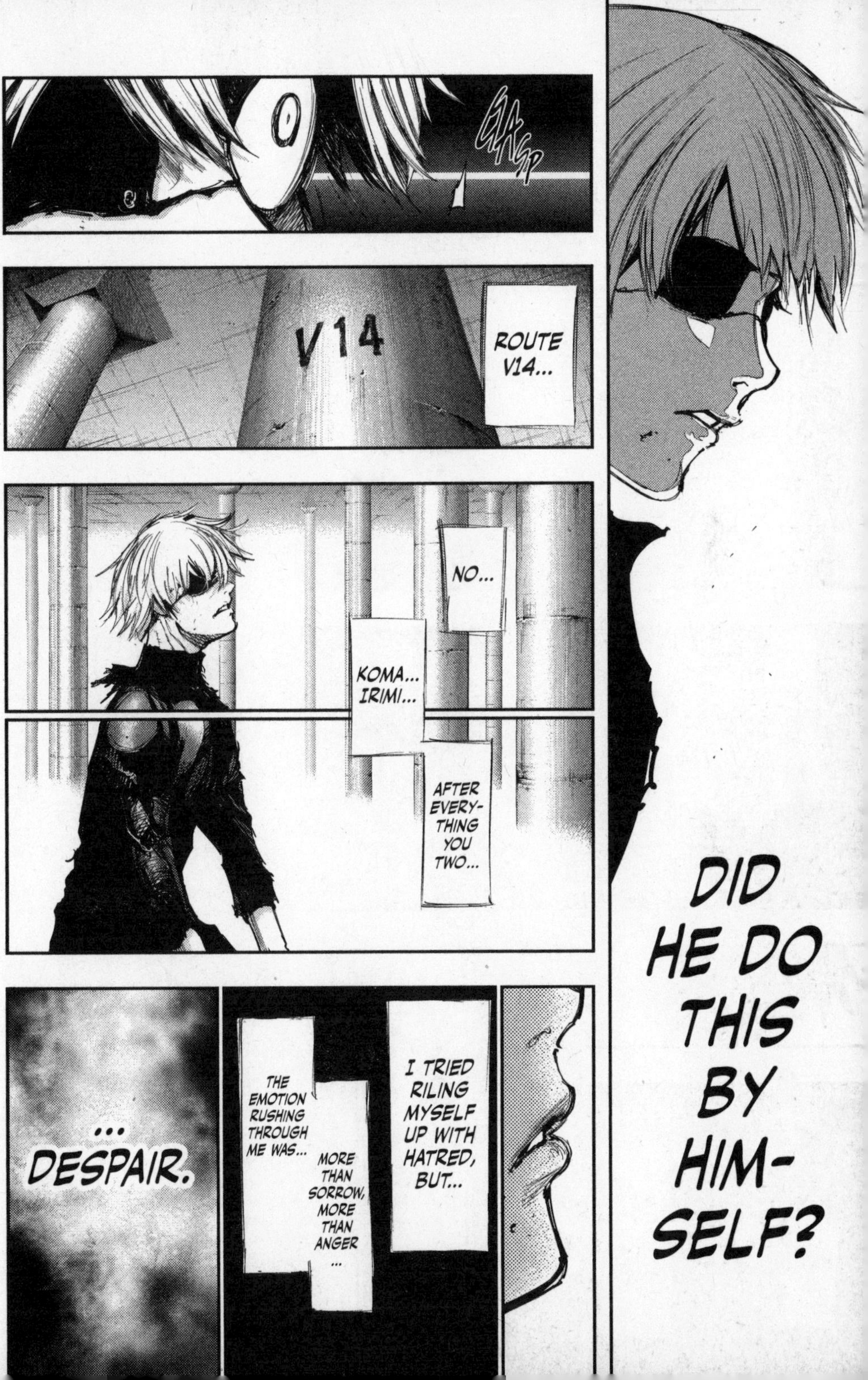
DID HE DO THIS BY HIM-SELF?
GASP
ROUTE V14...
V14
NO...
KOMA... IRIMI...
AFTER EVERY-THING YOU TWO...
I TRIED RILING MYSELF UP WITH HATRED, BUT...
THE EMOTION RUSHING THROUGH ME WAS...
MORE THAN SORROW, MORE THAN ANGER ...
... DESPAIR.

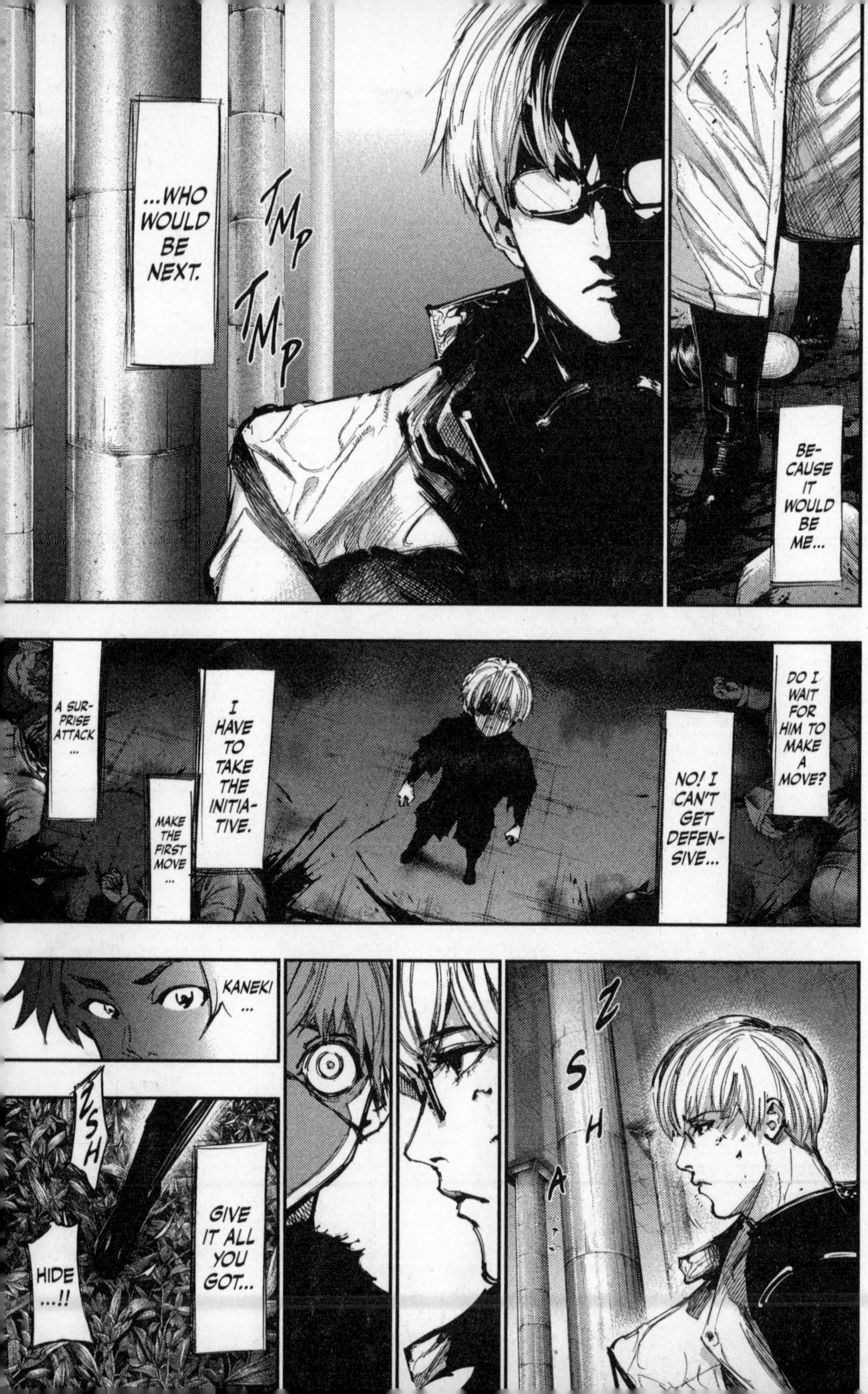
BE-CAUSE IT WOULD BE ME...
...WHO WOULD BE NEXT.
TMP TMP
DO I WAIT FOR HIM TO MAKE A MOVE?
NO! I CAN'T GET DEFEN-SIVE...
I HAVE TO TAKE THE INITIA-TIVE.
A SUR-PRISE ATTACK...
MAKE THE FIRST MOVE...
ZSHA
GIVE IT ALL YOU GOT...
KANEKI...
ZSH
HIDE...!!

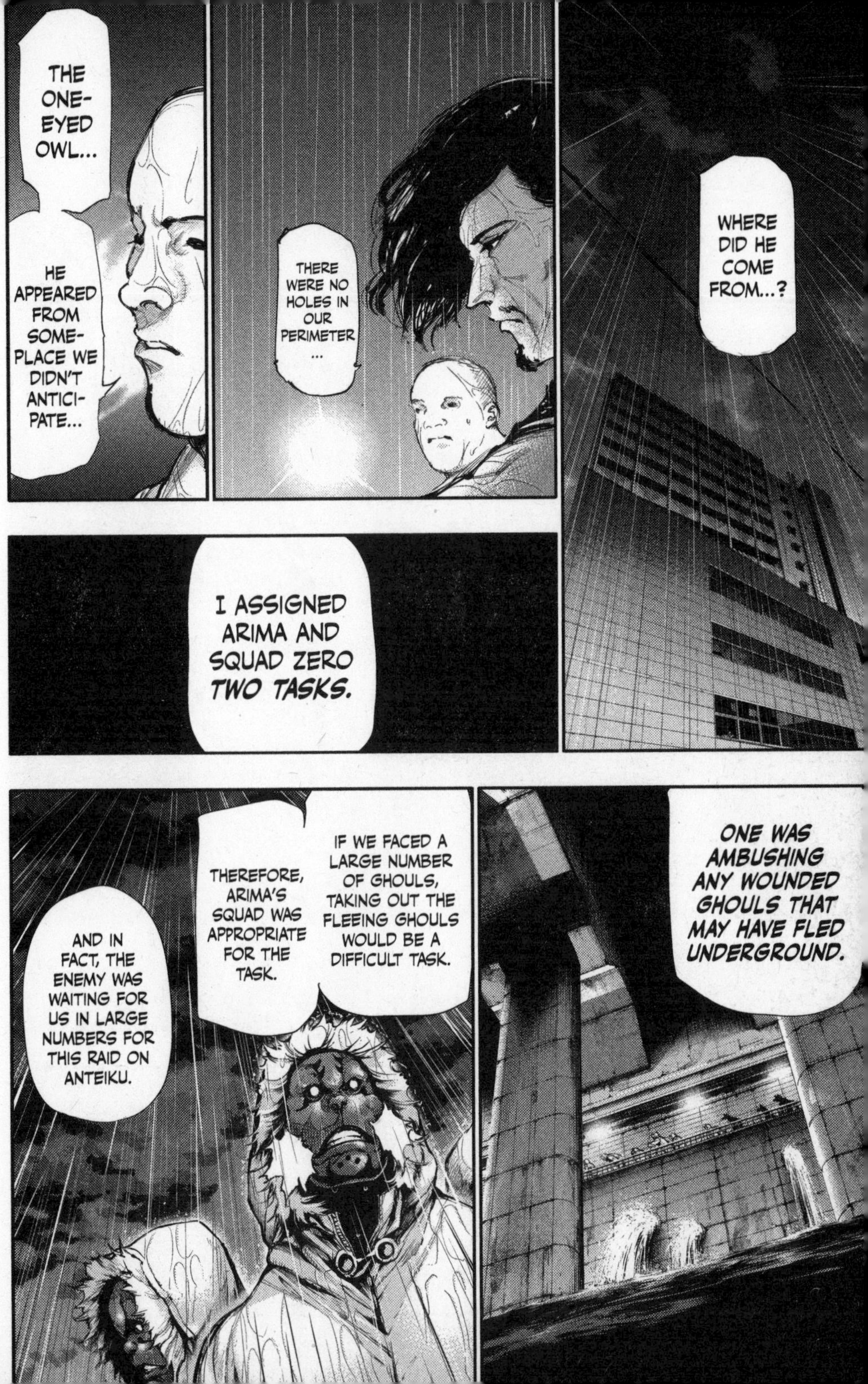
WHERE DID HE COME FROM...?
THERE WERE NO HOLES IN OUR PERIMETER...
THE ONE-EYED OWL...
HE APPEARED FROM SOMEPLACE WE DIDN'T ANTICIPATE...
I ASSIGNED ARIMA AND SQUAD ZERO *TWO TASKS.*
ONE WAS AMBUSHING ANY WOUNDED GHOULS THAT MAY HAVE FLED UNDERGROUND.
IF WE FACED A LARGE NUMBER OF GHOULS, TAKING OUT THE FLEEING GHOULS WOULD BE A DIFFICULT TASK.
THEREFORE, ARIMA'S SQUAD WAS APPROPRIATE FOR THE TASK.
AND IN FACT, THE ENEMY WAS WAITING FOR US IN LARGE NUMBERS FOR THIS RAID ON ANTEIKU.

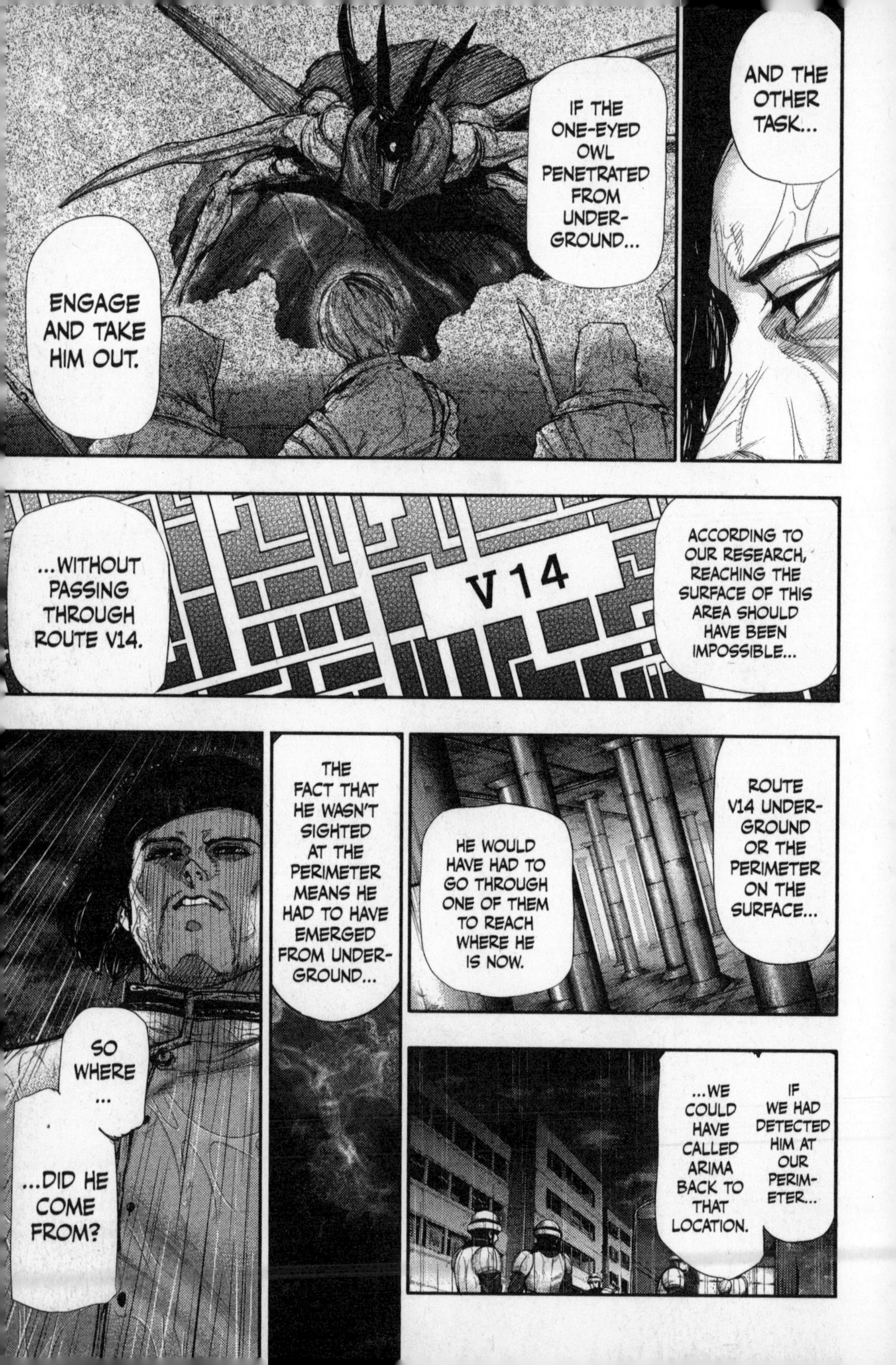
AND THE OTHER TASK...
IF THE ONE-EYED OWL PENETRATED FROM UNDER-GROUND...
ENGAGE AND TAKE HIM OUT.
ACCORDING TO OUR RESEARCH, REACHING THE SURFACE OF THIS AREA SHOULD HAVE BEEN IMPOSSIBLE...
V 14
...WITHOUT PASSING THROUGH ROUTE V14.
ROUTE V14 UNDER-GROUND OR THE PERIMETER ON THE SURFACE...
HE WOULD HAVE HAD TO GO THROUGH ONE OF THEM TO REACH WHERE HE IS NOW.
THE FACT THAT HE WASN'T SIGHTED AT THE PERIMETER MEANS HE HAD TO HAVE EMERGED FROM UNDER-GROUND...
SO WHERE ...
...DID HE COME FROM?
IF WE HAD DETECTED HIM AT OUR PERIM-ETER...
...WE COULD HAVE CALLED ARIMA BACK TO THAT LOCATION.

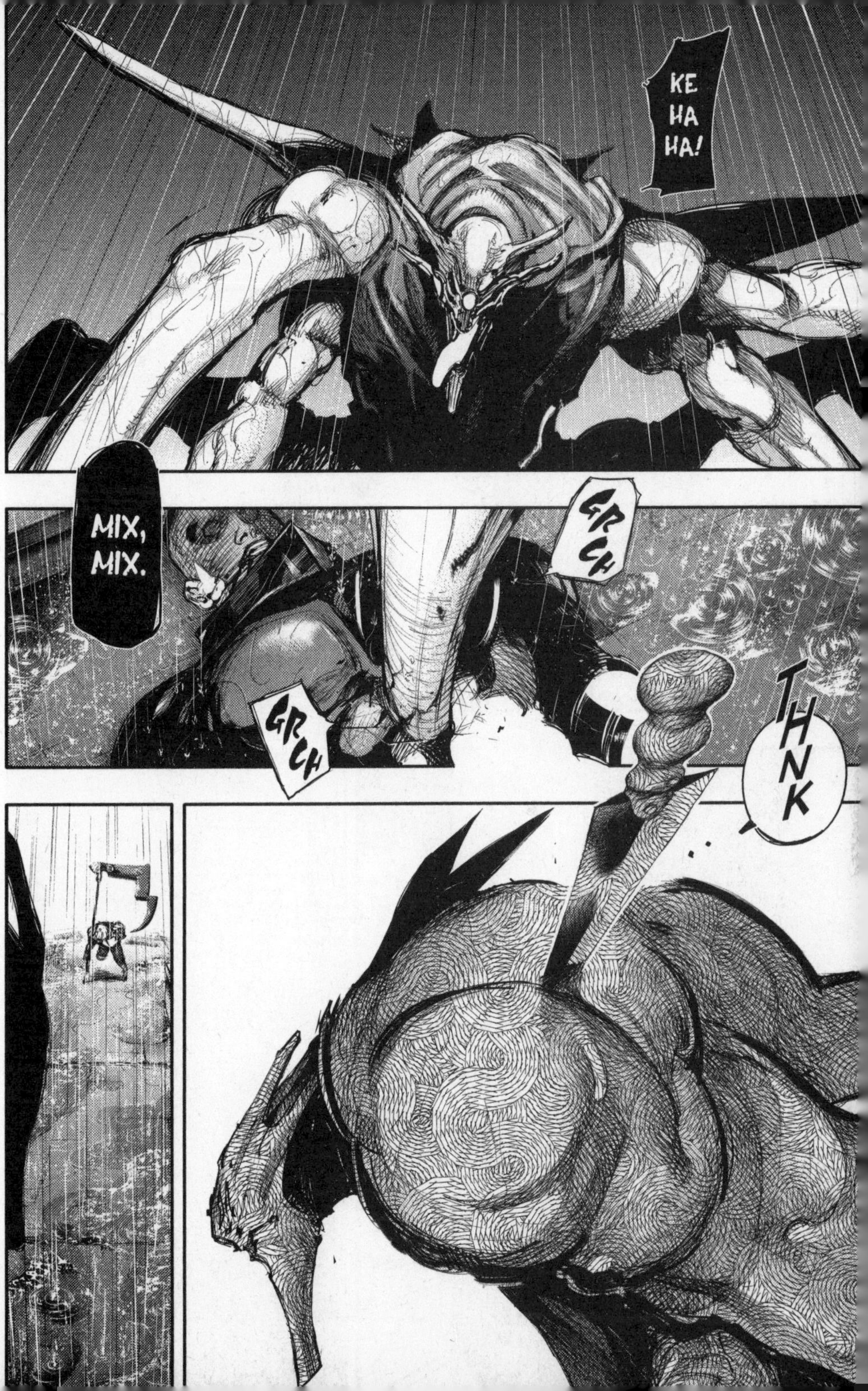
KE HA HA!
GRCH
MIX, MIX.
GRCH
THNK

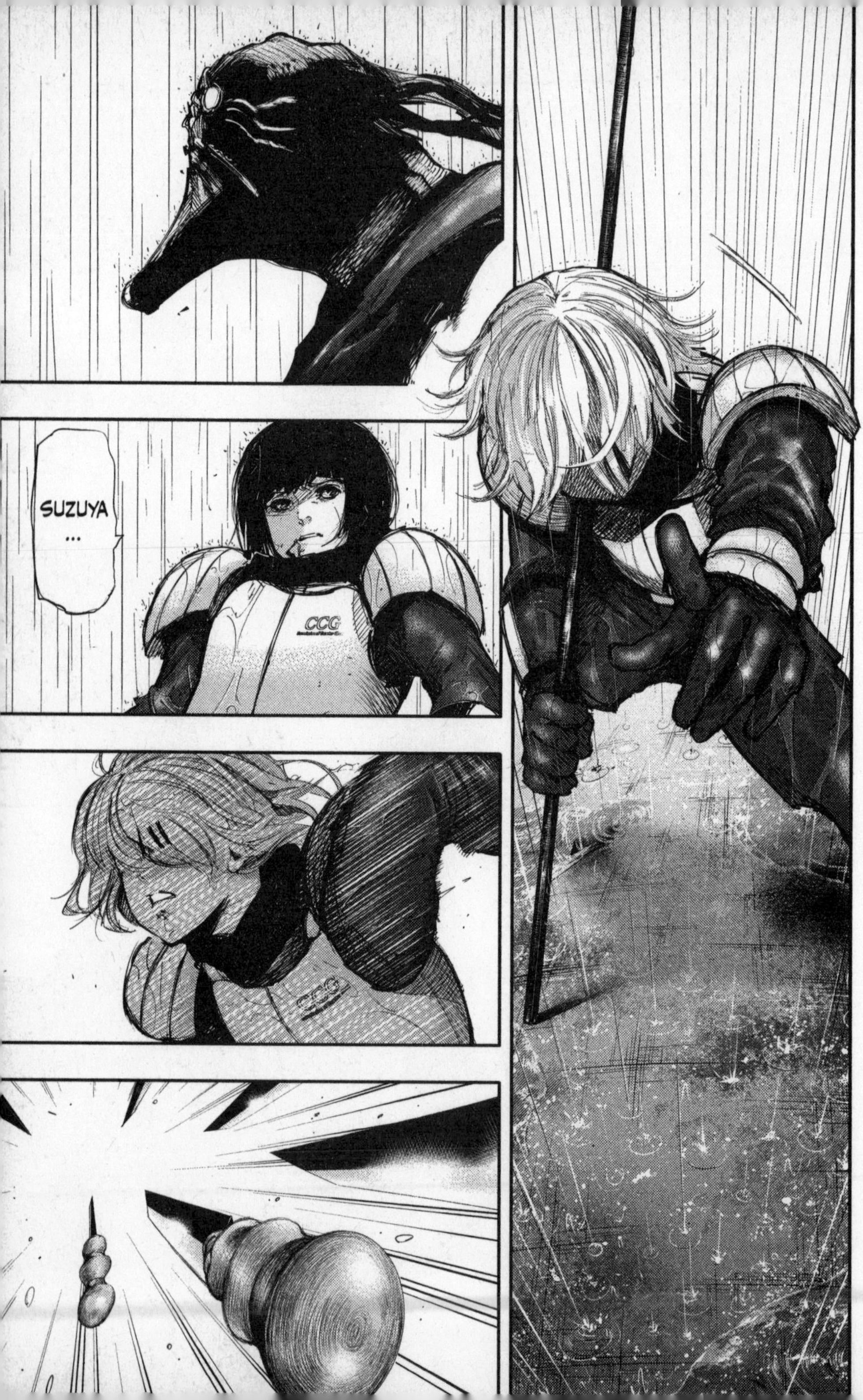
SUZUYA ...

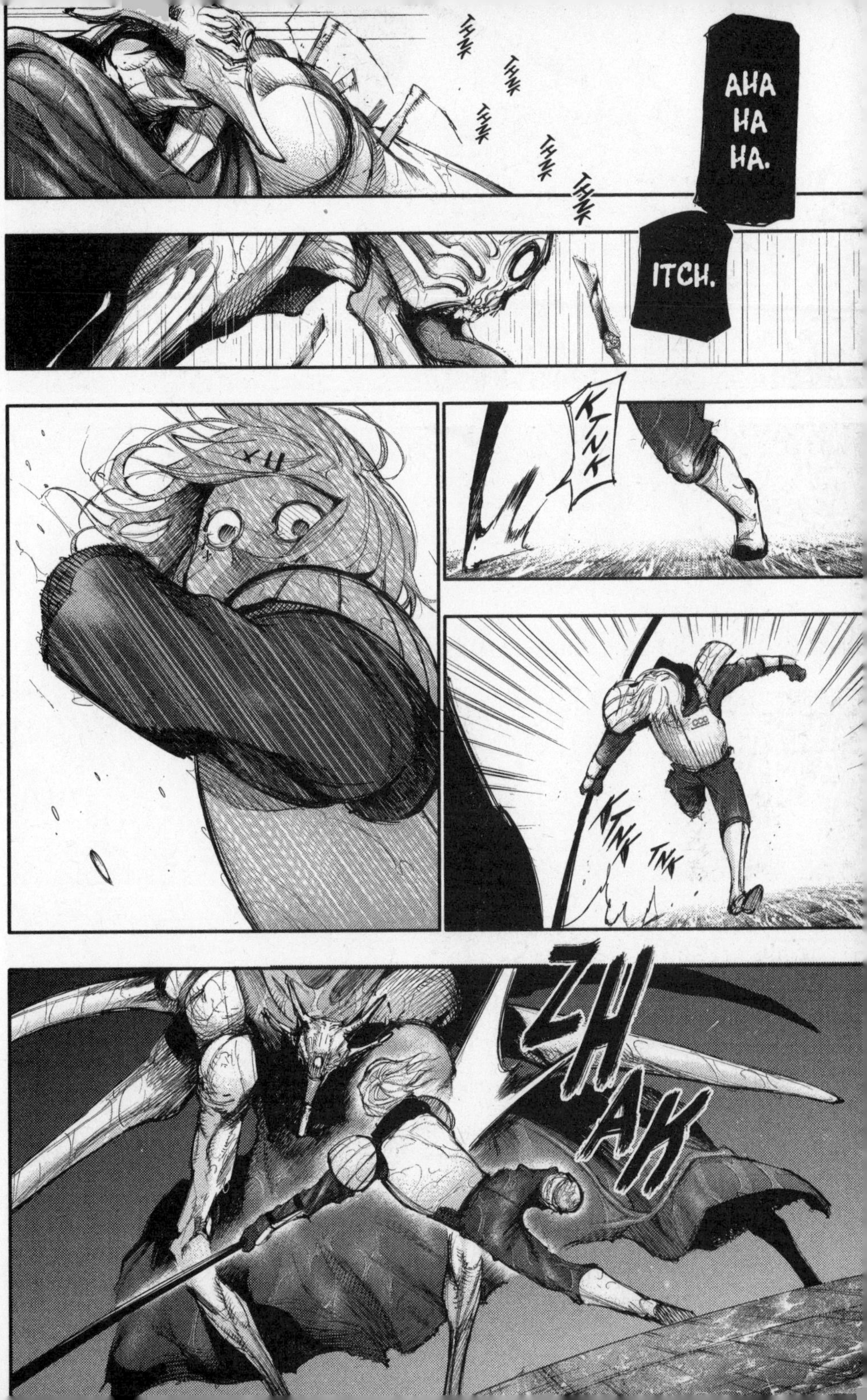
AHA HA HA.
THNK
THNK
THNK
THNK
THNK
ITCH.
KTINK
KTINK
TNK
ZHAK

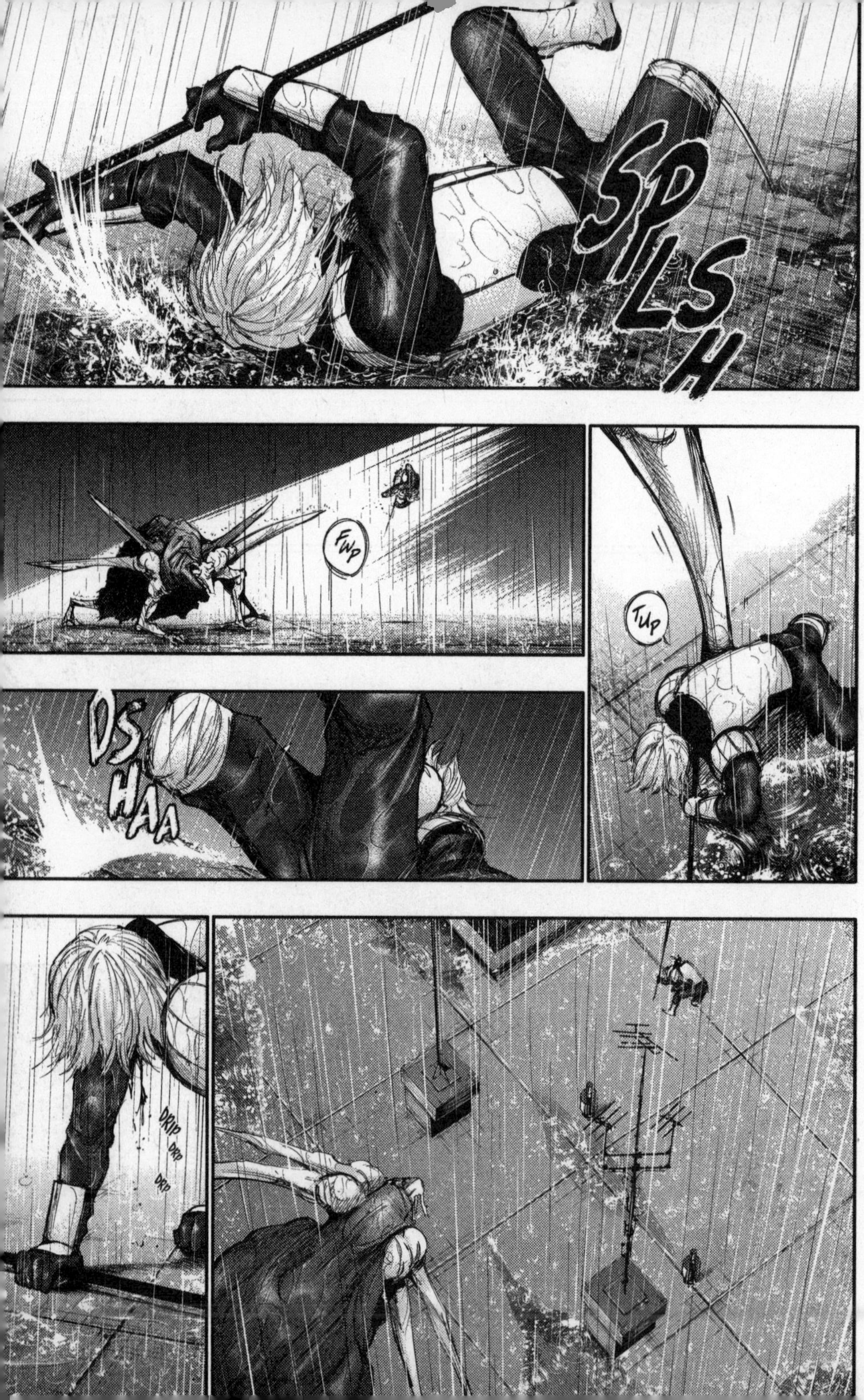
SPLSH
TUP
FWP
DSHAA
DRIP DRIP DRIP

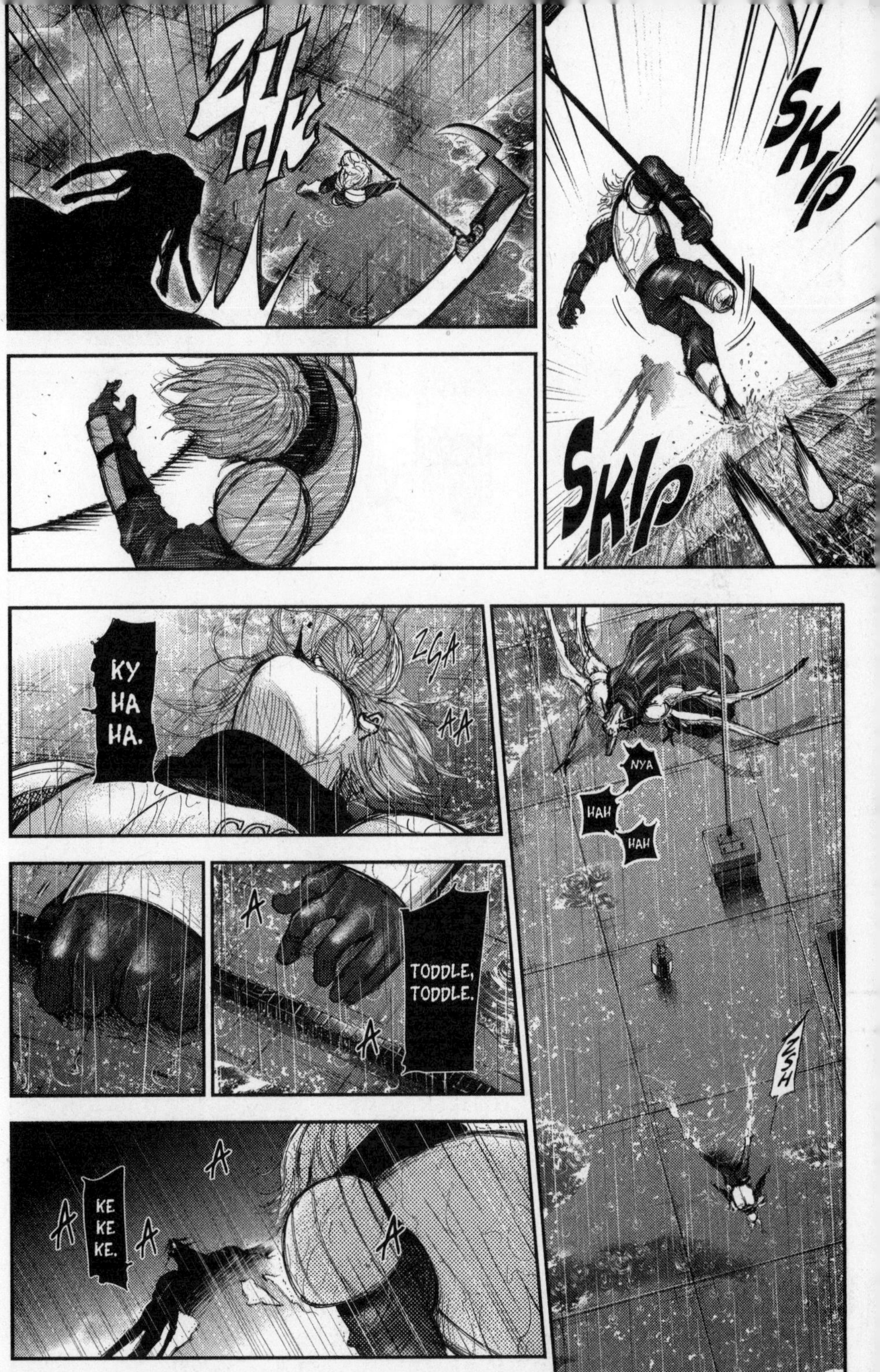
SKIP
SKIP
ZHK
NYA
HAH
HAH
ZSH
KY HA HA.
ZGA
AA
A
TODDLE, TODDLE.
A
A
KE KE KE.
A
A
A
A

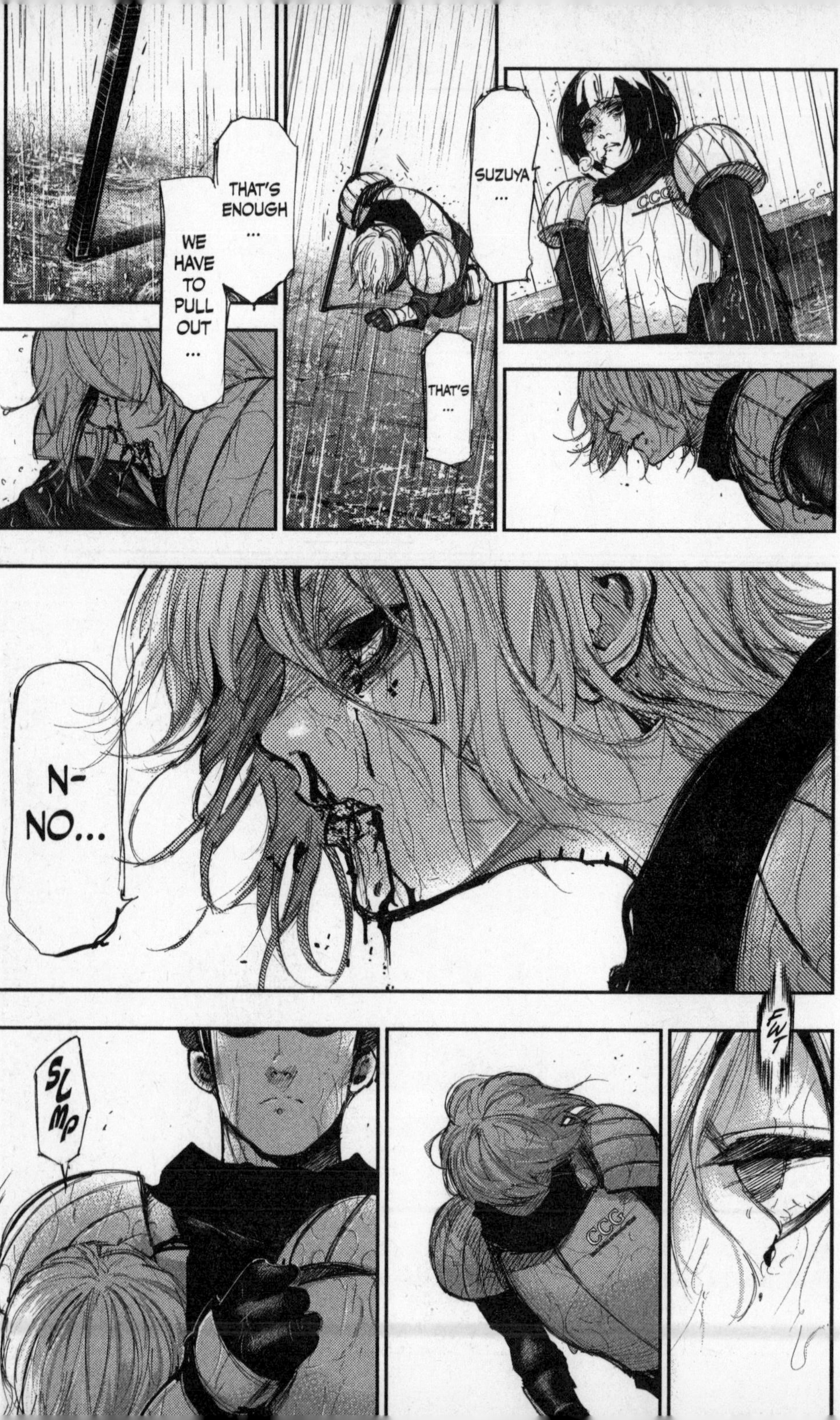
SUZUYA...
THAT'S...
THAT'S ENOUGH... WE HAVE TO PULL OUT...
N-NO...
FWT
SLUMP

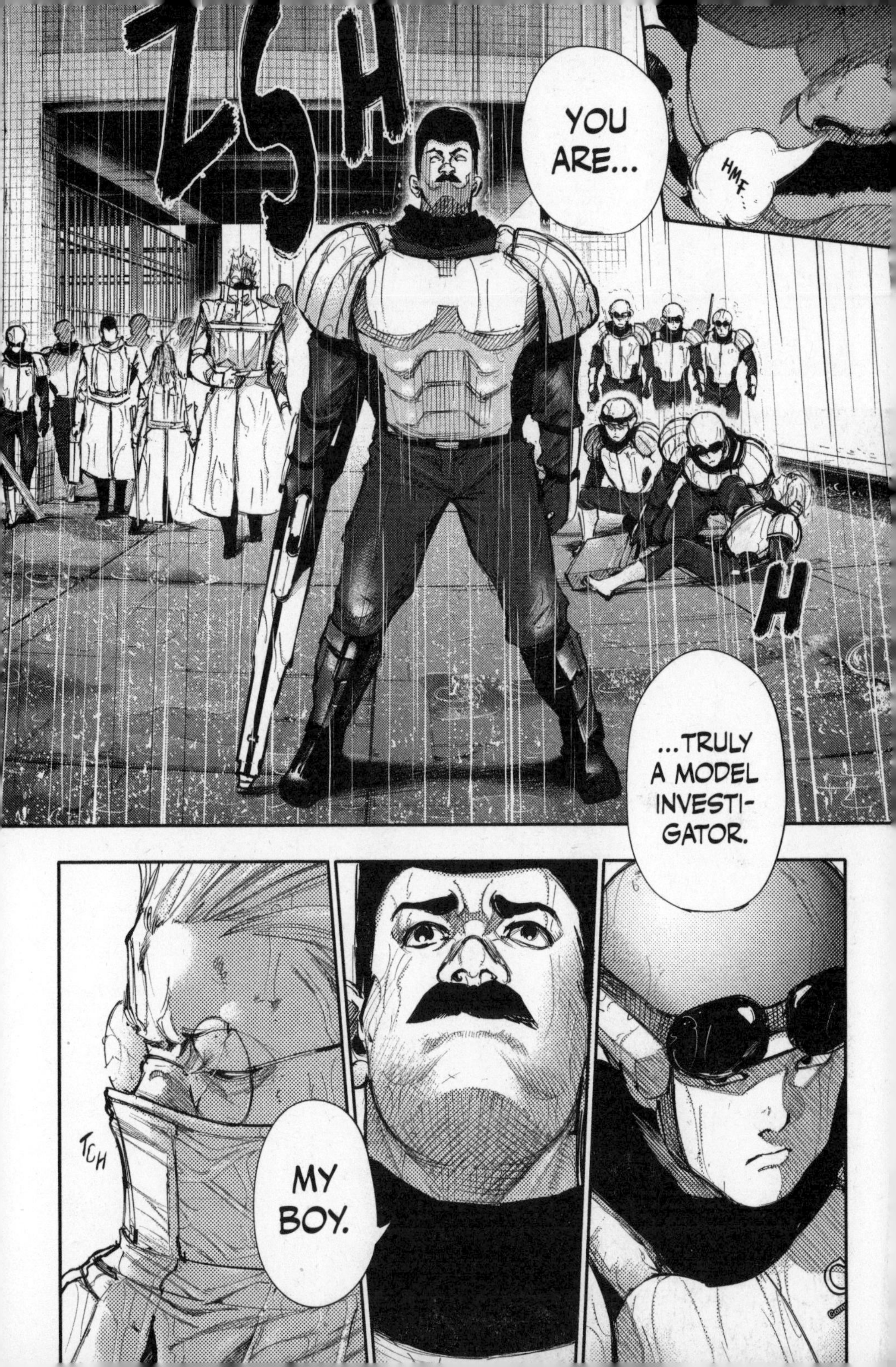
HMF...
YOU ARE...
ZSH
H
...TRULY A MODEL INVESTIGATOR.
MY BOY.
TCH

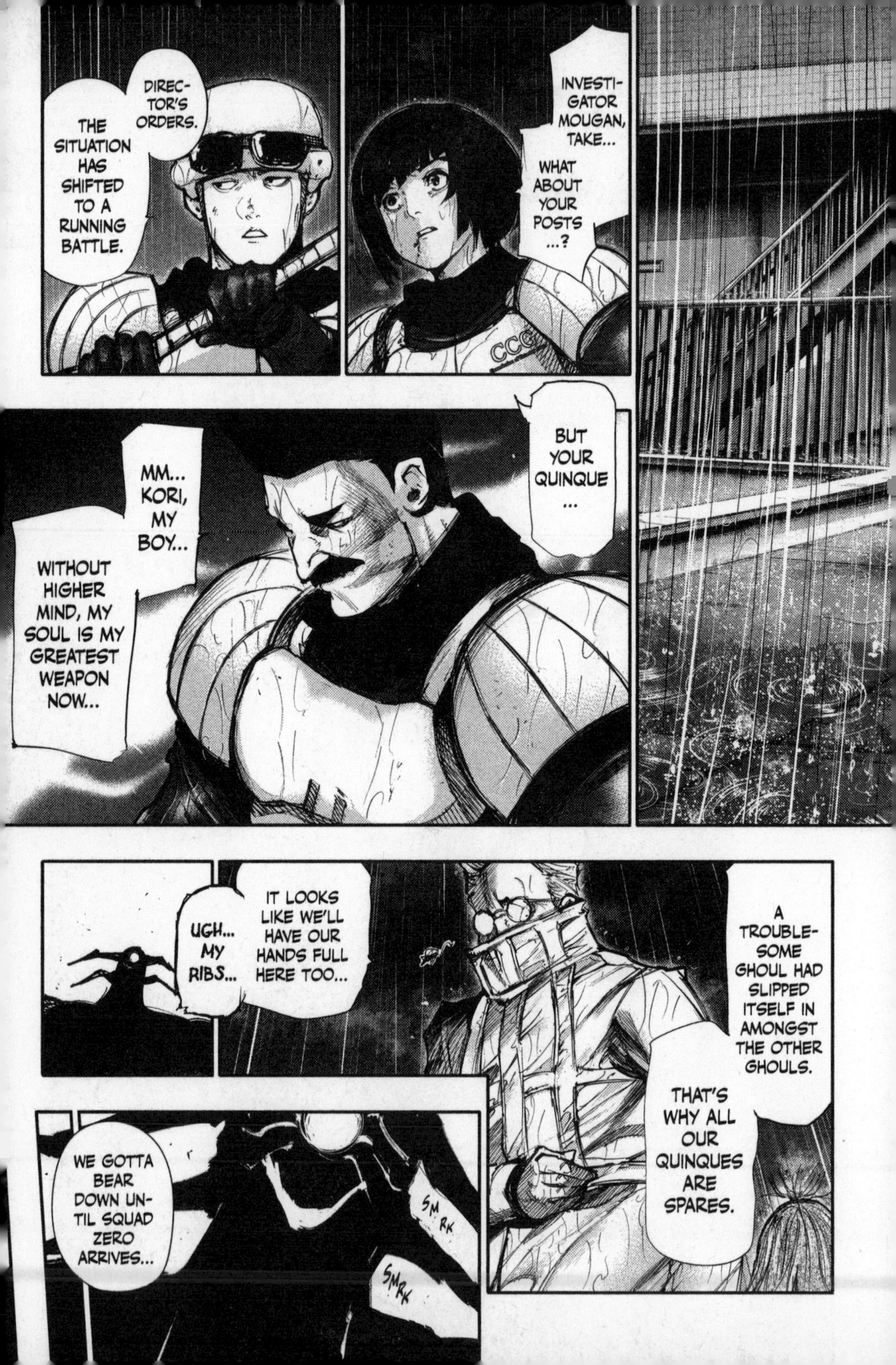
INVESTIGATOR MOUGAN, TAKE...
WHAT ABOUT YOUR POSTS ...?
DIRECTOR'S ORDERS.
THE SITUATION HAS SHIFTED TO A RUNNING BATTLE.
BUT YOUR QUINQUE ...
MM... KORI, MY BOY...
WITHOUT HIGHER MIND, MY SOUL IS MY GREATEST WEAPON NOW...
A TROUBLESOME GHOUL HAD SLIPPED ITSELF IN AMONGST THE OTHER GHOULS.
THAT'S WHY ALL OUR QUINQUES ARE SPARES.
IT LOOKS LIKE WE'LL HAVE OUR HANDS FULL HERE TOO...
UGH... MY RIBS...
WE GOTTA BEAR DOWN UNTIL SQUAD ZERO ARRIVES...
SMRK
SMRK

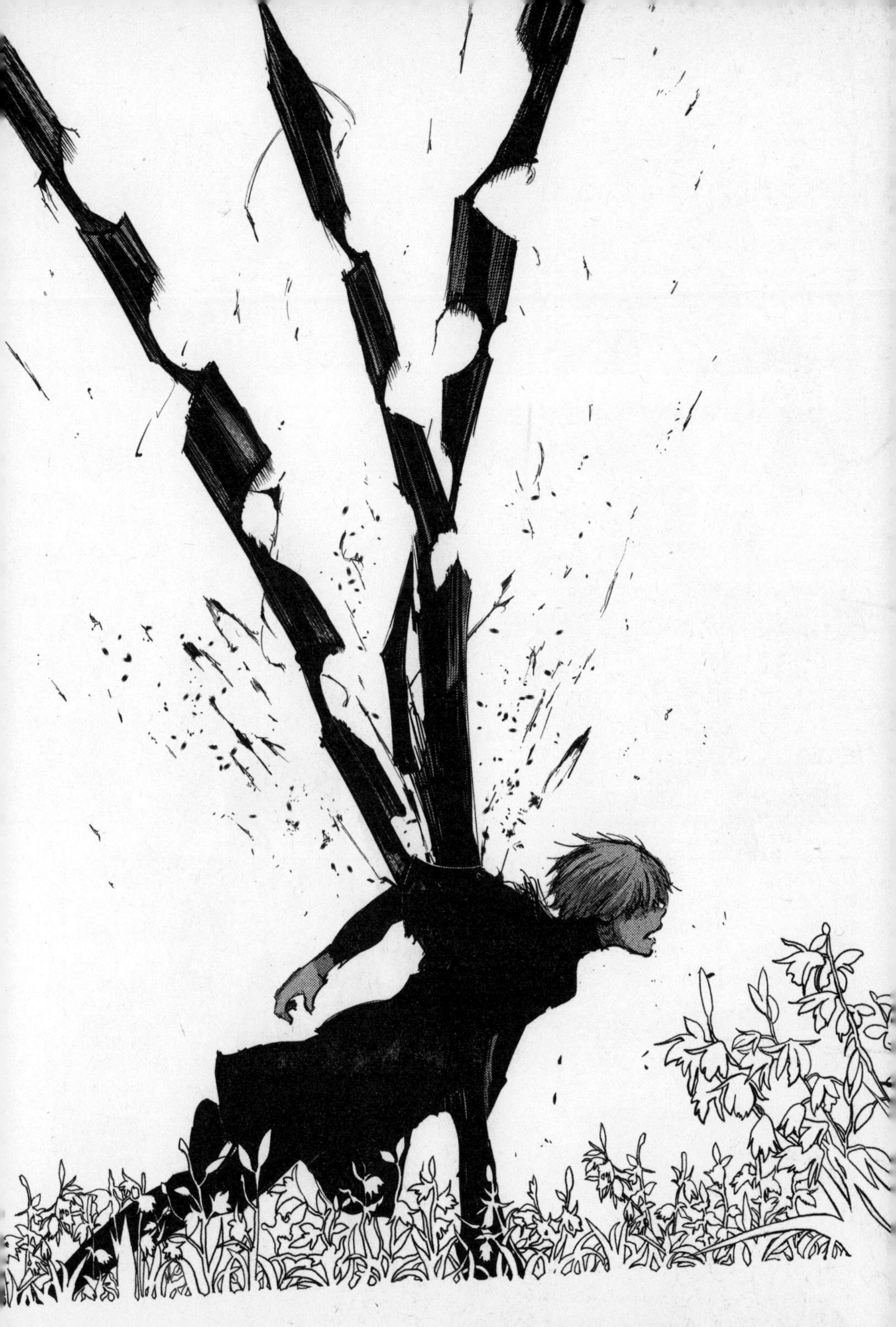

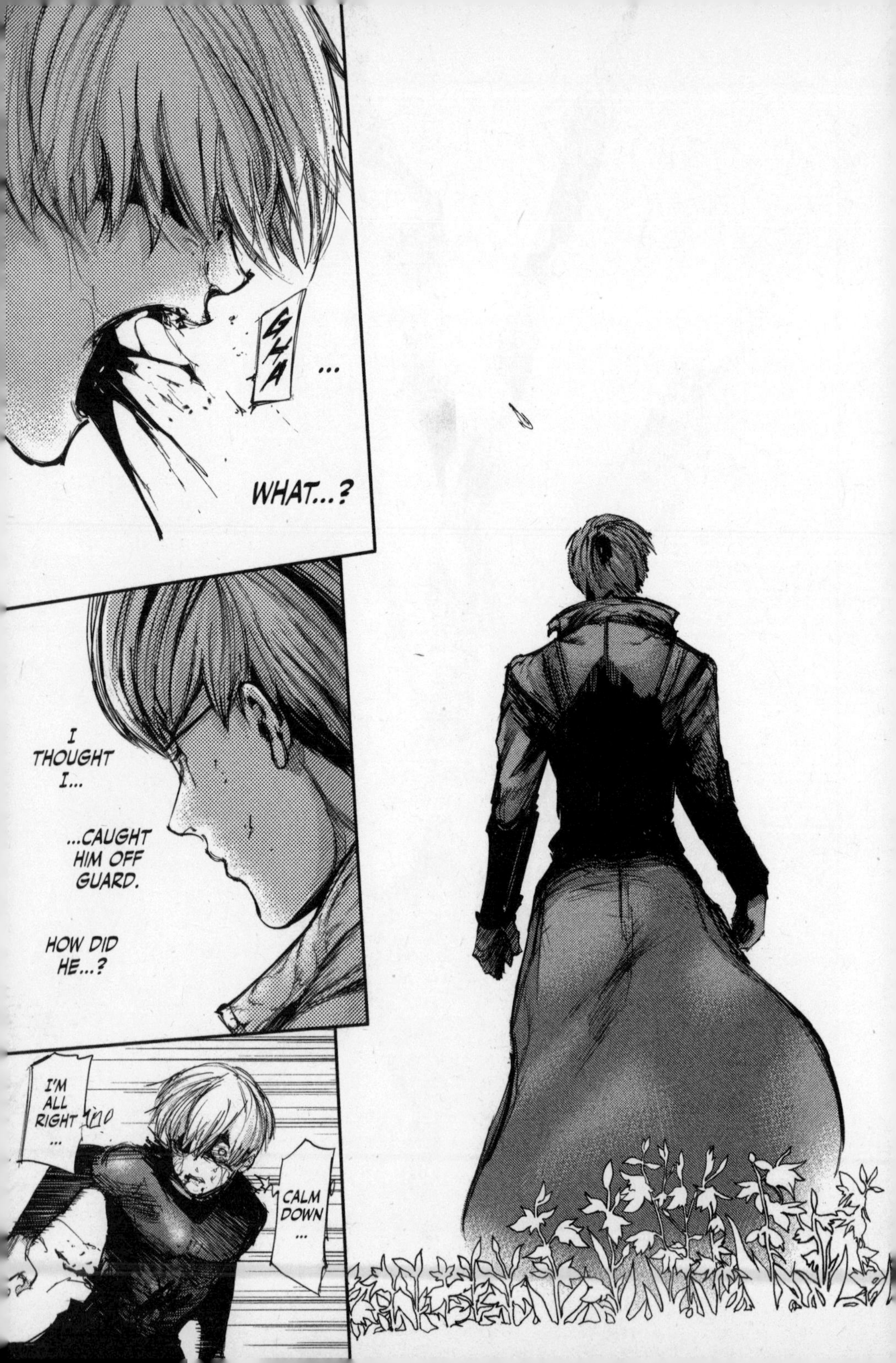
GHA
...
WHAT...?
I THOUGHT I...
...CAUGHT HIM OFF GUARD.
HOW DID HE...?
CALM DOWN...
I'M ALL RIGHT...

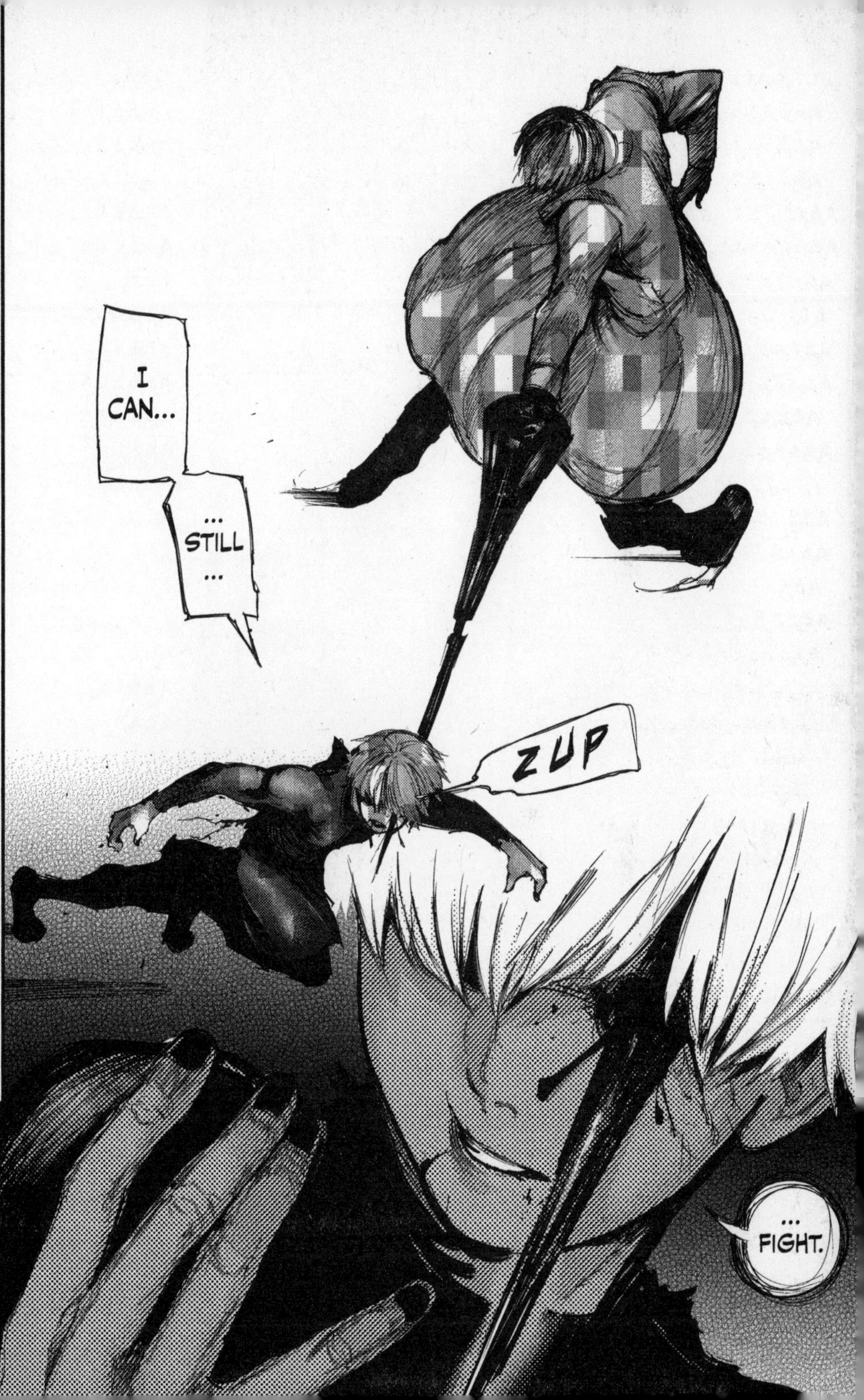
I CAN...
...STILL...
ZUP
...FIGHT.

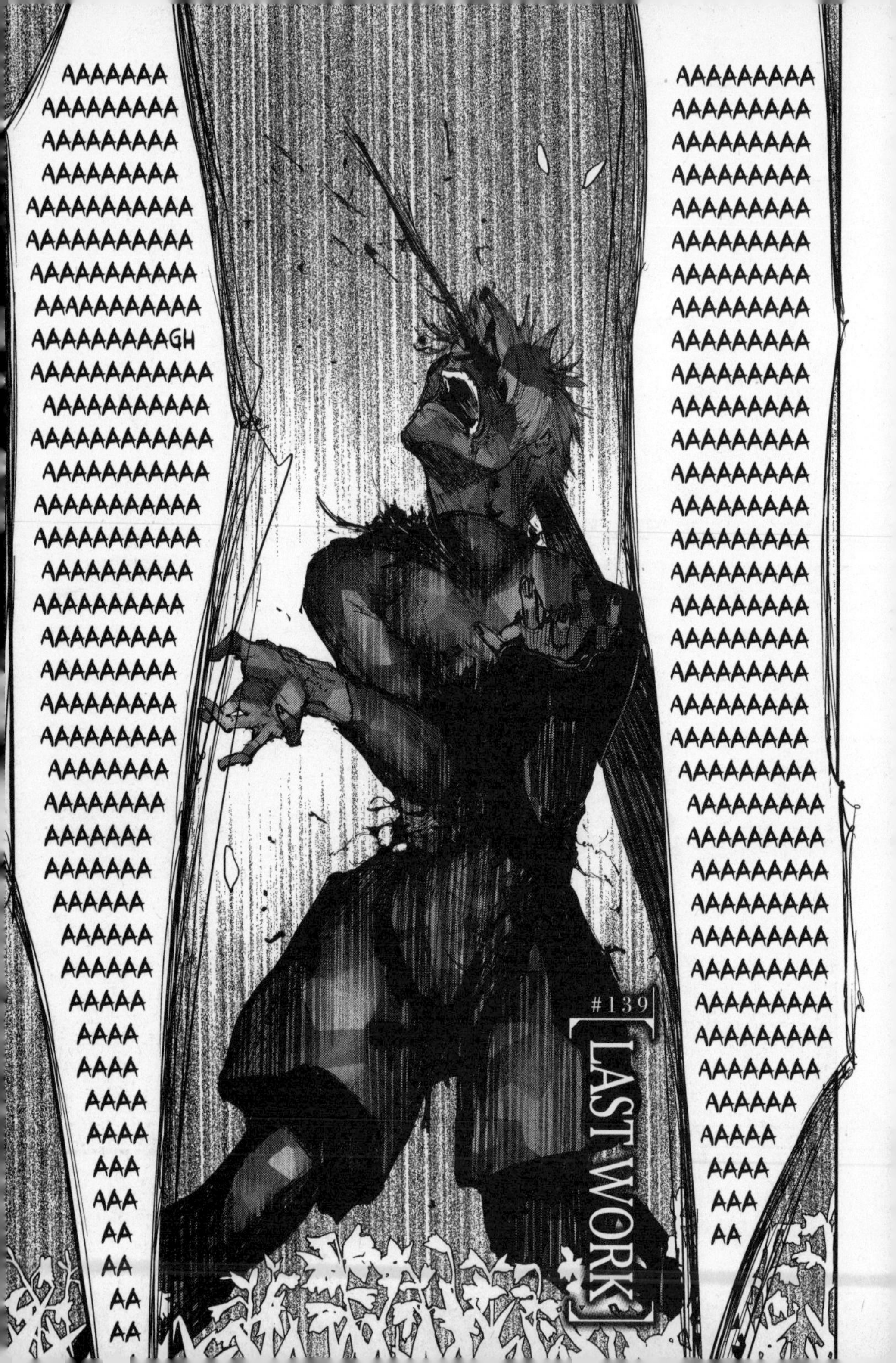
AAAAAAAAA
AAAAAAAAA
AAAAAAAAA
AAAAAAAAA
AAAAAAAAA
AAAAAAAAA
AAAAAAAAA
AAAAAAAAA
AAAAAAAAA
AAAAAAAAA
AAAAAAAAA
AAAAAAAAA
AAAAAAAAA
AAAAAAAAA
AAAAAAAAA
AAAAAAAAA
AAAAAAAAA
AAAAAAAAA
AAAAAAAAA
AAAAAAAAA
AAAAAAAAA
AAAAAAAAA
AAAAAAAAA
AAAAAAAAA
AAAAAAAAA
AAAAAAAAA
AAAAAAAAA
AAAAAAAAAA
AAAAAAAAAA
AAAAAAAA
AAAAAA
AAAAA
AAAA
AAA
AA
#139
[LAST WORK]
AAAAAAA
AAAAAAAAA
AAAAAAAAA
AAAAAAAAA
AAAAAAAAAAAA
AAAAAAAAAAA
AAAAAAAAAAA
AAAAAAAAAAA
AAAAAAAAAAGH
AAAAAAAAAAAAA
AAAAAAAAAAA
AAAAAAAAAAAAA
AAAAAAAAAAA
AAAAAAAAAAA
AAAAAAAAAAA
AAAAAAAAAA
AAAAAAAAAA
AAAAAAAAA
AAAAAAAAA
AAAAAAAAA
AAAAAAAAA
AAAAAAAA
AAAAAAAA
AAAAAAA
AAAAAAA
AAAAAA
AAAAAA
AAAAAA
AAAAA
AAAA
AAAA
AAAA
AAAA
AAA
AAA
AA
AA
AA
AA

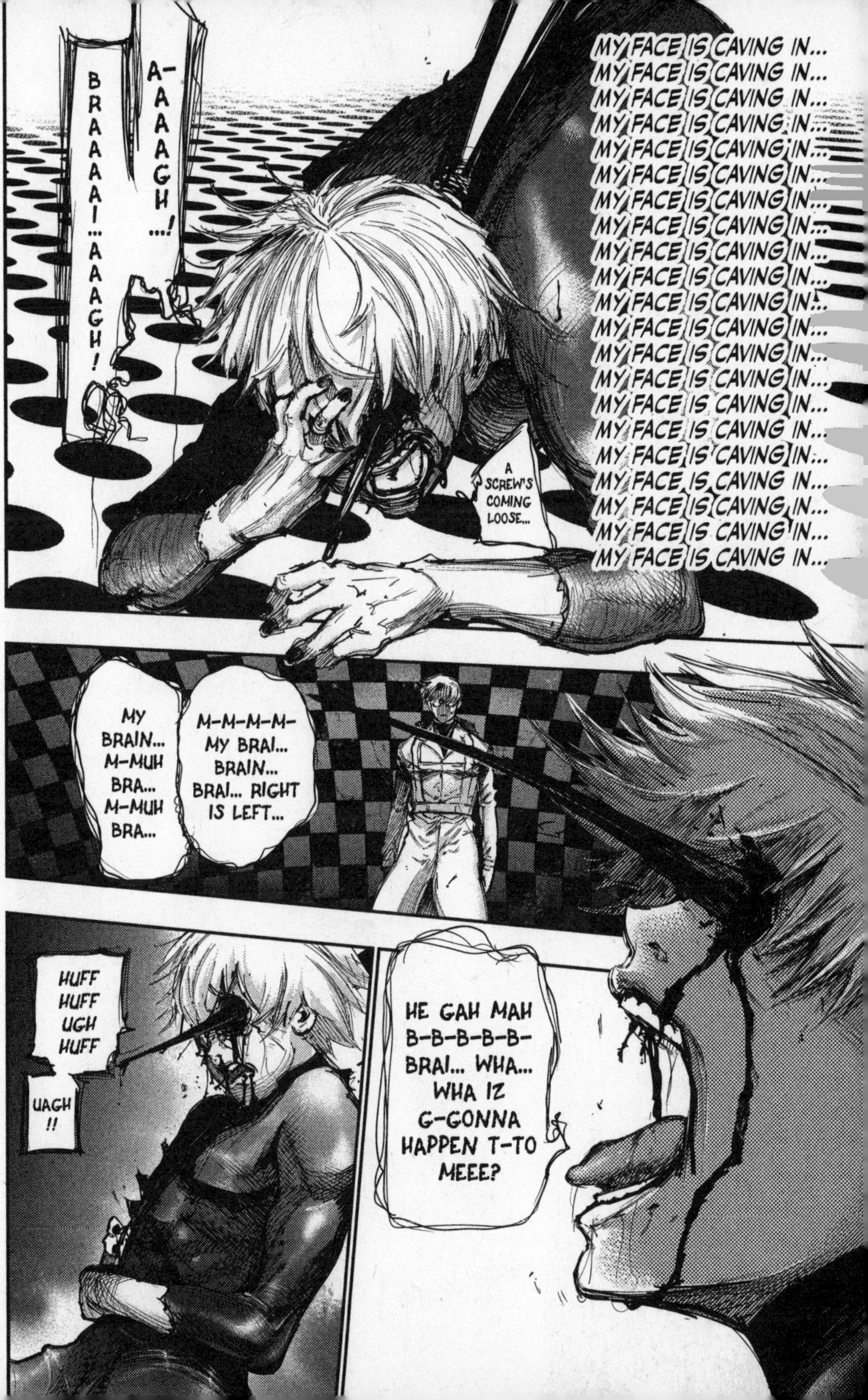
MY FACE IS CAVING IN...
MY FACE IS CAVING IN...
MY FACE IS CAVING IN...
MY FACE IS CAVING IN...
MY FACE IS CAVING IN...
MY FACE IS CAVING IN...
MY FACE IS CAVING IN...
MY FACE IS CAVING IN...
MY FACE IS CAVING IN...
MY FACE IS CAVING IN...
MY FACE IS CAVING IN...
MY FACE IS CAVING IN...
MY FACE IS CAVING IN...
MY FACE IS CAVING IN...
MY FACE IS CAVING IN...
MY FACE IS CAVING IN...
MY FACE IS CAVING IN...
MY FACE IS CAVING IN...
MY FACE IS CAVING IN...
MY FACE IS CAVING IN...
MY FACE IS CAVING IN...
A SCREW'S COMING LOOSE...
A-AAAAGH ...!
BRAAAAAI... AAAAGH!
M-M-M-M-MY BRAI... BRAIN... BRAI... RIGHT IS LEFT...
MY BRAIN... M-MUH BRA... M-MUH BRA...
HE GAH MAH B-B-B-B-B-BRAI... WHA... WHA IZ G-GONNA HAPPEN T-TO MEEE?
HUFF HUFF UGH HUFF
UAGH !!

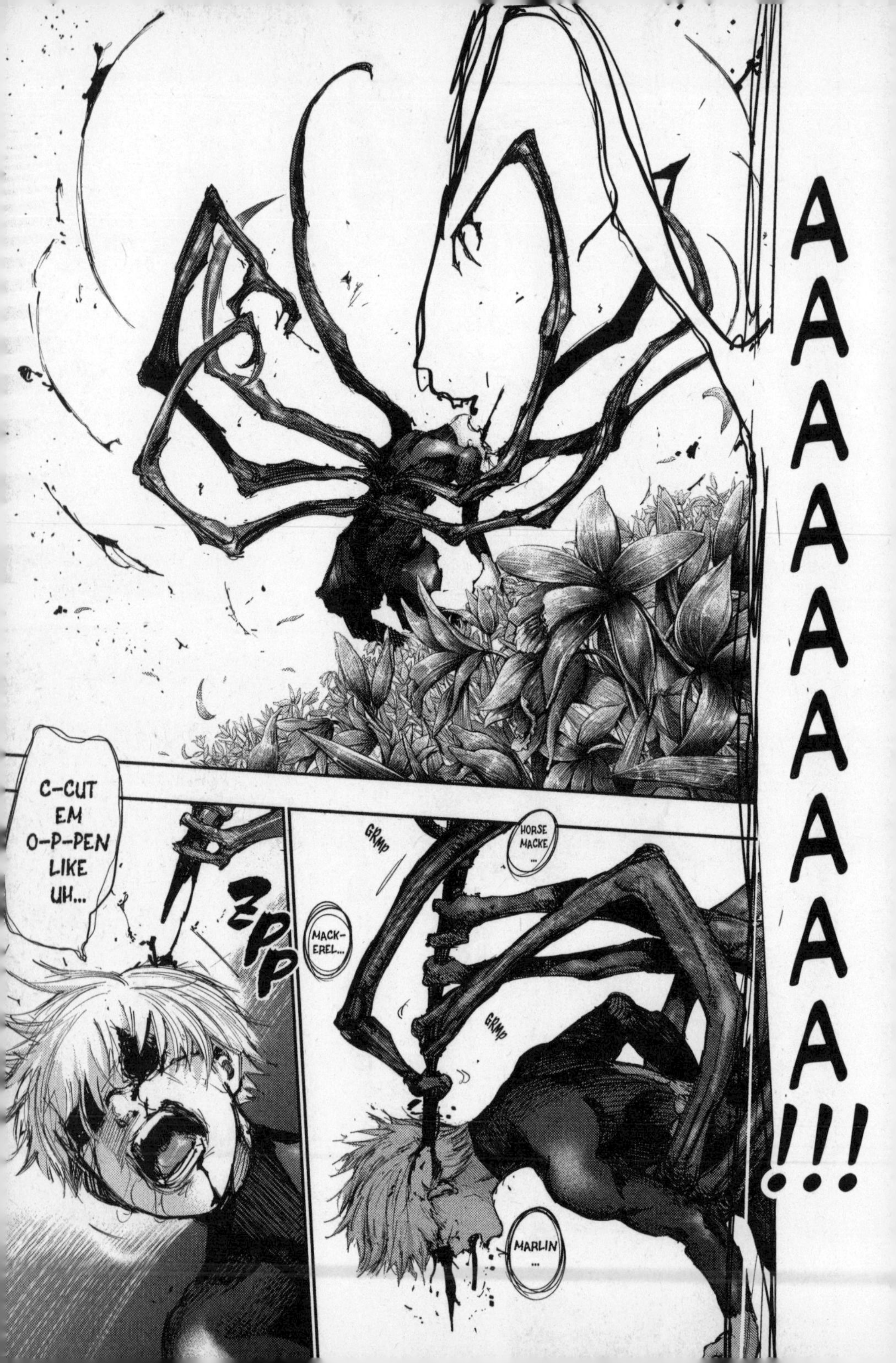
AAAAAAAAA!!!
HORSE MACKE...
GRMP
MACK-EREL...
GRMP
MARLIN...
C-CUT EM O-P-PEN LIKE UH...
ZPP

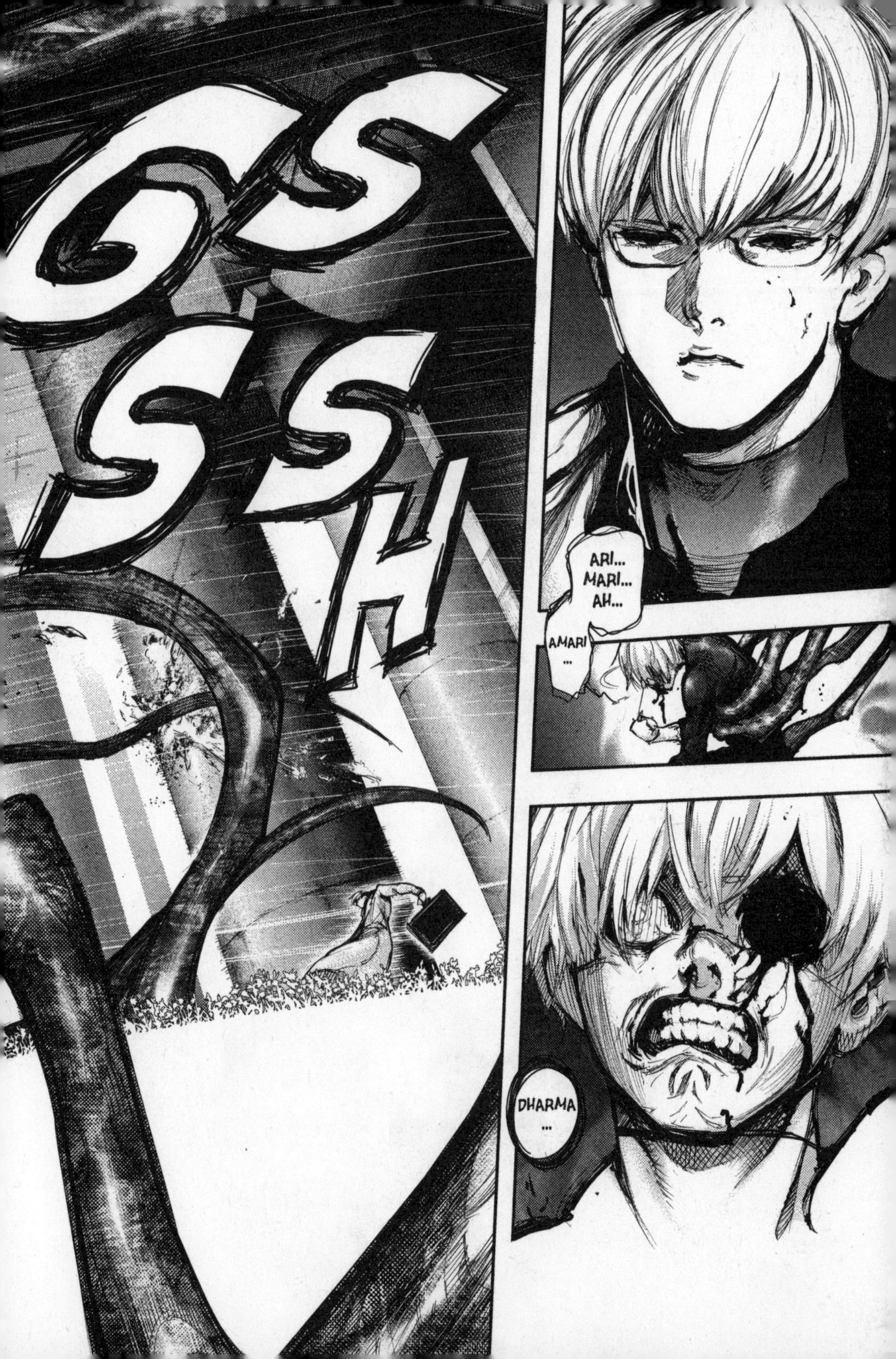
ARI... MARI... AH...
AMARI...
DHARMA...
GSSSHH

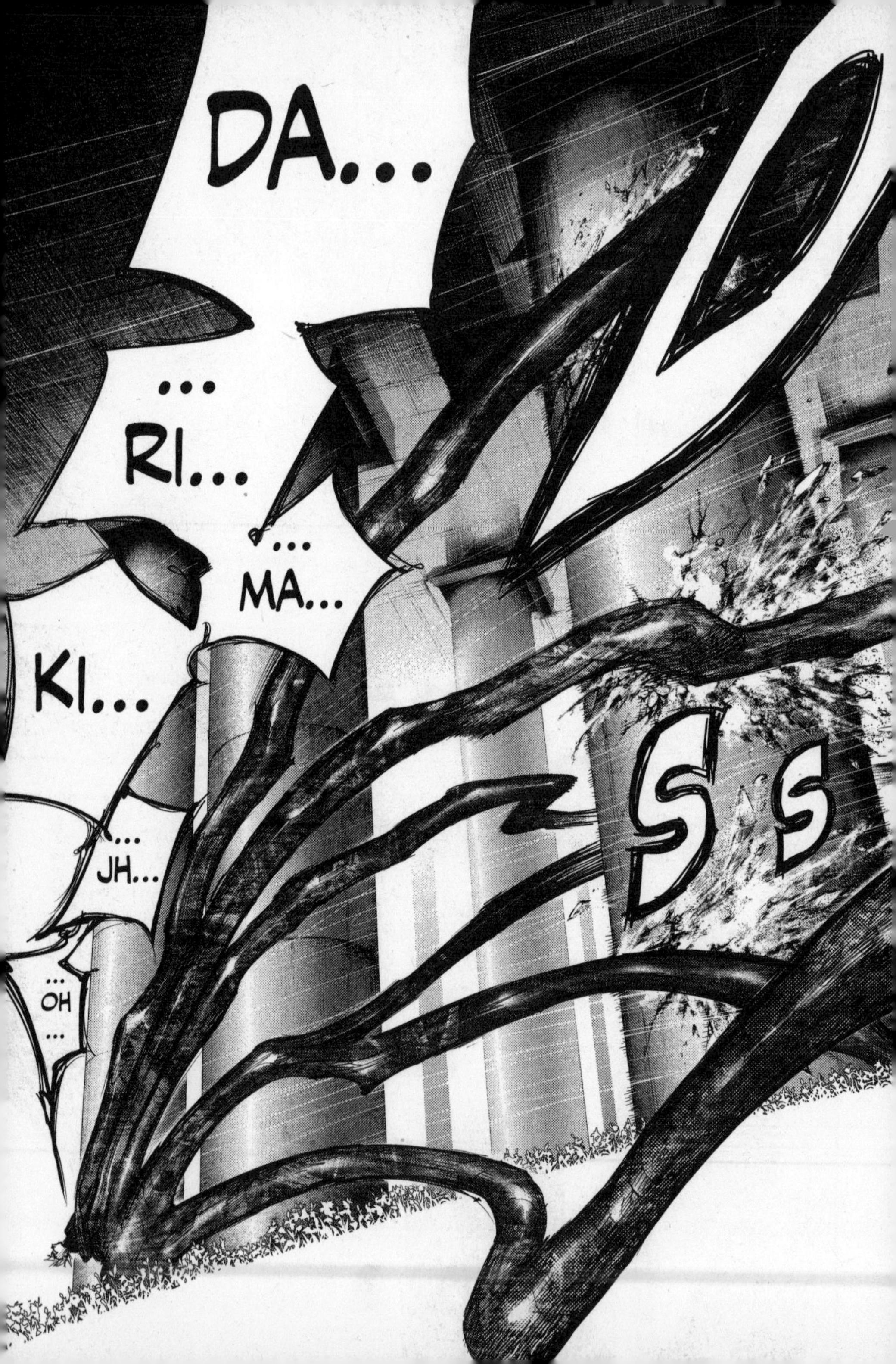
DA...
...RI...
...MA...
KI...
...JH...
...OH...
SS

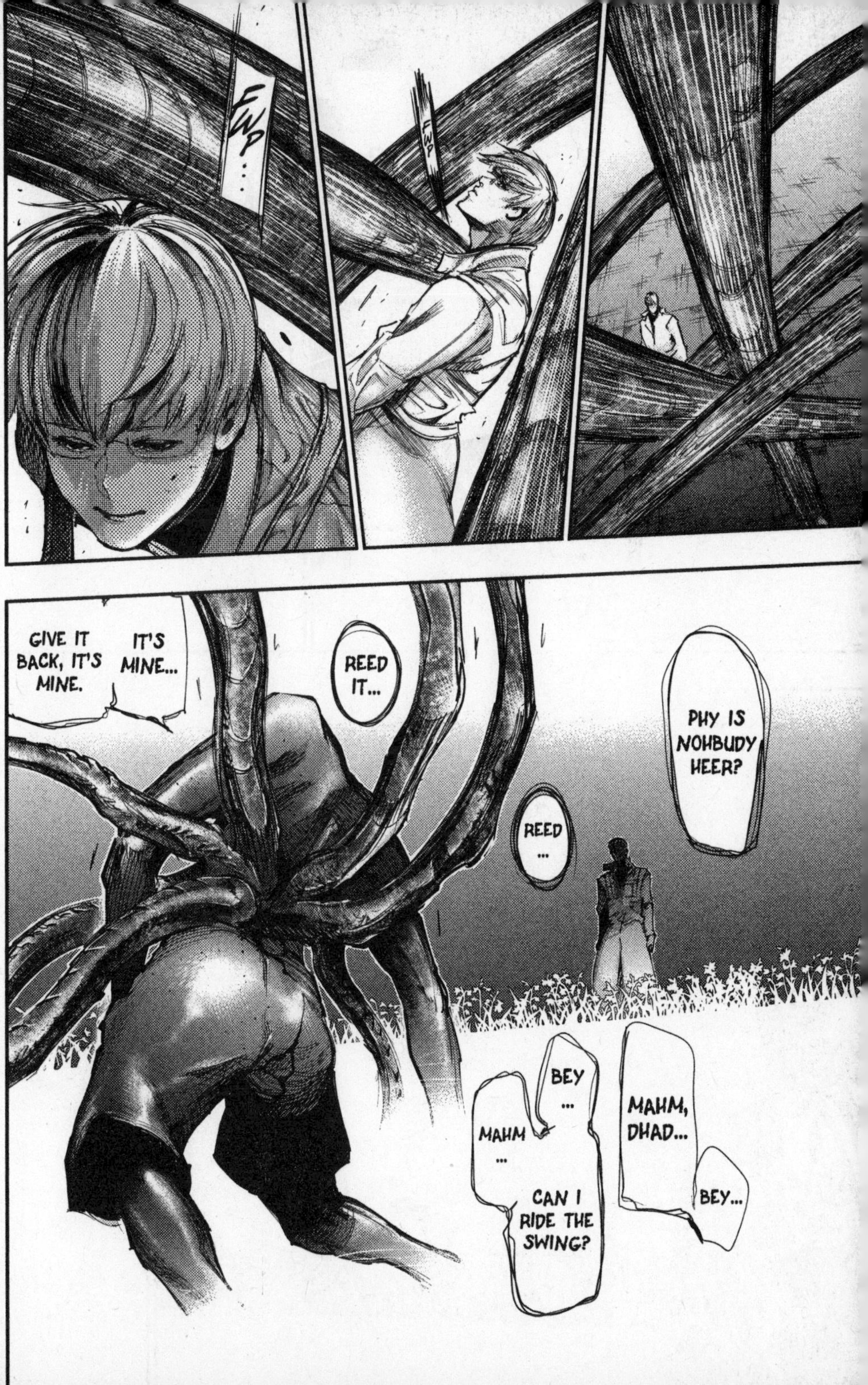
FWP
FWP...
PHY IS NOHBUDY HEER?
REED ...
REED IT...
IT'S MINE...
GIVE IT BACK, IT'S MINE.
MAHM, DHAD...
BEY...
BEY ...
MAHM ...
CAN I RIDE THE SWING?

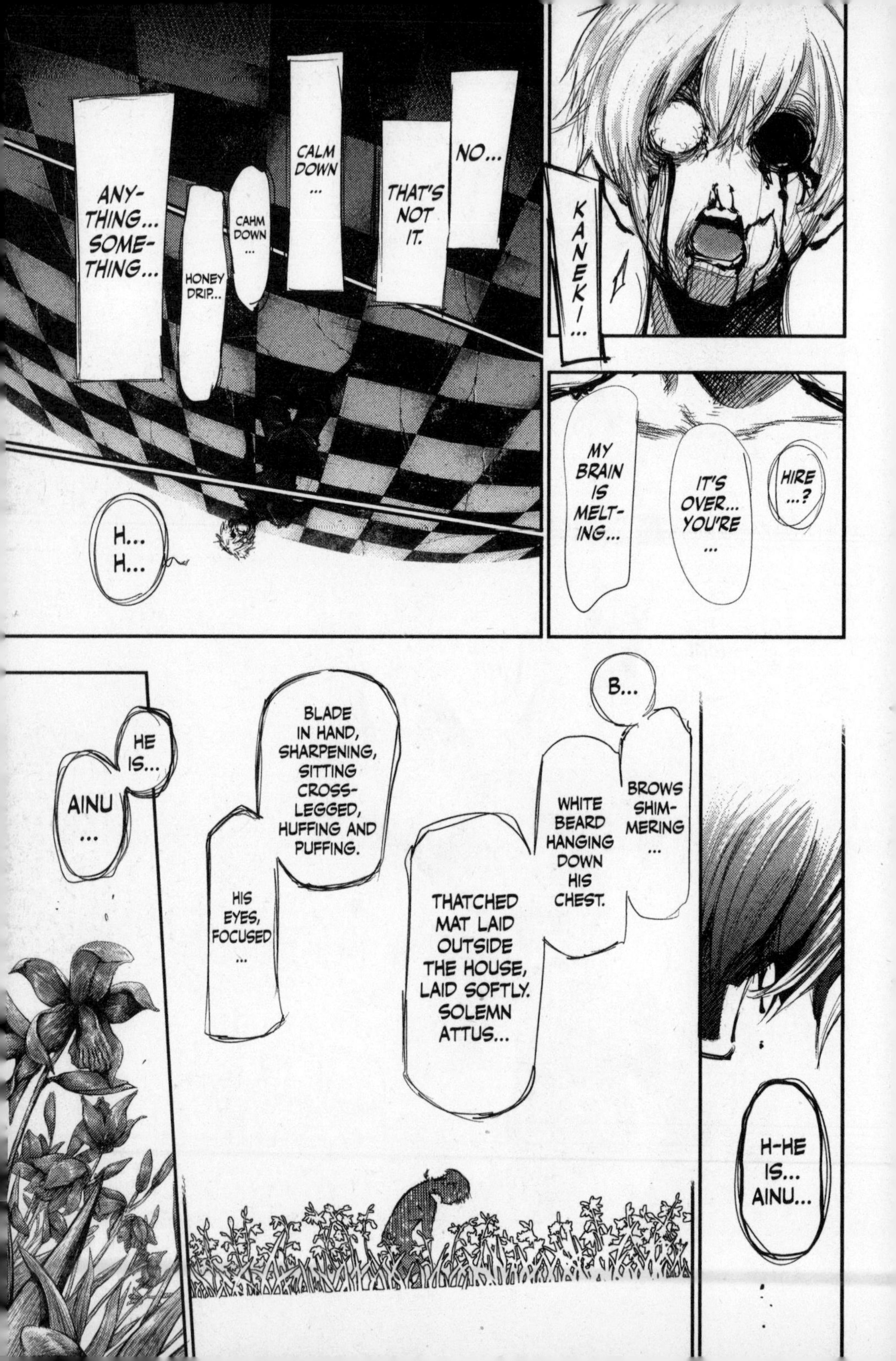
KANEKI...
HIRE...?
IT'S OVER... YOU'RE ...
MY BRAIN IS MELTING...
NO...
THAT'S NOT IT.
CALM DOWN ...
CAHM DOWN ...
HONEY DRIP...
ANYTHING... SOMETHING...
H... H...
H-HE IS... AINU...
B...
BROWS SHIMMERING ...
WHITE BEARD HANGING DOWN HIS CHEST.
THATCHED MAT LAID OUTSIDE THE HOUSE, LAID SOFTLY. SOLEMN ATTUS...
BLADE IN HAND, SHARPENING, SITTING CROSS-LEGGED, HUFFING AND PUFFING.
HIS EYES, FOCUSED ...
HE IS...
AINU ...

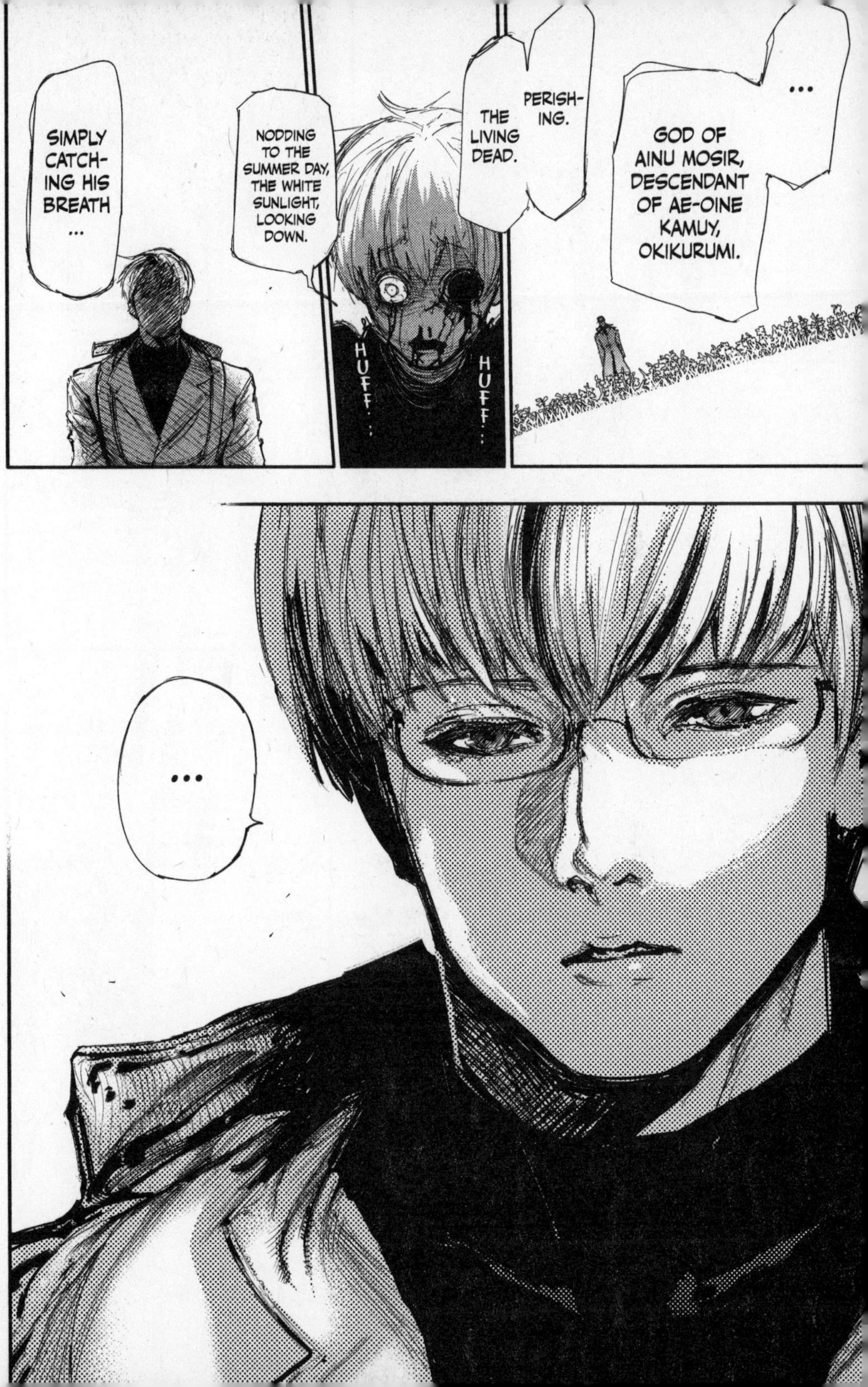
...
GOD OF AINU MOSIR, DESCENDANT OF AE-OINE KAMUY, OKIKURUMI.
PERISHING.
THE LIVING DEAD.
HUFF...
HUFF...
NODDING TO THE SUMMER DAY, THE WHITE SUNLIGHT, LOOKING DOWN.
SIMPLY CATCHING HIS BREATH...
...

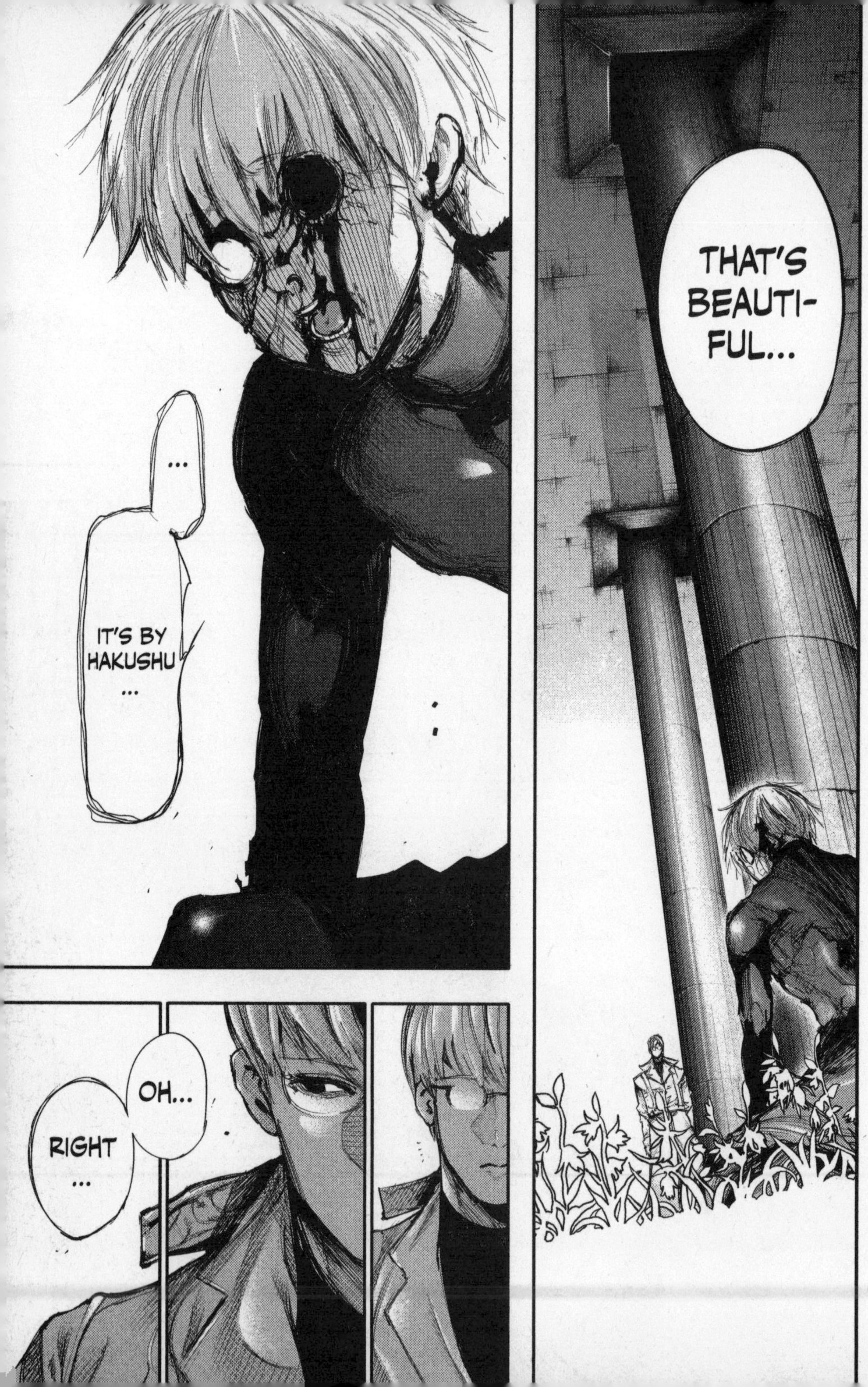
THAT'S BEAUTI-FUL...
...
IT'S BY HAKUSHU ...
OH...
RIGHT ...

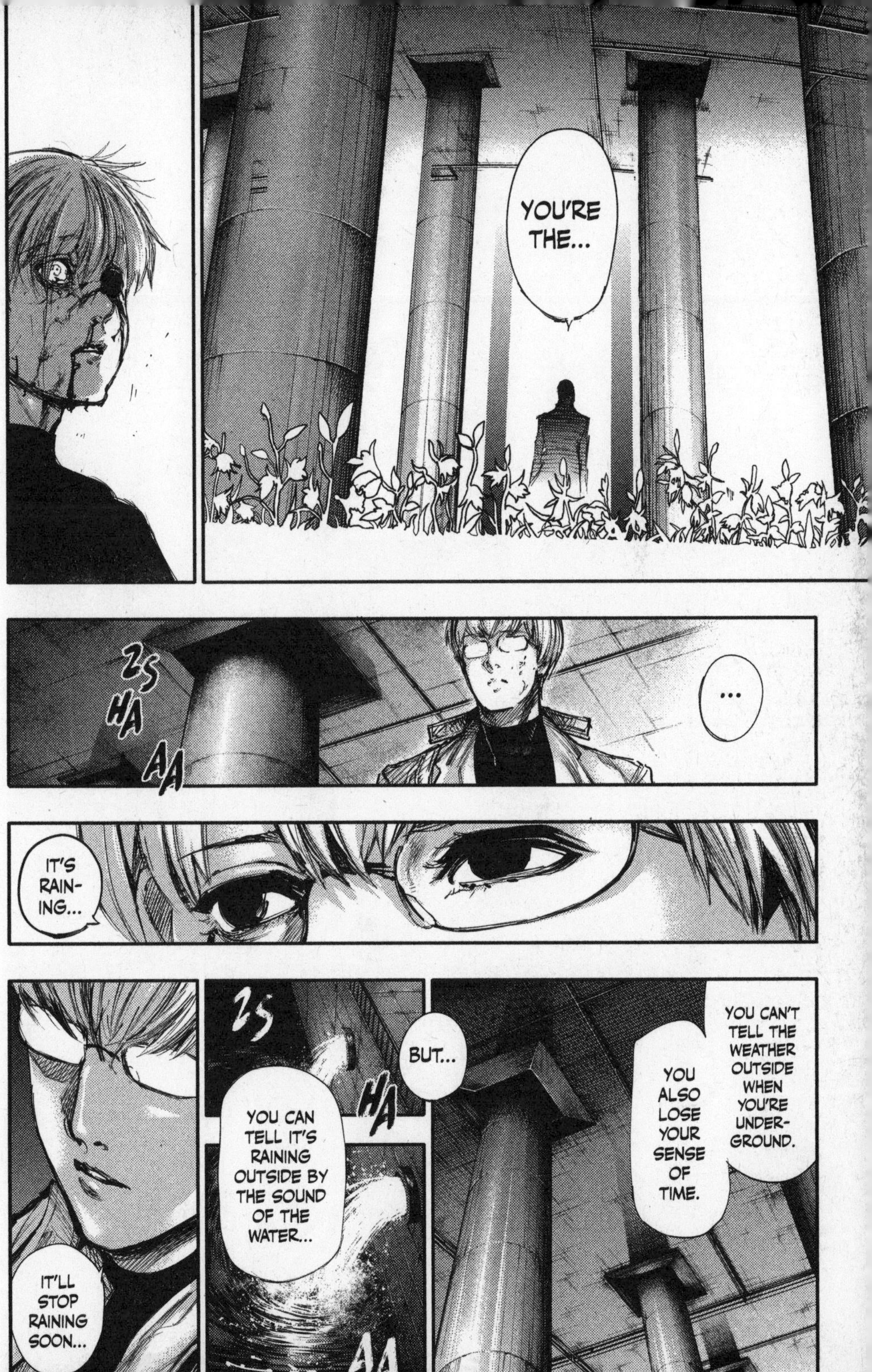
YOU'RE THE...
...
ZS HA AA
IT'S RAINING...
YOU CAN'T TELL THE WEATHER OUTSIDE WHEN YOU'RE UNDERGROUND.
YOU ALSO LOSE YOUR SENSE OF TIME.
BUT...
ZS HA
YOU CAN TELL IT'S RAINING OUTSIDE BY THE SOUND OF THE WATER...
AA
IT'LL STOP RAINING SOON...

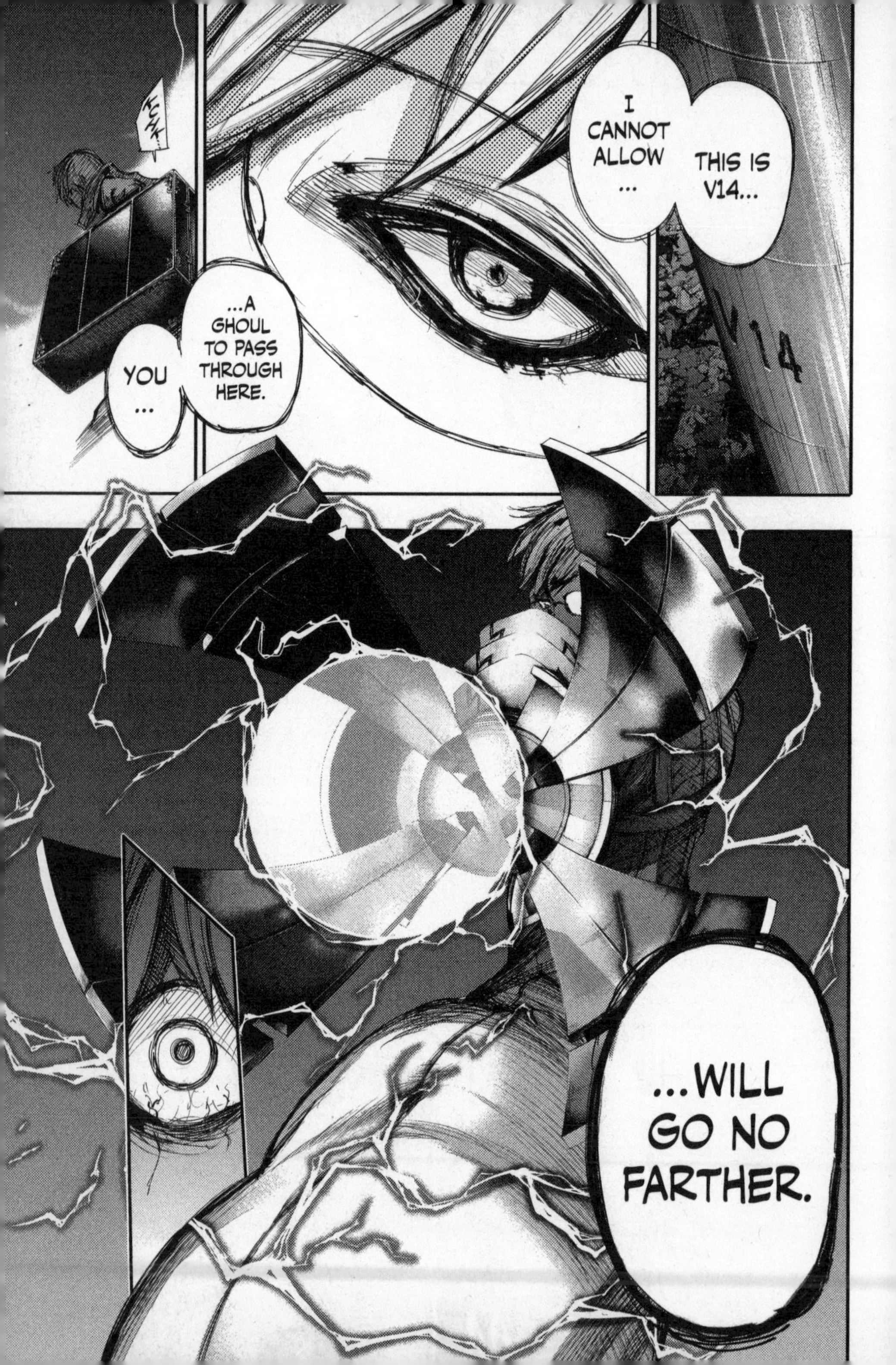
THIS IS V14...
I CANNOT ALLOW ...
...A GHOUL TO PASS THROUGH HERE.
V14
KUHK...
YOU ...
...WILL GO NO FARTHER.

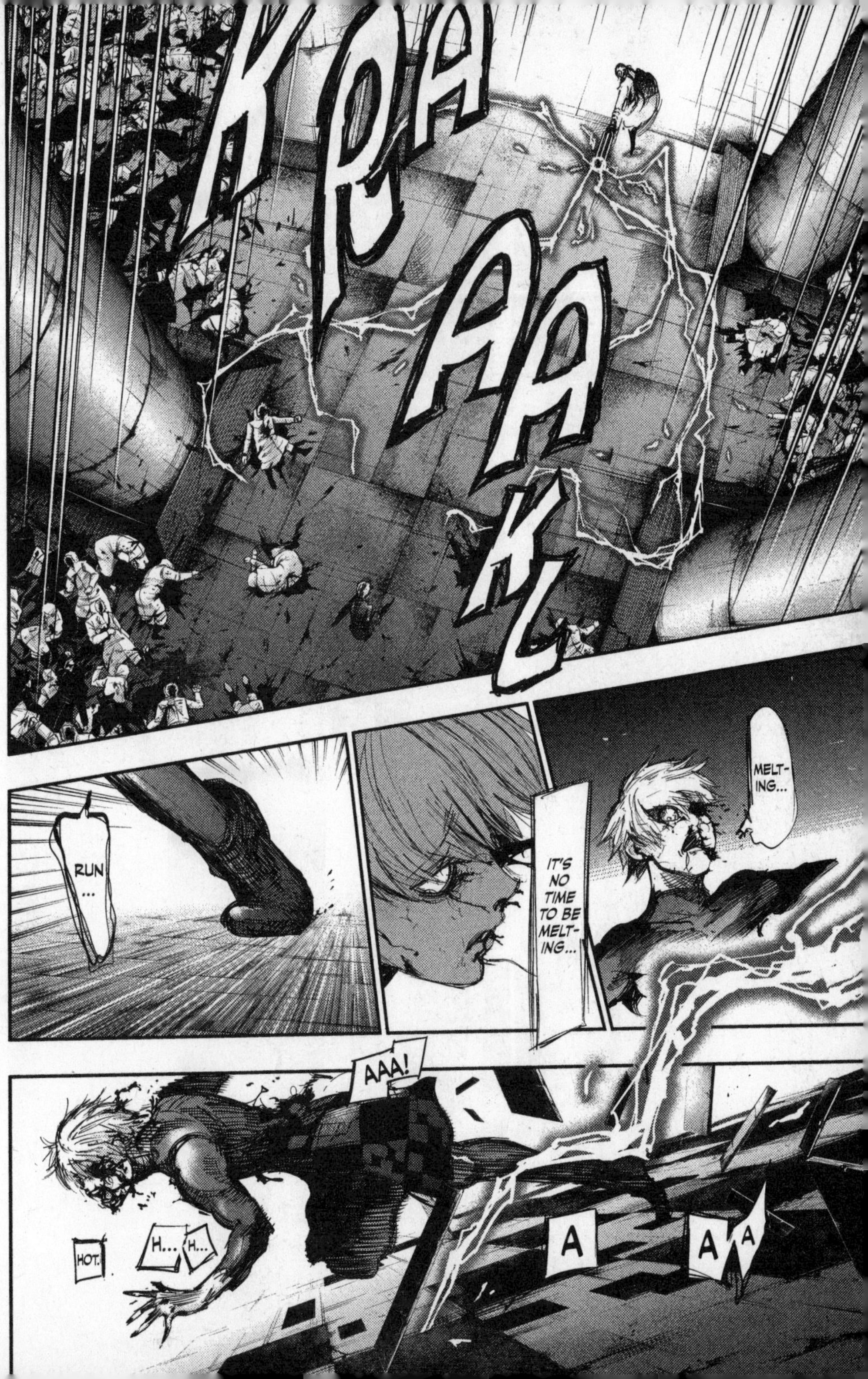
KRAAAKL
MELT-ING...
IT'S NO TIME TO BE MELT-ING...
RUN...
AAA!
A A A
H... H...
HOT.

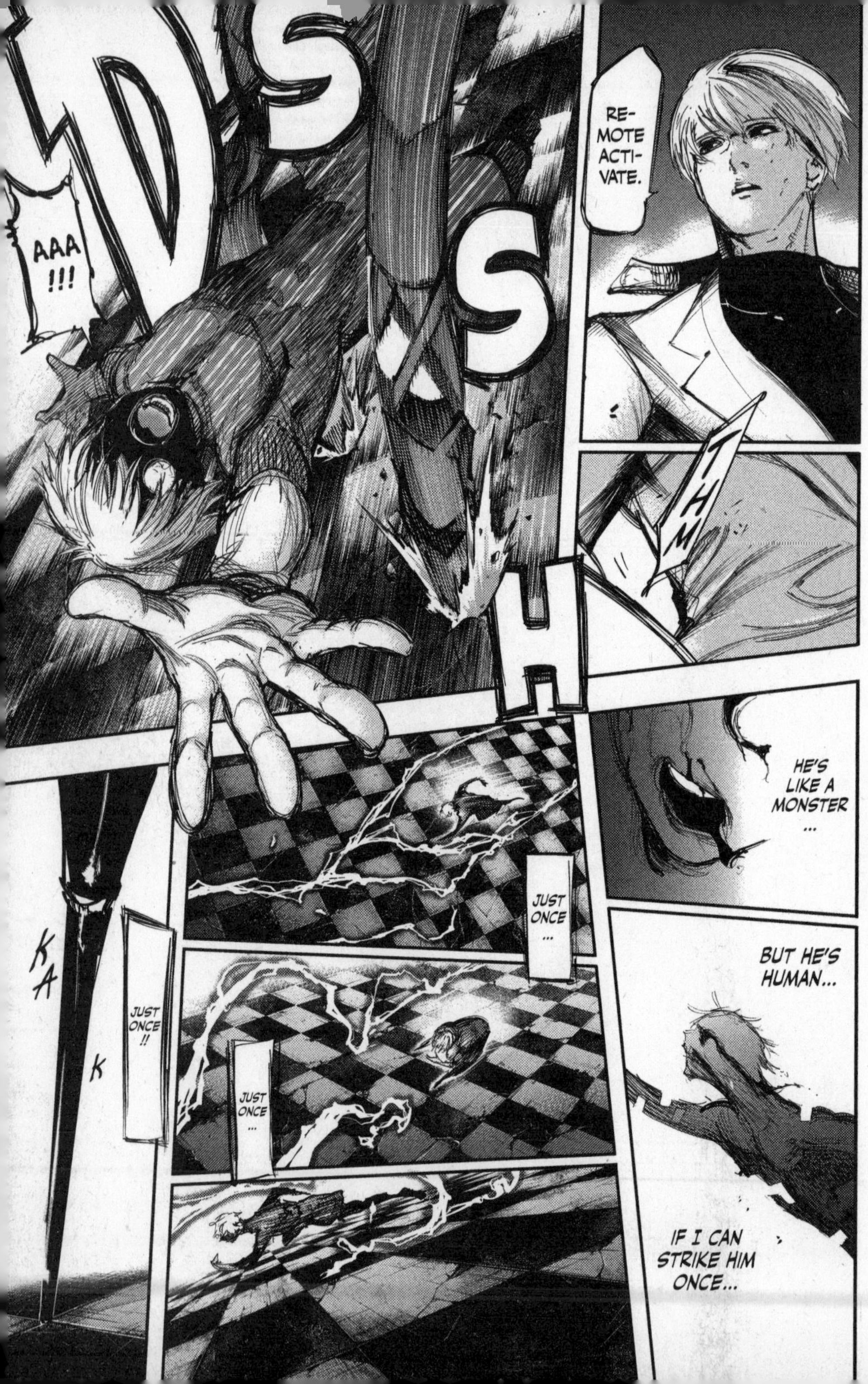
RE-MOTE ACTI-VATE.
THM
DOSS
AAA!!!
HE'S LIKE A MONSTER...
BUT HE'S HUMAN...
IF I CAN STRIKE HIM ONCE...
JUST ONCE...
JUST ONCE...
JUST ONCE!!
KAK

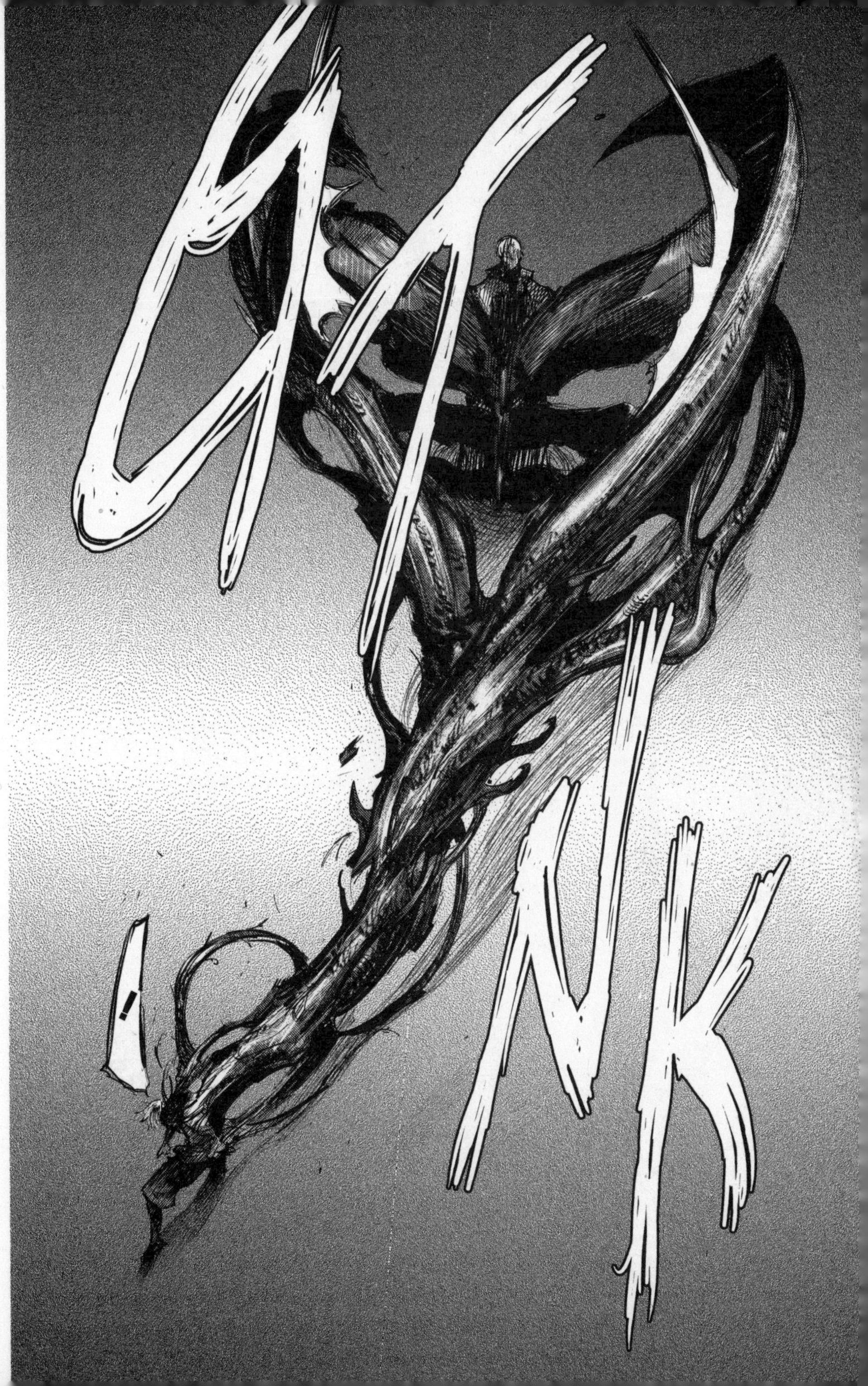

CHINK
!

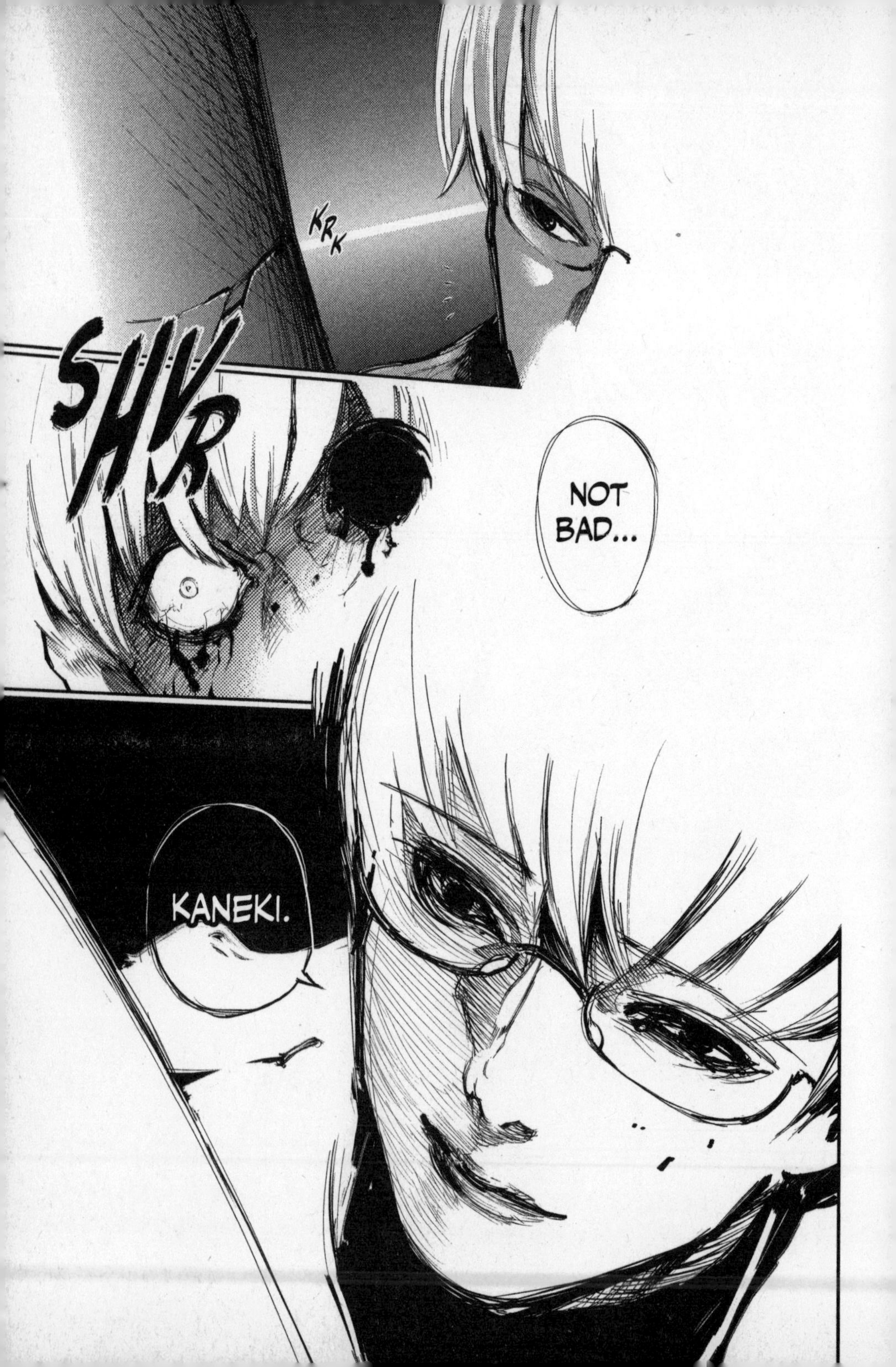
KRK
SHVR
NOT BAD...
KANEKI.

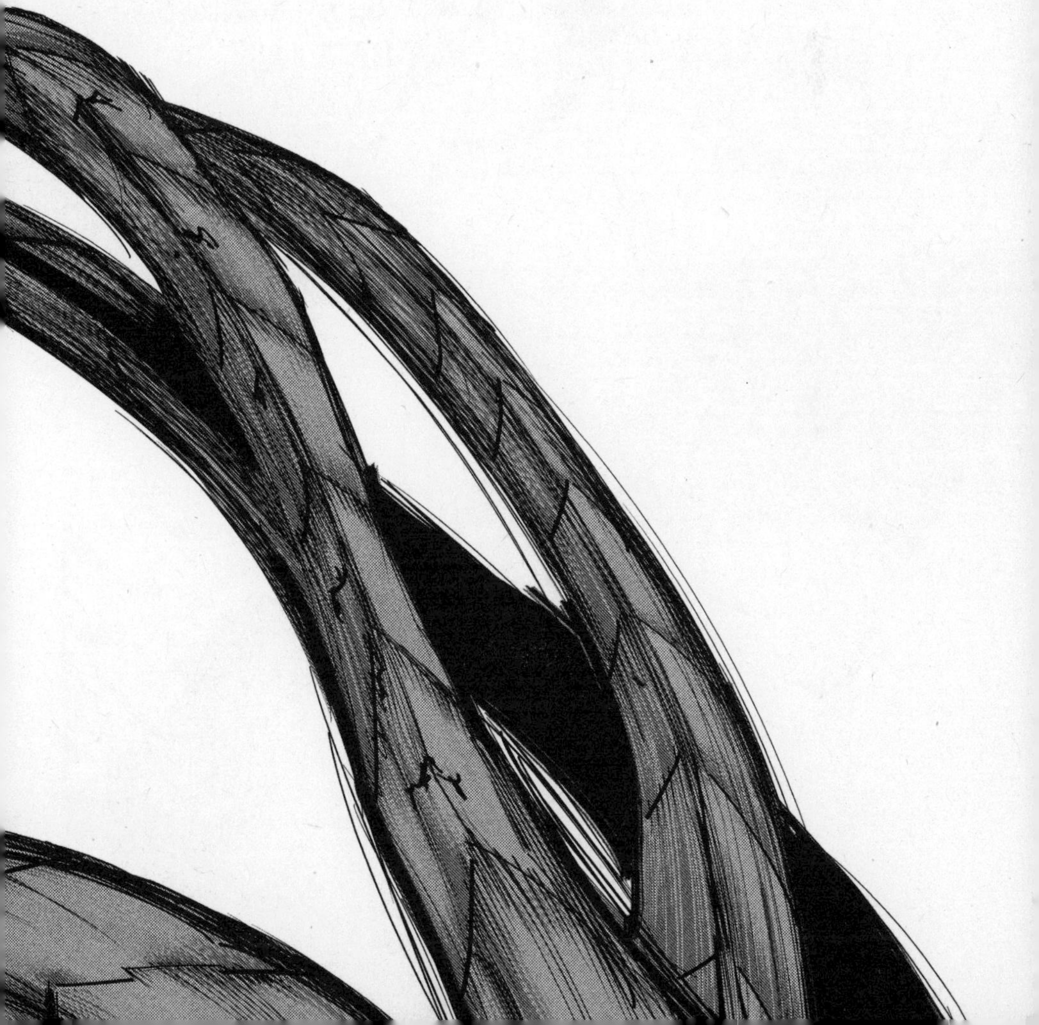

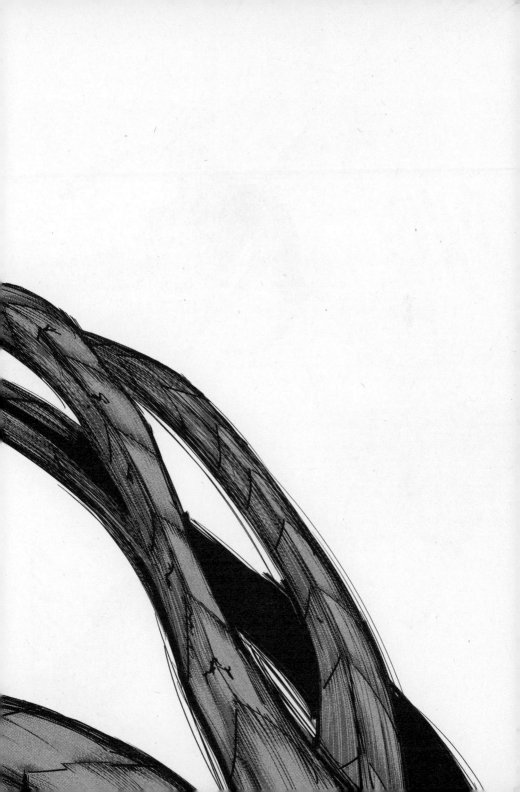

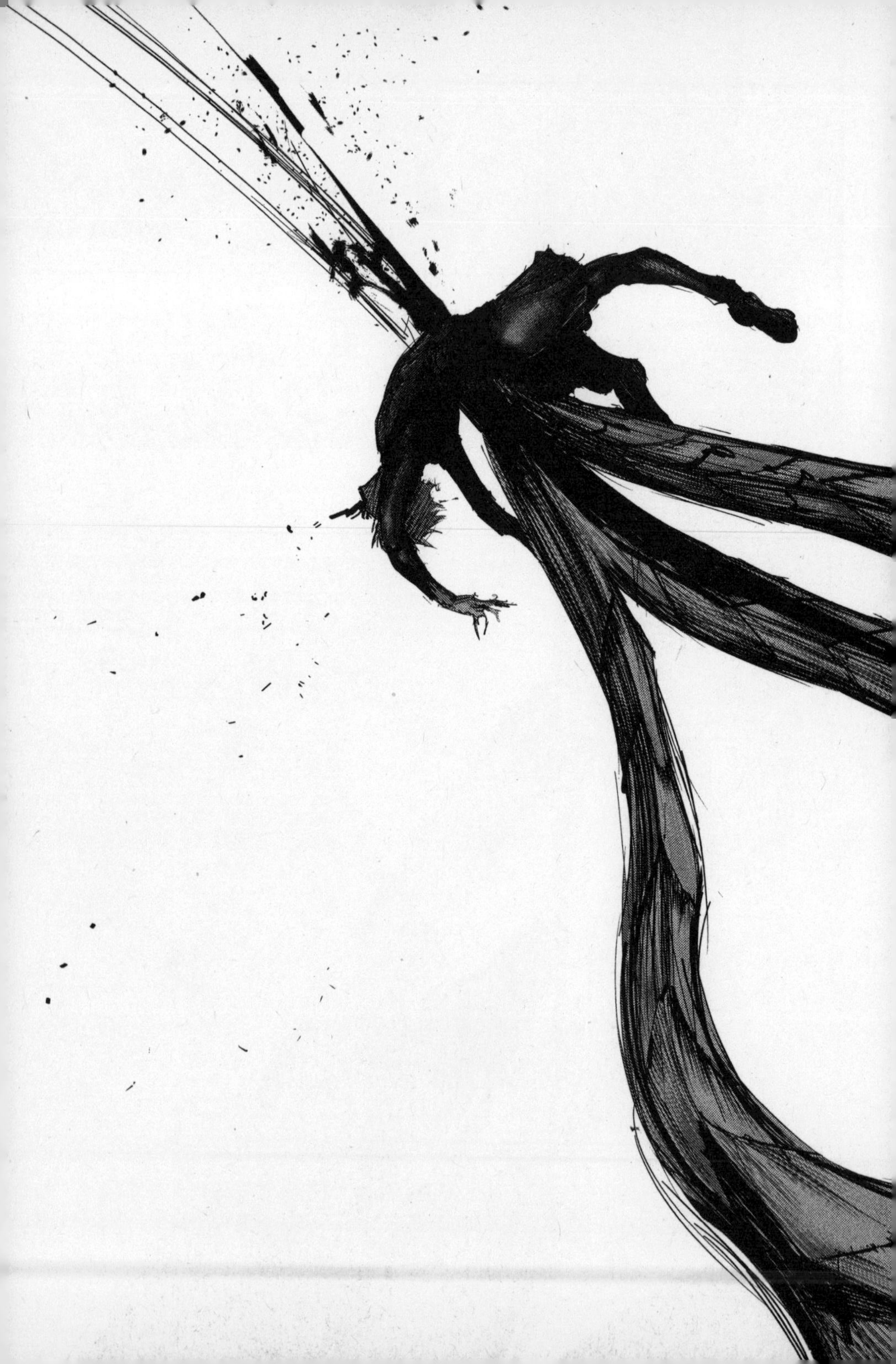

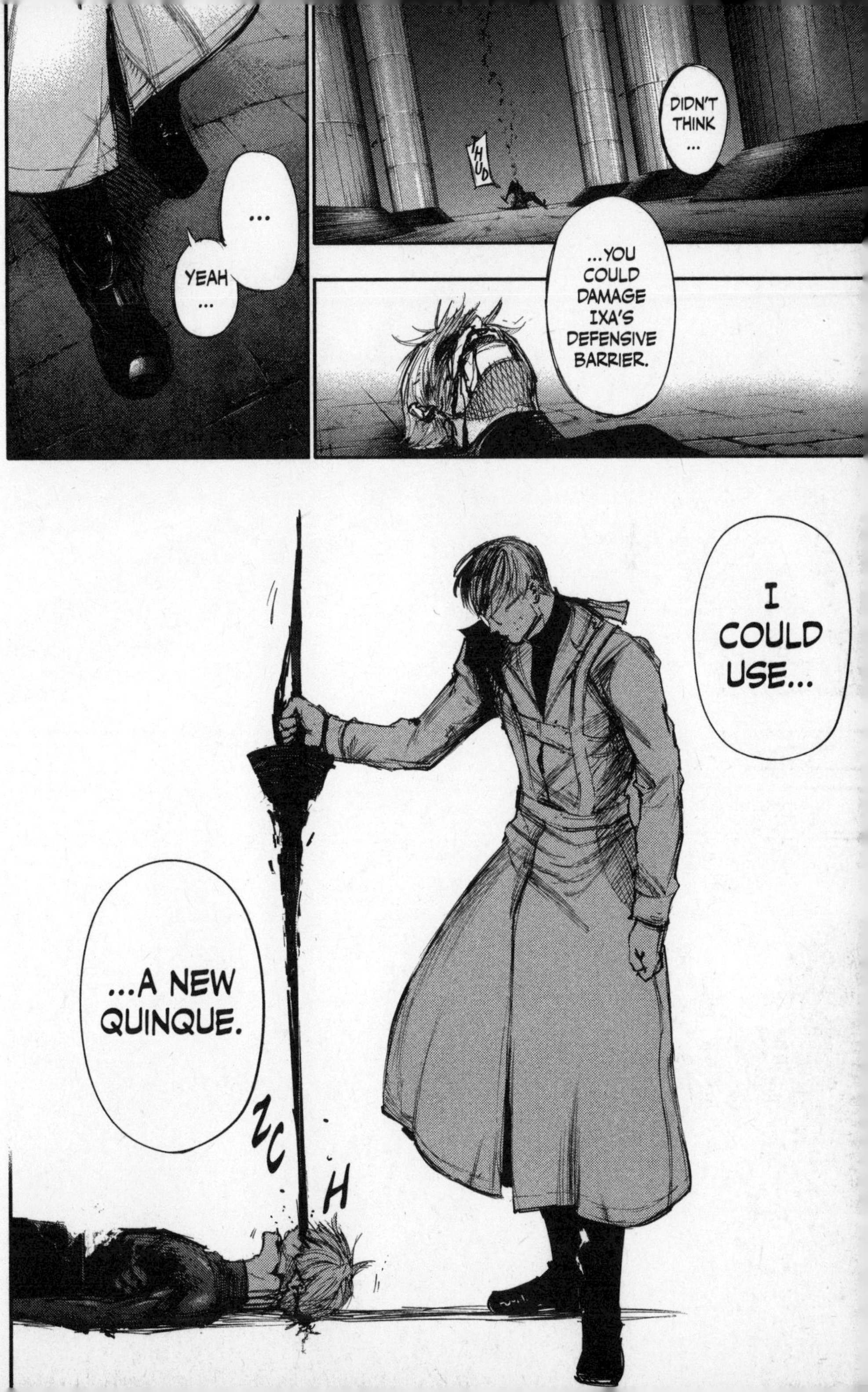
THUD
DIDN'T THINK ...
...YOU COULD DAMAGE IXA'S DEFENSIVE BARRIER.
...
YEAH ...
I COULD USE...
...A NEW QUINQUE.
ZCH

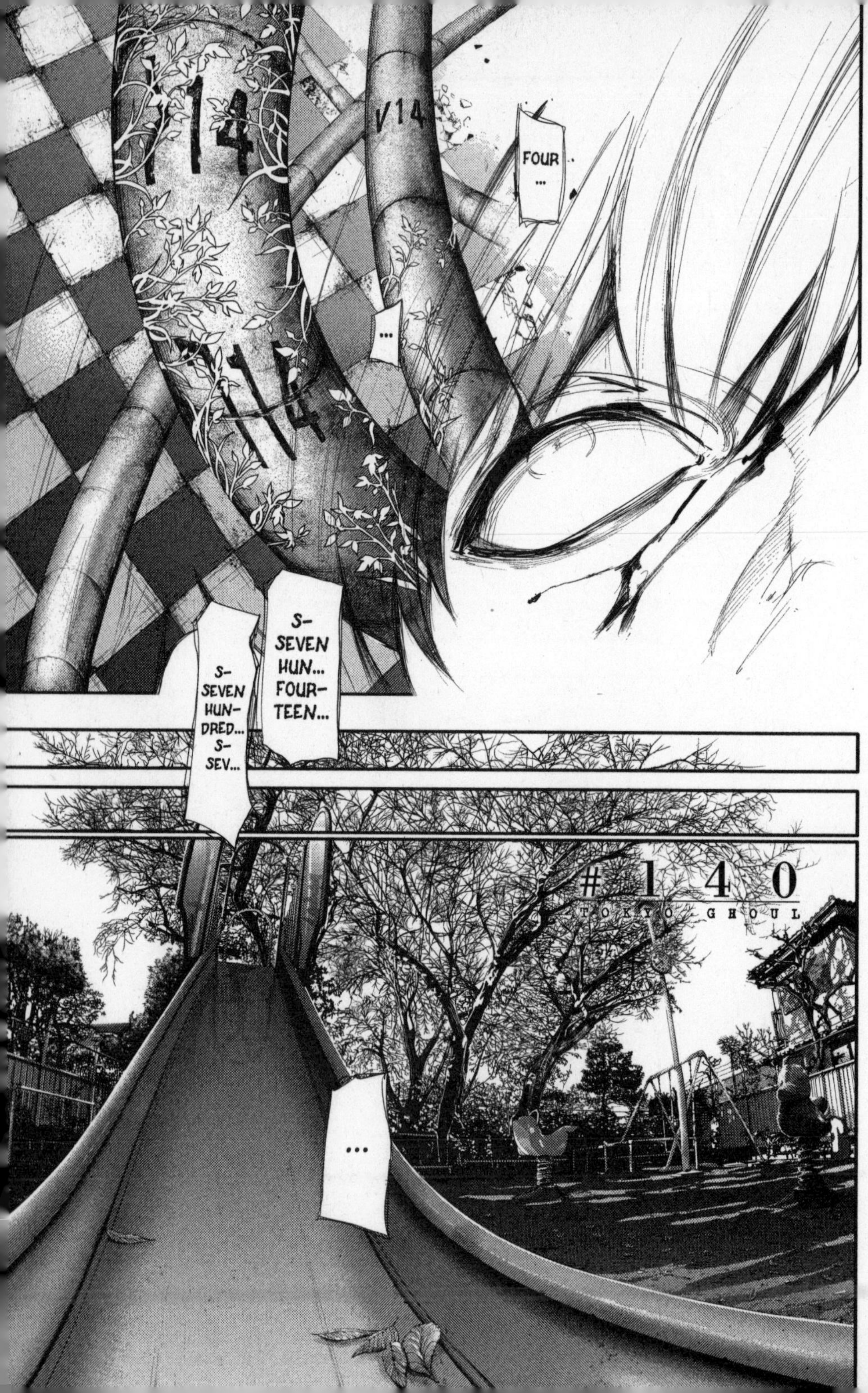
FOUR...
...
S-SEVEN HUN... FOURTEEN...
S-SEVEN HUNDRED... S-SEV...
#140
TOKYO GHOUL
...

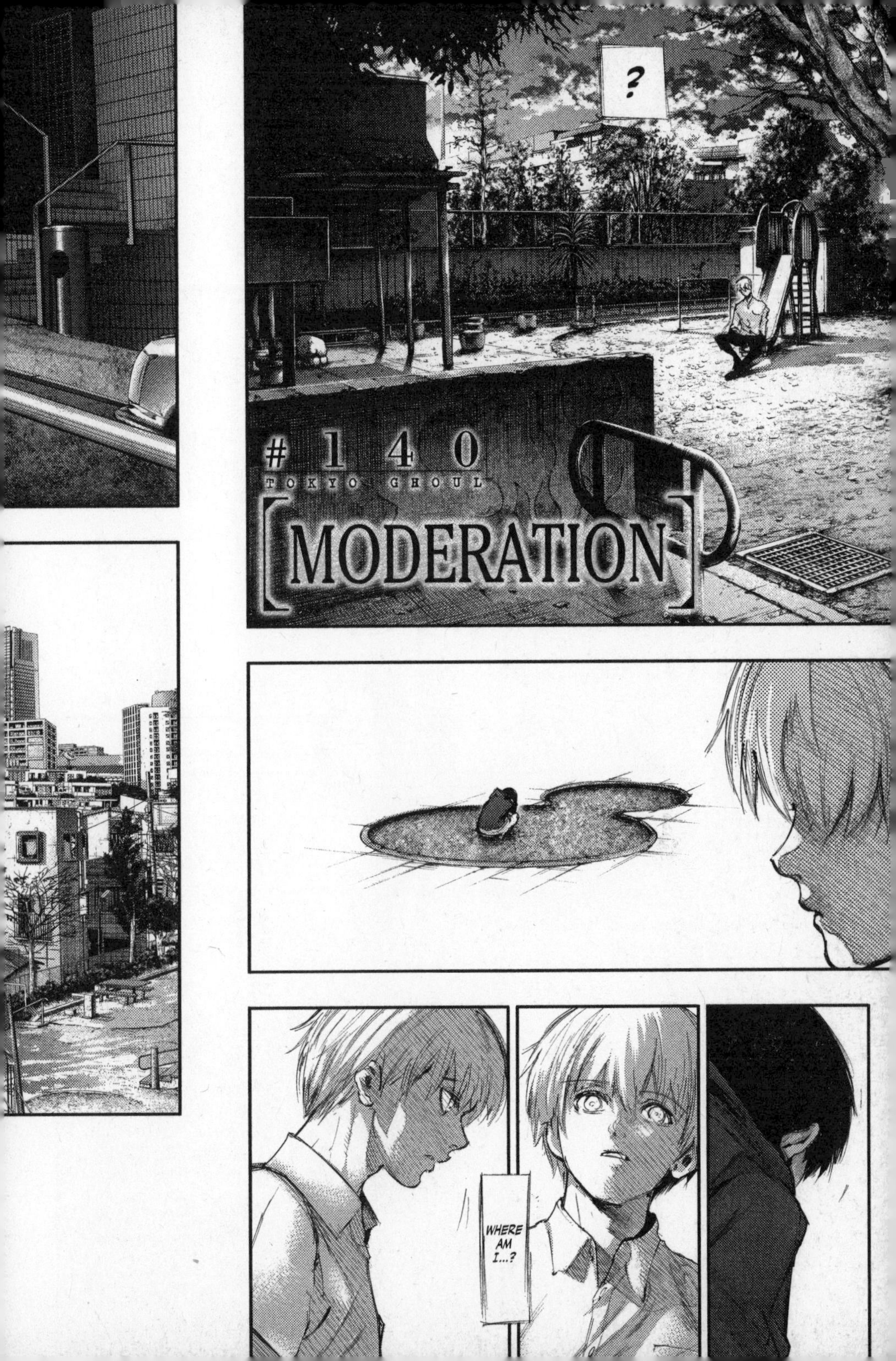
?
#140
TOKYO GHOUL
MODERATION
WHERE AM I...?

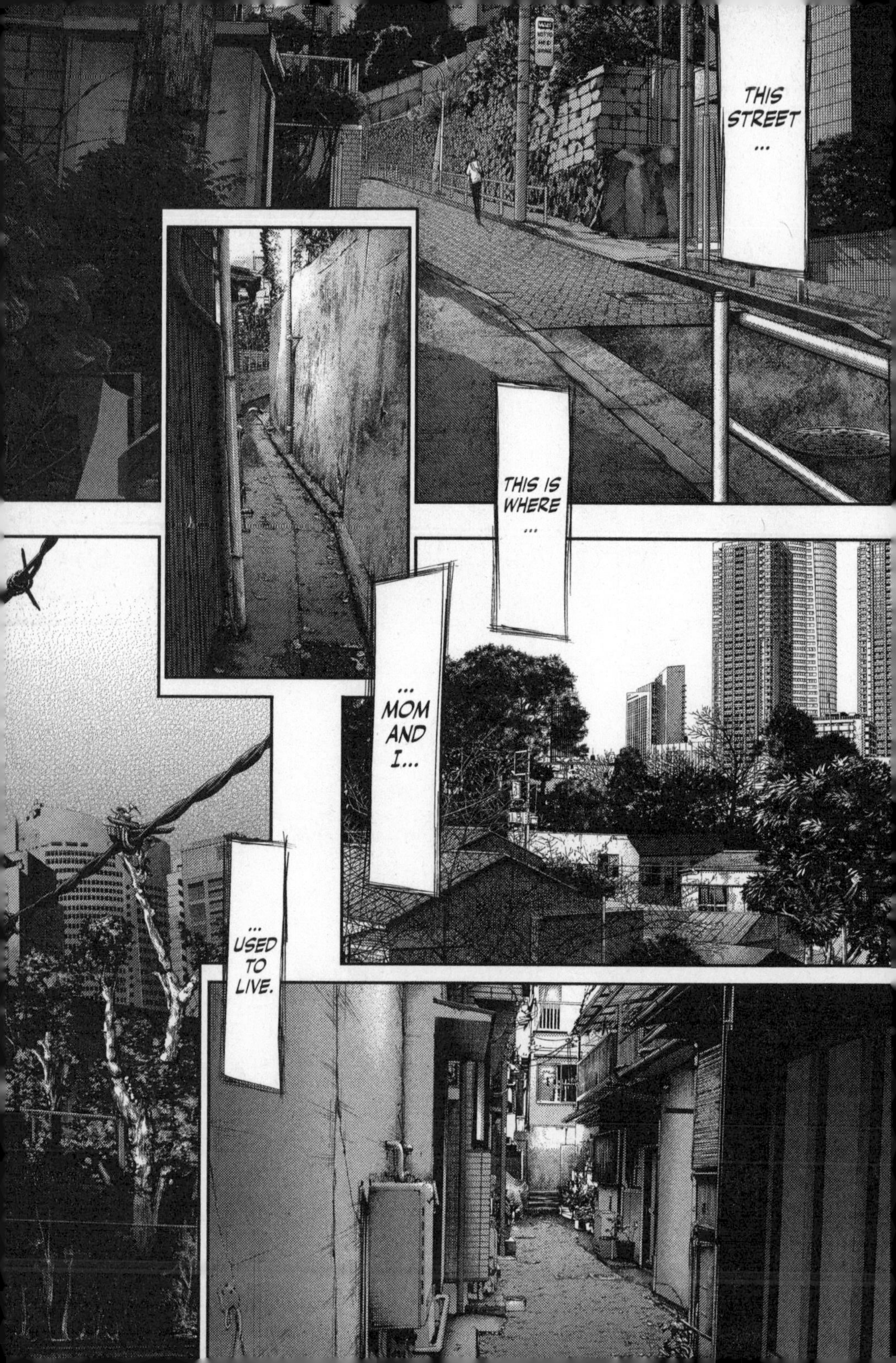
THIS STREET ...
THIS IS WHERE ...
... MOM AND I...
... USED TO LIVE.

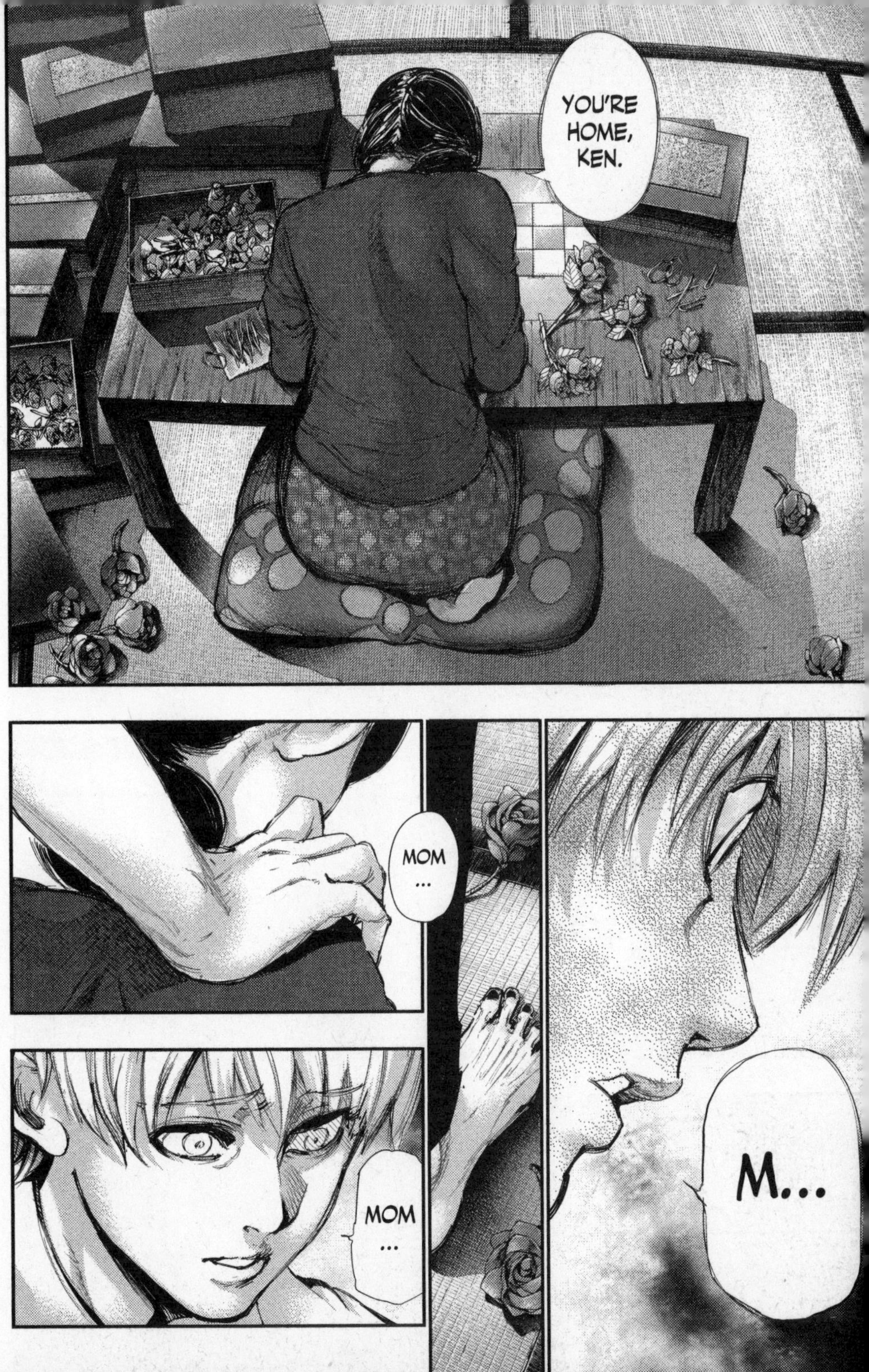
YOU'RE HOME, KEN.
M...
MOM ...
MOM ...

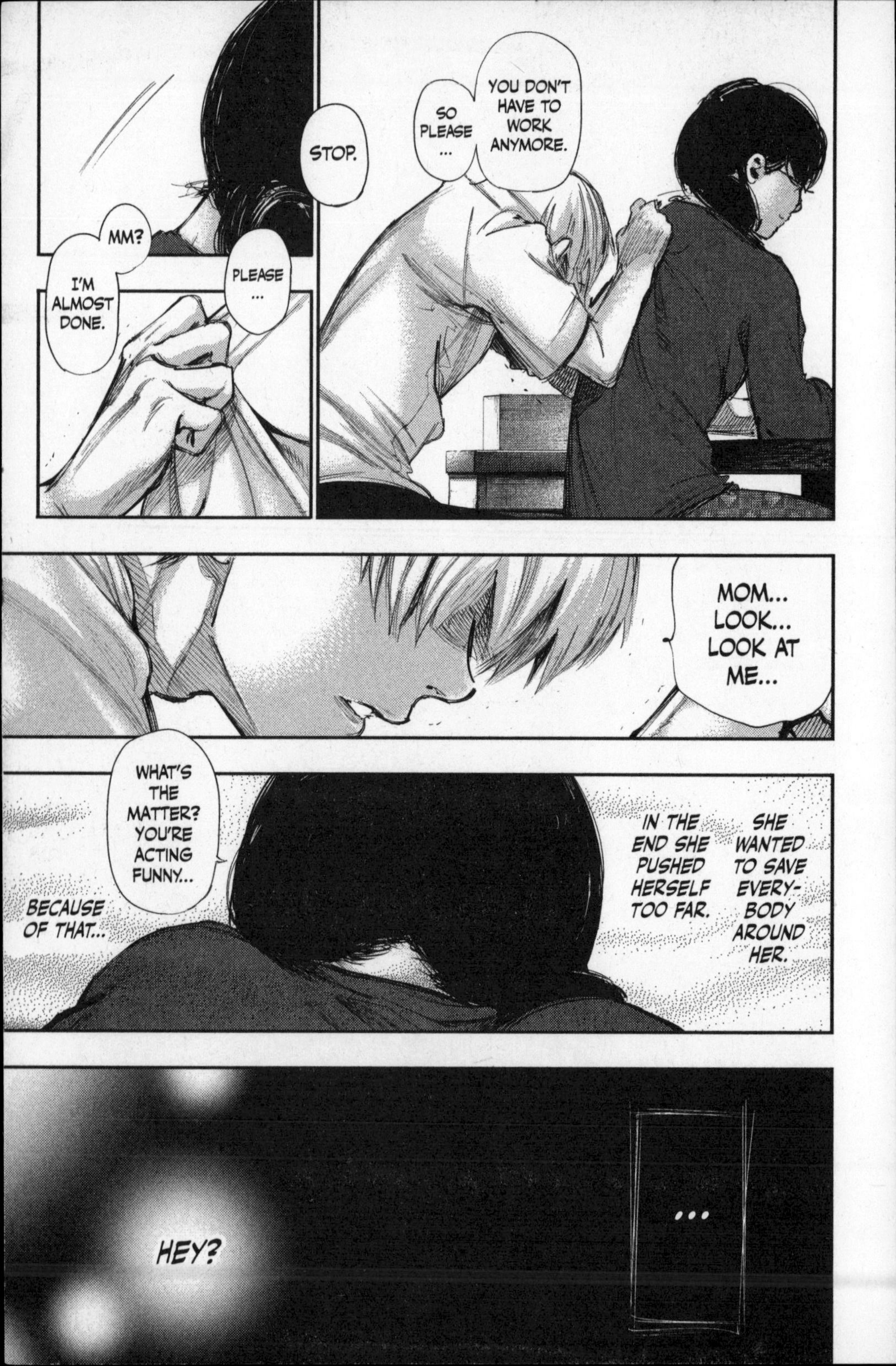
YOU DON'T HAVE TO WORK ANYMORE.
SO PLEASE ...
STOP.
MM?
PLEASE ...
I'M ALMOST DONE.
MOM... LOOK... LOOK AT ME...
SHE WANTED TO SAVE EVERY-BODY AROUND HER.
IN THE END SHE PUSHED HERSELF TOO FAR.
WHAT'S THE MATTER? YOU'RE ACTING FUNNY...
BECAUSE OF THAT...
...
HEY?

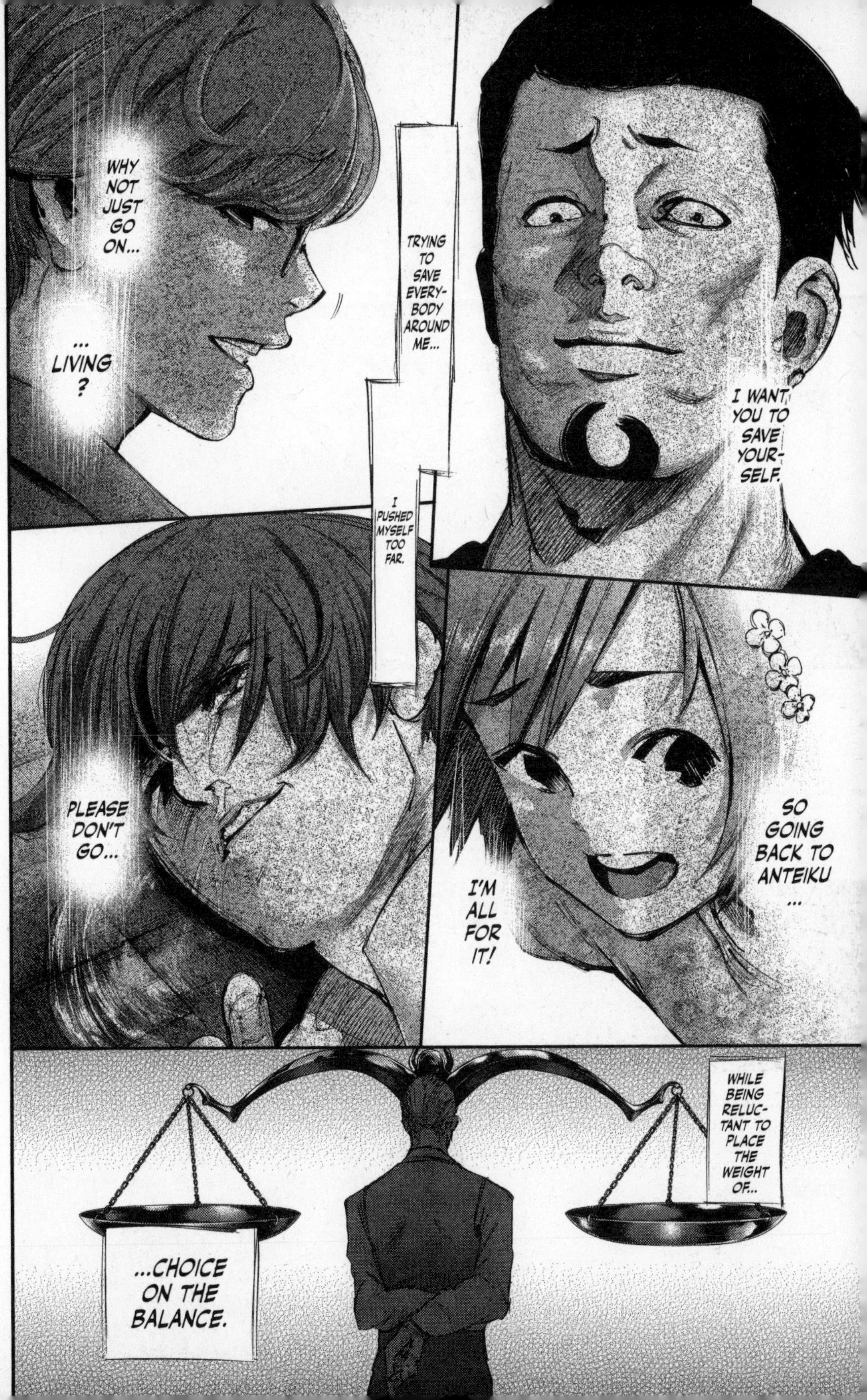
I WANT YOU TO SAVE YOURSELF.
TRYING TO SAVE EVERYBODY AROUND ME...
WHY NOT JUST GO ON...
...LIVING?
I PUSHED MYSELF TOO FAR.
SO GOING BACK TO ANTEIKU...
I'M ALL FOR IT!
PLEASE DON'T GO...
WHILE BEING RELUCTANT TO PLACE THE WEIGHT OF...
...CHOICE ON THE BALANCE.

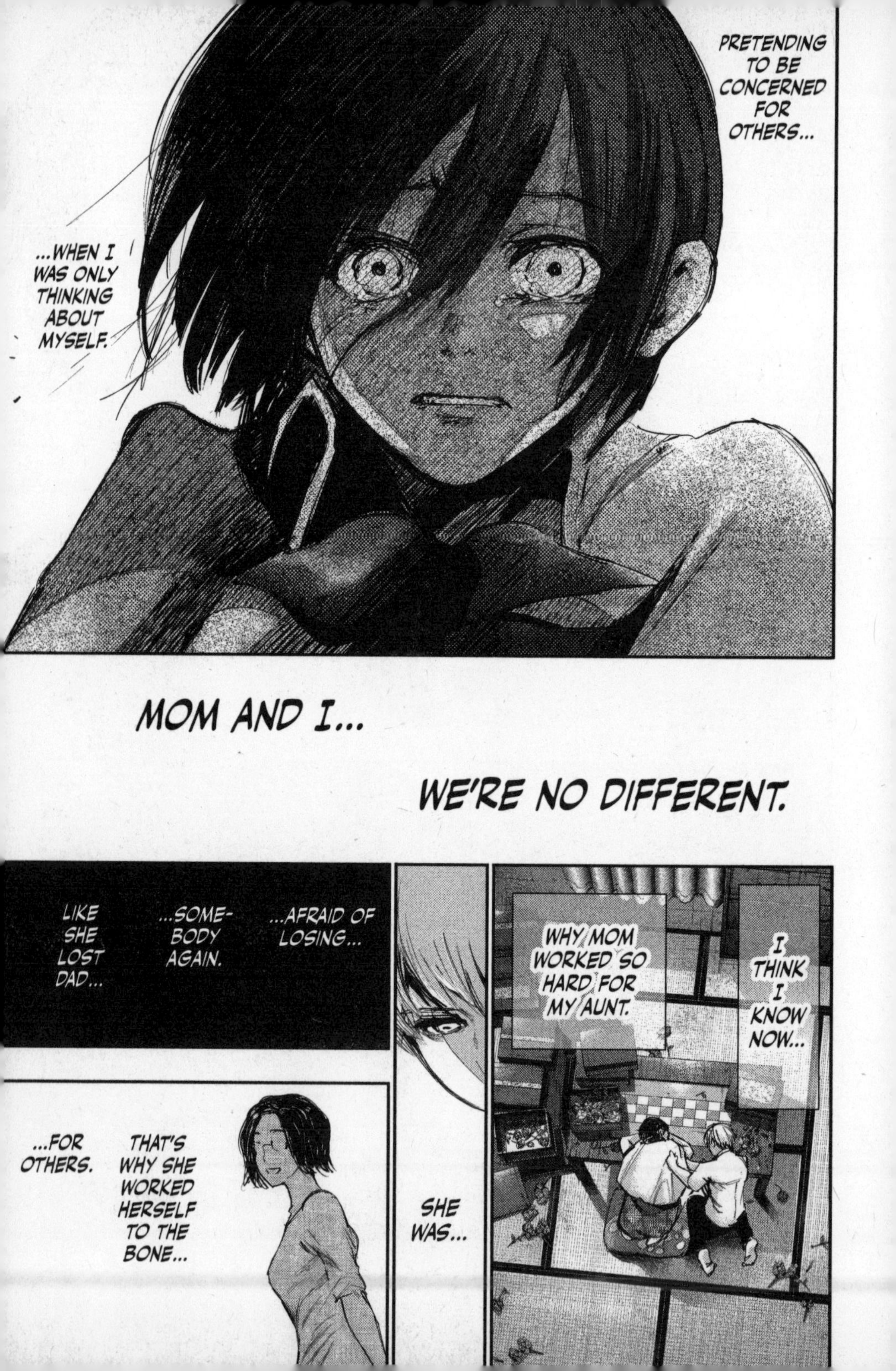
PRETENDING TO BE CONCERNED FOR OTHERS...
...WHEN I WAS ONLY THINKING ABOUT MYSELF.
MOM AND I...
WE'RE NO DIFFERENT.
I THINK I KNOW NOW...
WHY MOM WORKED SO HARD FOR MY AUNT.
SHE WAS...
...AFRAID OF LOSING...
...SOME-BODY AGAIN.
LIKE SHE LOST DAD...
THAT'S WHY SHE WORKED HERSELF TO THE BONE...
...FOR OTHERS.

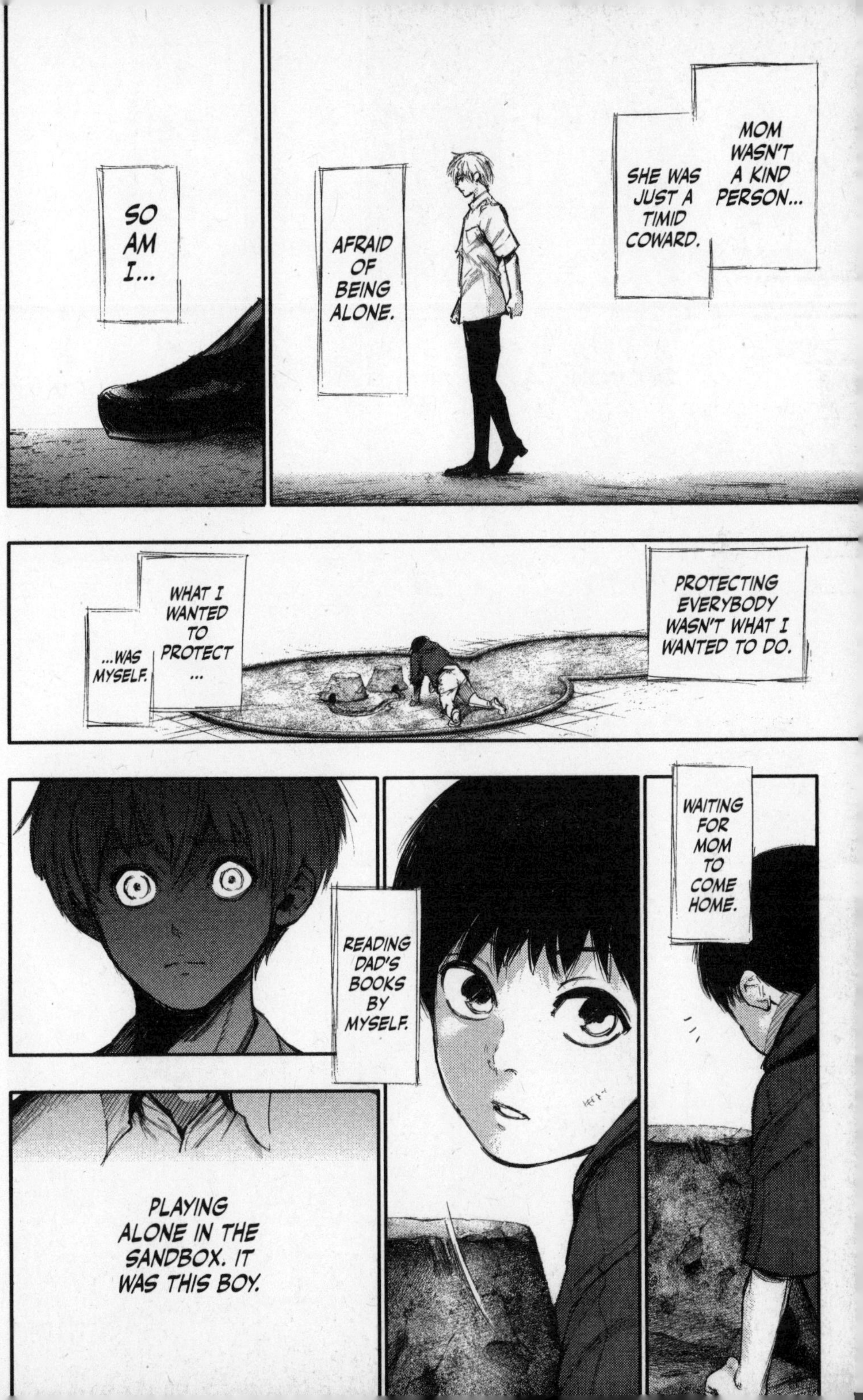
MOM WASN'T A KIND PERSON...
SHE WAS JUST A TIMID COWARD.
AFRAID OF BEING ALONE.
SO AM I...
PROTECTING EVERYBODY WASN'T WHAT I WANTED TO DO.
WHAT I WANTED TO PROTECT...
...WAS MYSELF.
WAITING FOR MOM TO COME HOME.
READING DAD'S BOOKS BY MYSELF.
PLAYING ALONE IN THE SANDBOX. IT WAS THIS BOY.

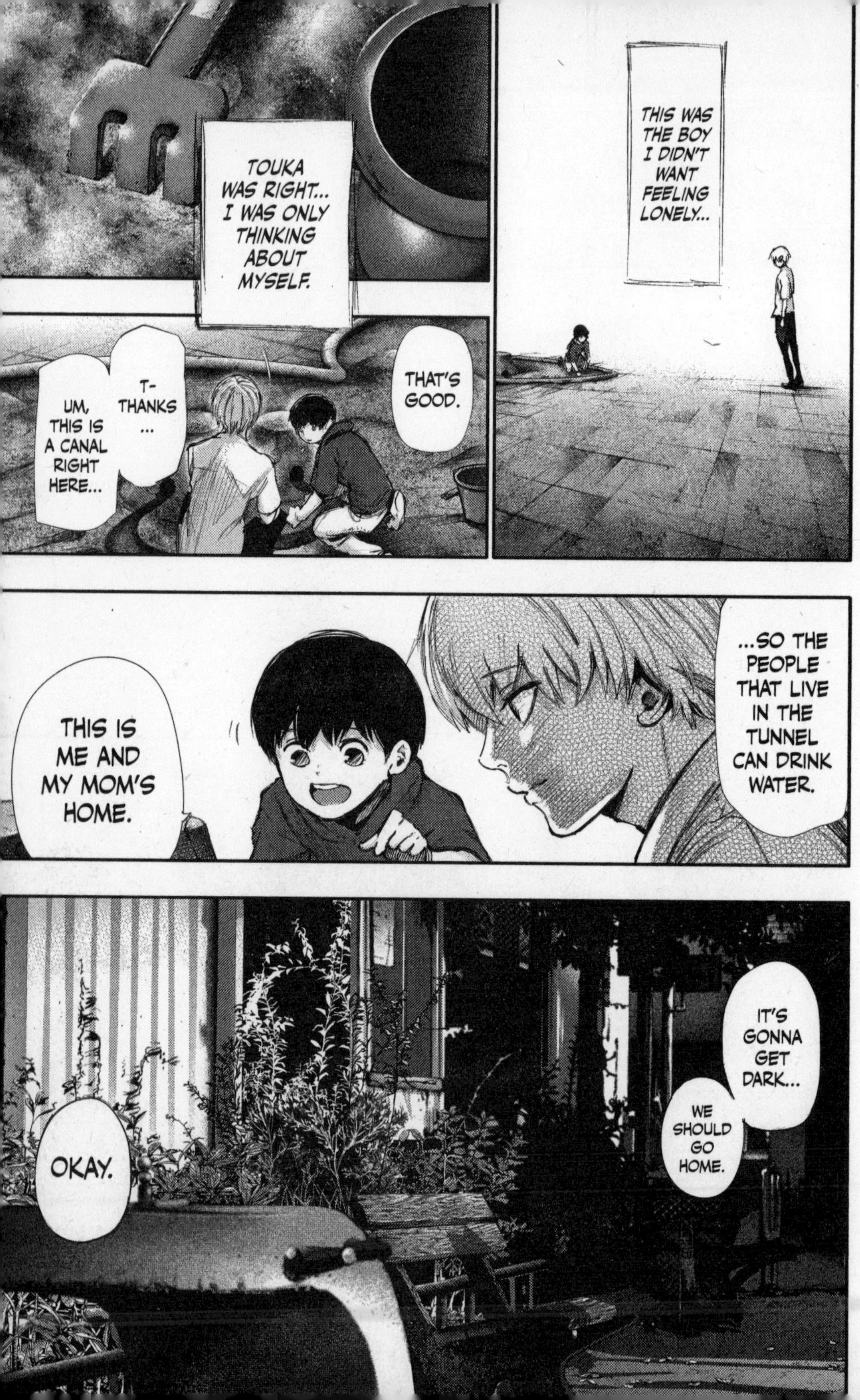
THIS WAS THE BOY I DIDN'T WANT FEELING LONELY...
TOUKA WAS RIGHT... I WAS ONLY THINKING ABOUT MYSELF.
THAT'S GOOD.
T-THANKS...
UM, THIS IS A CANAL RIGHT HERE...
...SO THE PEOPLE THAT LIVE IN THE TUNNEL CAN DRINK WATER.
THIS IS ME AND MY MOM'S HOME.
IT'S GONNA GET DARK...
WE SHOULD GO HOME.
OKAY.

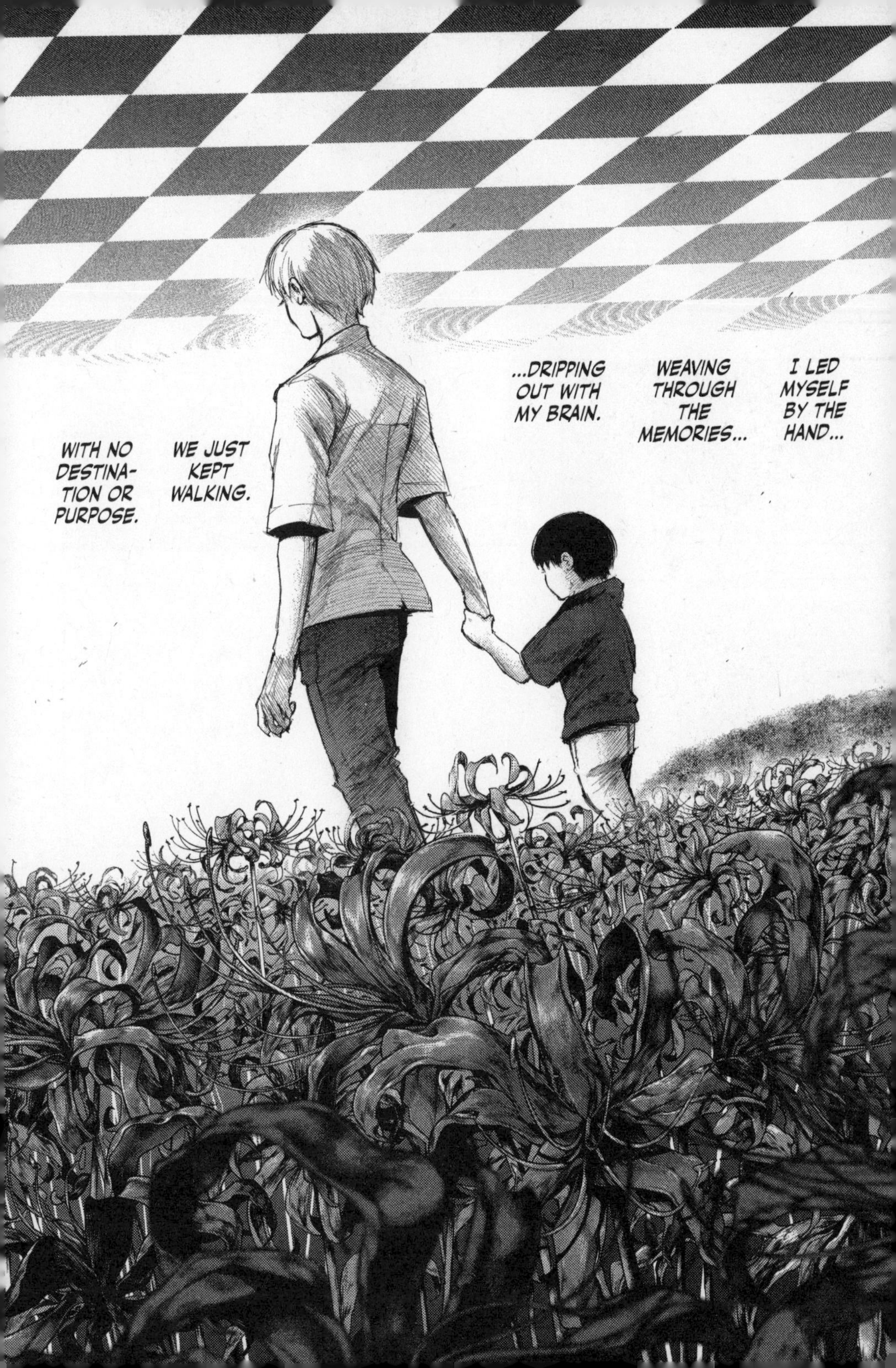
I LED MYSELF BY THE HAND...
WEAVING THROUGH THE MEMORIES...
...DRIPPING OUT WITH MY BRAIN.
WE JUST KEPT WALKING.
WITH NO DESTINATION OR PURPOSE.

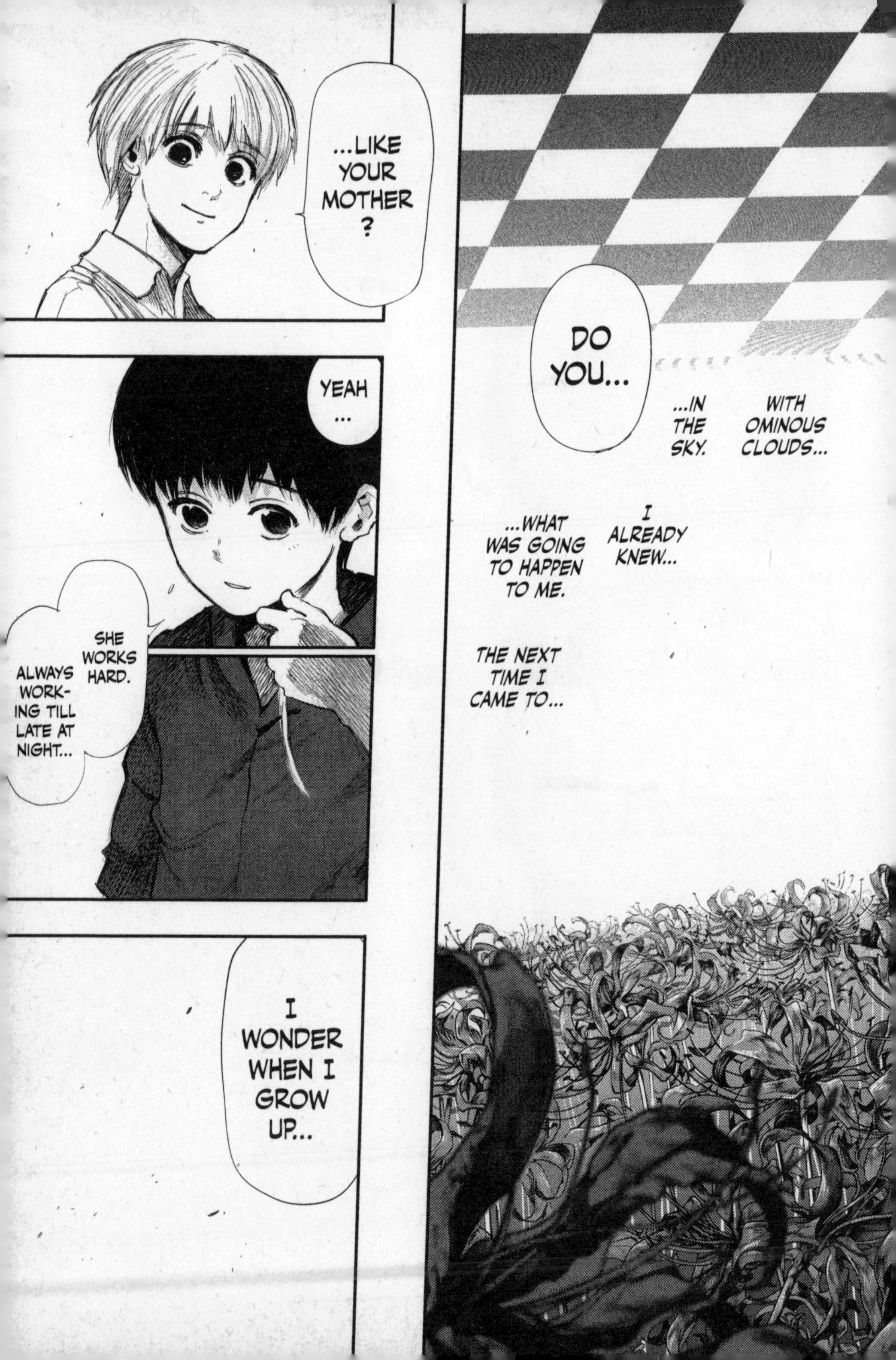
DO YOU...
WITH OMINOUS CLOUDS...
...IN THE SKY.
I ALREADY KNEW...
...WHAT WAS GOING TO HAPPEN TO ME.
THE NEXT TIME I CAME TO...
...LIKE YOUR MOTHER?
YEAH...
SHE WORKS HARD.
ALWAYS WORKING TILL LATE AT NIGHT...
I WONDER WHEN I GROW UP...

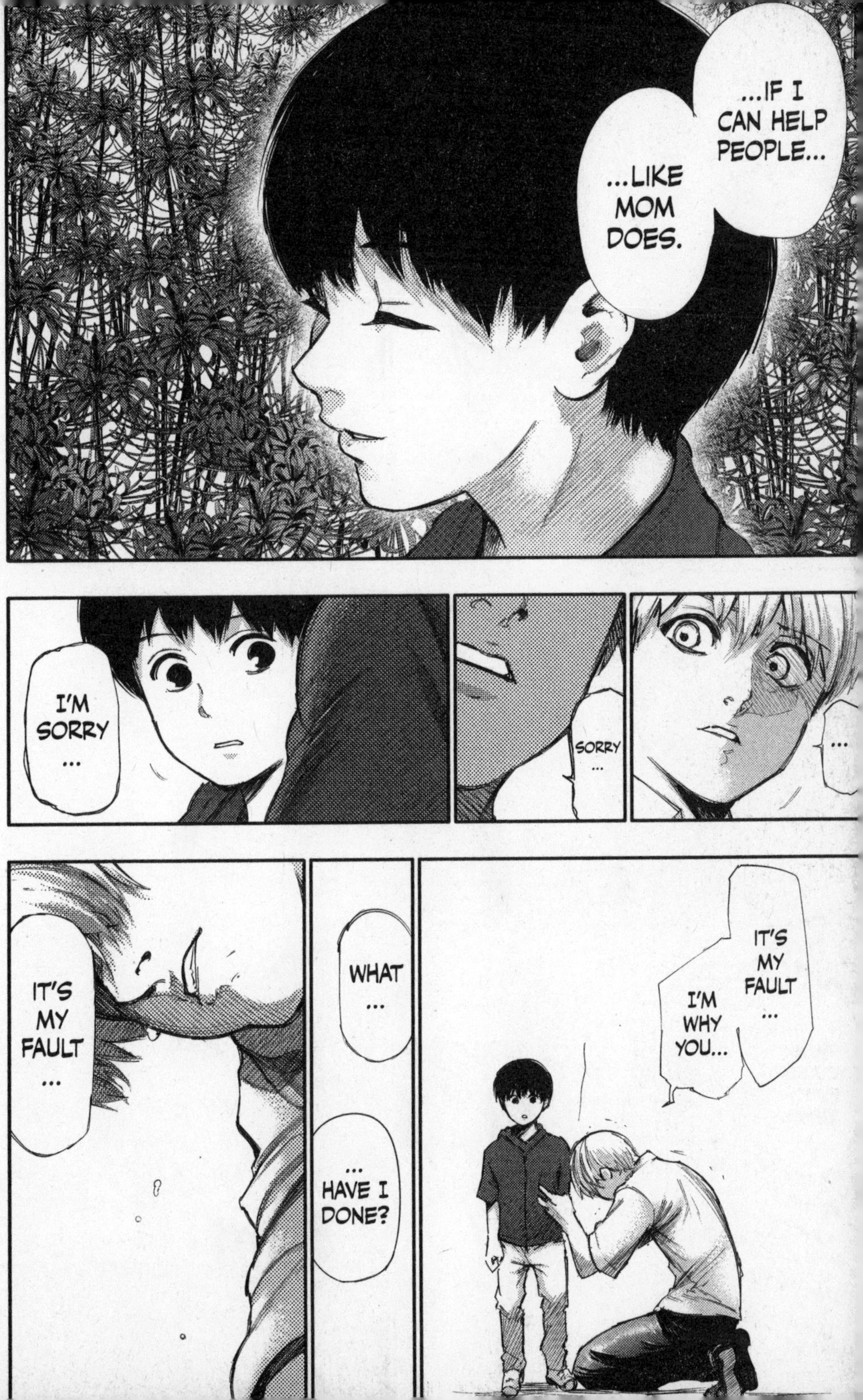
...IF I CAN HELP PEOPLE...
...LIKE MOM DOES.
...
SORRY ...
I'M SORRY ...
IT'S MY FAULT ...
I'M WHY YOU...
WHAT ...
... HAVE I DONE?
IT'S MY FAULT ...

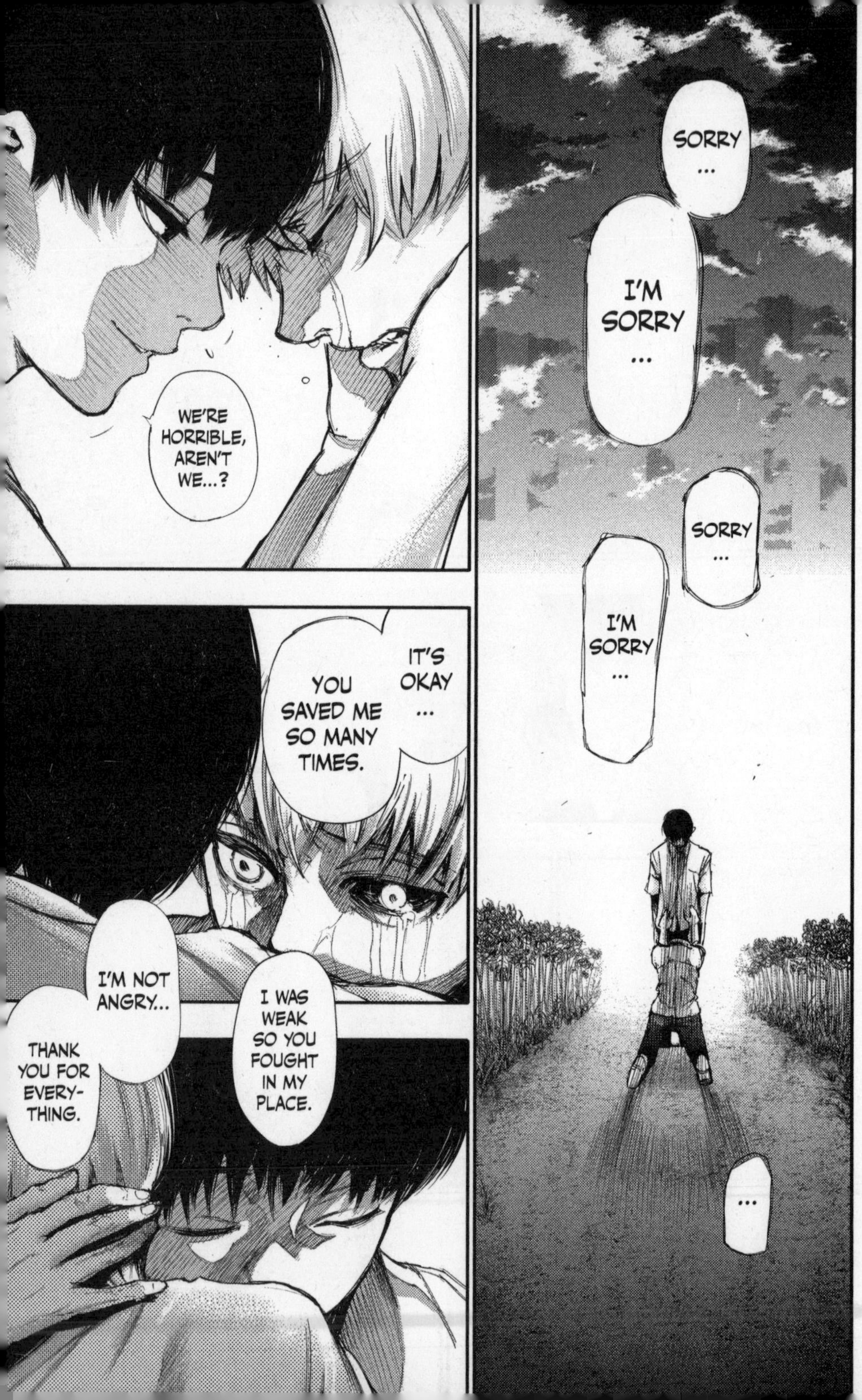
SORRY...
I'M SORRY...
SORRY...
I'M SORRY...
...
WE'RE HORRIBLE, AREN'T WE...?
IT'S OKAY...
YOU SAVED ME SO MANY TIMES.
I WAS WEAK SO YOU FOUGHT IN MY PLACE.
I'M NOT ANGRY...
THANK YOU FOR EVERY-THING.

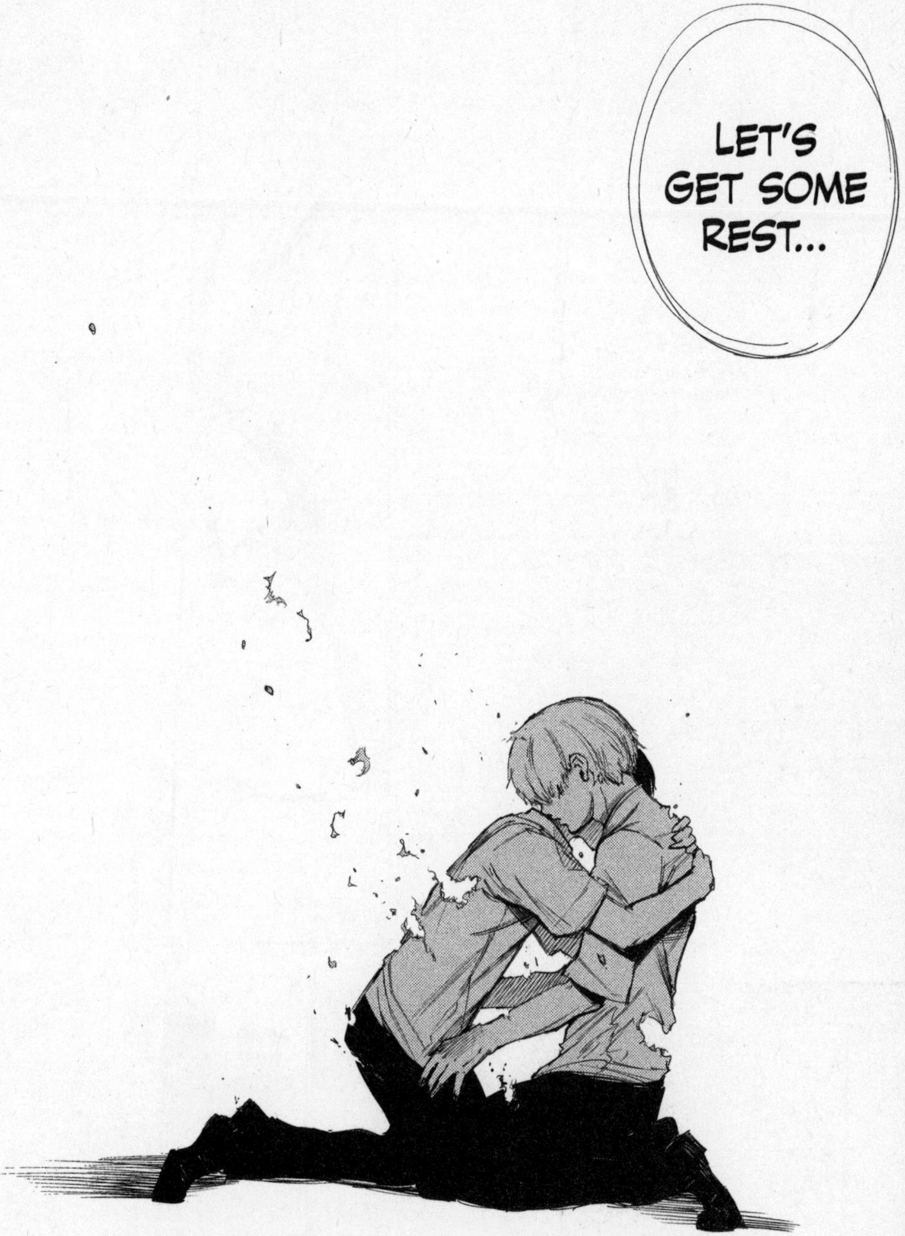
LET'S GET SOME REST...

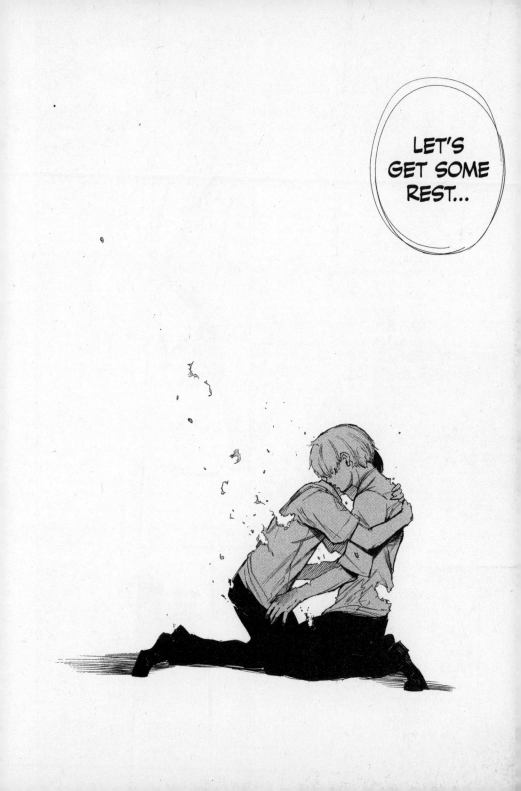

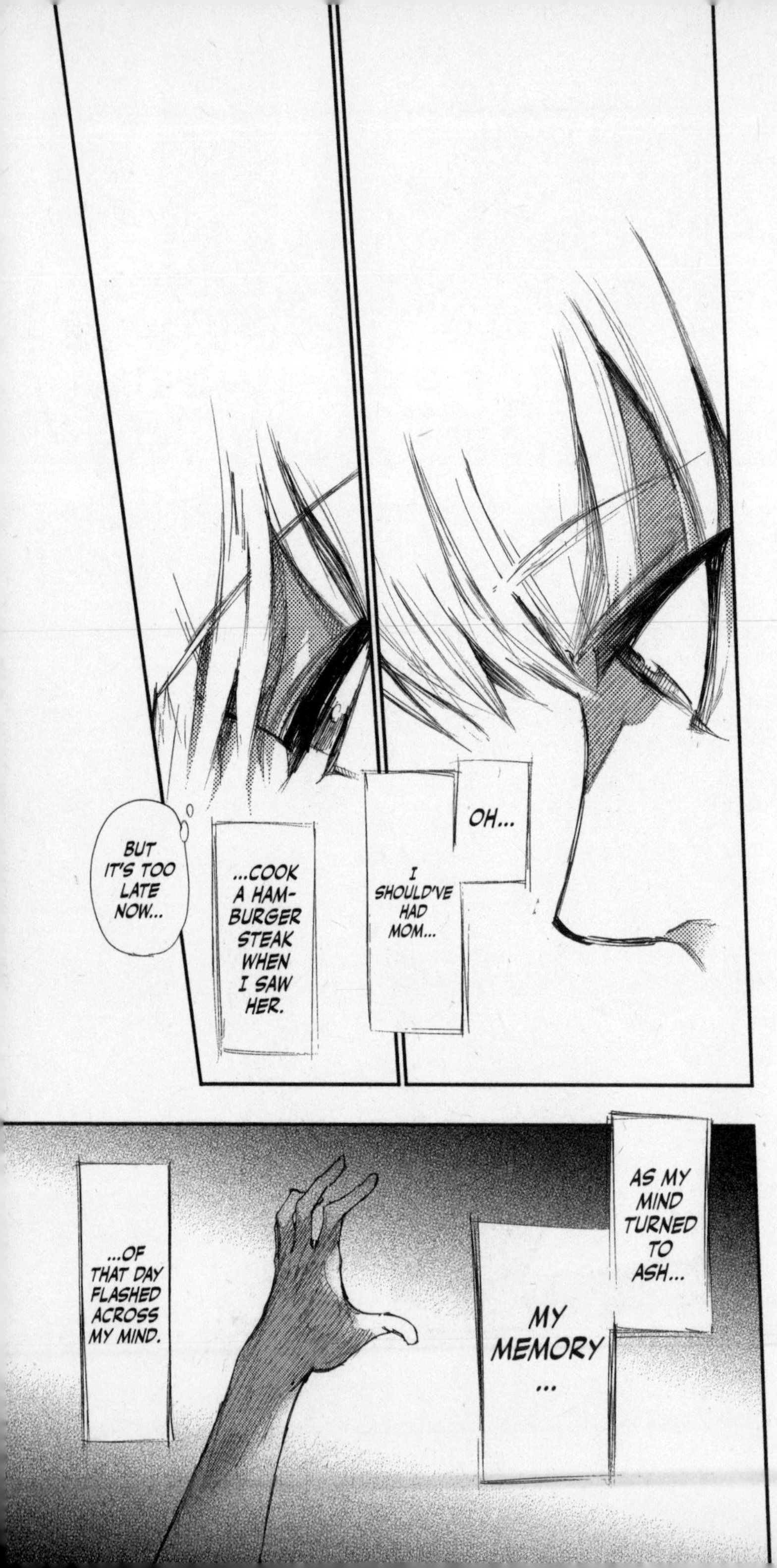
OH...
I SHOULD'VE HAD MOM...
...COOK A HAMBURGER STEAK WHEN I SAW HER.
BUT IT'S TOO LATE NOW...
AS MY MIND TURNED TO ASH...
MY MEMORY...
...OF THAT DAY FLASHED ACROSS MY MIND.

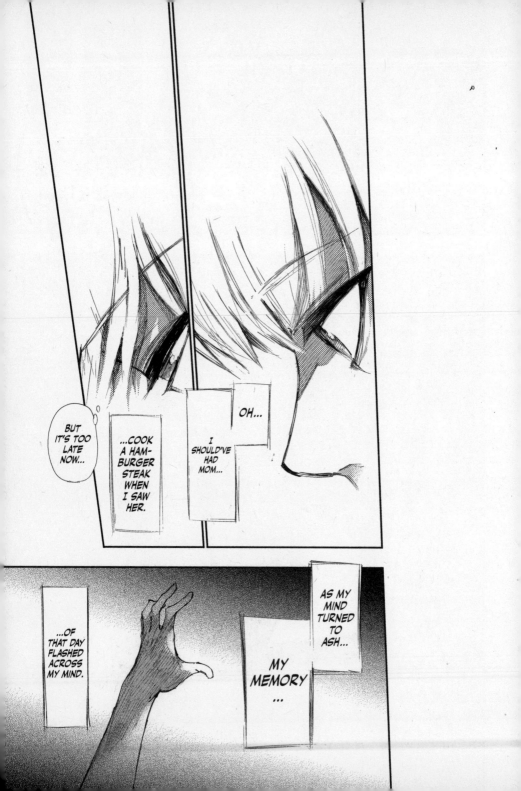

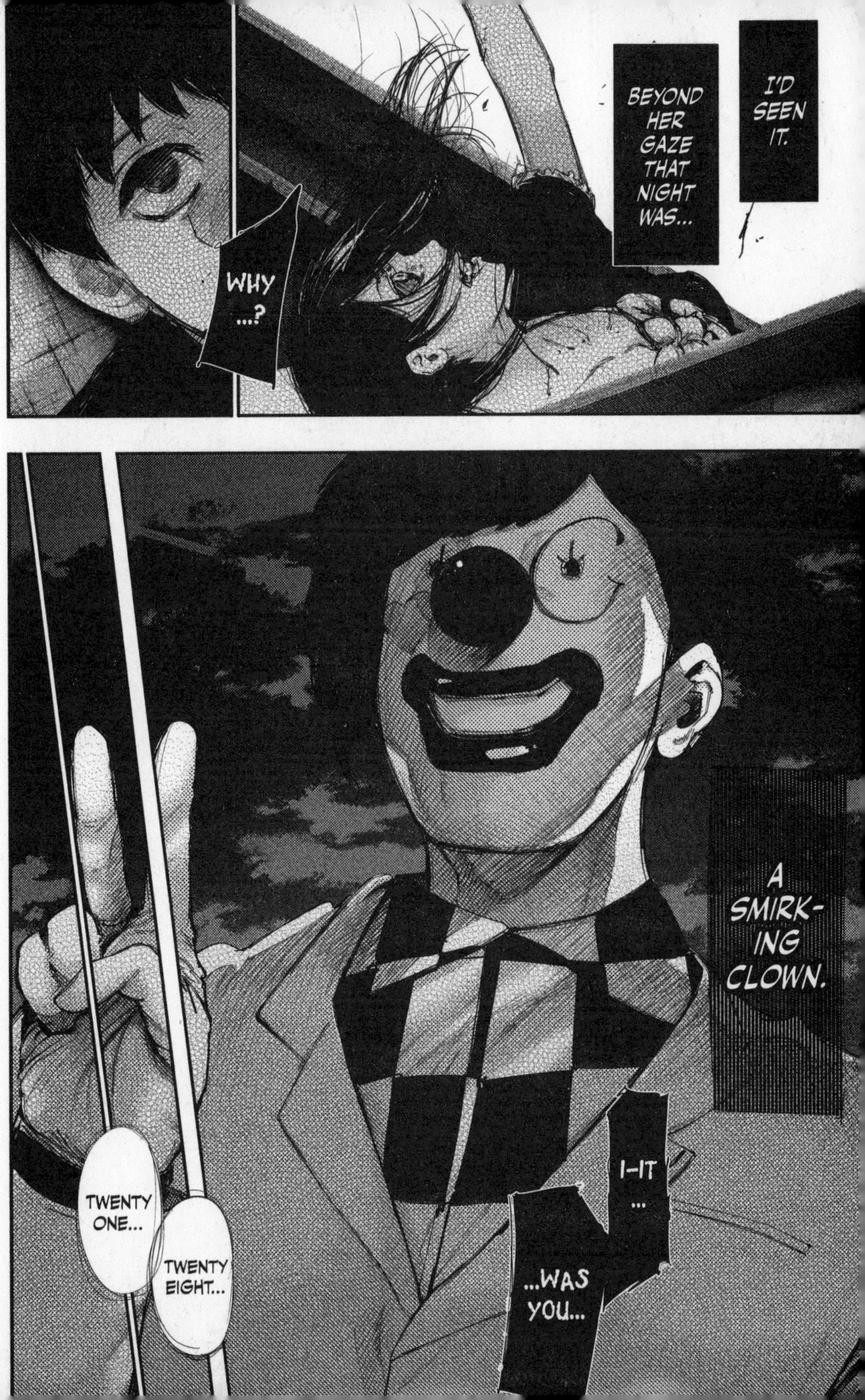
I'D SEEN IT.
BEYOND HER GAZE THAT NIGHT WAS...
WHY ...?
A SMIRKING CLOWN.
I-IT ...
...WAS YOU...
TWENTY ONE...
TWENTY EIGHT...

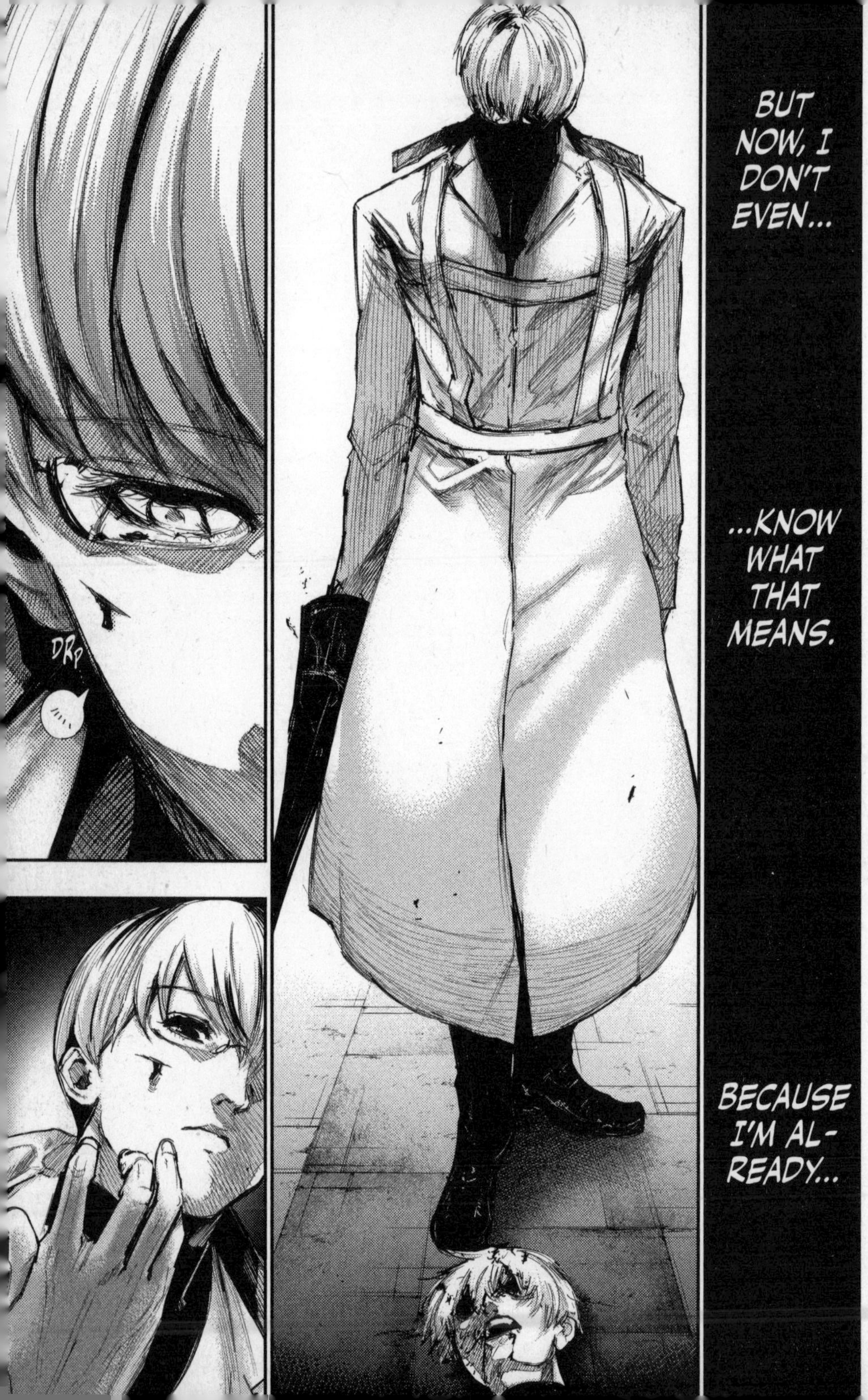
BUT NOW, I DON'T EVEN...
...KNOW WHAT THAT MEANS.
BECAUSE I'M AL-READY...
DRP

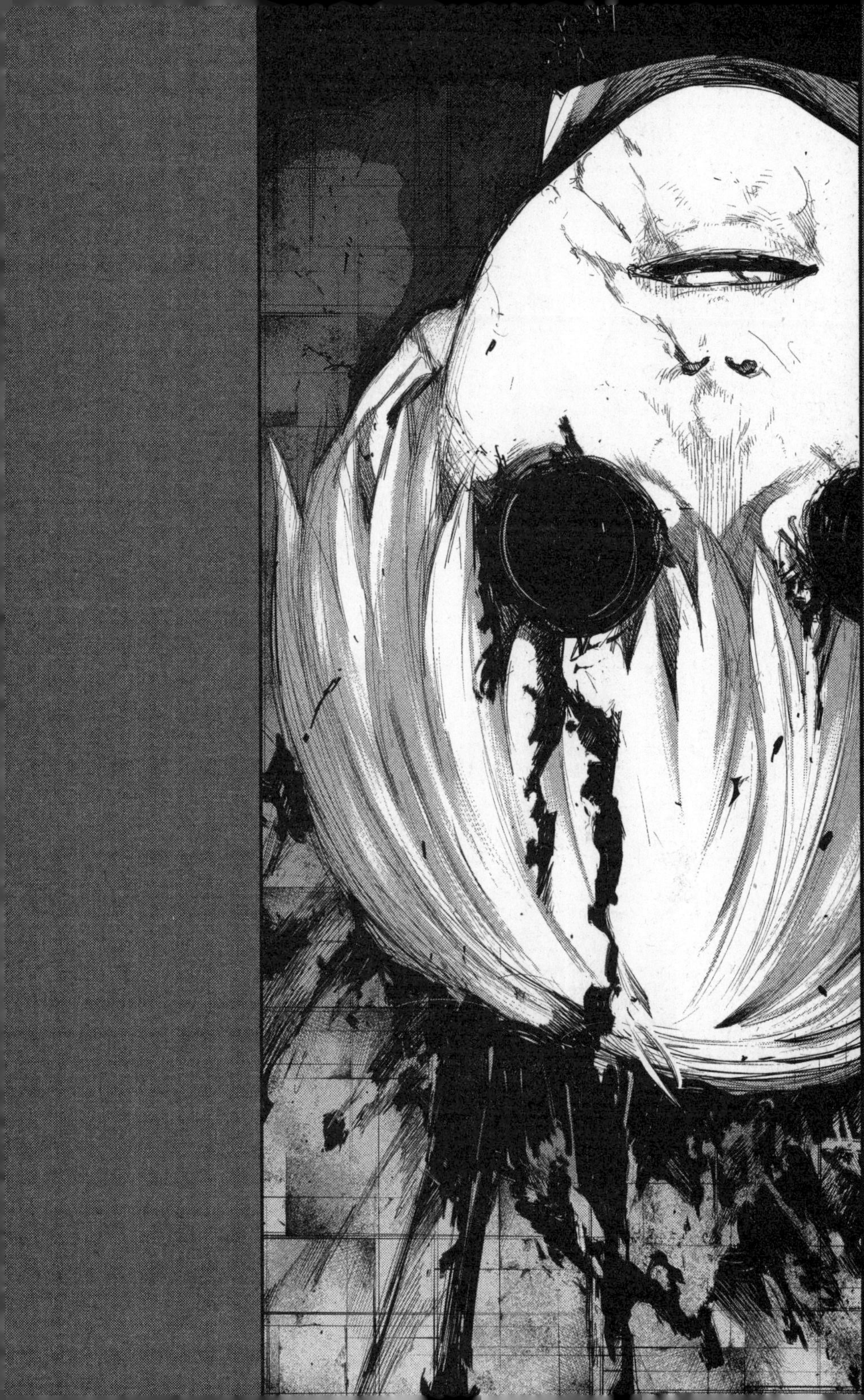

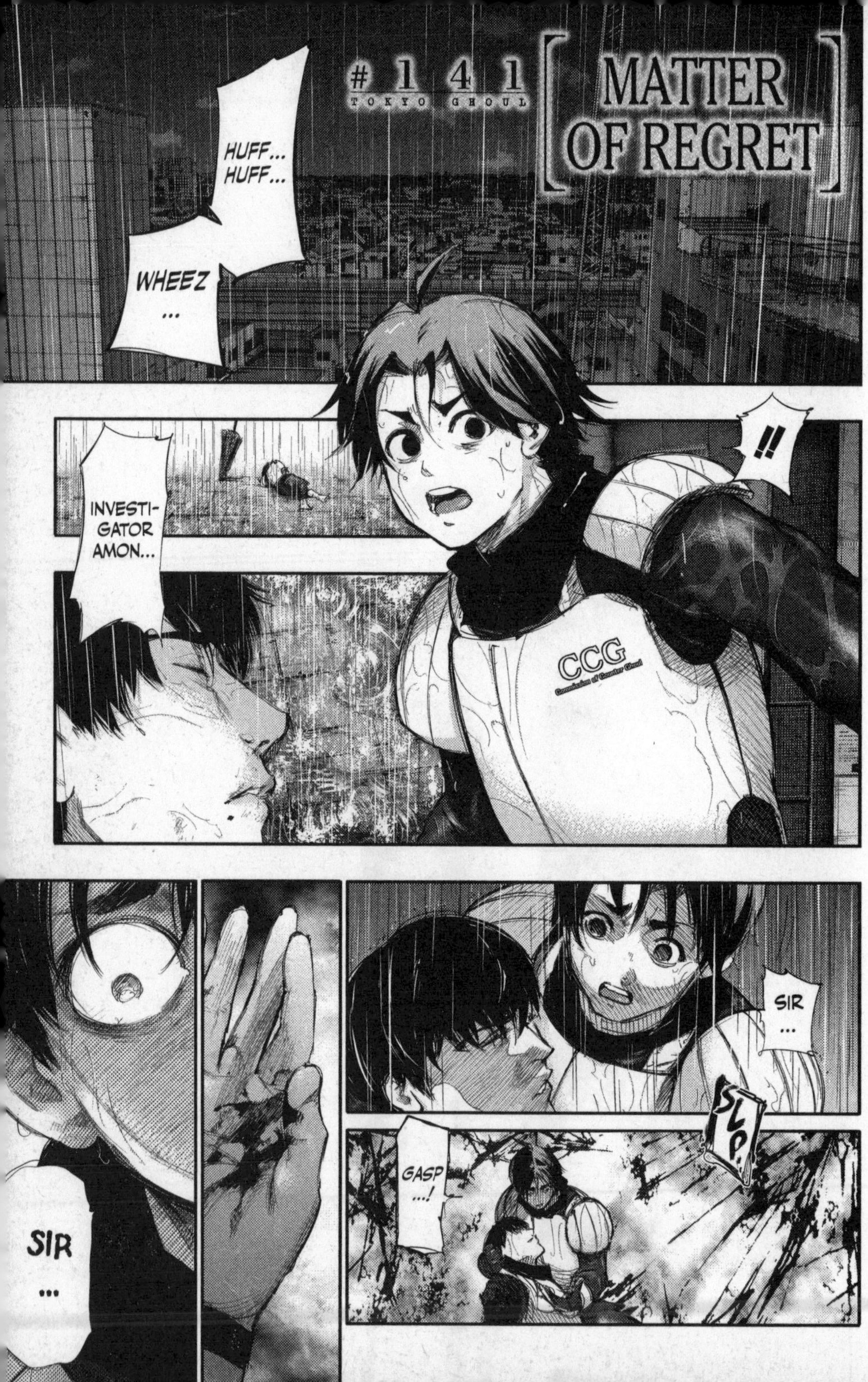

#141
TOKYO GHOUL
MATTER OF REGRET
HUFF... HUFF...
WHEEZ ...
!!
INVESTI-GATOR AMON...
CCG
Commission of Counter Ghoul
SIR ...
SLP
GASP ...!
SIR ...

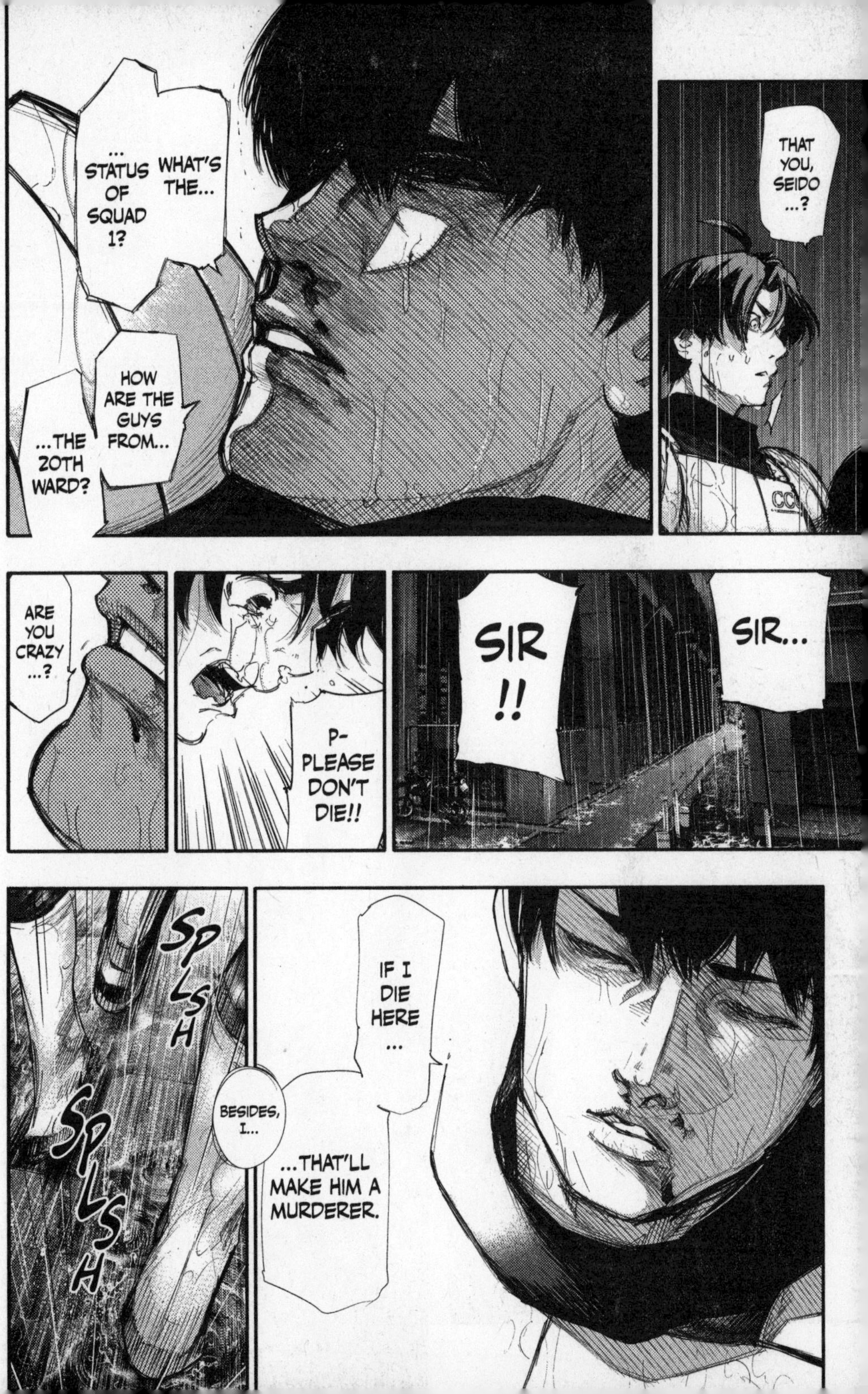
THAT YOU, SEIDO ...?
WHAT'S THE...
... STATUS OF SQUAD 1?
HOW ARE THE GUYS FROM...
...THE 20TH WARD?
SIR...
SIR !!
P-PLEASE DON'T DIE!!
ARE YOU CRAZY ...?
IF I DIE HERE ...
...THAT'LL MAKE HIM A MURDERER.
BESIDES, I...
SPLSH
SPLSH

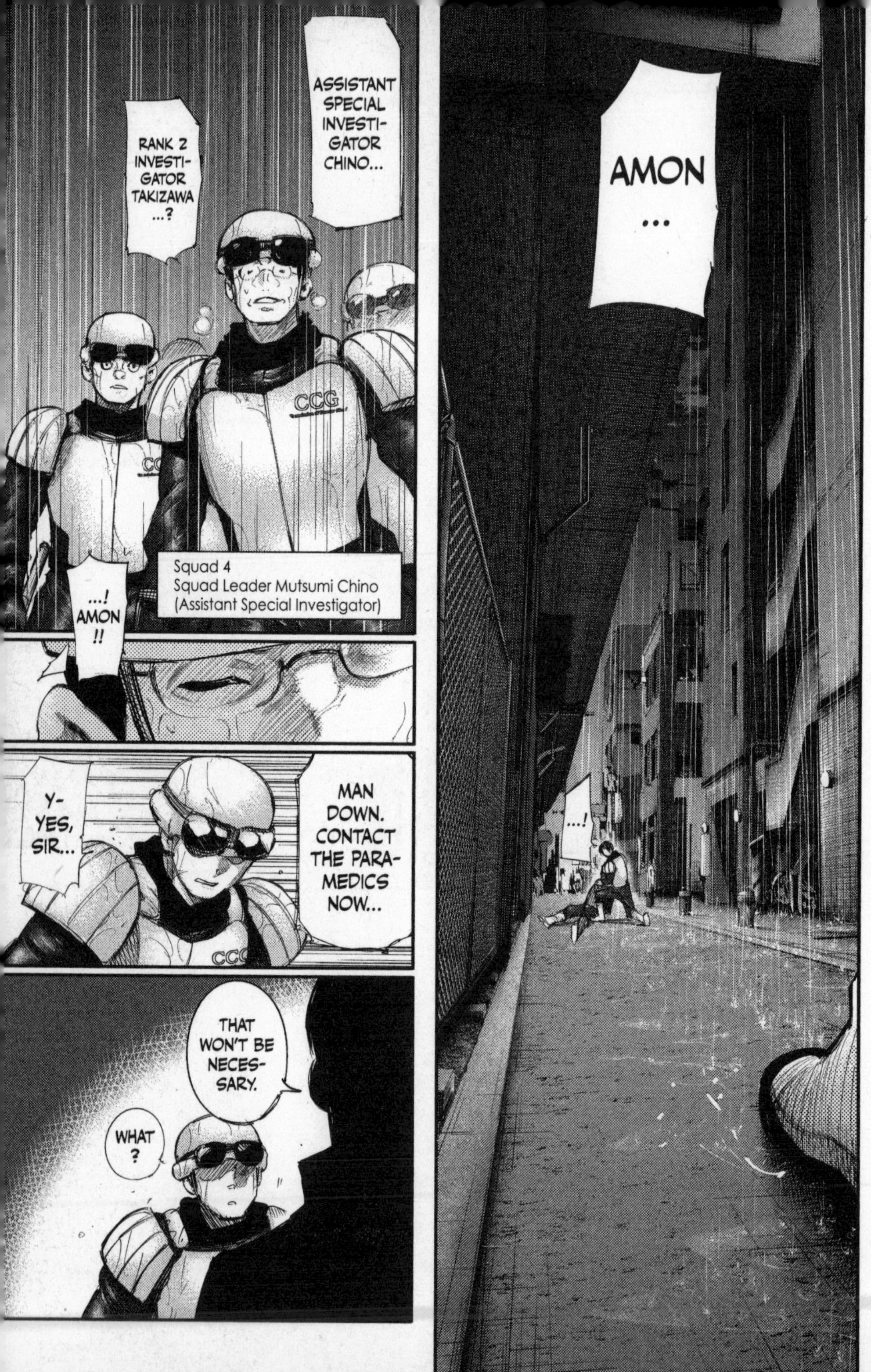
AMON...
...!
ASSISTANT SPECIAL INVESTIGATOR CHINO...
RANK 2 INVESTIGATOR TAKIZAWA...?
Squad 4 Squad Leader Mutsumi Chino (Assistant Special Investigator)
...! AMON!!
MAN DOWN. CONTACT THE PARAMEDICS NOW...
Y-YES, SIR...
THAT WON'T BE NECESSARY.
WHAT?

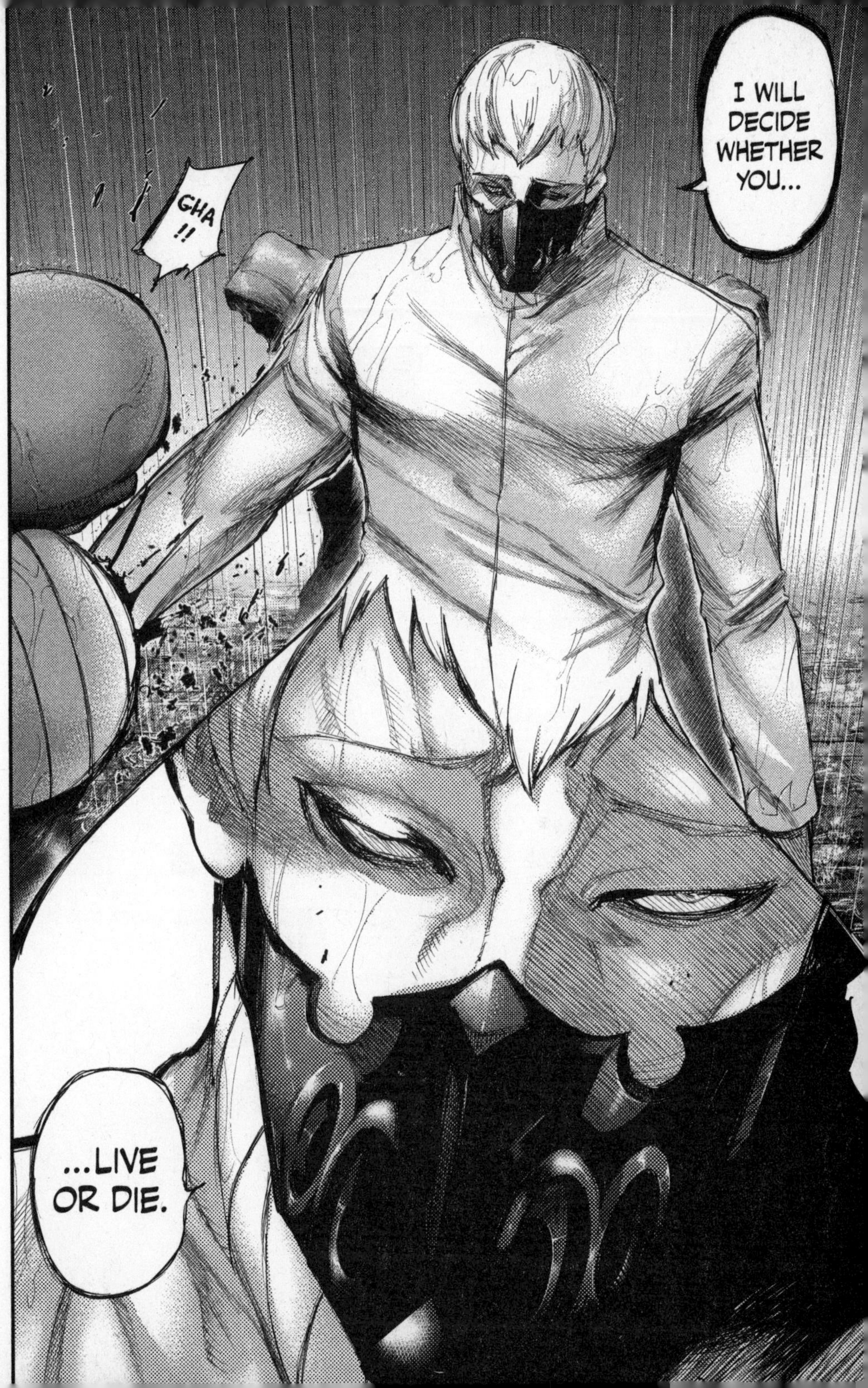
I WILL DECIDE WHETHER YOU...
GHA !!
...LIVE OR DIE.

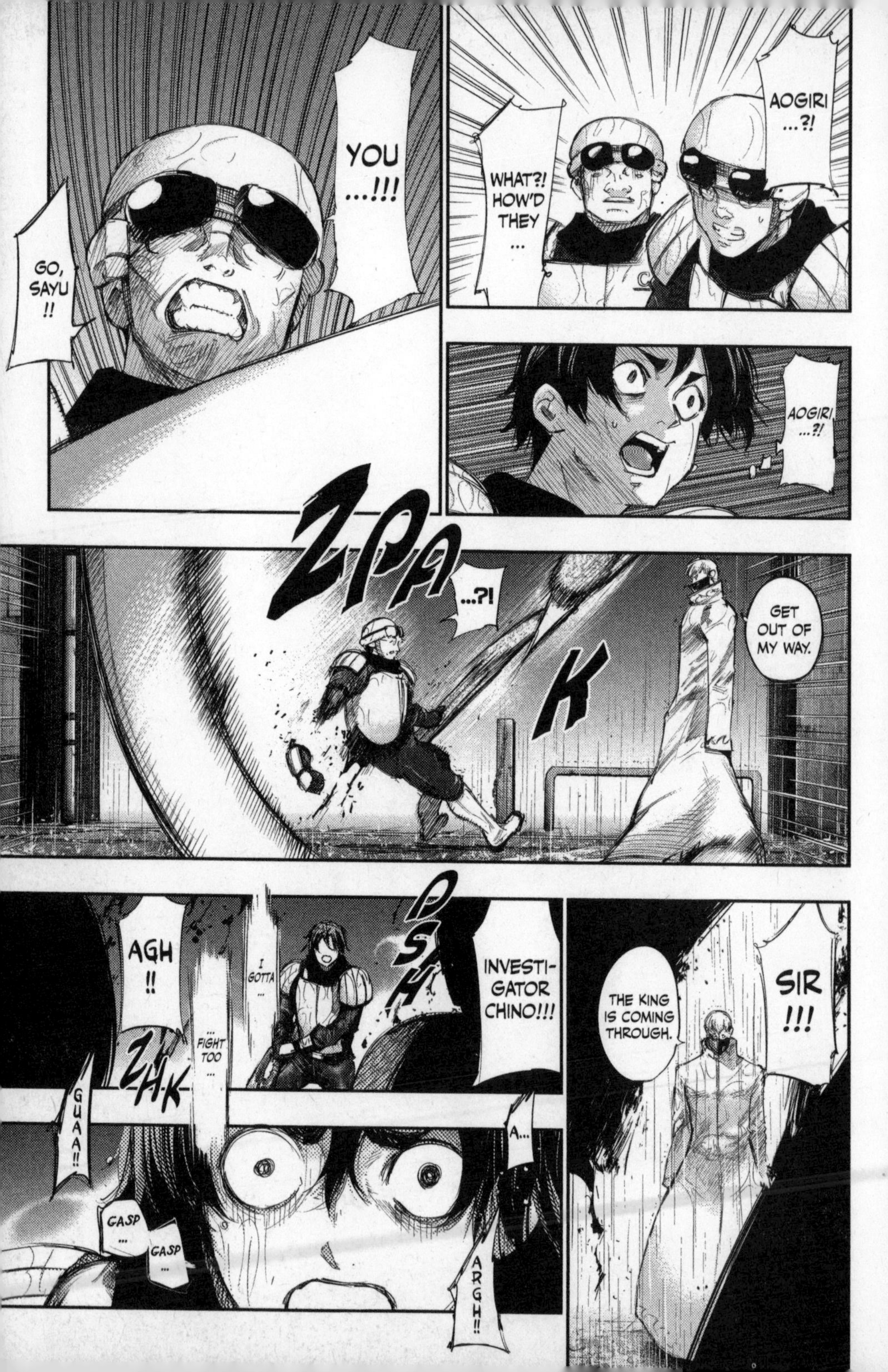
AOGIRI ...?!
WHAT?! HOW'D THEY ...
AOGIRI ...?!
YOU ...!!!
GO, SAYU !!
ZPAK
...?!
GET OUT OF MY WAY.
SIR !!!
THE KING IS COMING THROUGH.
INVESTI-GATOR CHINO!!!
PSH
I GOTTA ...
... FIGHT TOO ...
AGH !!
ZHK
GUAAA!!
A...
ARGH!!
GASP ...
GASP ...

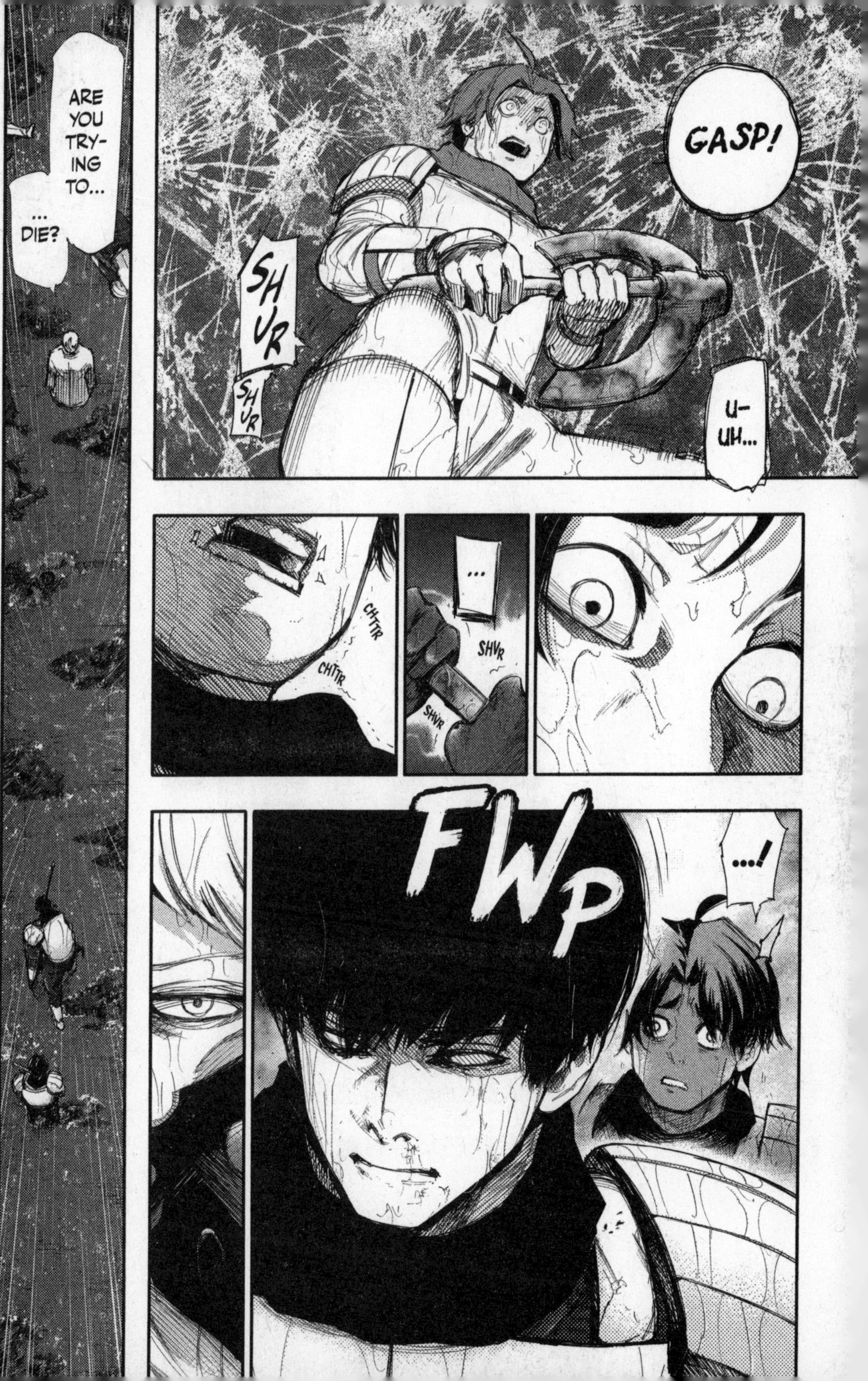
GASP!
U-UH...
SHUR
SHUR
...
SHVR
SHVR
CHTTR
CHTTR
...!
FWP
ARE YOU TRYING TO...
... DIE?

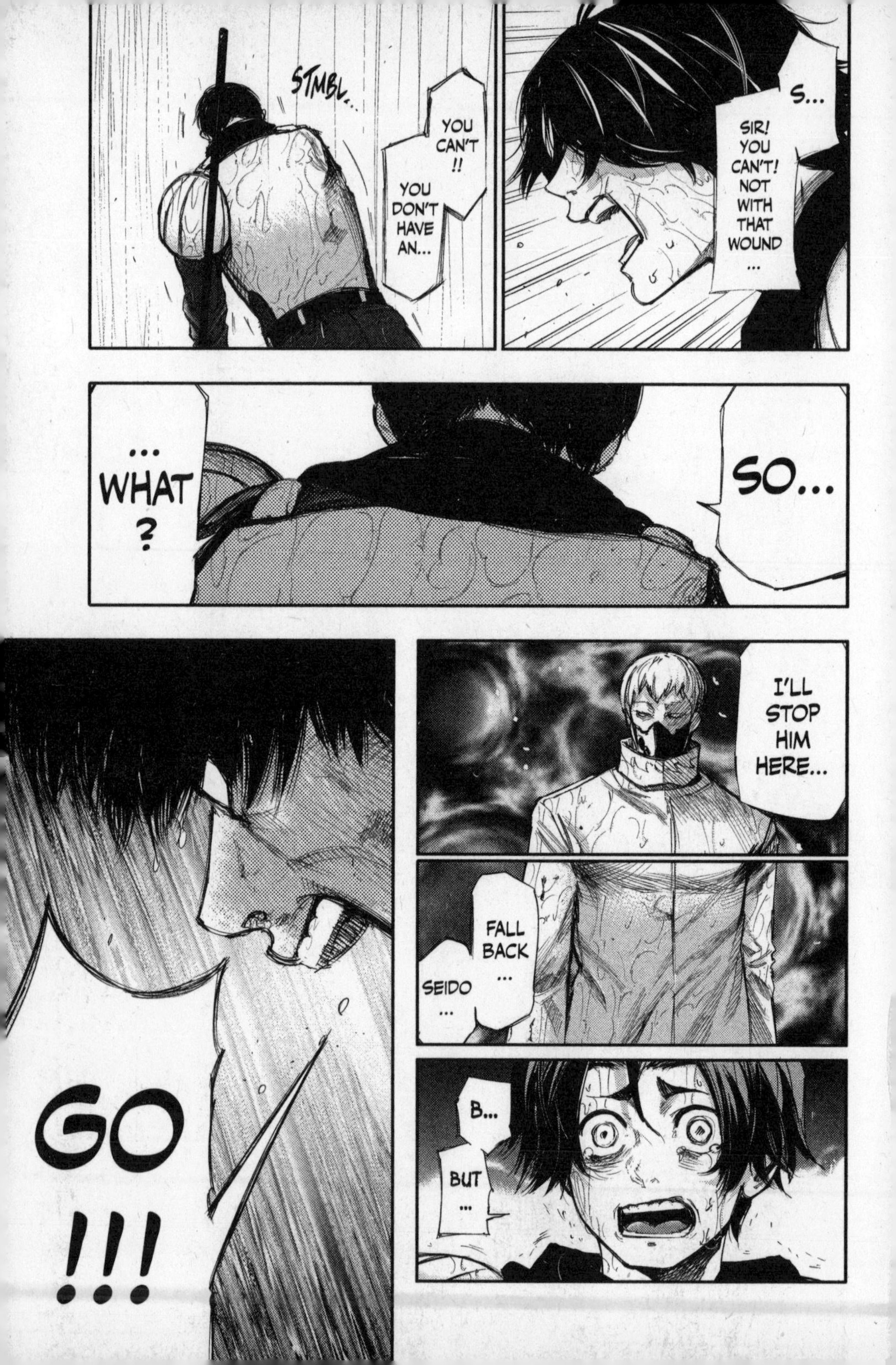
S...
SIR! YOU CAN'T! NOT WITH THAT WOUND ...
YOU CAN'T !!
YOU DON'T HAVE AN...
STMBL...
SO...
... WHAT ?
I'LL STOP HIM HERE...
FALL BACK ...
SEIDO ...
B...
BUT ...
GO !!!

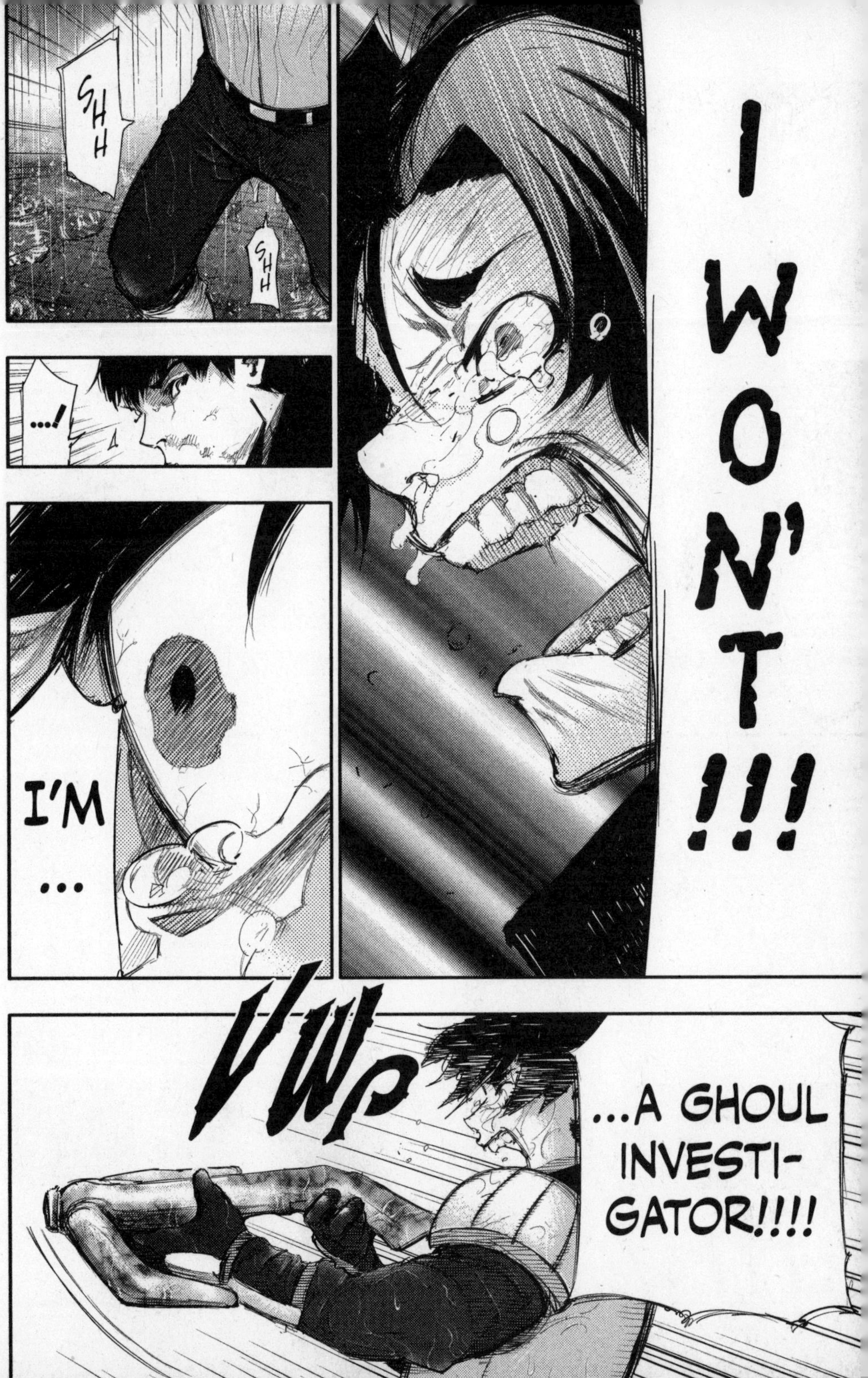
I WON'T!!!
SHH
SHH
...!
I'M ...
...A GHOUL INVESTI-GATOR!!!!
VWP

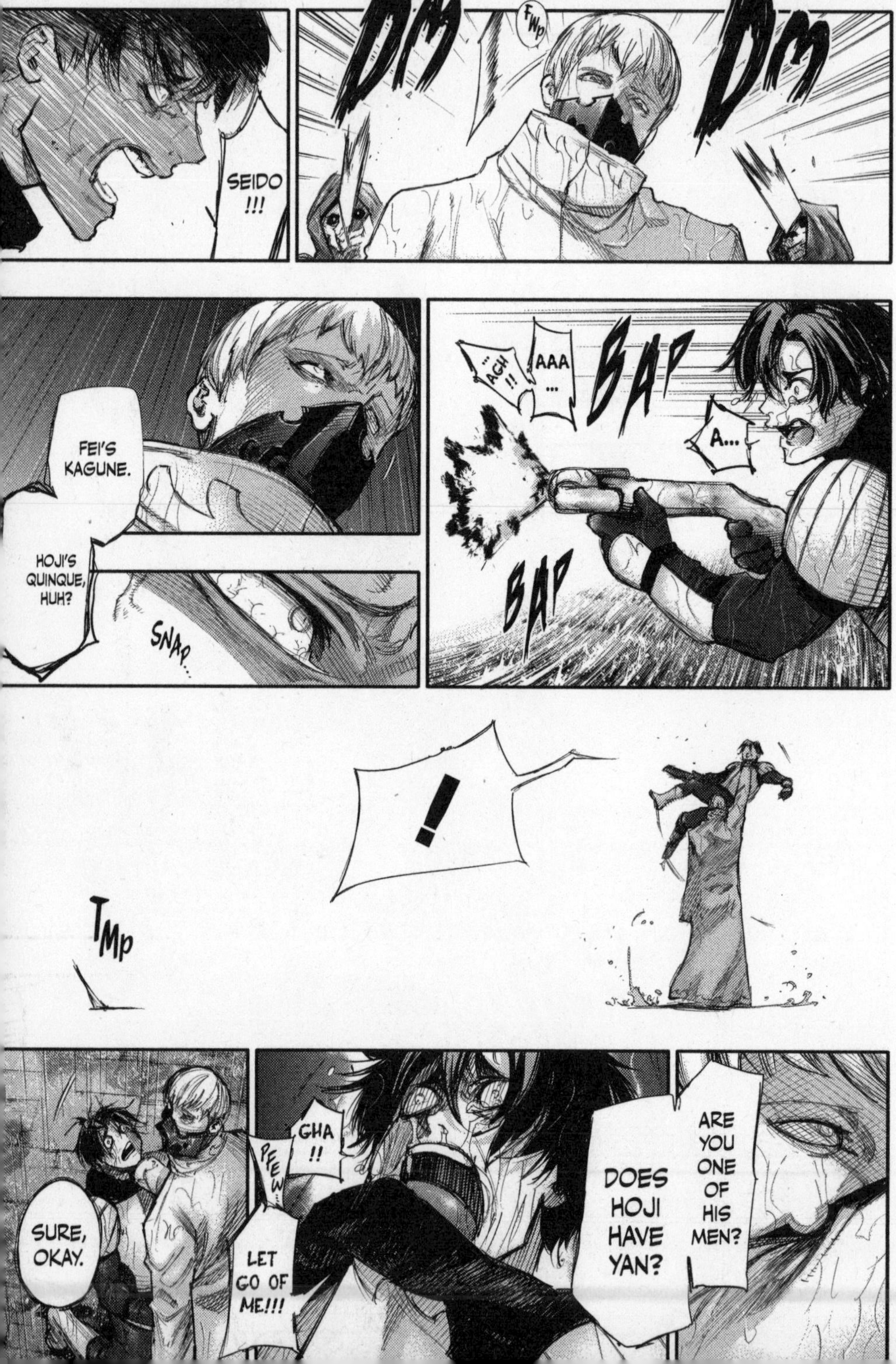
DM
FWP
DM
SEIDO !!!
BAP
AAA ...
... AGH !!
A...
BAP
FEI'S KAGUNE.
HOJI'S QUINQUE, HUH?
SNAP...
!
TMP
ARE YOU ONE OF HIS MEN?
DOES HOJI HAVE YAN?
GHA !!
PFEW...
LET GO OF ME!!!
SURE, OKAY.

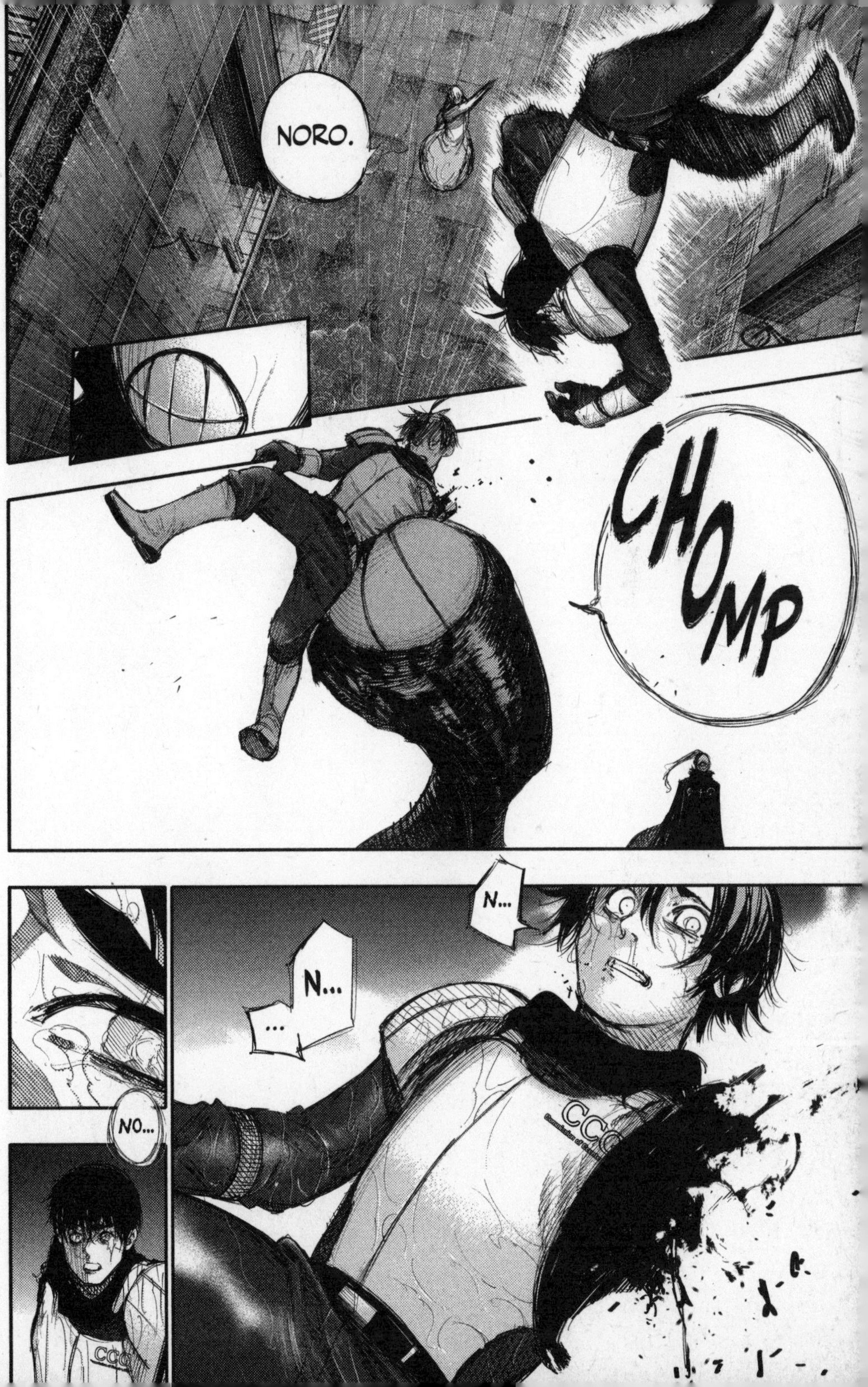
NORO.
CHOMP
N...
N...
...
NO...

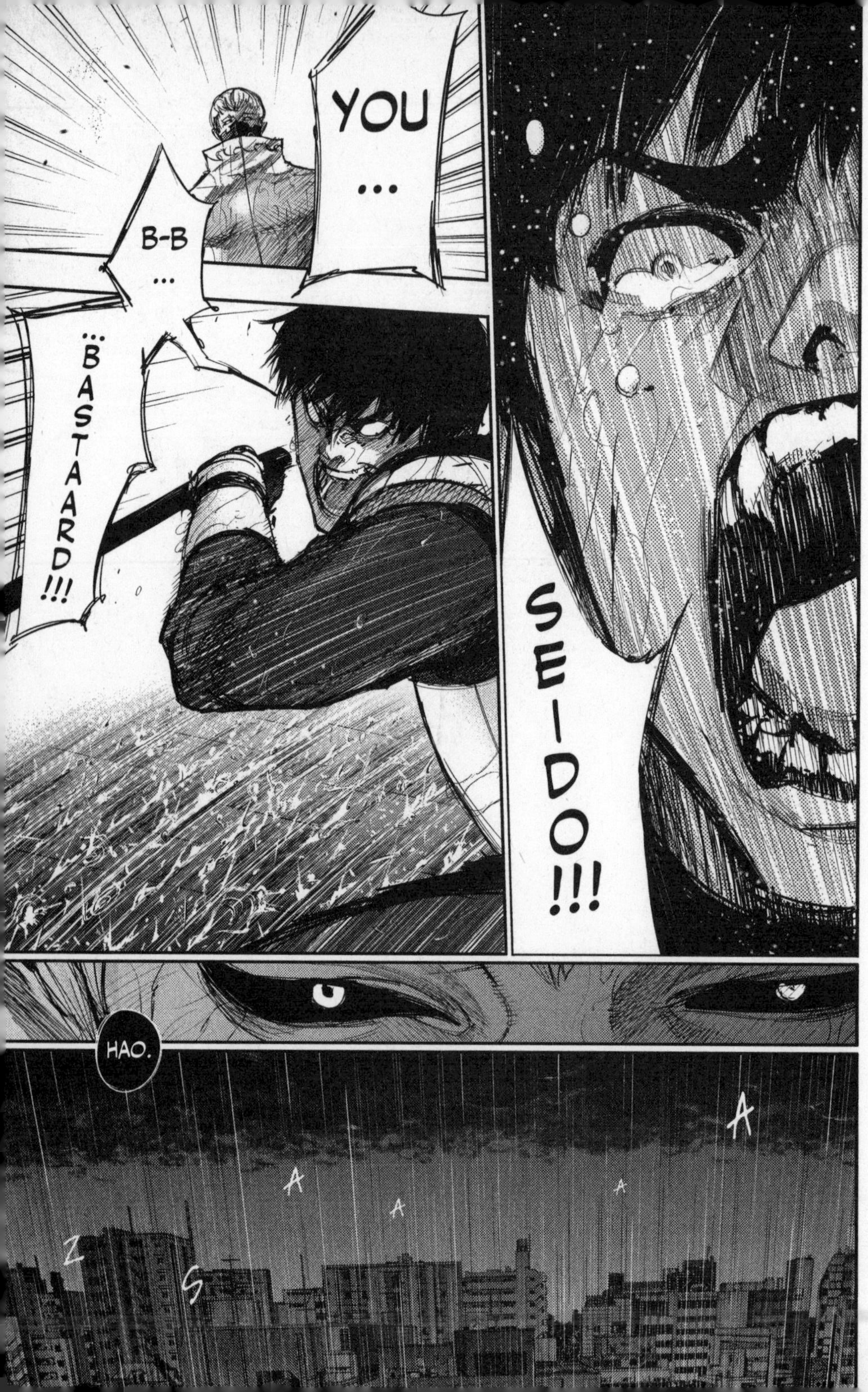
SEIDO!!!
YOU...
B-B...
...BASTAARD!!!
HAO.
Z S A A A A

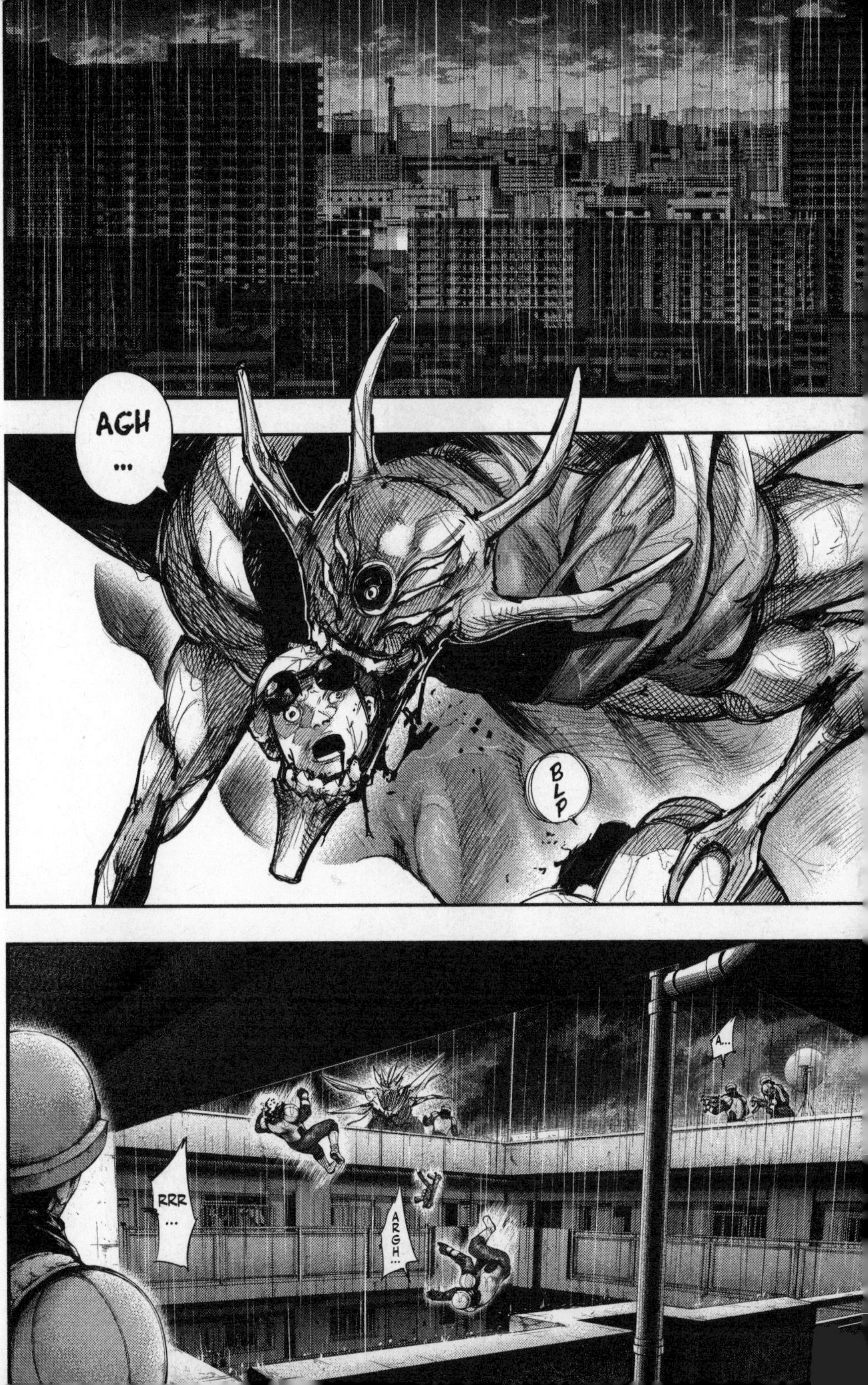
AGH
...
BLP
A...
ARGH...
RRR
...

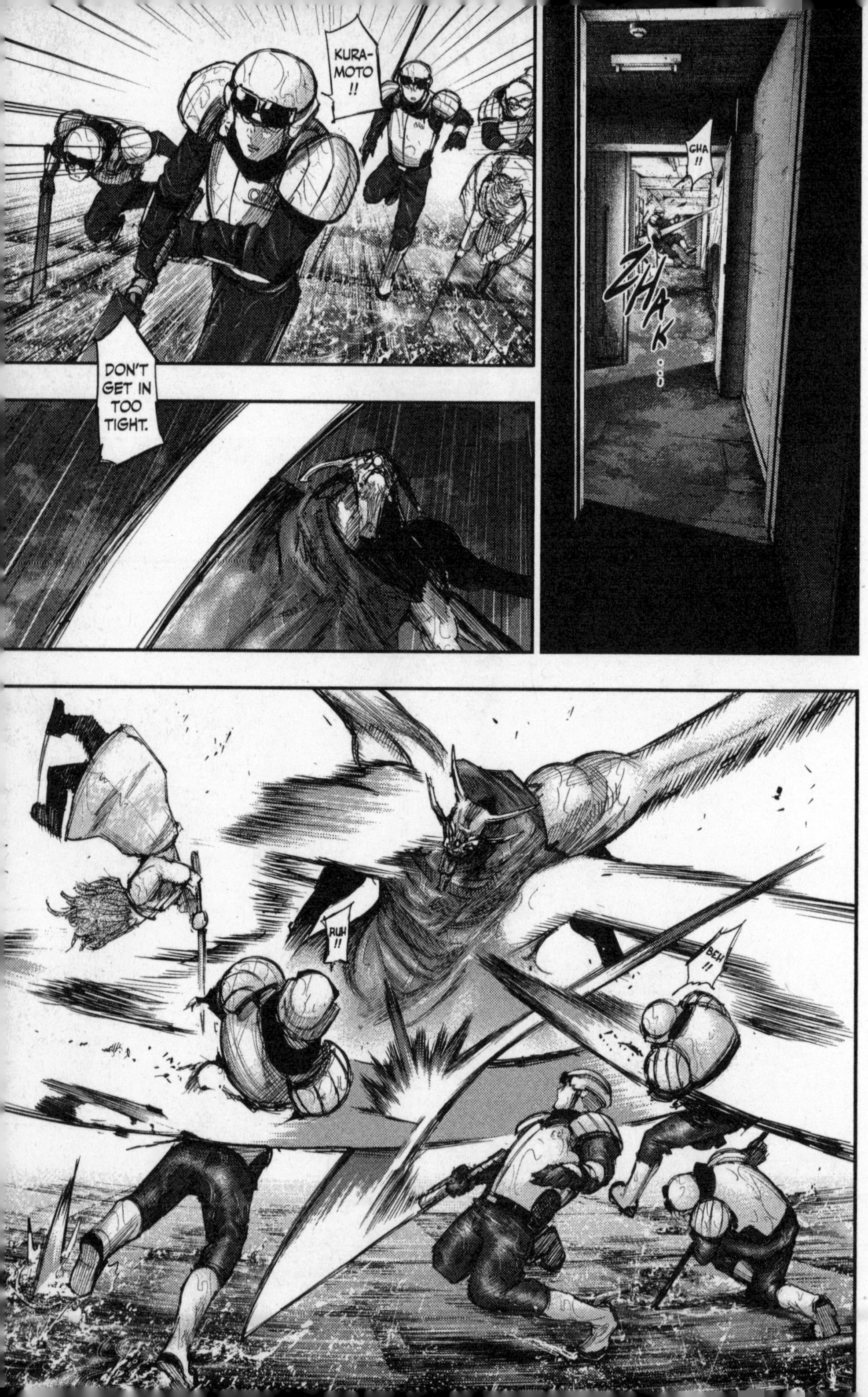
GHA!!
ZHAK...
KURA-MOTO!!
DON'T GET IN TOO TIGHT.
BEH!!
RUH!!

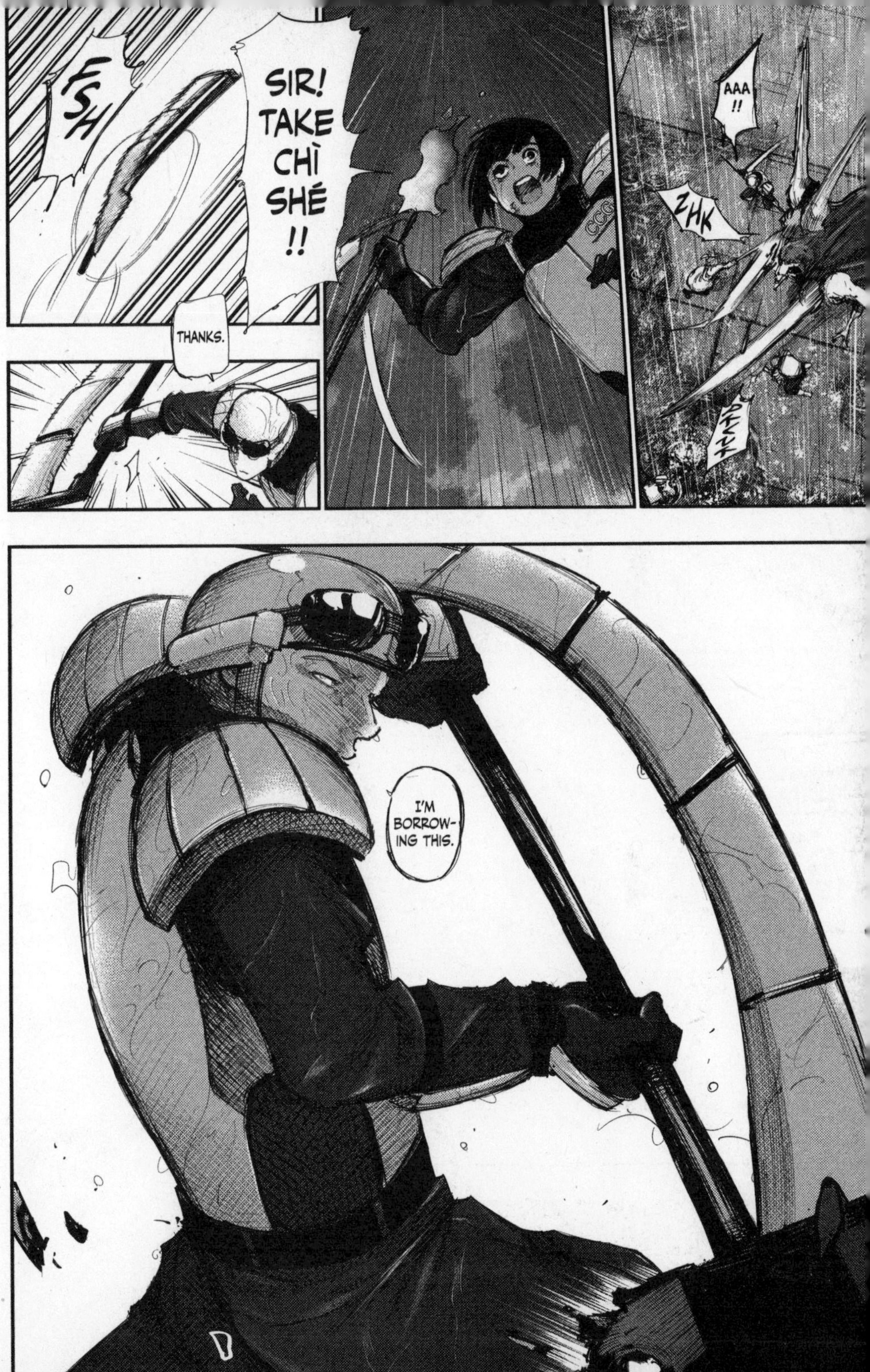
AAA!!
ZHK
SIR! TAKE CHÌ SHÉ!!
FSH
THANKS.
I'M BORROWING THIS.

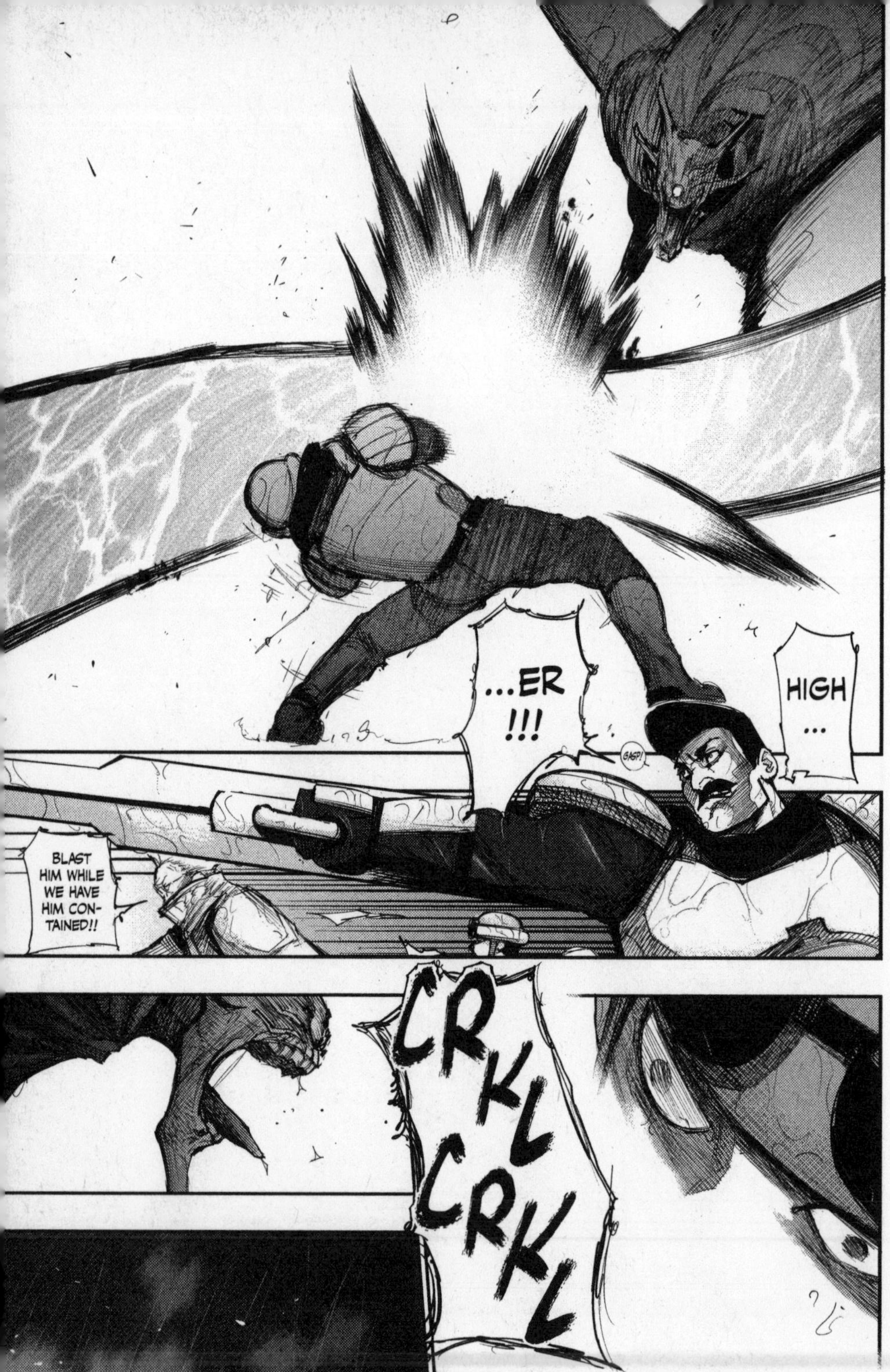
HIGH ...
...ER !!!
GASP!
BLAST HIM WHILE WE HAVE HIM CON-TAINED!!
CRKL CRKL

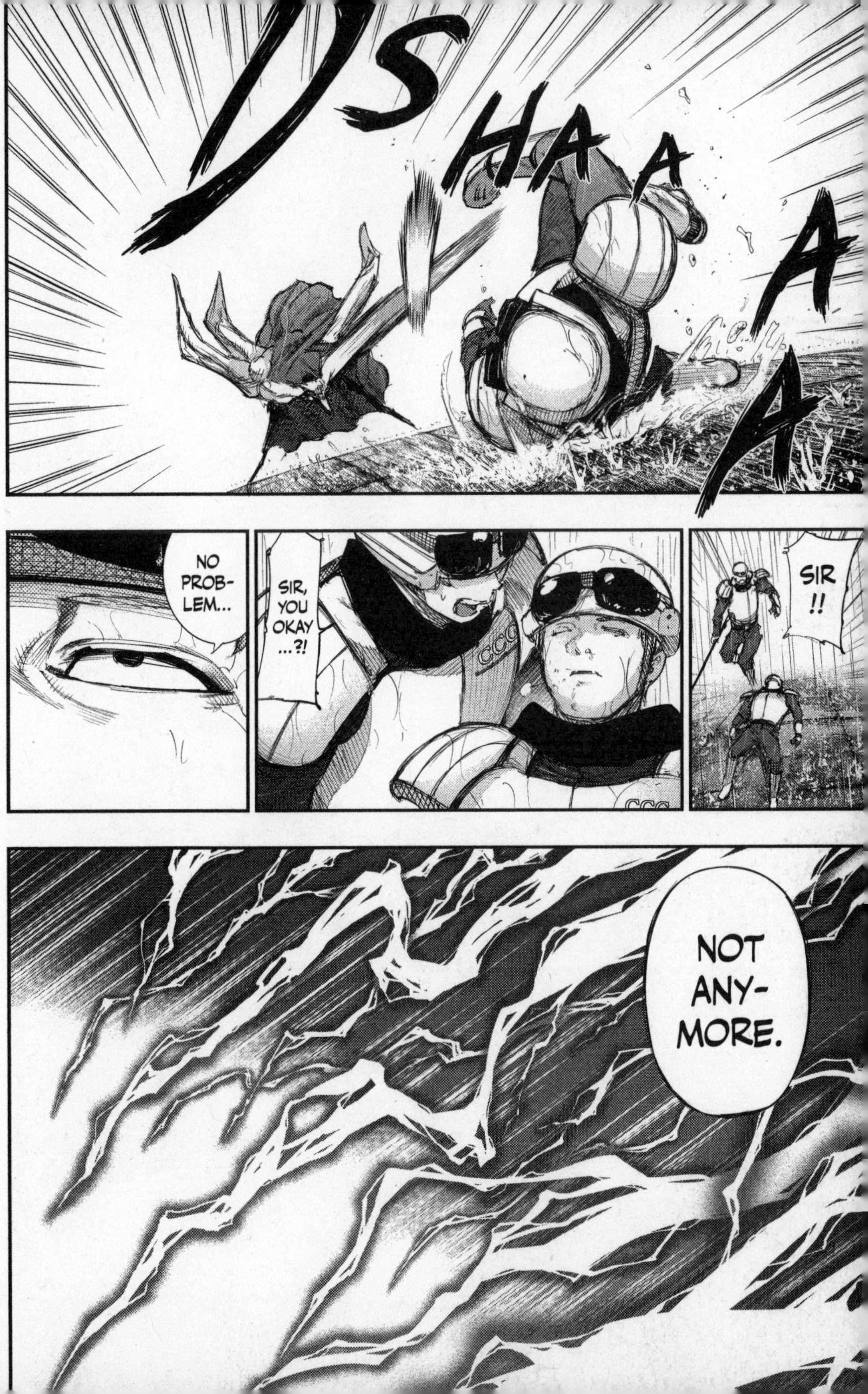
DSHAAAA
SIR !!
SIR, YOU OKAY ...?!
NO PROBLEM...
NOT ANYMORE.

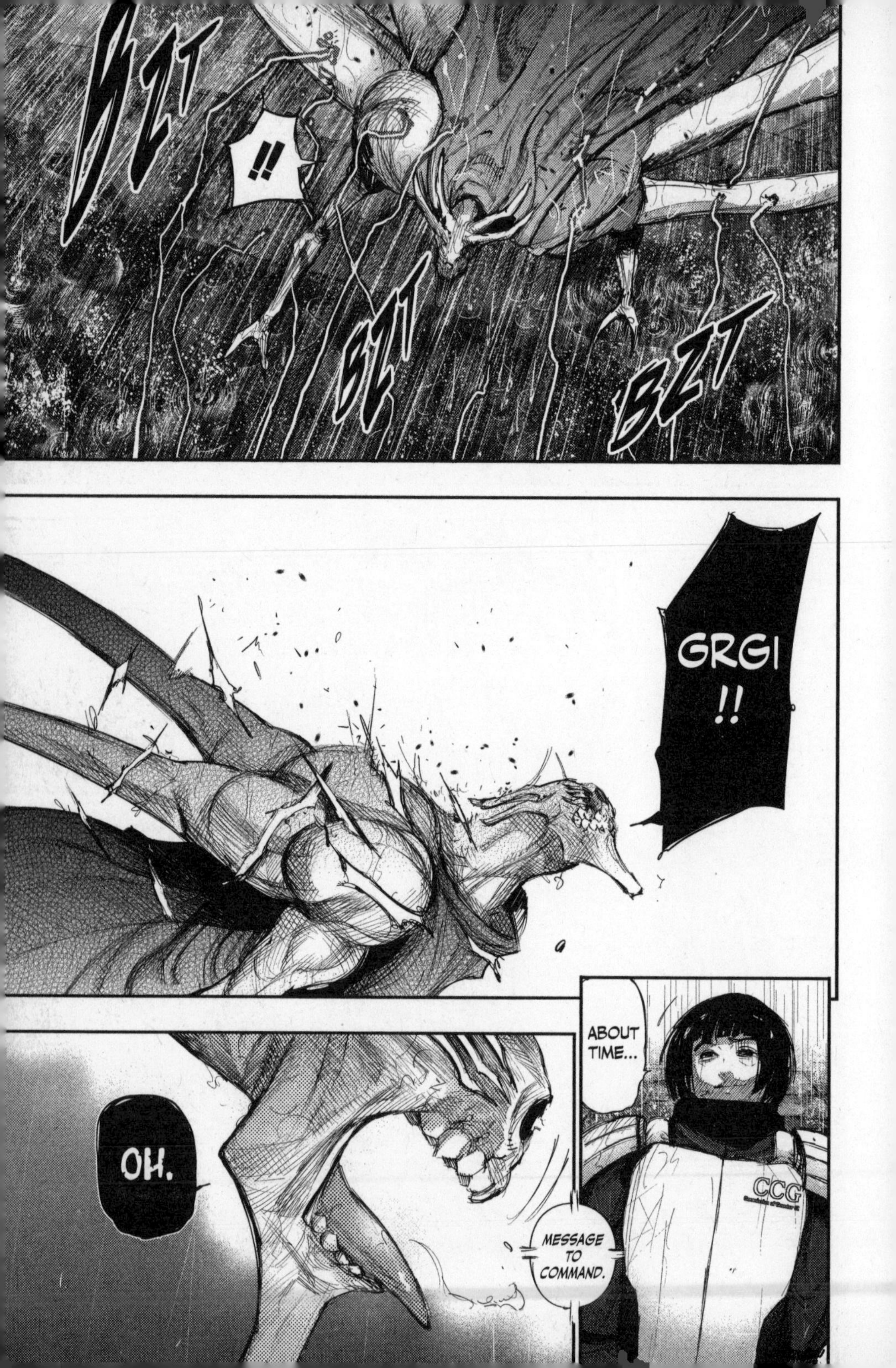
BZT
!!
BZT
BZT
GRGI !!
ABOUT TIME...
MESSAGE TO COMMAND.
OH.

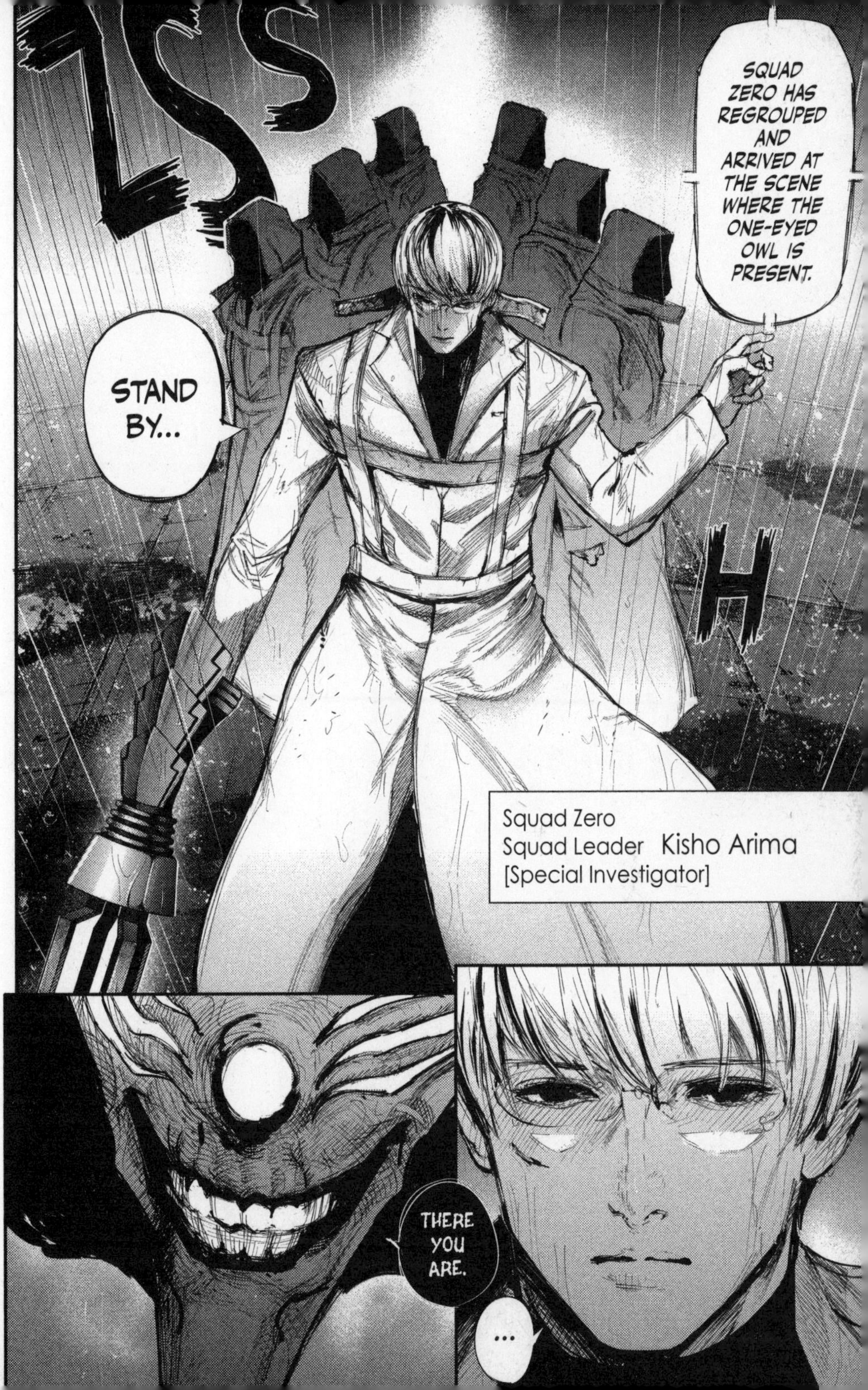
SQUAD ZERO HAS REGROUPED AND ARRIVED AT THE SCENE WHERE THE ONE-EYED OWL IS PRESENT.
STAND BY...
ZSSH
Squad Zero
Squad Leader Kisho Arima
[Special Investigator]
THERE YOU ARE.
...

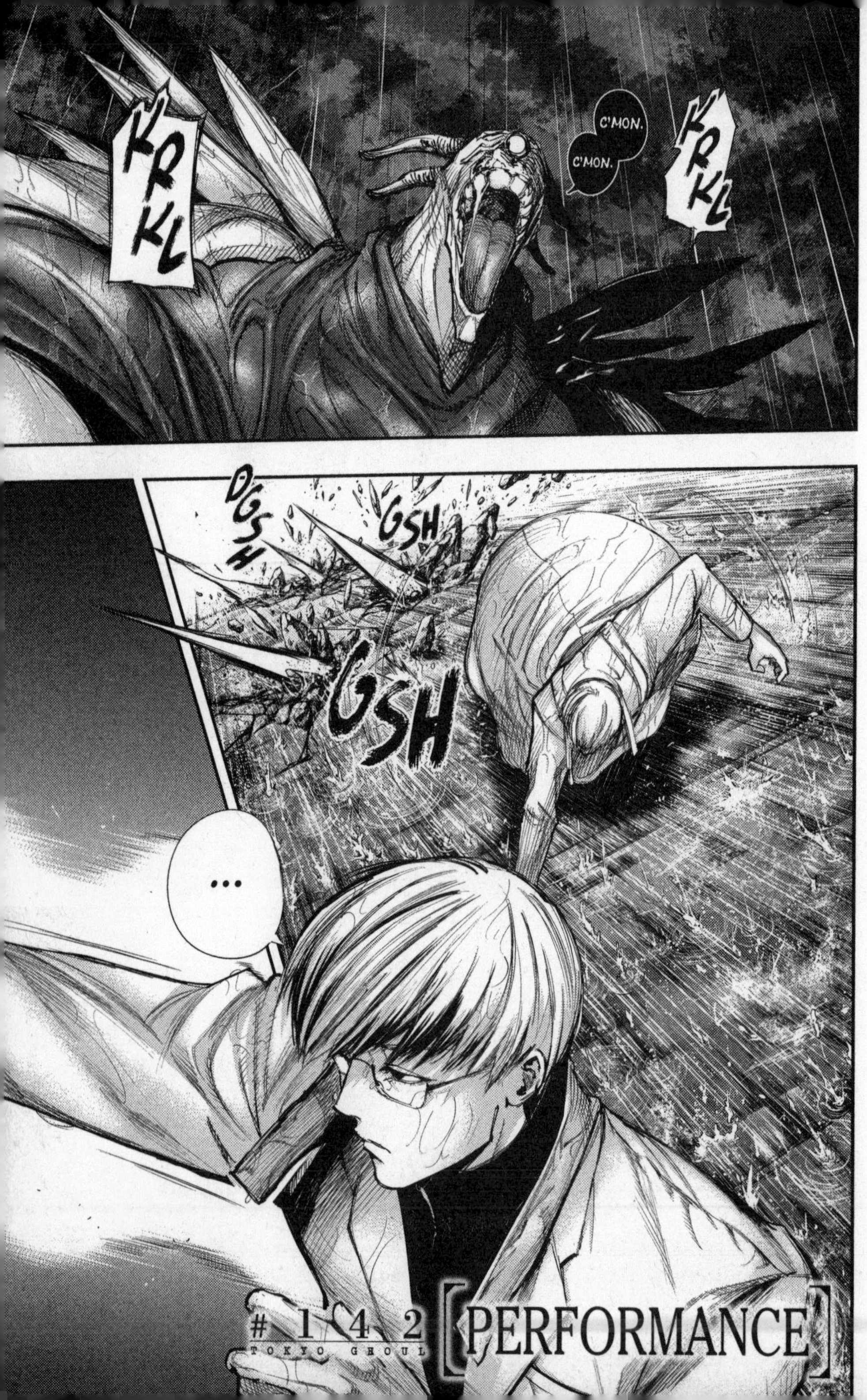
KRKL
C'MON.
C'MON.
KRKL
DGSH
GSH
GSH
...
#142 TOKYO GHOUL [PERFORMANCE]

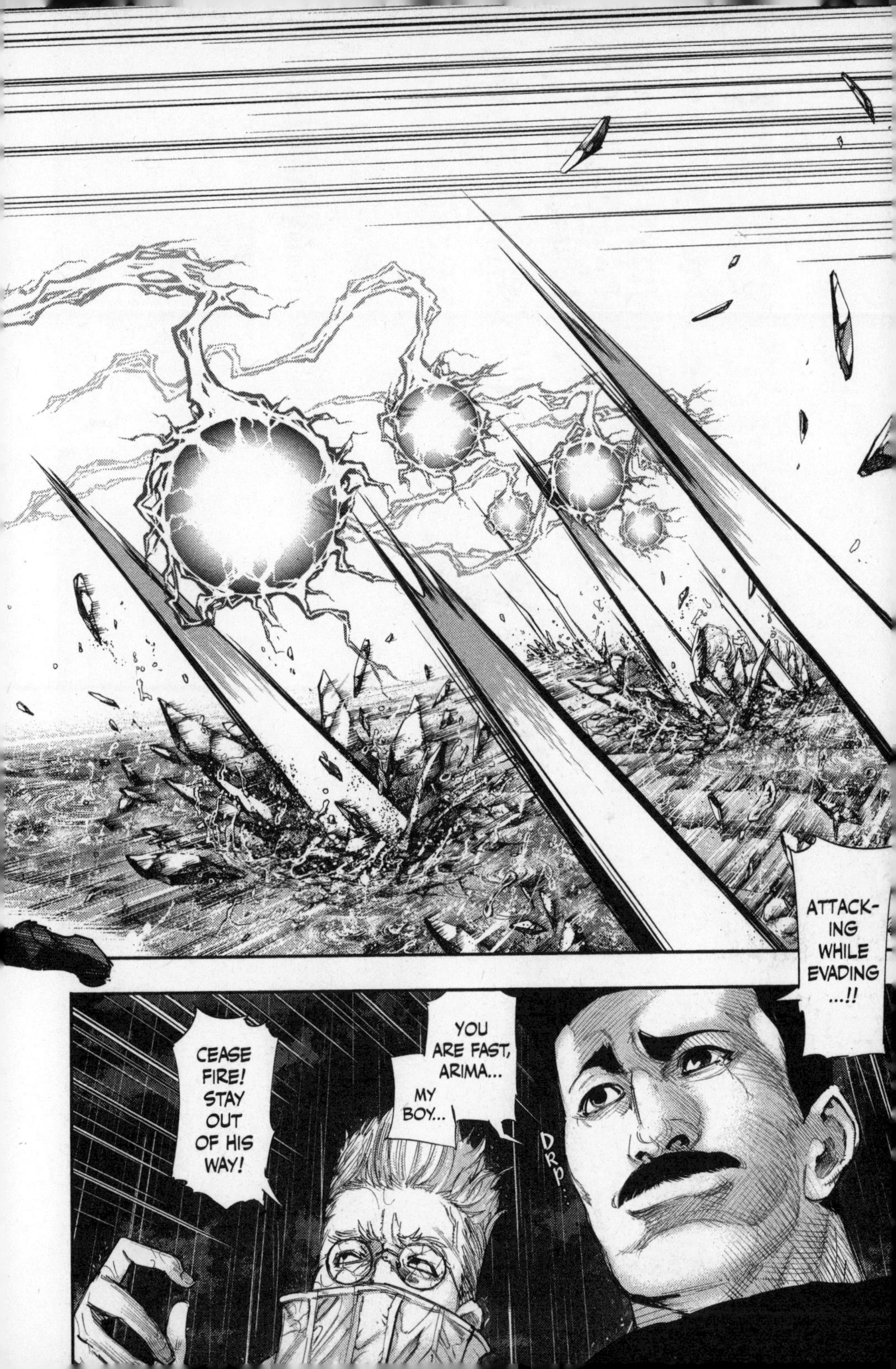
ATTACK-ING WHILE EVADING ...!!
YOU ARE FAST, ARIMA...
MY BOY...
DRP...
CEASE FIRE! STAY OUT OF HIS WAY!

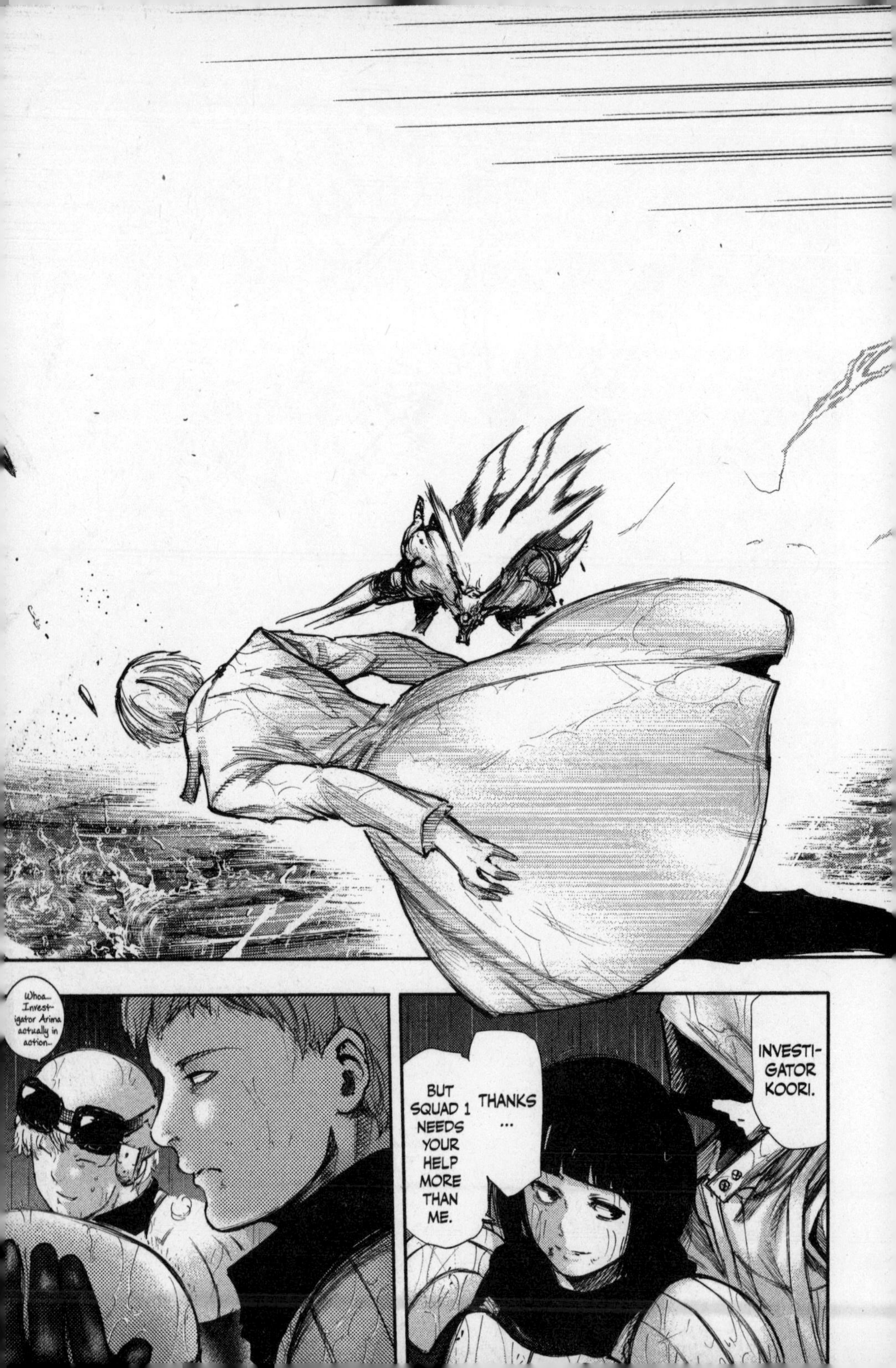
INVESTI-GATOR KOORI.
THANKS ...
BUT SQUAD 1 NEEDS YOUR HELP MORE THAN ME.
Whoa... Invest-igator Arima actually in action...

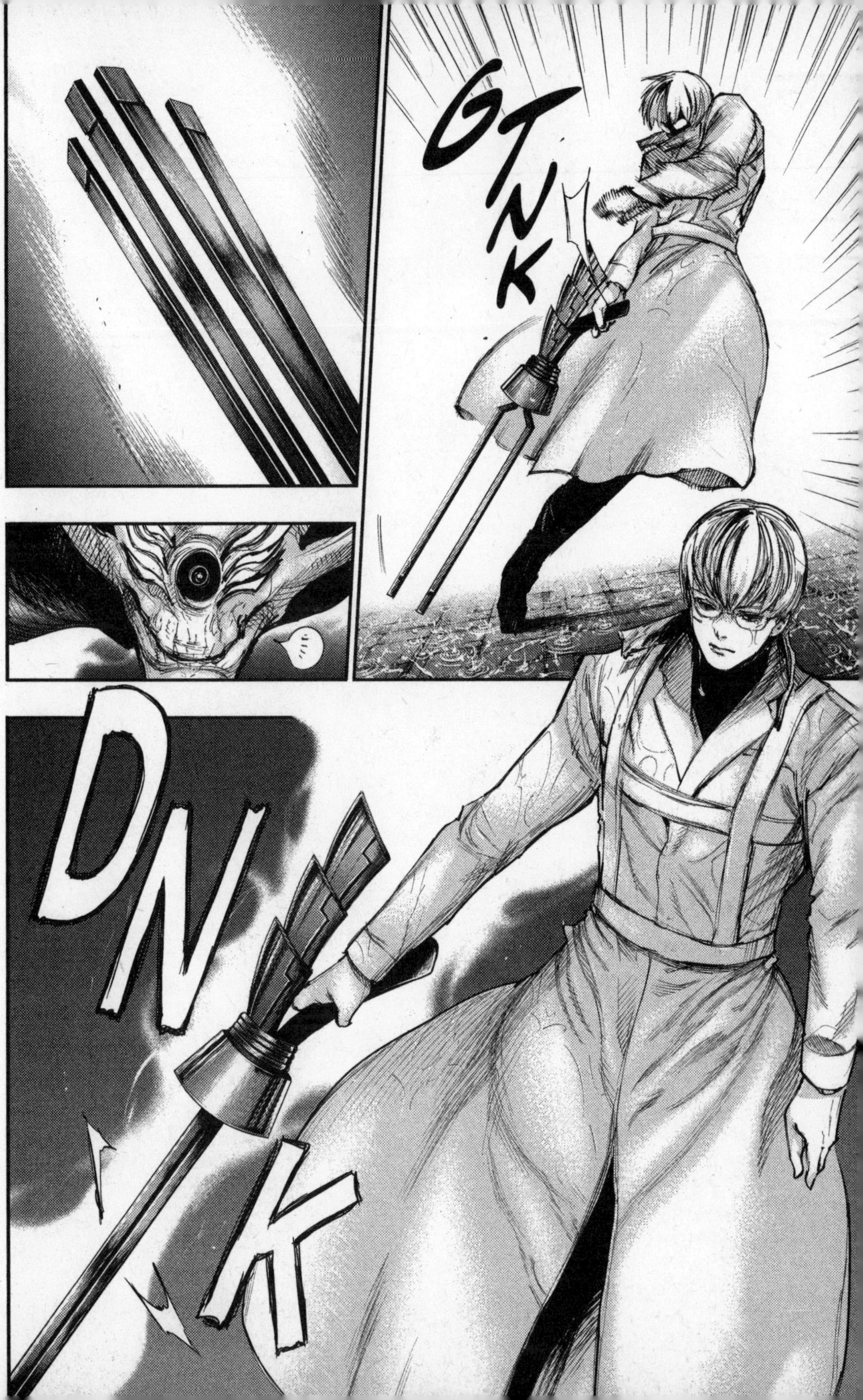
GTNK
...
DNK

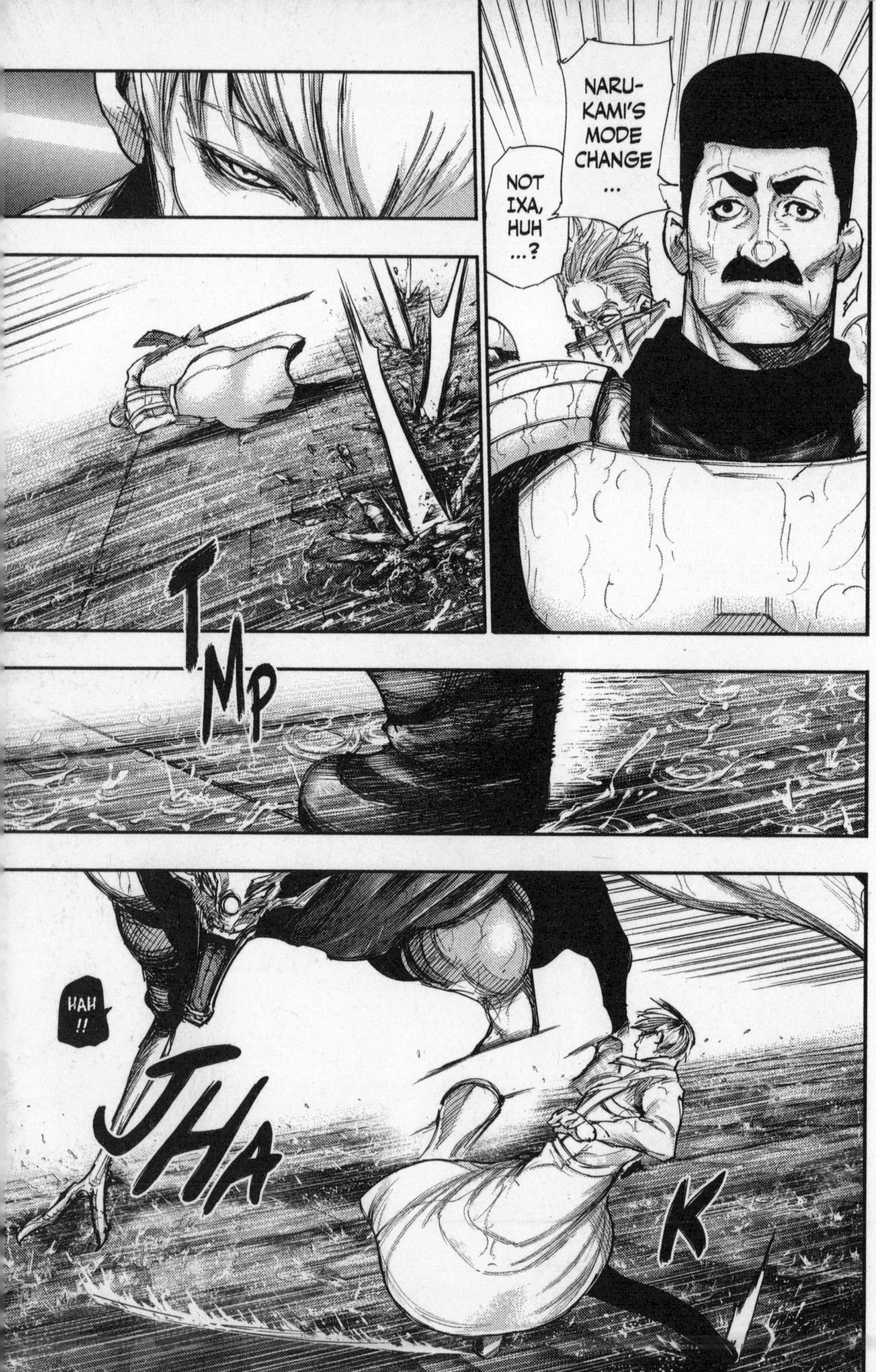
NARU-KAMI'S MODE CHANGE ...
NOT IXA, HUH ...?
TMP
HAH !!
JHAK

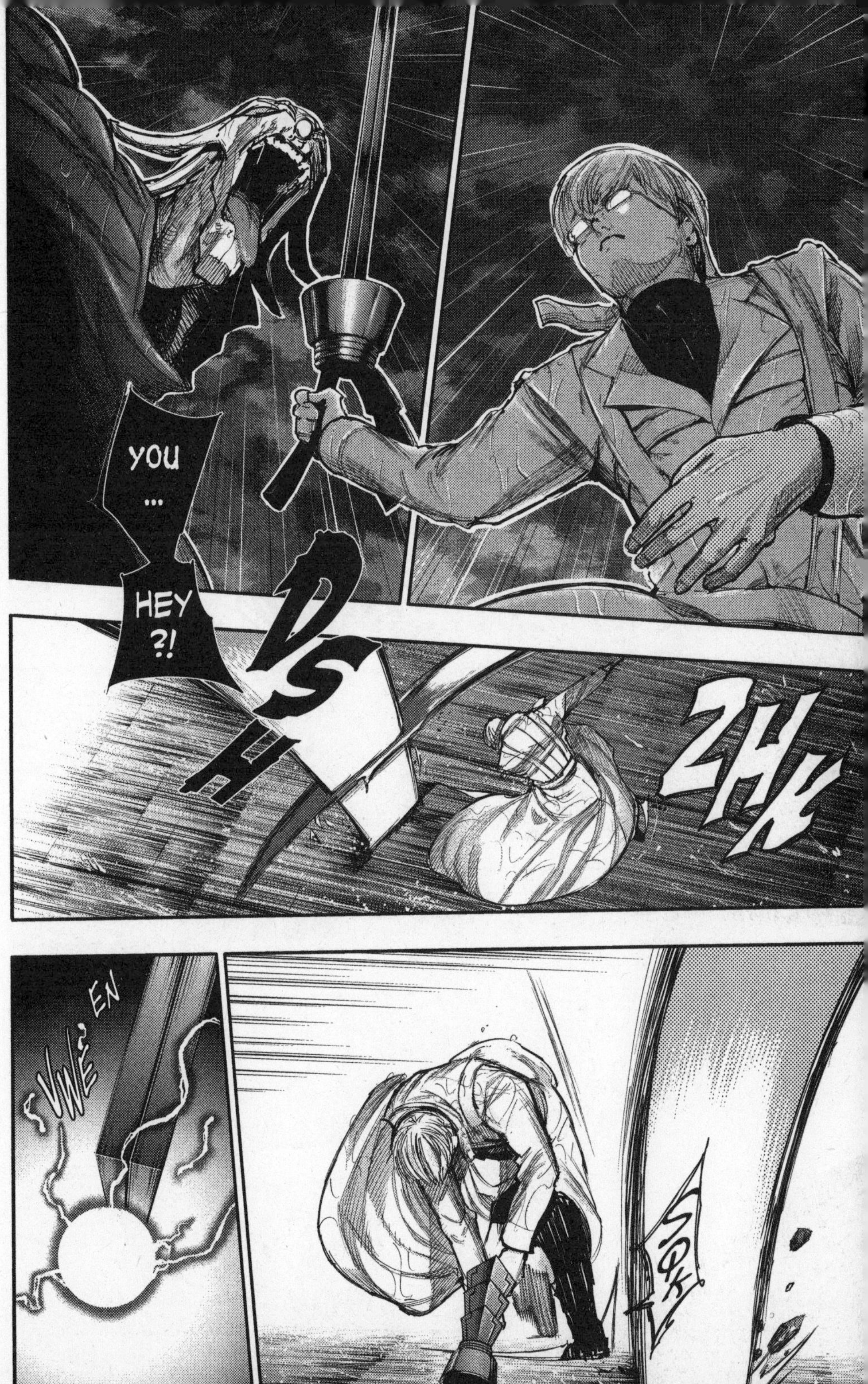
YOU ... HEY ?!
ZHK
DSH
SQK
VWEEN

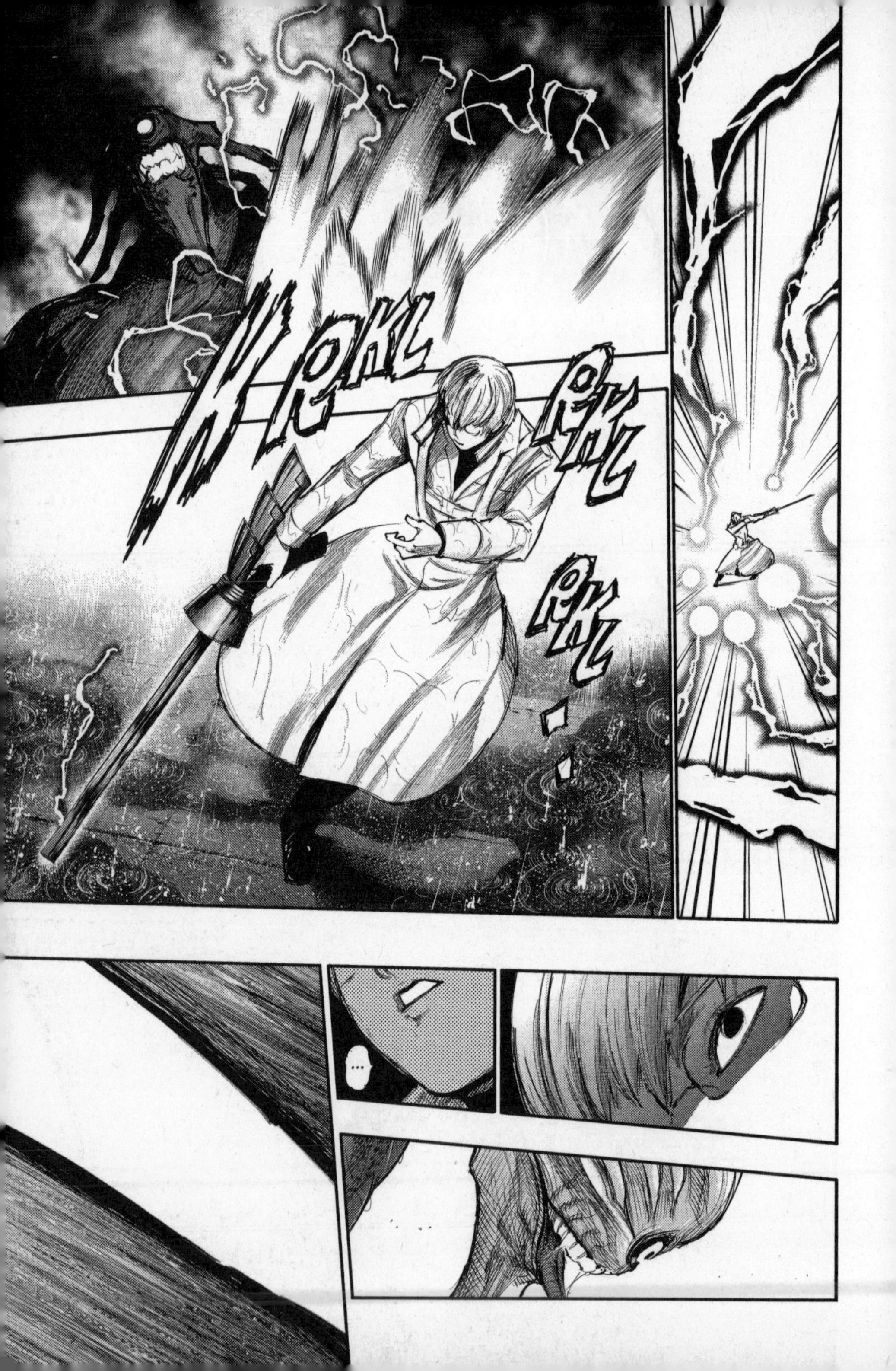
KRKL
RKL
RKL
...

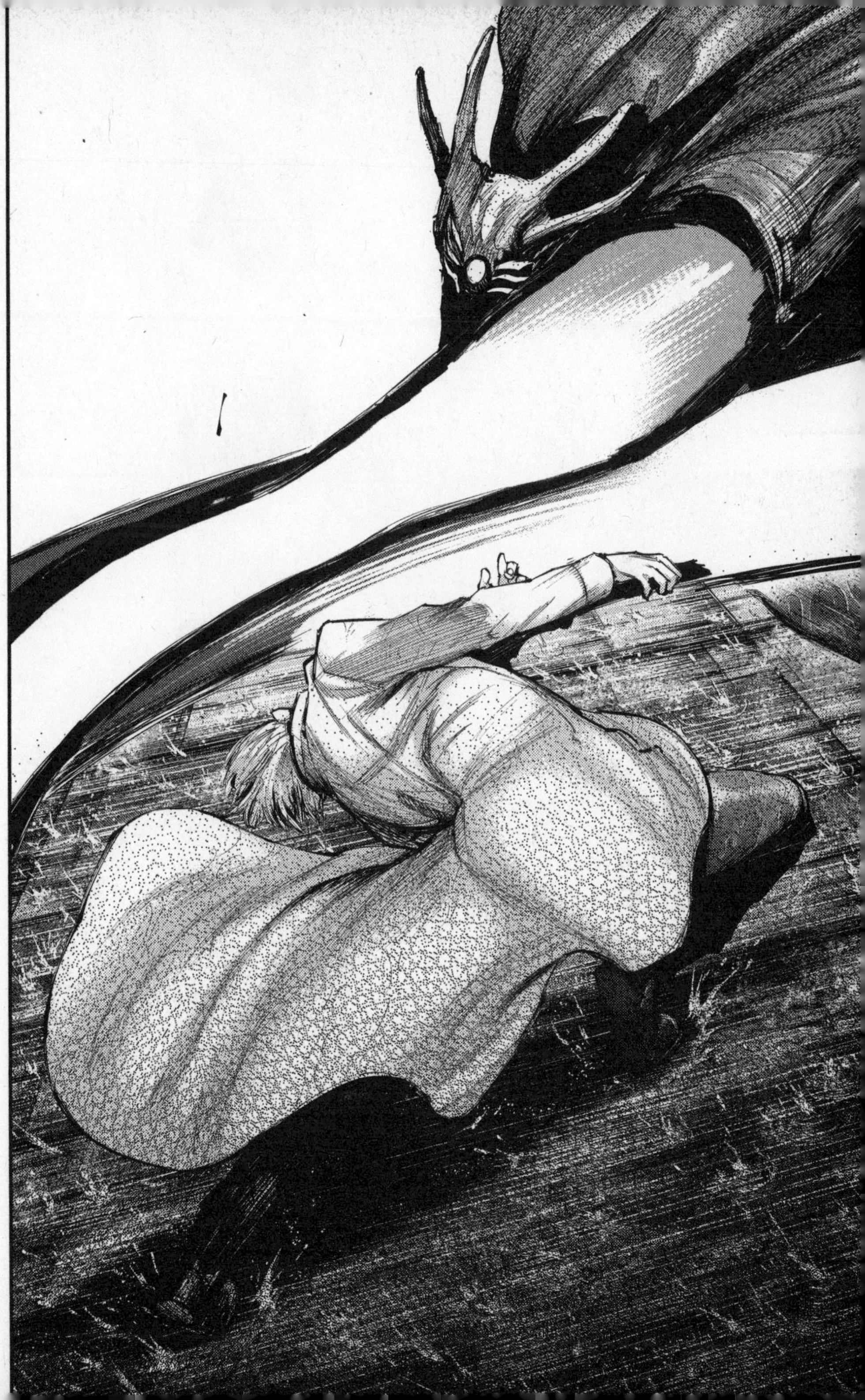

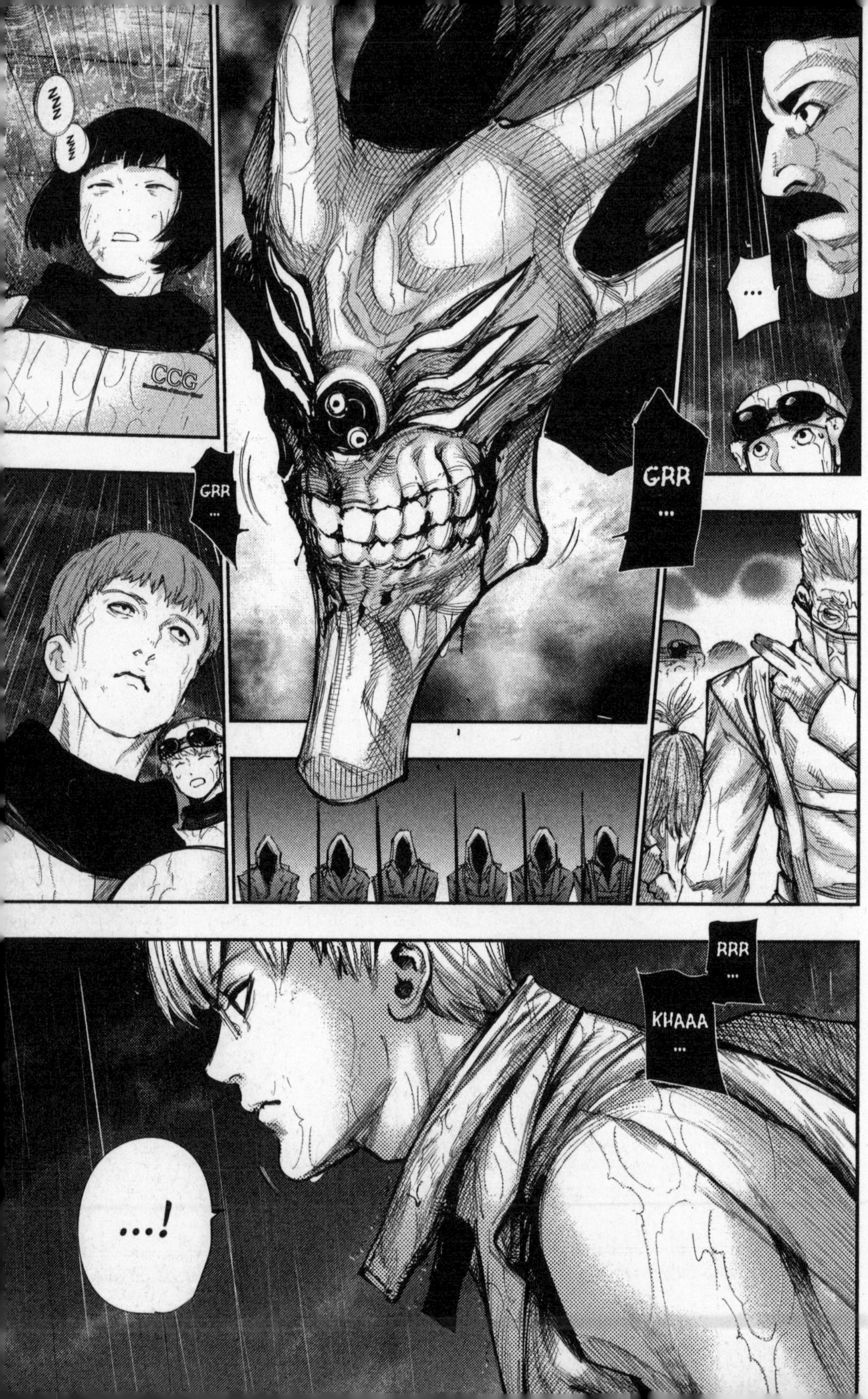
...
GRR ...
NNN NNN
GRR ...
RRR ...
KHAAA ...
...!

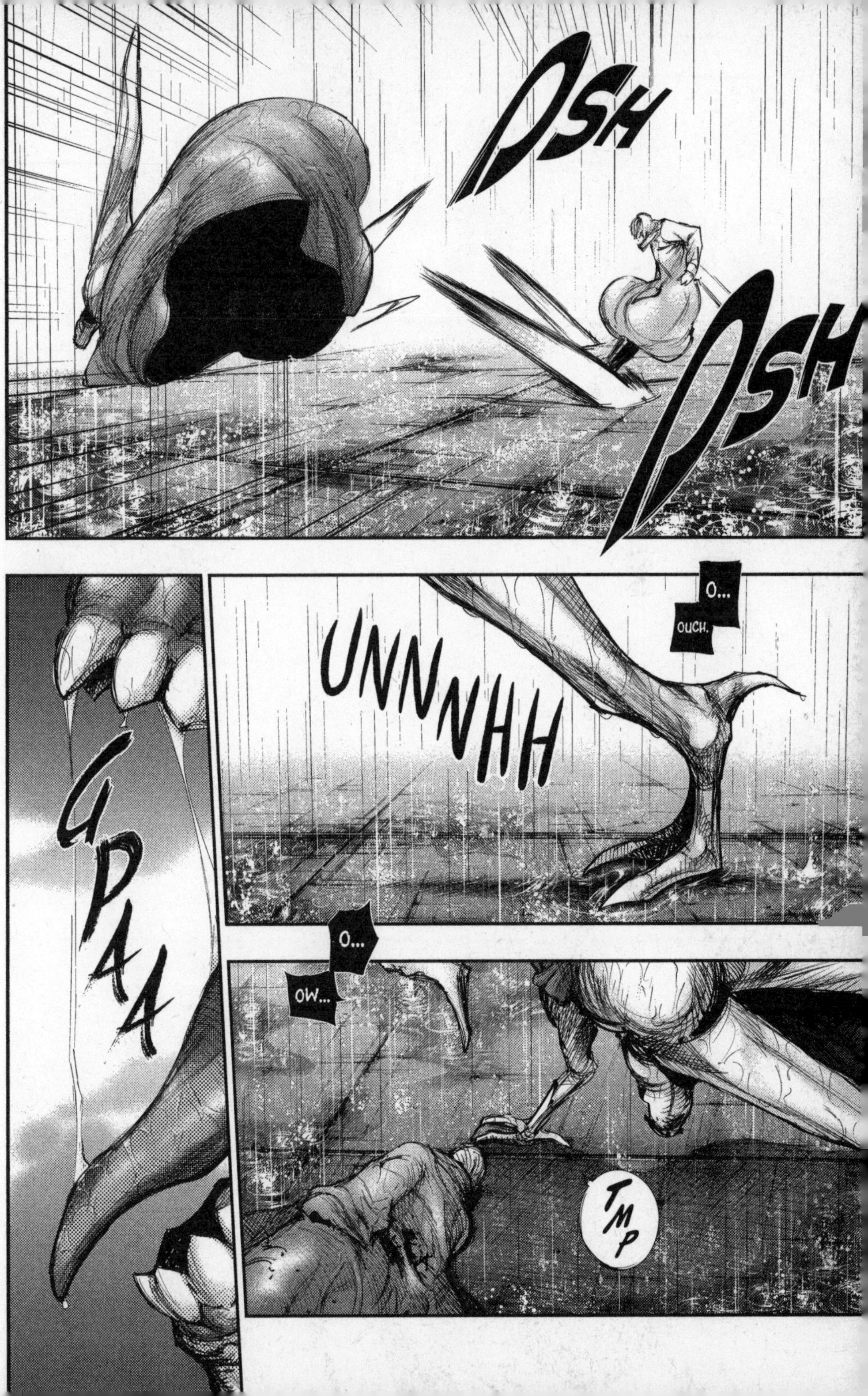
DSH
DSH
O...
OUCH.
UNNNHH
O...
OW...
TMP
GPAA

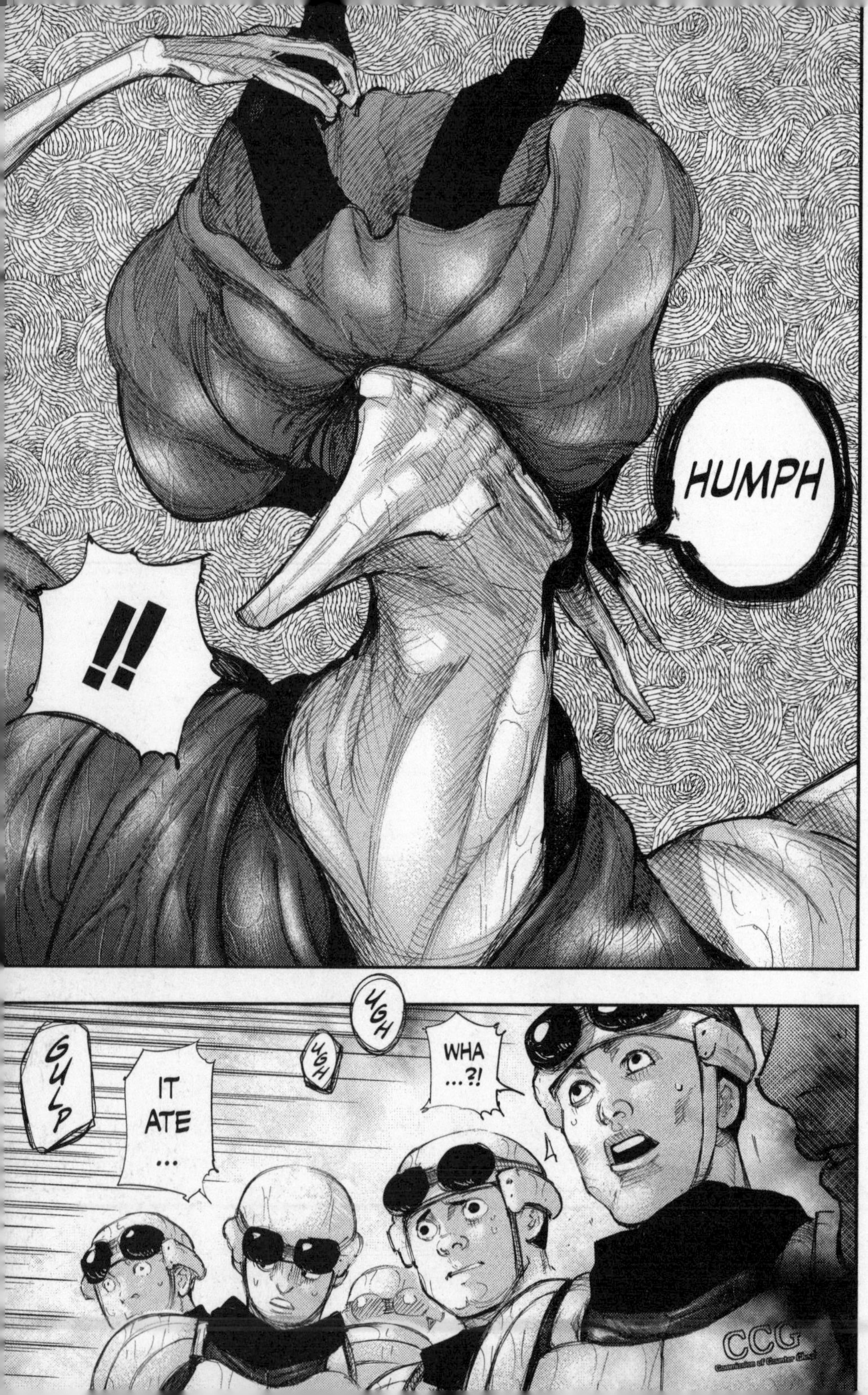
HUMPH
!!
WHA ...?!
UGH
UGH
IT ATE ...
GULP
CCG

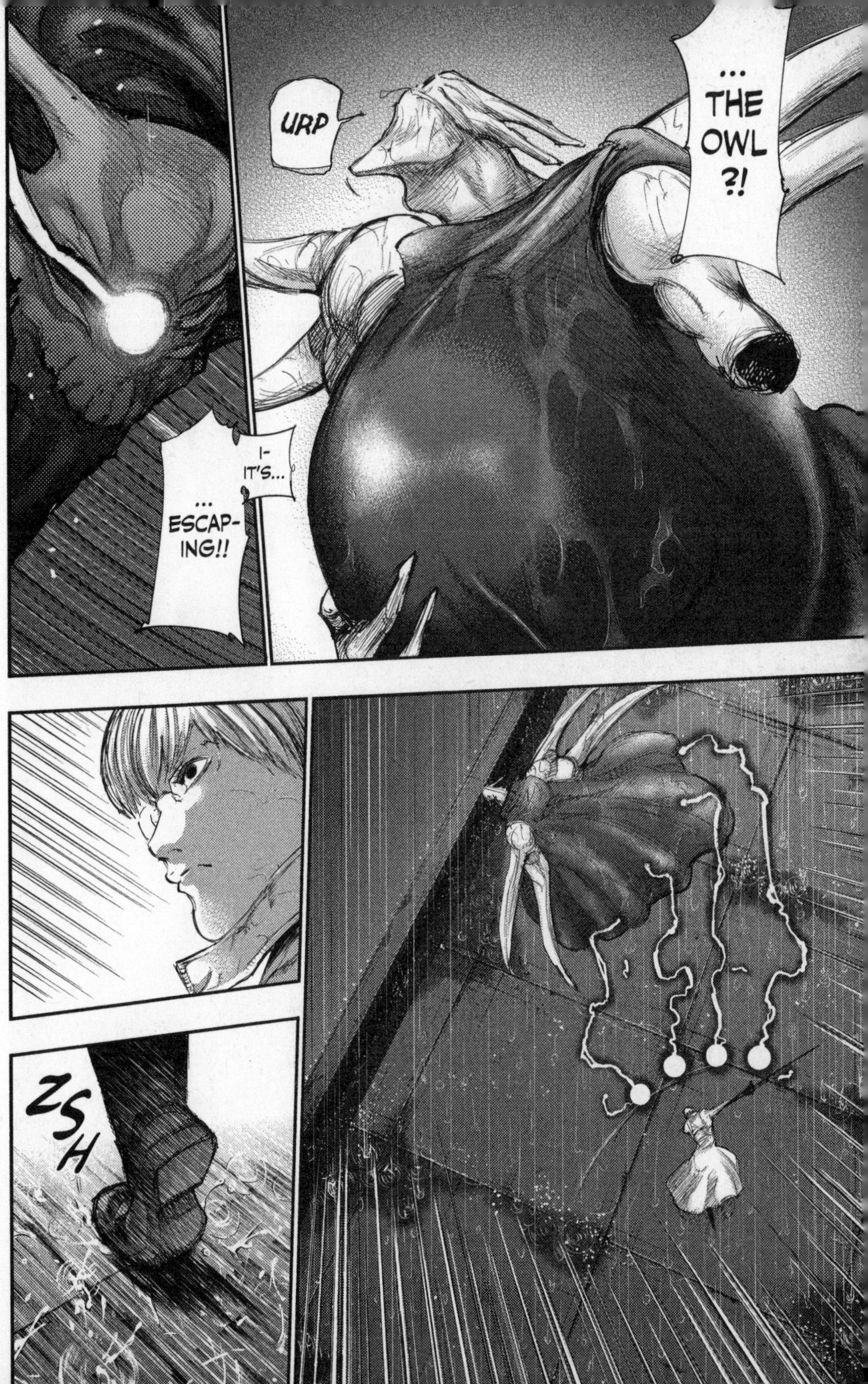
... THE OWL ?!
URP
I- IT'S...
... ESCAP-ING!!
ZSH

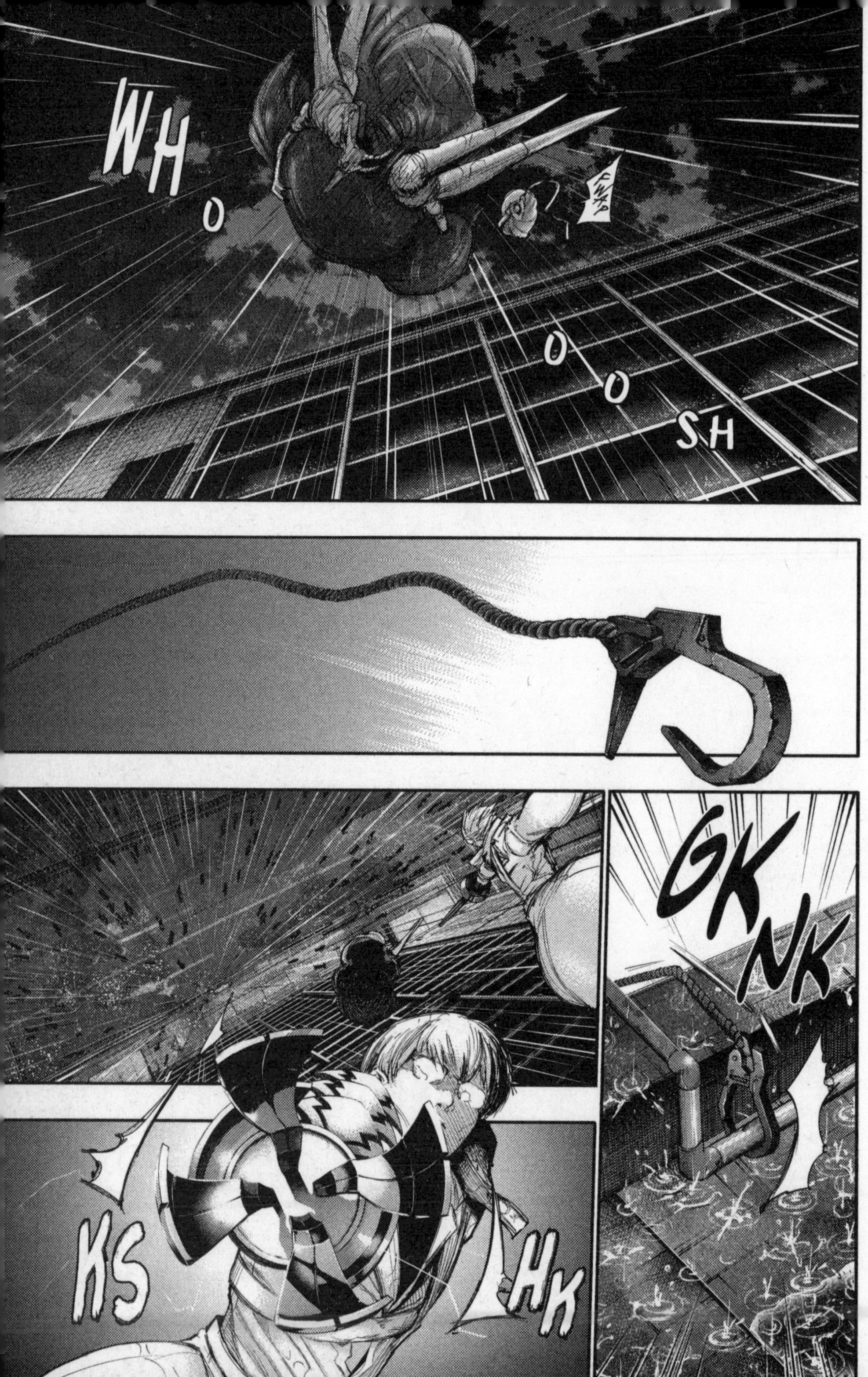
FWAP
WHOOOOSH
GKNK
KSHK

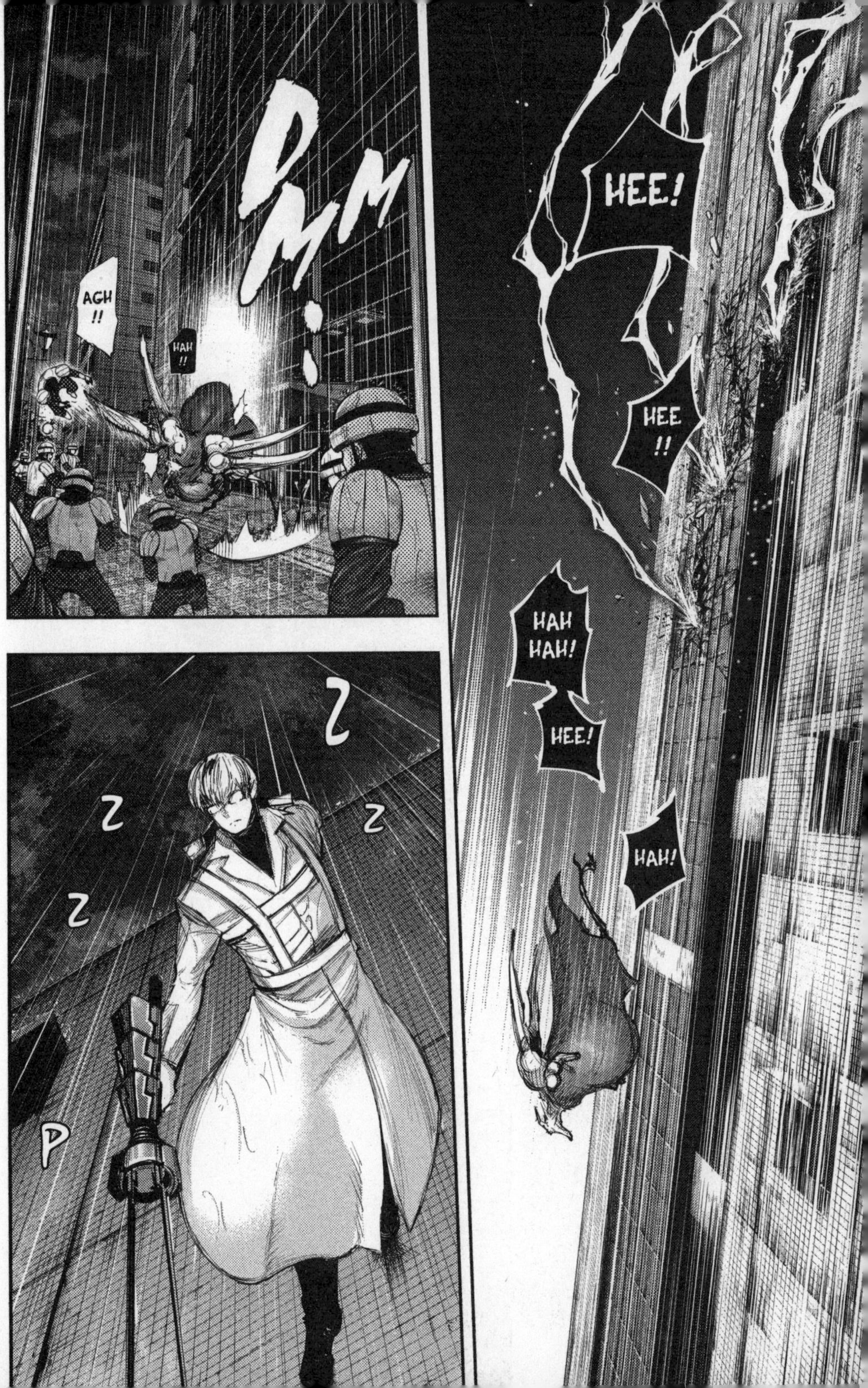
HEE!
HEE
!!
HAH
HAH!
HEE!
HAH!
DMM
AGH
!!
HAH
!!
Z
Z
Z
Z
P

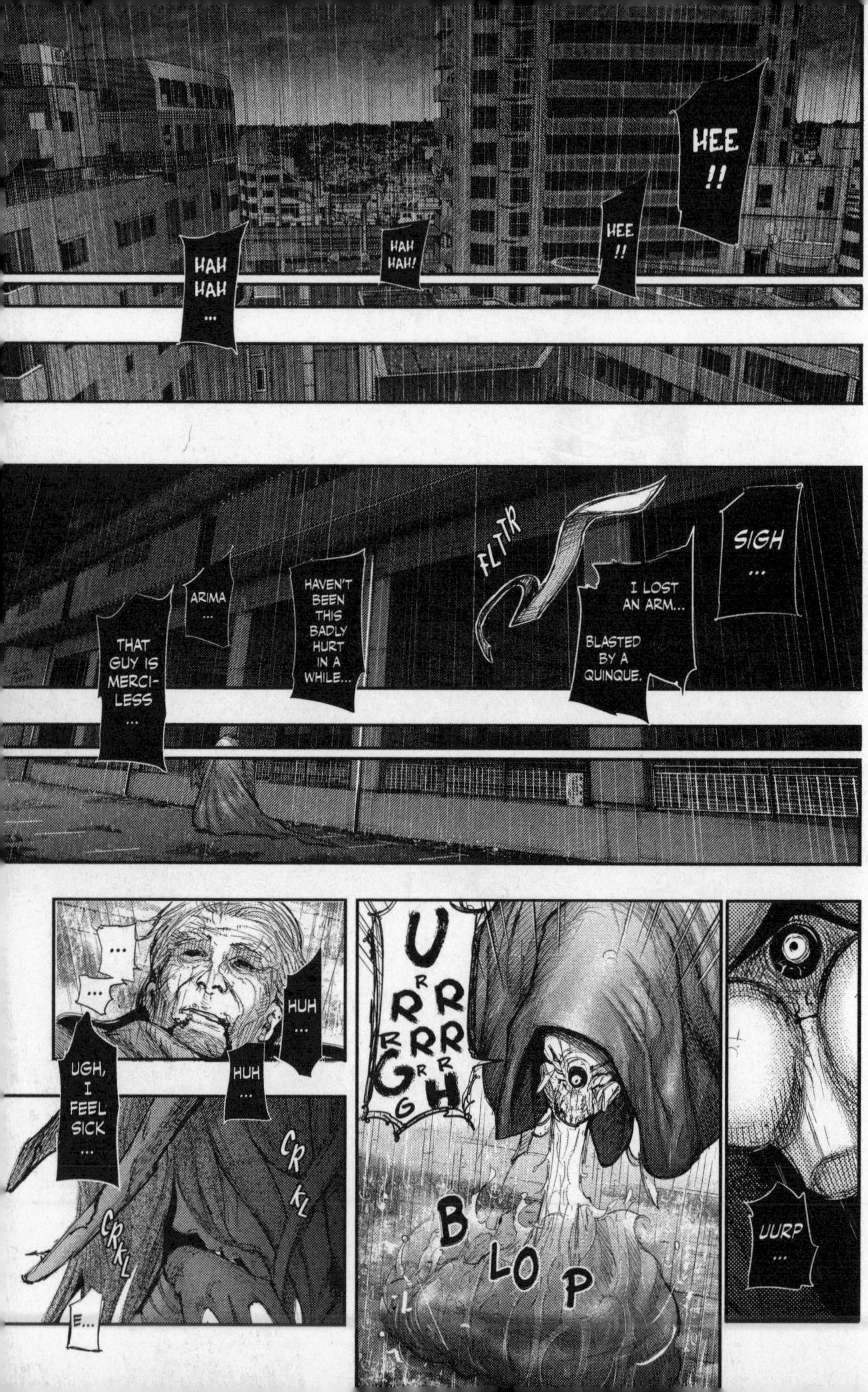
HEE!!
HEE!!
HAH HAH!
HAH HAH...
SIGH...
I LOST AN ARM...
BLASTED BY A QUINQUE.
FLTTR
HAVEN'T BEEN THIS BADLY HURT IN A WHILE...
ARIMA...
THAT GUY IS MERCI-LESS...
UURP...
URRRRRRRRGH
BLOP
HUH...
...
...
HUH...
UGH, I FEEL SICK...
CRKL
CRKL
E...

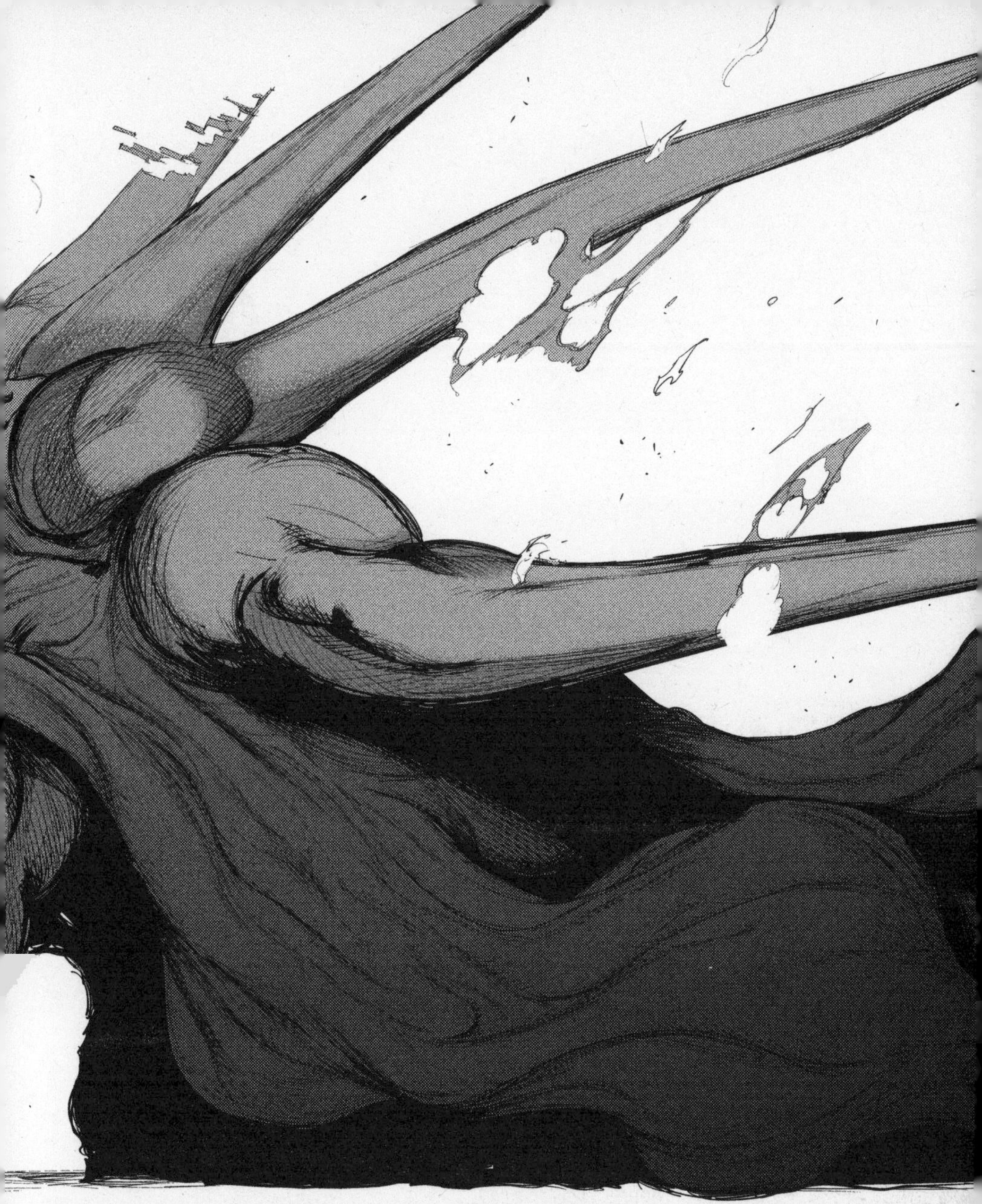

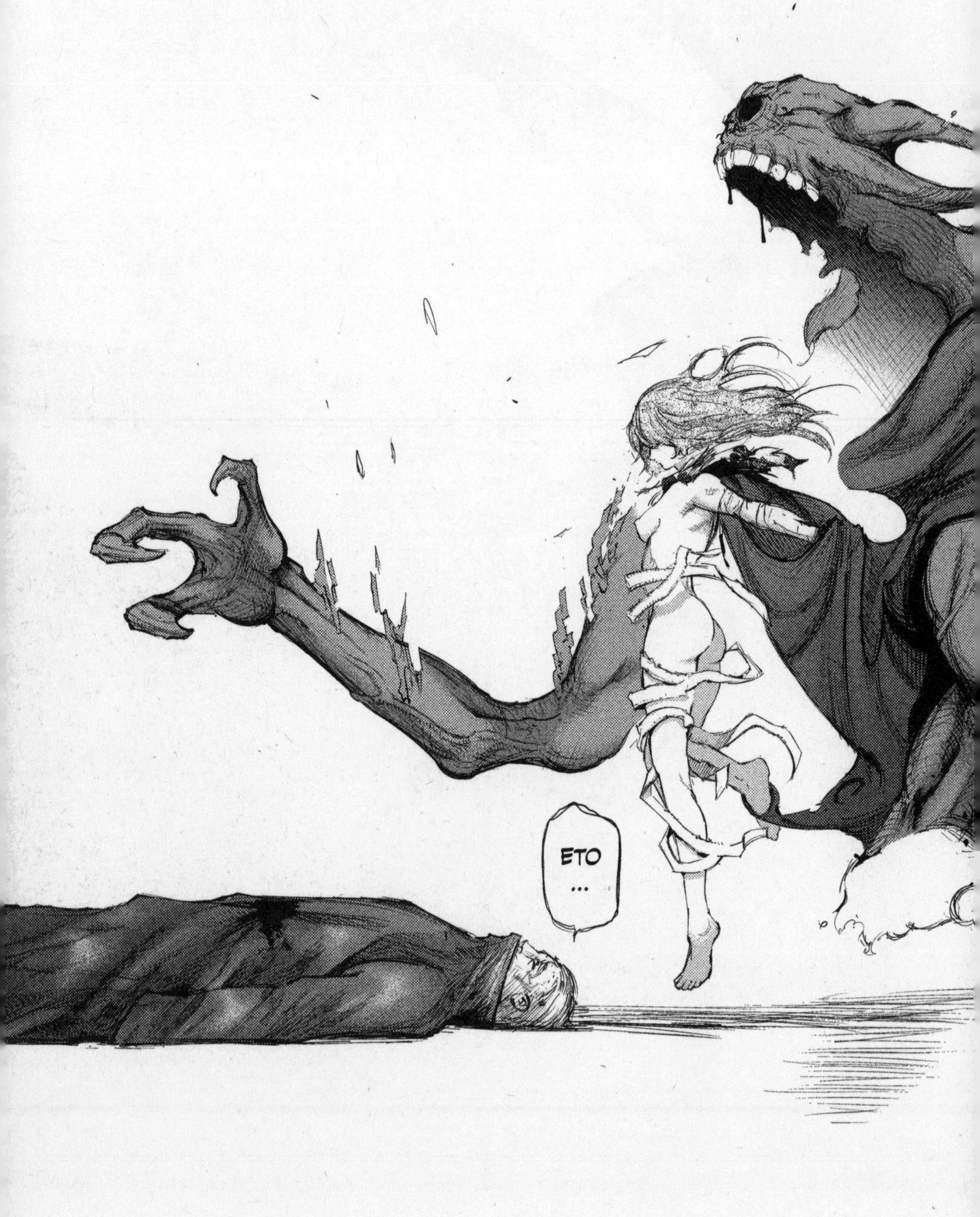
ETO
...

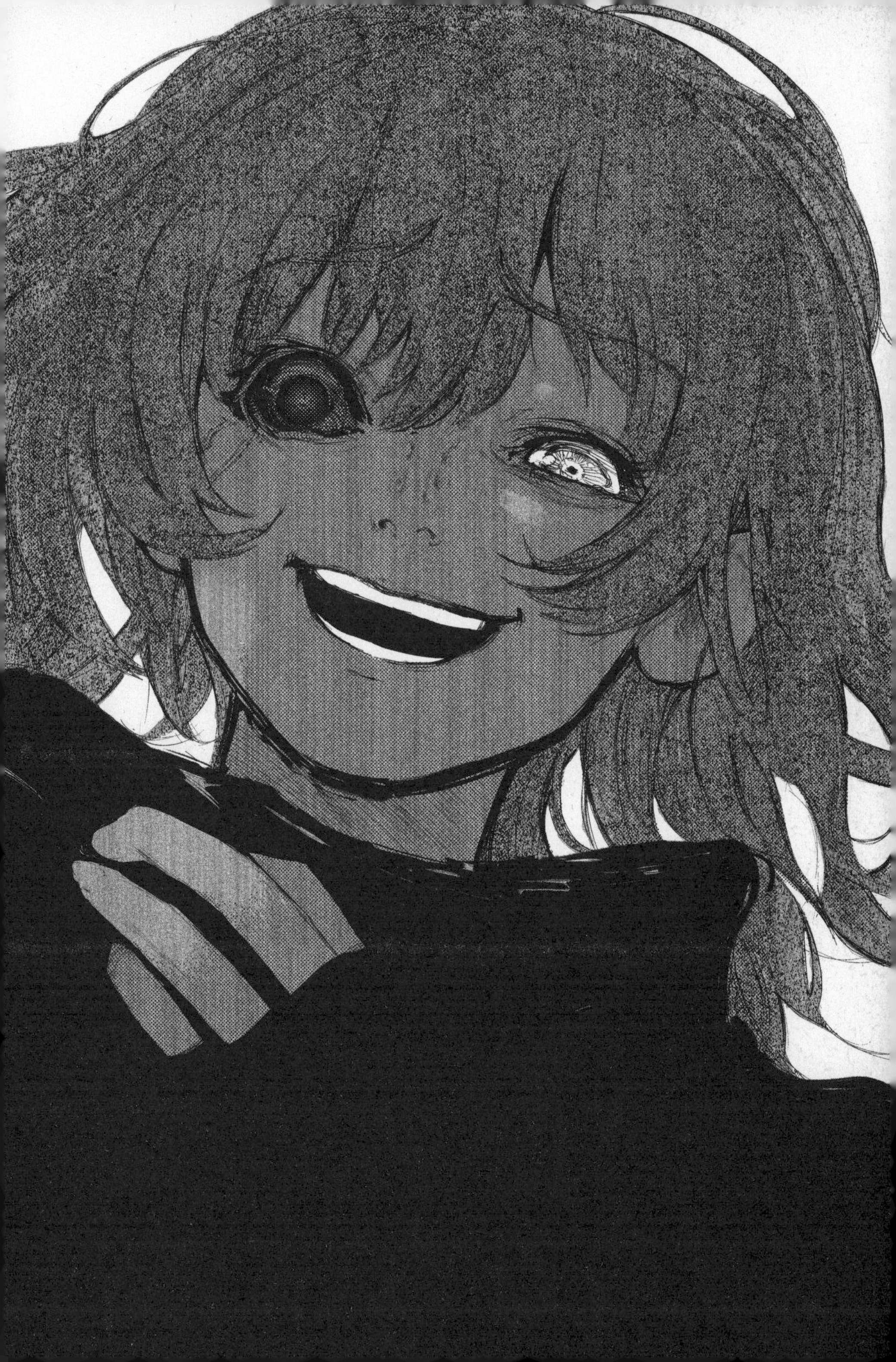

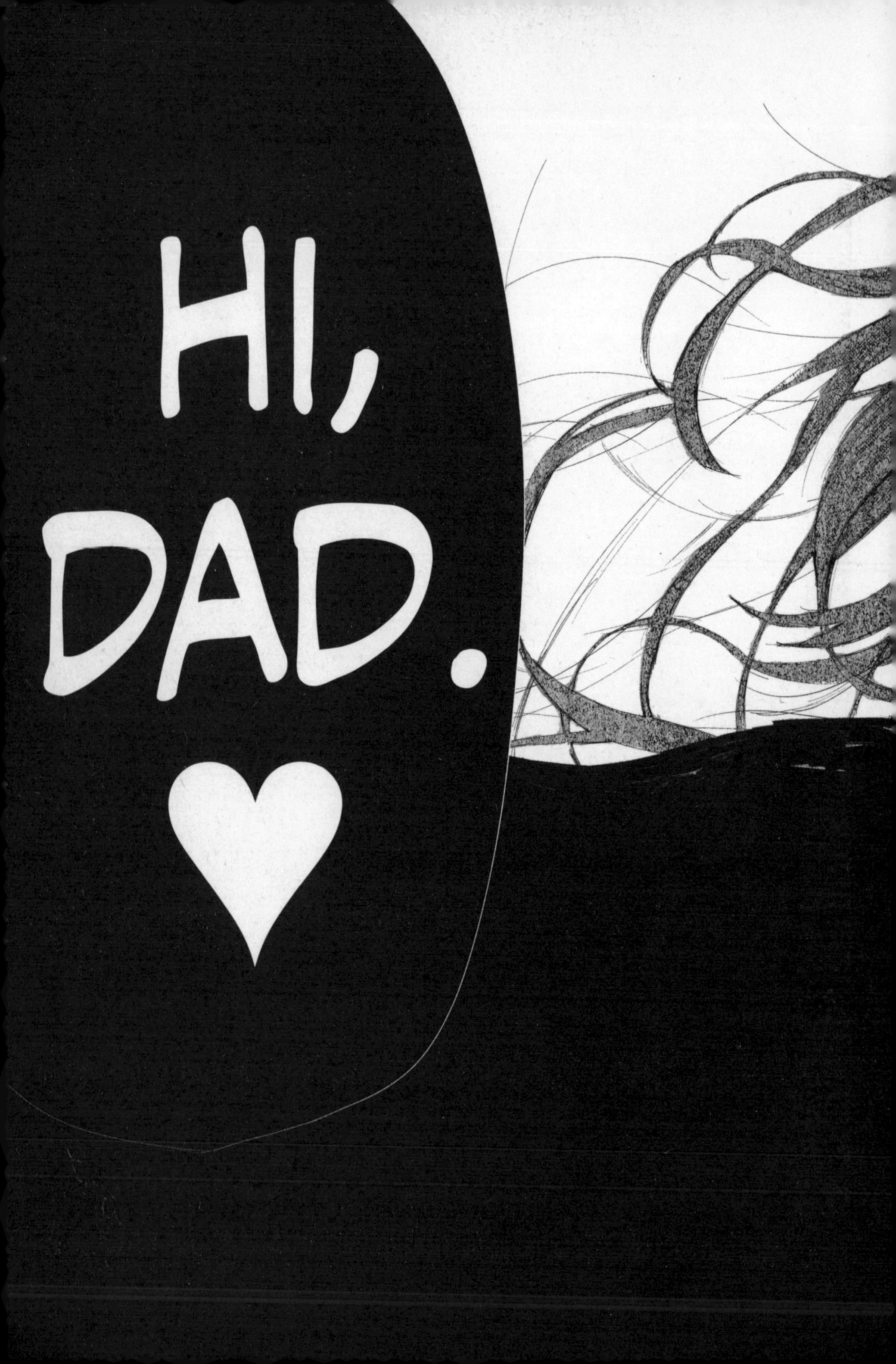
HI, DAD. ♥

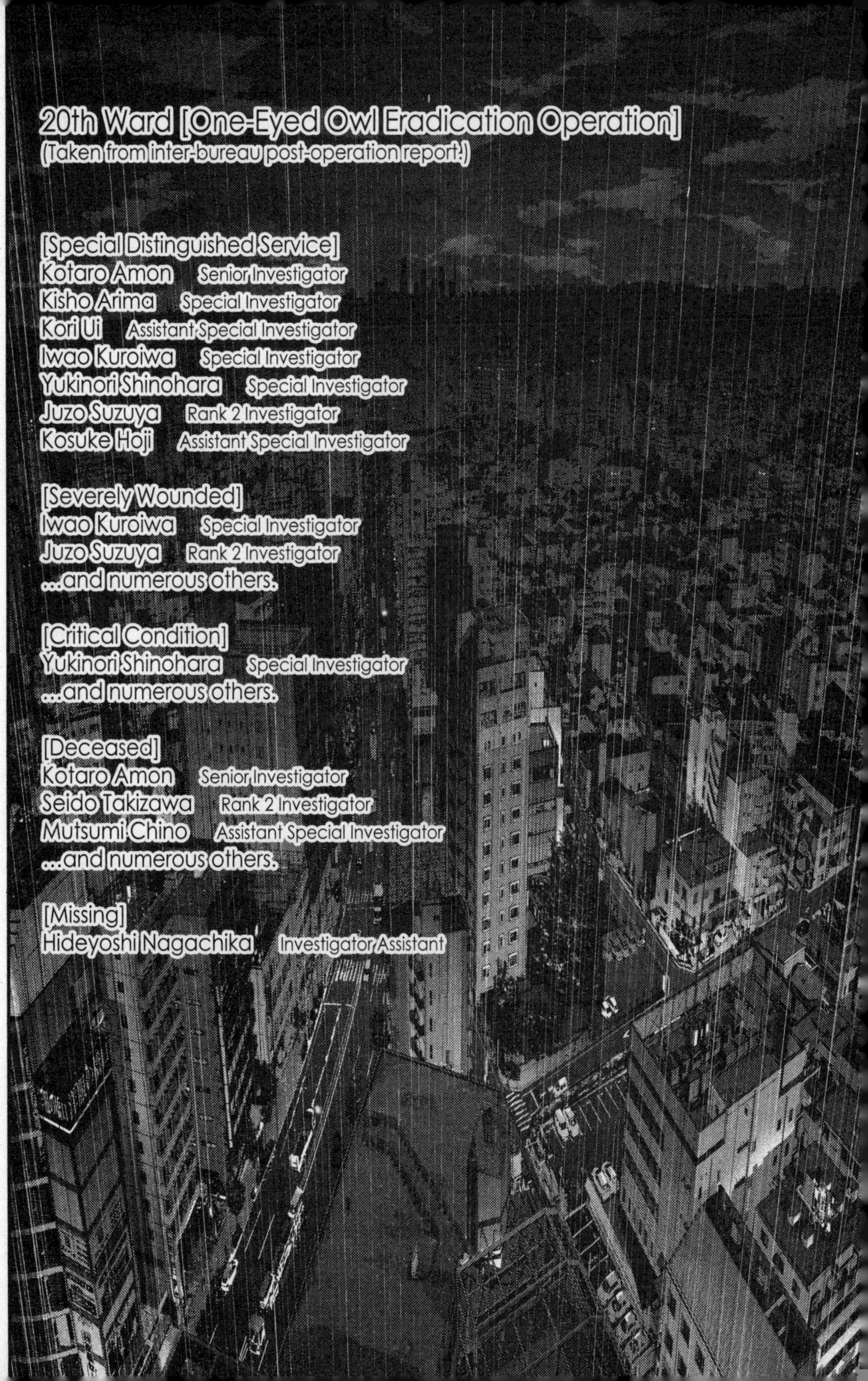
20th Ward [One-Eyed Owl Eradication Operation]
(Taken from inter-bureau post-operation report.)
[Special Distinguished Service]
Kotaro Amon Senior Investigator
Kisho Arima Special Investigator
Kori Ui Assistant Special Investigator
Iwao Kuroiwa Special Investigator
Yukinori Shinohara Special Investigator
Juzo Suzuya Rank 2 Investigator
Kosuke Hoji Assistant Special Investigator
[Severely Wounded]
Iwao Kuroiwa Special Investigator
Juzo Suzuya Rank 2 Investigator
...and numerous others.
[Critical Condition]
Yukinori Shinohara Special Investigator
...and numerous others.
[Deceased]
Kotaro Amon Senior Investigator
Seido Takizawa Rank 2 Investigator
Mutsumi Chino Assistant Special Investigator
...and numerous others.
[Missing]
Hideyoshi Nagachika Investigator Assistant

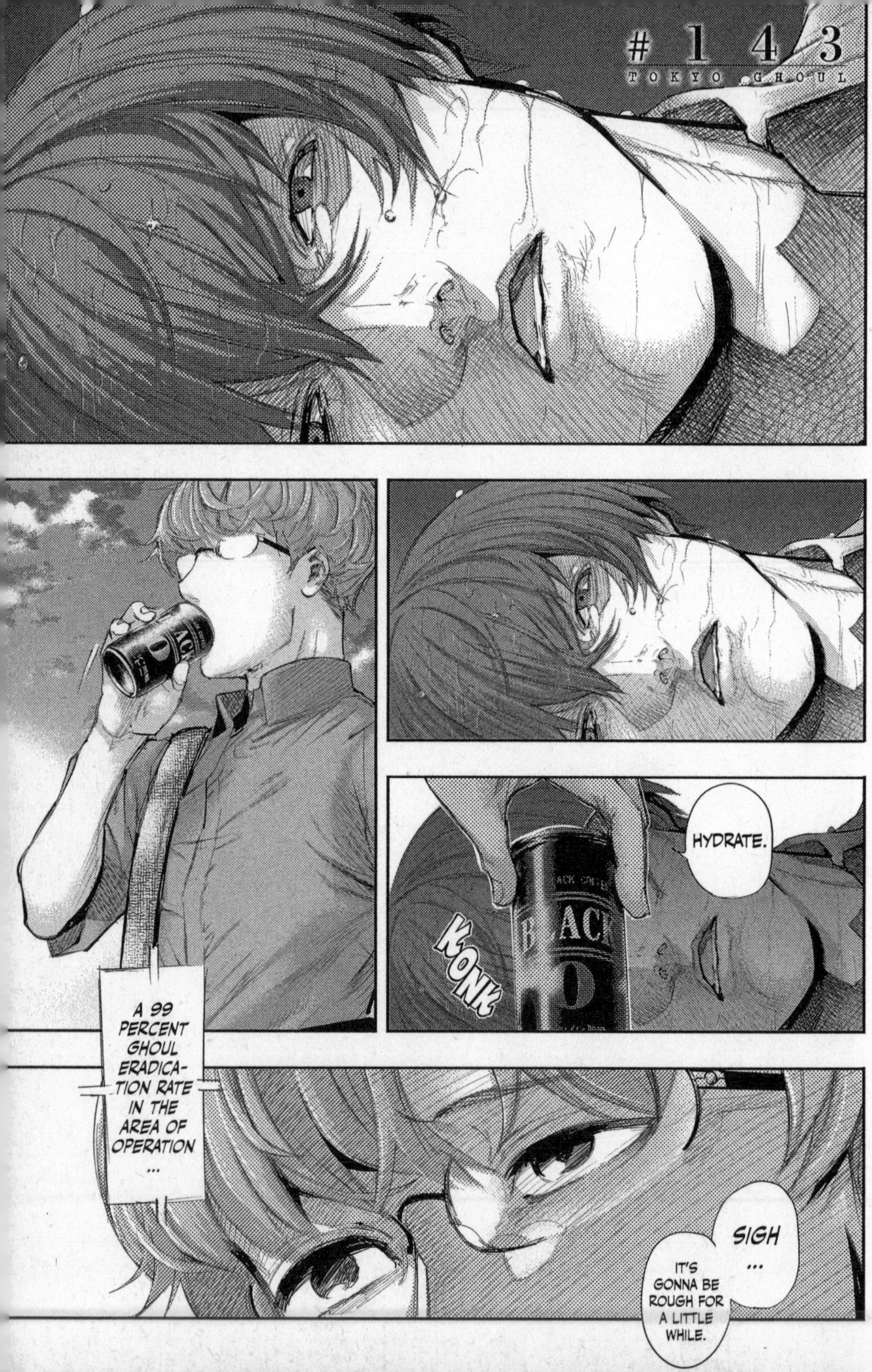
#143
TOKYO GHOUL
HYDRATE.
KONK
A 99 PERCENT GHOUL ERADICATION RATE IN THE AREA OF OPERATION ...
SIGH ...
IT'S GONNA BE ROUGH FOR A LITTLE WHILE.

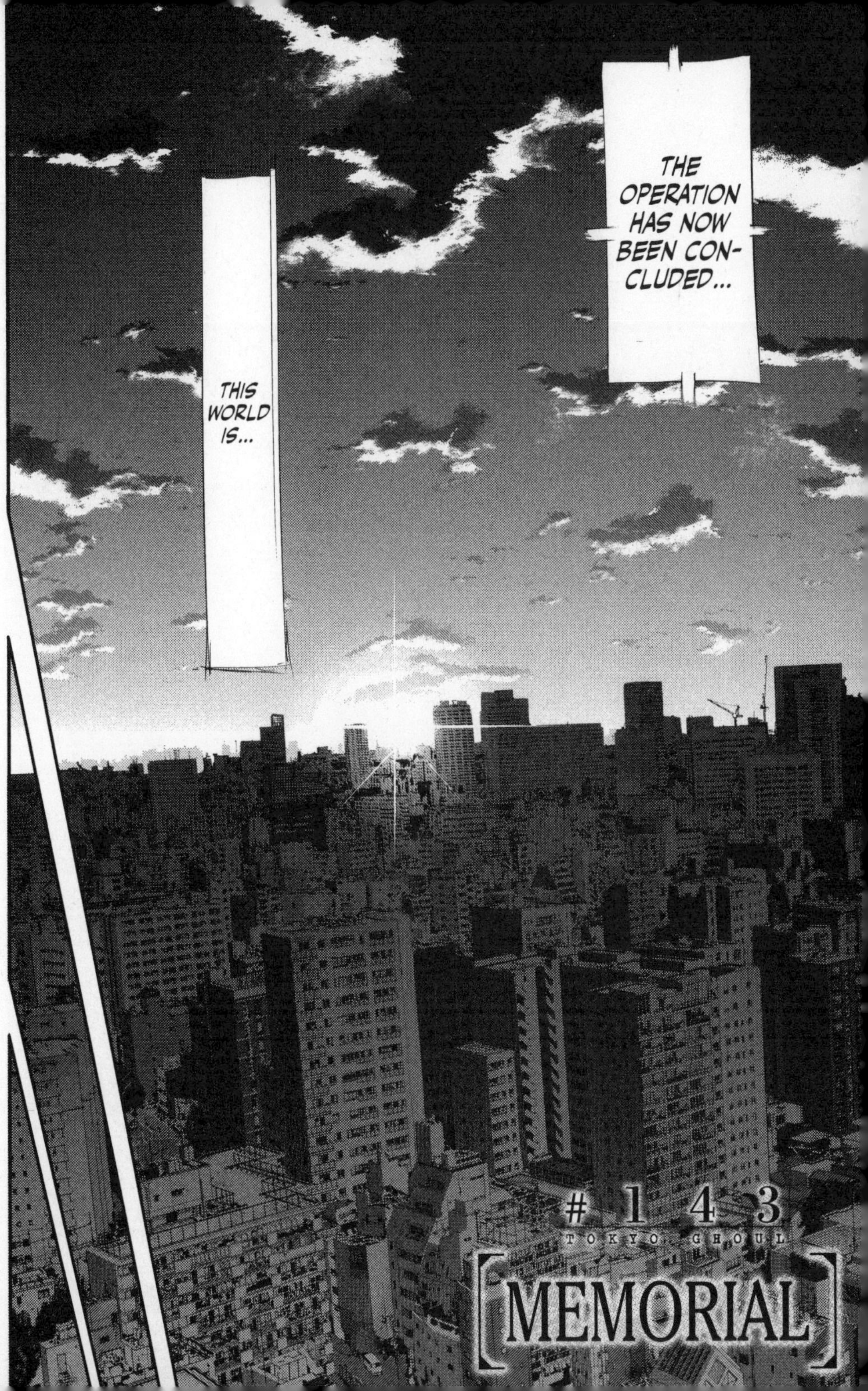
THE OPERATION HAS NOW BEEN CON- CLUDED...
THIS WORLD IS...
#143
TOKYO GHOUL
[MEMORIAL]

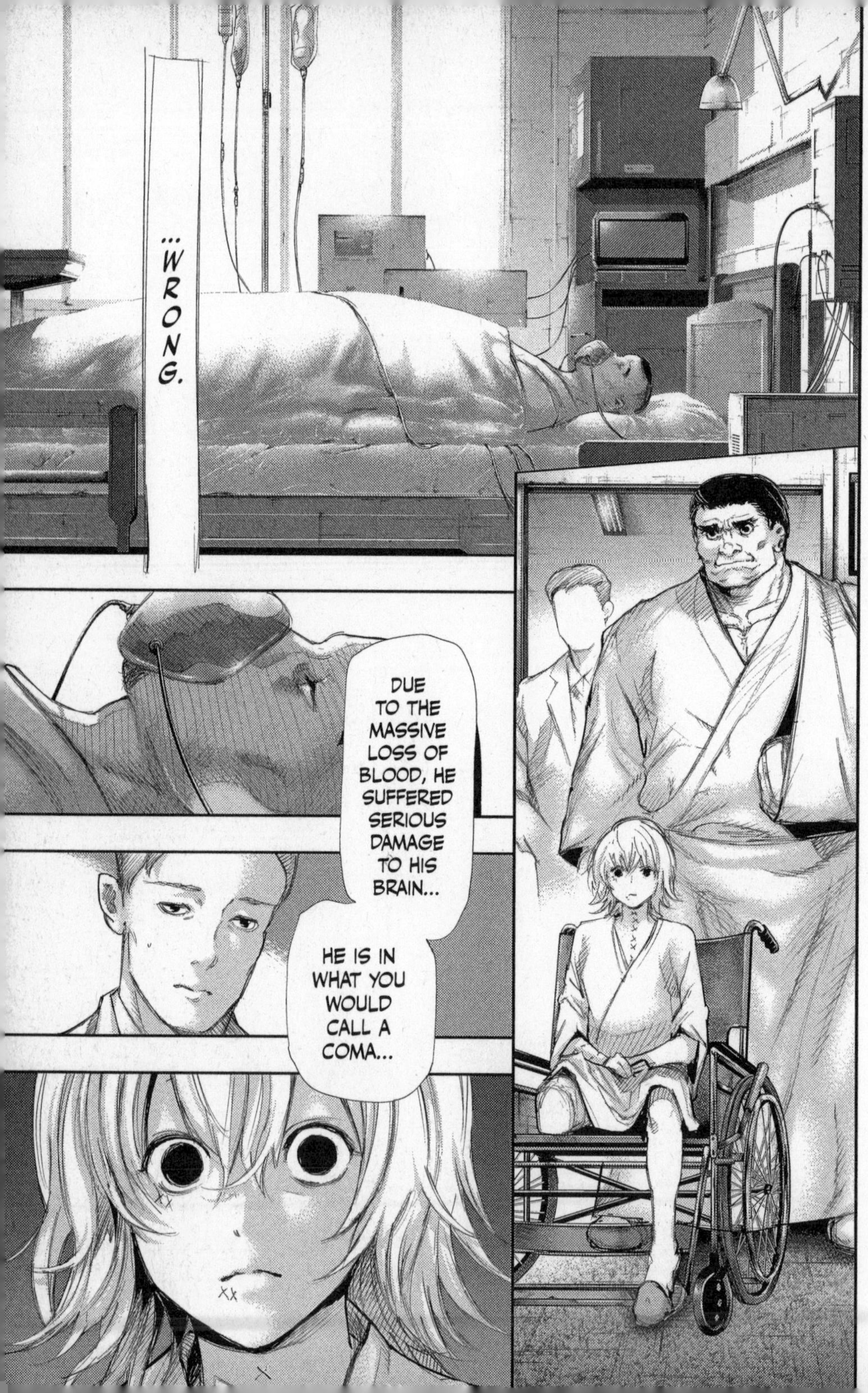
...WRONG.
DUE TO THE MASSIVE LOSS OF BLOOD, HE SUFFERED SERIOUS DAMAGE TO HIS BRAIN...
HE IS IN WHAT YOU WOULD CALL A COMA...

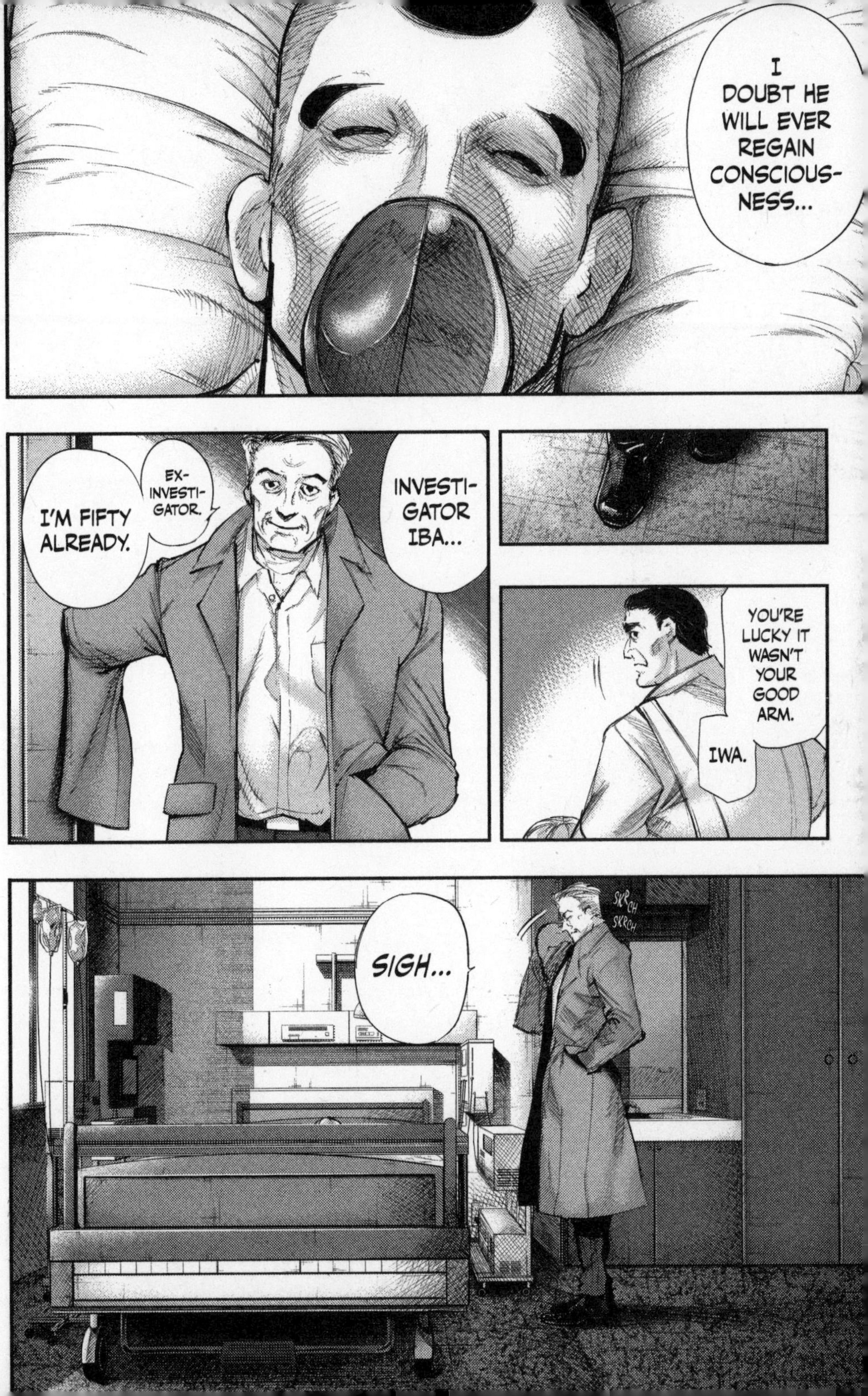
I DOUBT HE WILL EVER REGAIN CONSCIOUSNESS...
YOU'RE LUCKY IT WASN'T YOUR GOOD ARM.
IWA.
INVESTIGATOR IBA...
EX-INVESTIGATOR.
I'M FIFTY ALREADY.
SKRCH SKRCH
SIGH...

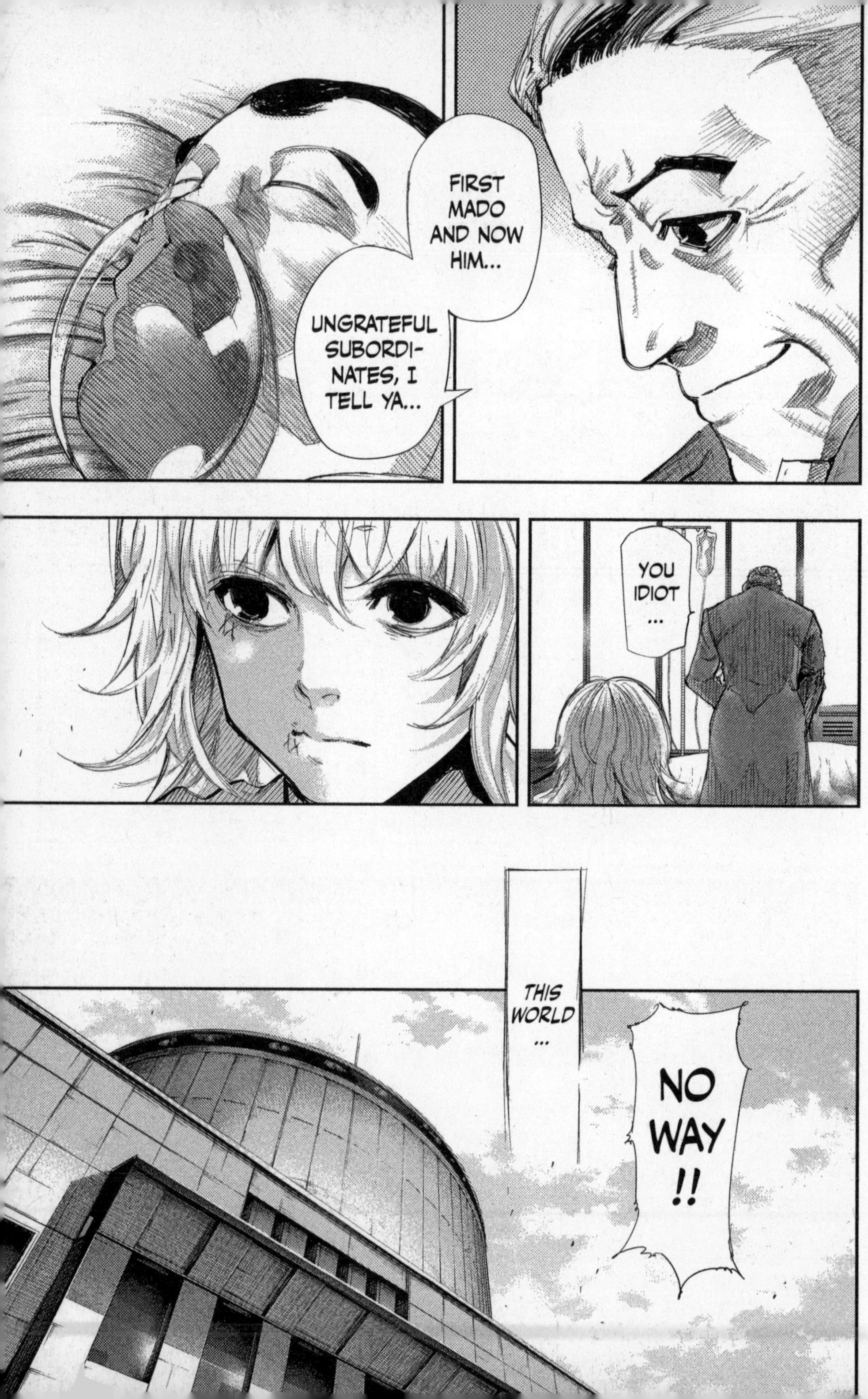
FIRST MADO AND NOW HIM...
UNGRATEFUL SUBORDI-NATES, I TELL YA...
YOU IDIOT ...
THIS WORLD ...
NO WAY !!

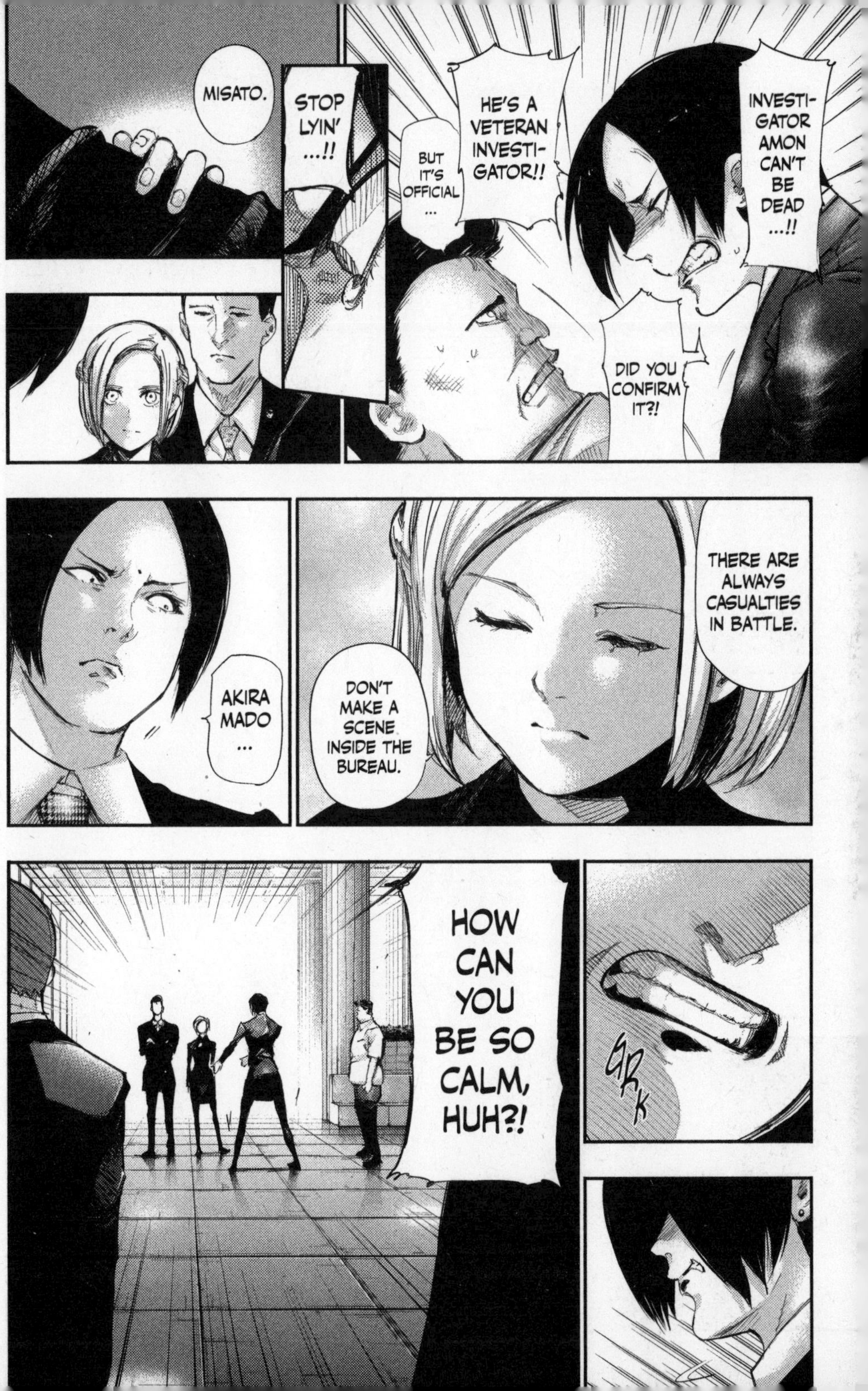
INVESTIGATOR AMON CAN'T BE DEAD ...!!
HE'S A VETERAN INVESTIGATOR!!
DID YOU CONFIRM IT?!
BUT IT'S OFFICIAL ...
STOP LYIN' ...!!
MISATO.
THERE ARE ALWAYS CASUALTIES IN BATTLE.
DON'T MAKE A SCENE INSIDE THE BUREAU.
AKIRA MADO ...
GRK
HOW CAN YOU BE SO CALM, HUH?!

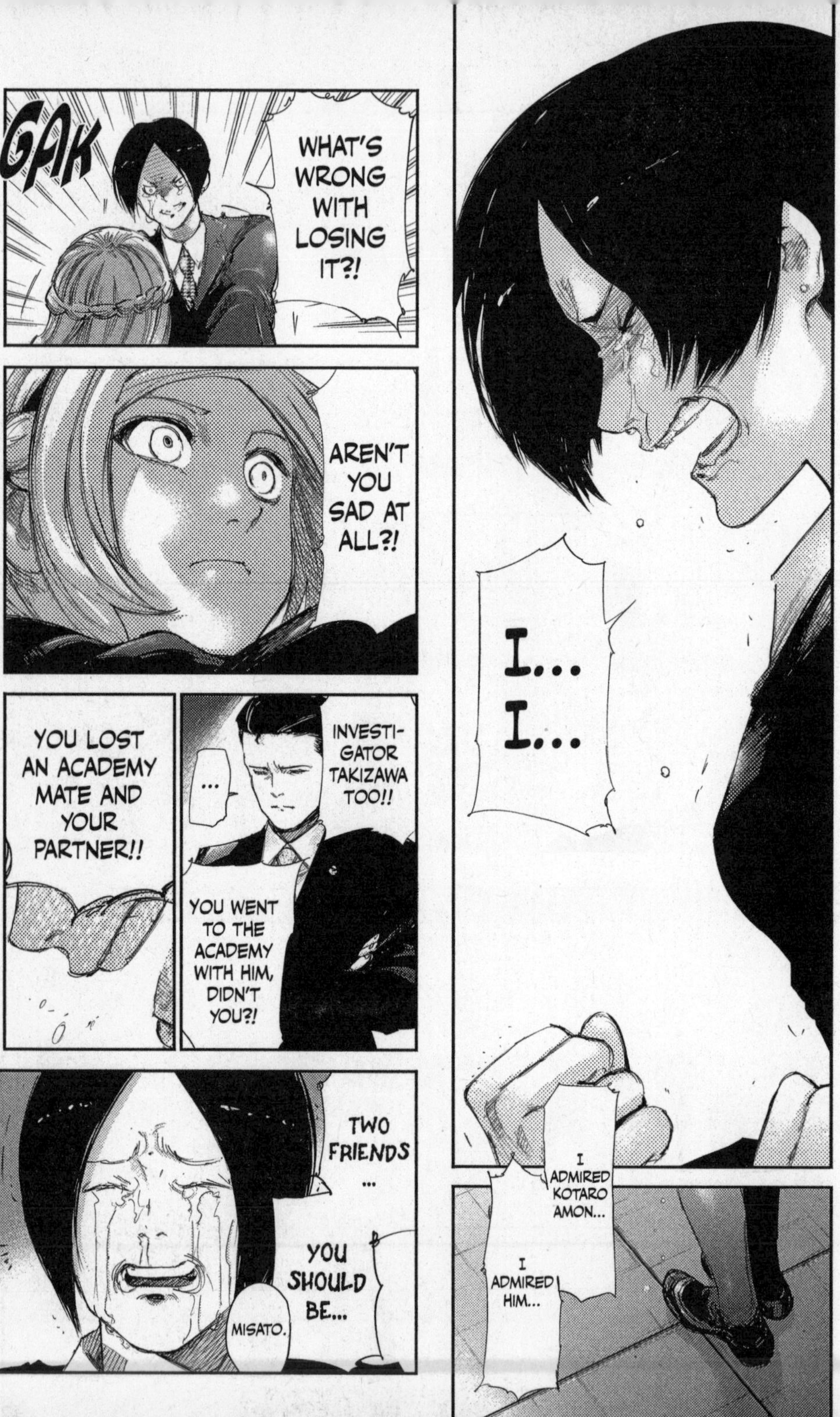
I...
I...
I ADMIRED KOTARO AMON...
I ADMIRED HIM...
GAK
WHAT'S WRONG WITH LOSING IT?!
AREN'T YOU SAD AT ALL?!
INVESTI-GATOR TAKIZAWA TOO!!
...
YOU WENT TO THE ACADEMY WITH HIM, DIDN'T YOU?!
YOU LOST AN ACADEMY MATE AND YOUR PARTNER!!
TWO FRIENDS...
YOU SHOULD BE...
MISATO.

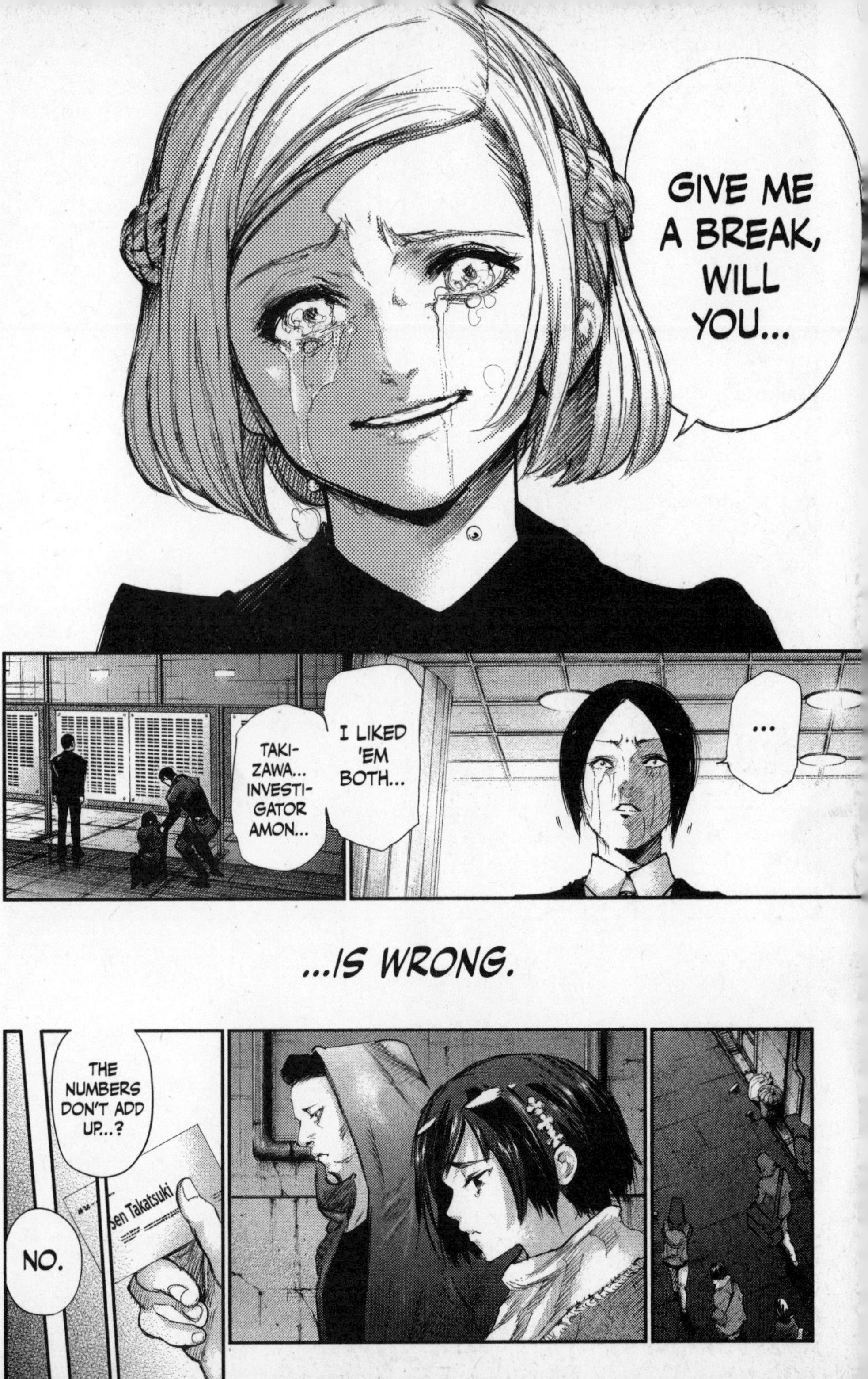
GIVE ME A BREAK, WILL YOU...
...
I LIKED 'EM BOTH...
TAKI-ZAWA... INVESTI-GATOR AMON...
...IS WRONG.
THE NUMBERS DON'T ADD UP...?
NO.

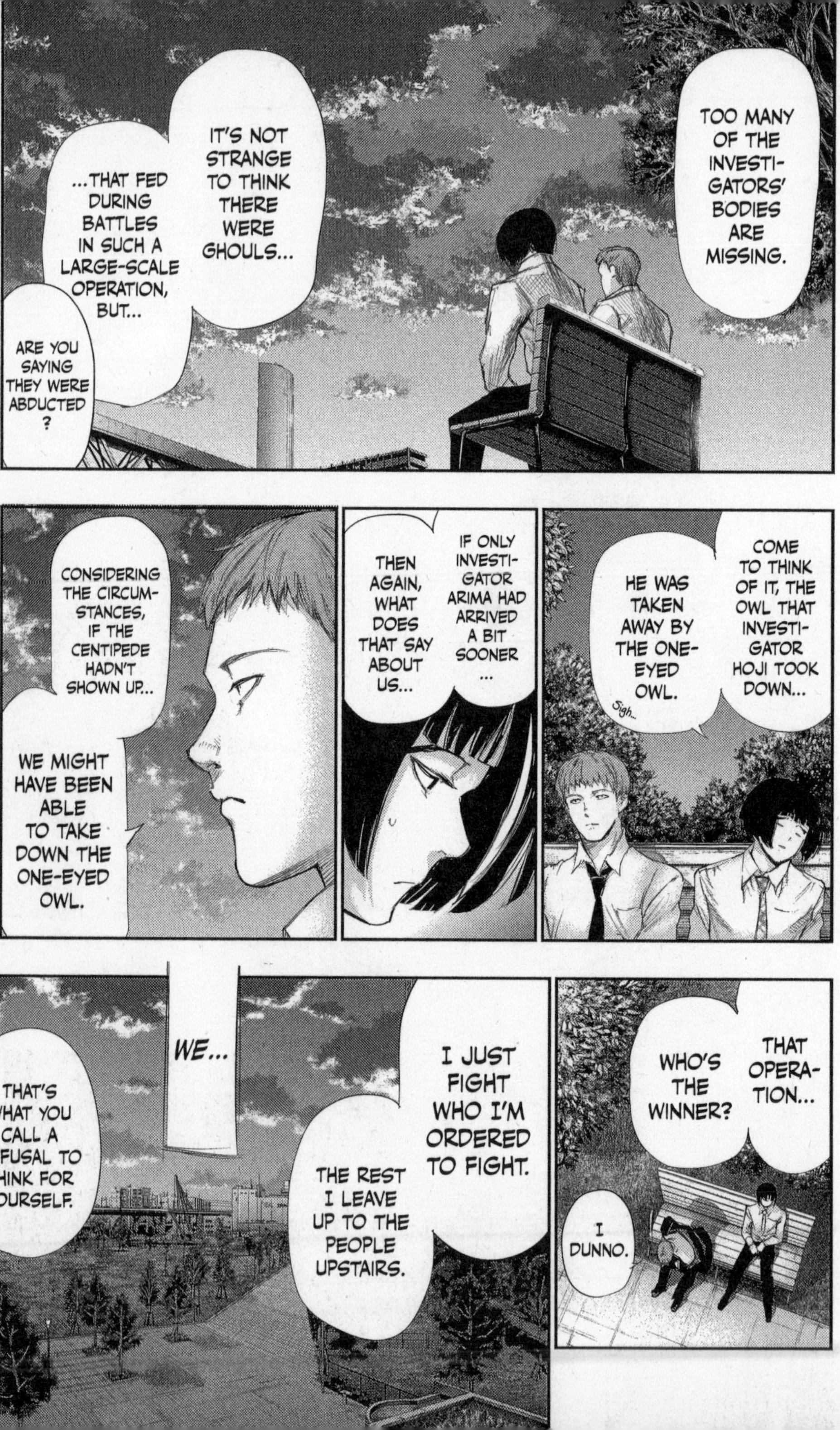

TOO MANY OF THE INVESTIGATORS' BODIES ARE MISSING.
IT'S NOT STRANGE TO THINK THERE WERE GHOULS...
...THAT FED DURING BATTLES IN SUCH A LARGE-SCALE OPERATION, BUT...
ARE YOU SAYING THEY WERE ABDUCTED?
COME TO THINK OF IT, THE OWL THAT INVESTIGATOR HOJI TOOK DOWN...
HE WAS TAKEN AWAY BY THE ONE-EYED OWL.
Sigh...
IF ONLY INVESTIGATOR ARIMA HAD ARRIVED A BIT SOONER...
THEN AGAIN, WHAT DOES THAT SAY ABOUT US...
CONSIDERING THE CIRCUMSTANCES, IF THE CENTIPEDE HADN'T SHOWN UP...
WE MIGHT HAVE BEEN ABLE TO TAKE DOWN THE ONE-EYED OWL.
THAT OPERATION...
WHO'S THE WINNER?
I DUNNO.
I JUST FIGHT WHO I'M ORDERED TO FIGHT.
THE REST I LEAVE UP TO THE PEOPLE UPSTAIRS.
WE...
THAT'S WHAT YOU CALL A REFUSAL TO THINK FOR YOURSELF.

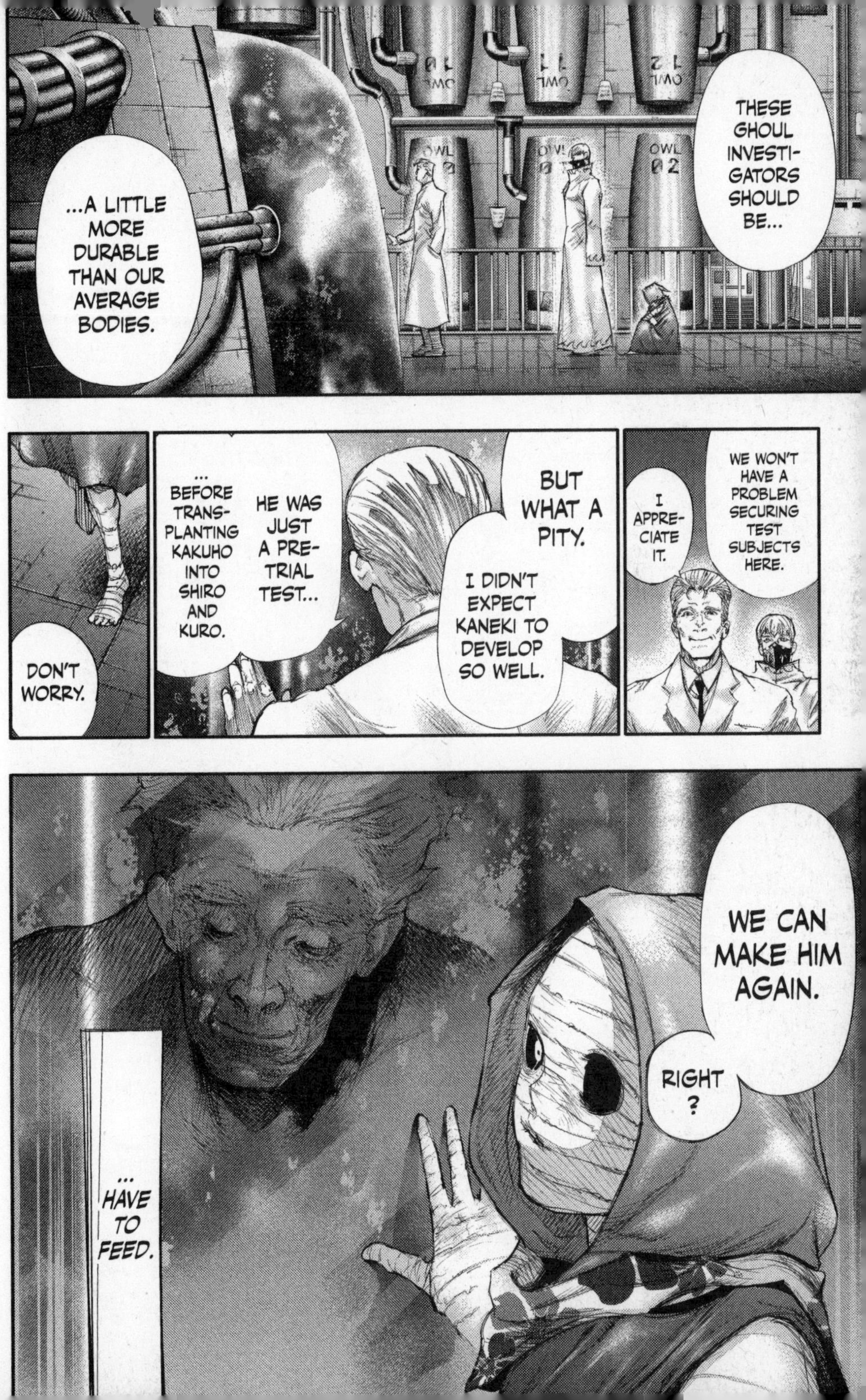
THESE GHOUL INVESTIGATORS SHOULD BE...
...A LITTLE MORE DURABLE THAN OUR AVERAGE BODIES.
WE WON'T HAVE A PROBLEM SECURING TEST SUBJECTS HERE.
I APPRECIATE IT.
BUT WHAT A PITY.
I DIDN'T EXPECT KANEKI TO DEVELOP SO WELL.
HE WAS JUST A PRE-TRIAL TEST...
...BEFORE TRANSPLANTING KAKUHO INTO SHIRO AND KURO.
DON'T WORRY.
WE CAN MAKE HIM AGAIN.
RIGHT?
...HAVE TO FEED.

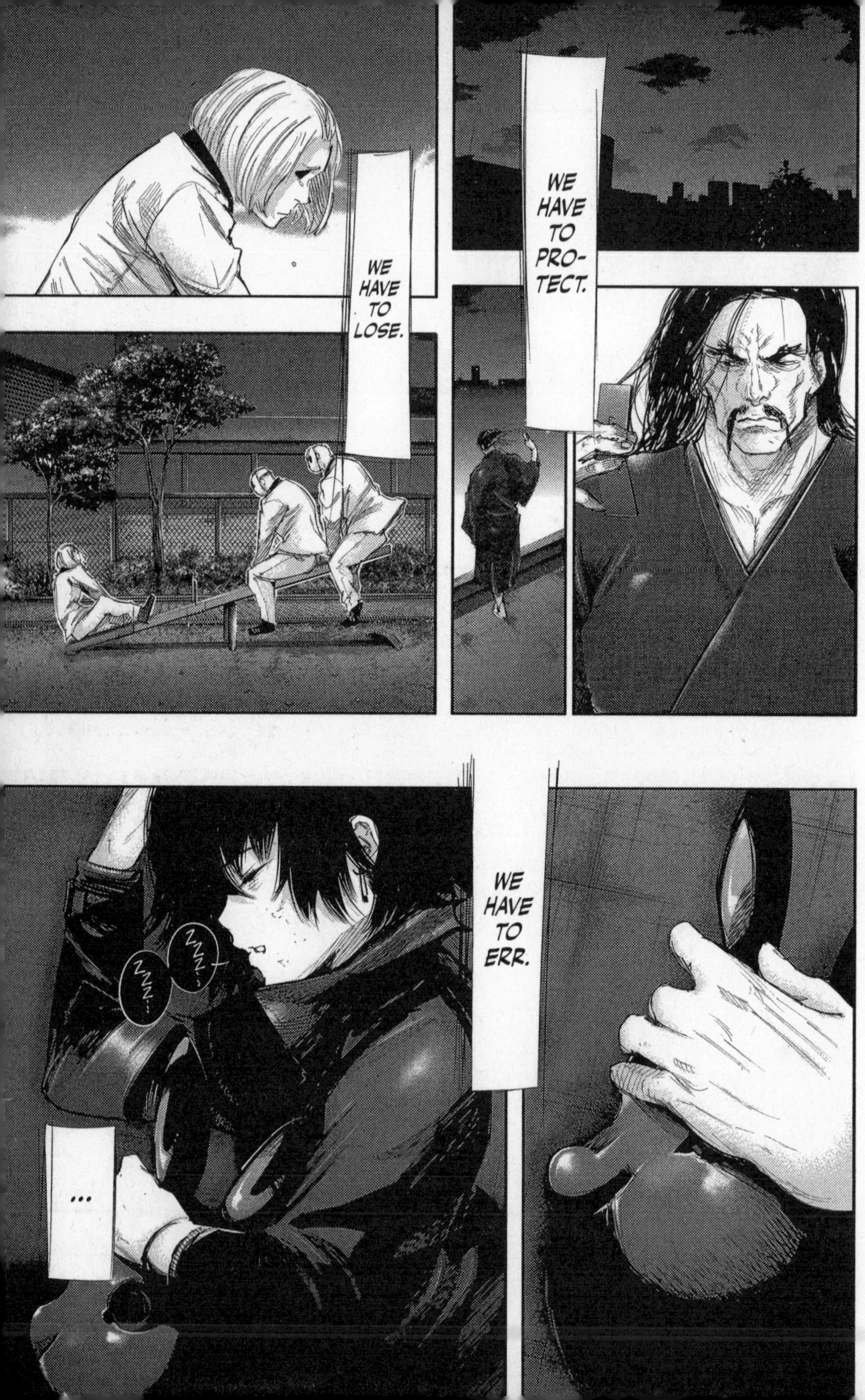
WE HAVE TO PROTECT.
WE HAVE TO LOSE.
WE HAVE TO ERR.
ZZZ...
ZZZ...
...

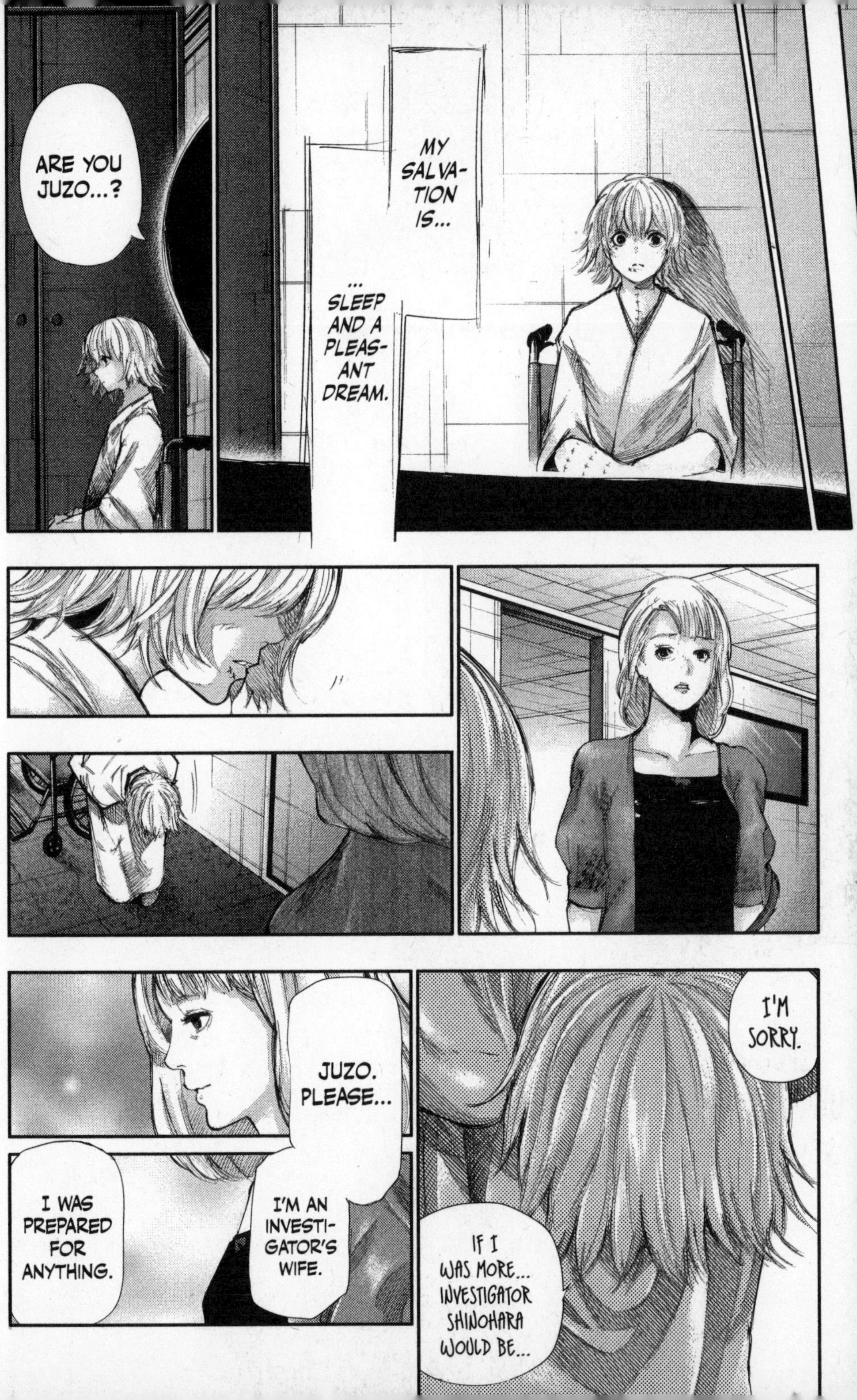
MY SALVATION IS...
...SLEEP AND A PLEASANT DREAM.
ARE YOU JUZO...?
I'M SORRY.
IF I WAS MORE... INVESTIGATOR SHINOHARA WOULD BE...
JUZO. PLEASE...
I'M AN INVESTIGATOR'S WIFE.
I WAS PREPARED FOR ANYTHING.

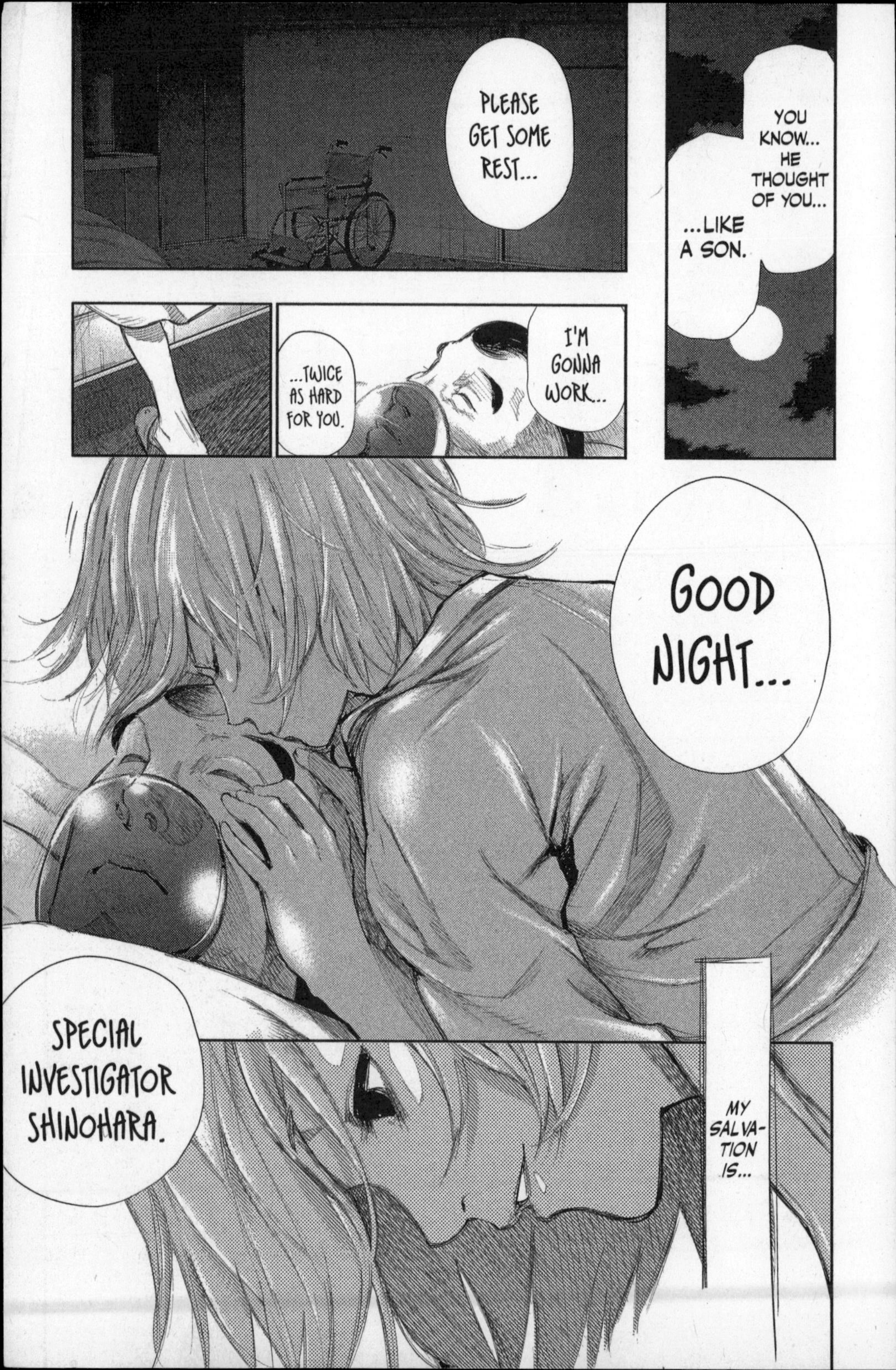

YOU KNOW... HE THOUGHT OF YOU...
...LIKE A SON.
PLEASE GET SOME REST...
I'M GONNA WORK...
...TWICE AS HARD FOR YOU.
GOOD NIGHT...
SPECIAL INVESTIGATOR SHINOHARA.
MY SALVA-TION IS...

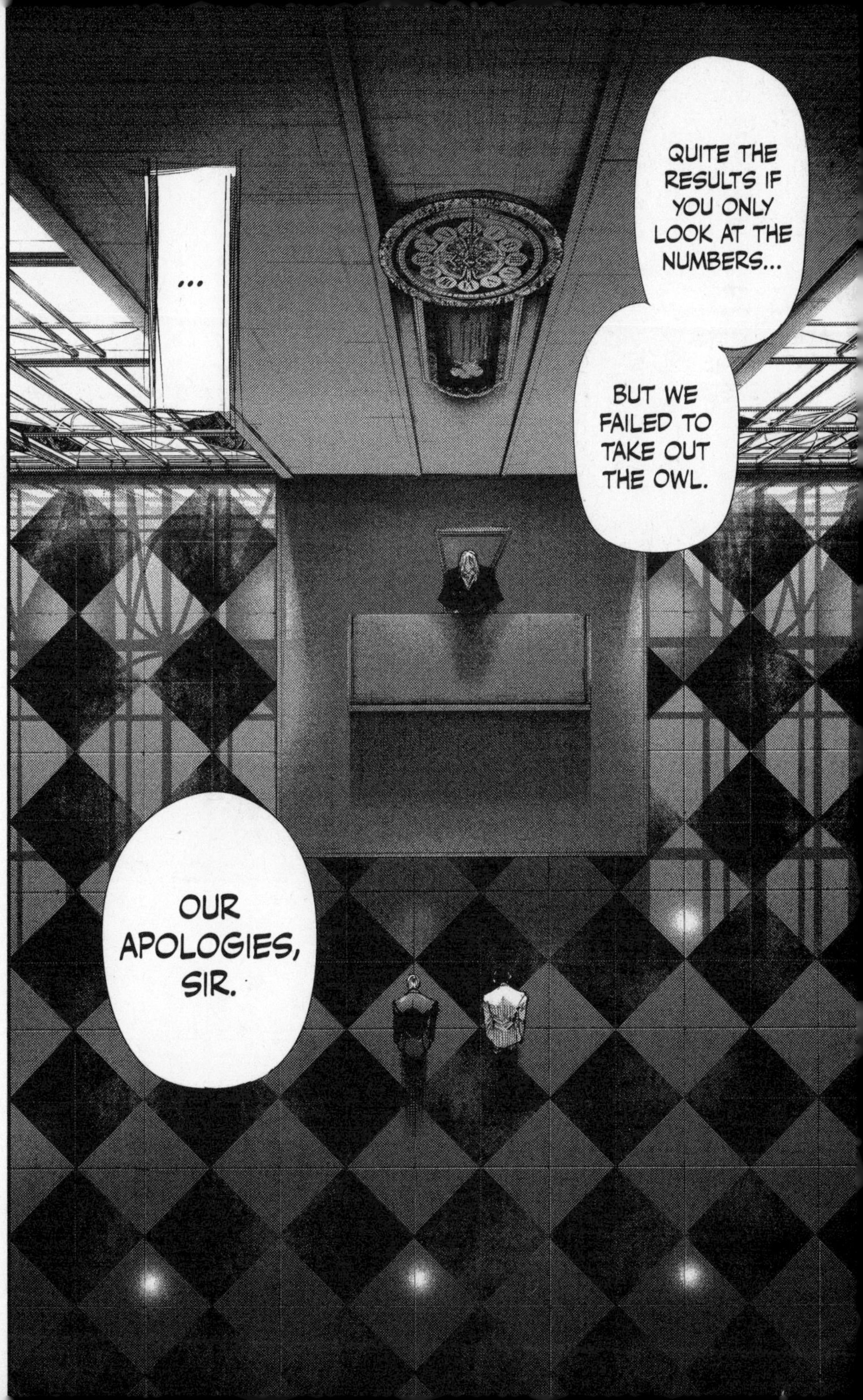
QUITE THE RESULTS IF YOU ONLY LOOK AT THE NUMBERS...
BUT WE FAILED TO TAKE OUT THE OWL.
...
OUR APOLOGIES, SIR.

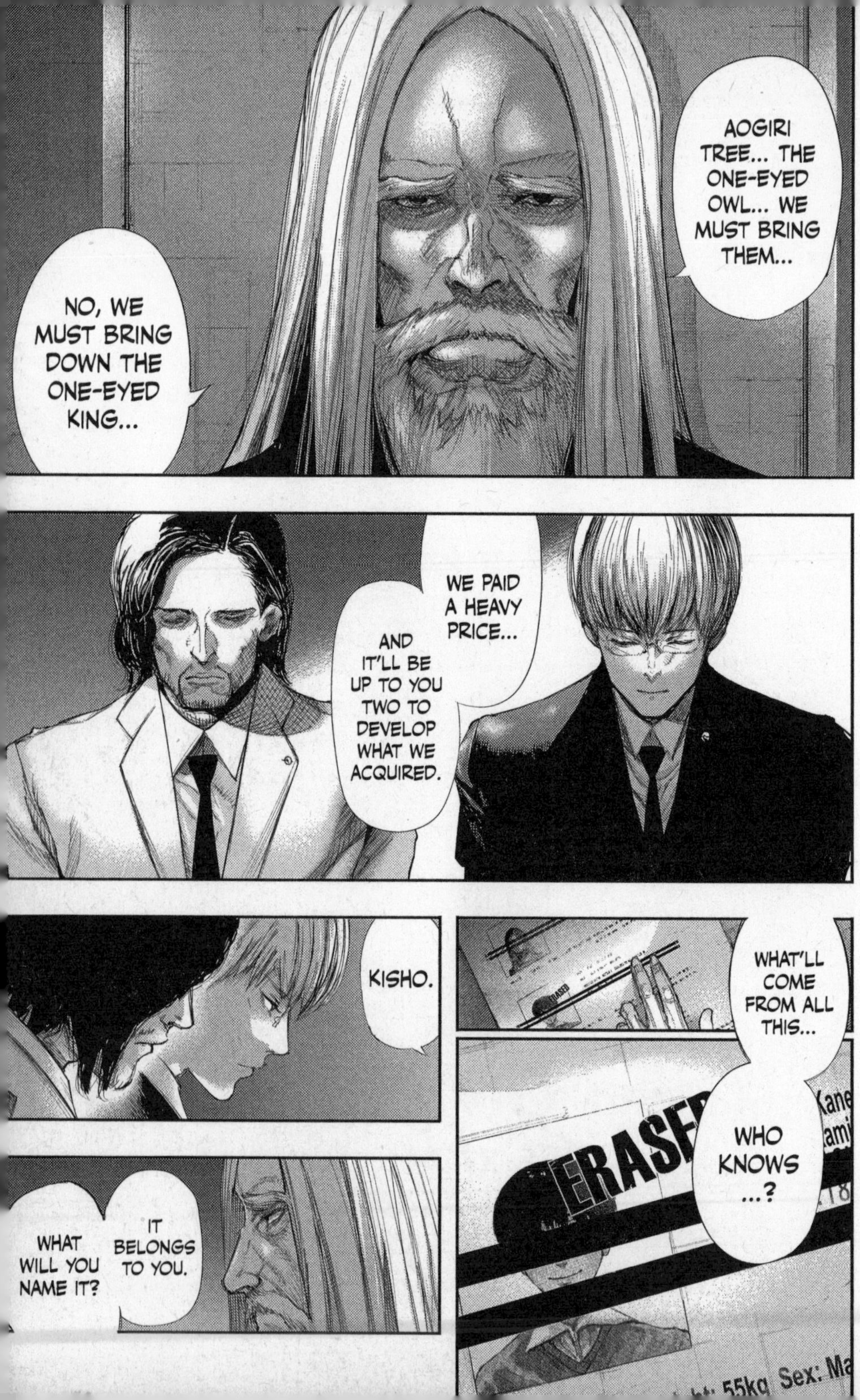
AOGIRI TREE... THE ONE-EYED OWL... WE MUST BRING THEM...
NO, WE MUST BRING DOWN THE ONE-EYED KING...
WE PAID A HEAVY PRICE...
AND IT'LL BE UP TO YOU TWO TO DEVELOP WHAT WE ACQUIRED.
WHAT'LL COME FROM ALL THIS...
WHO KNOWS ...?
KISHO.
IT BELONGS TO YOU.
WHAT WILL YOU NAME IT?

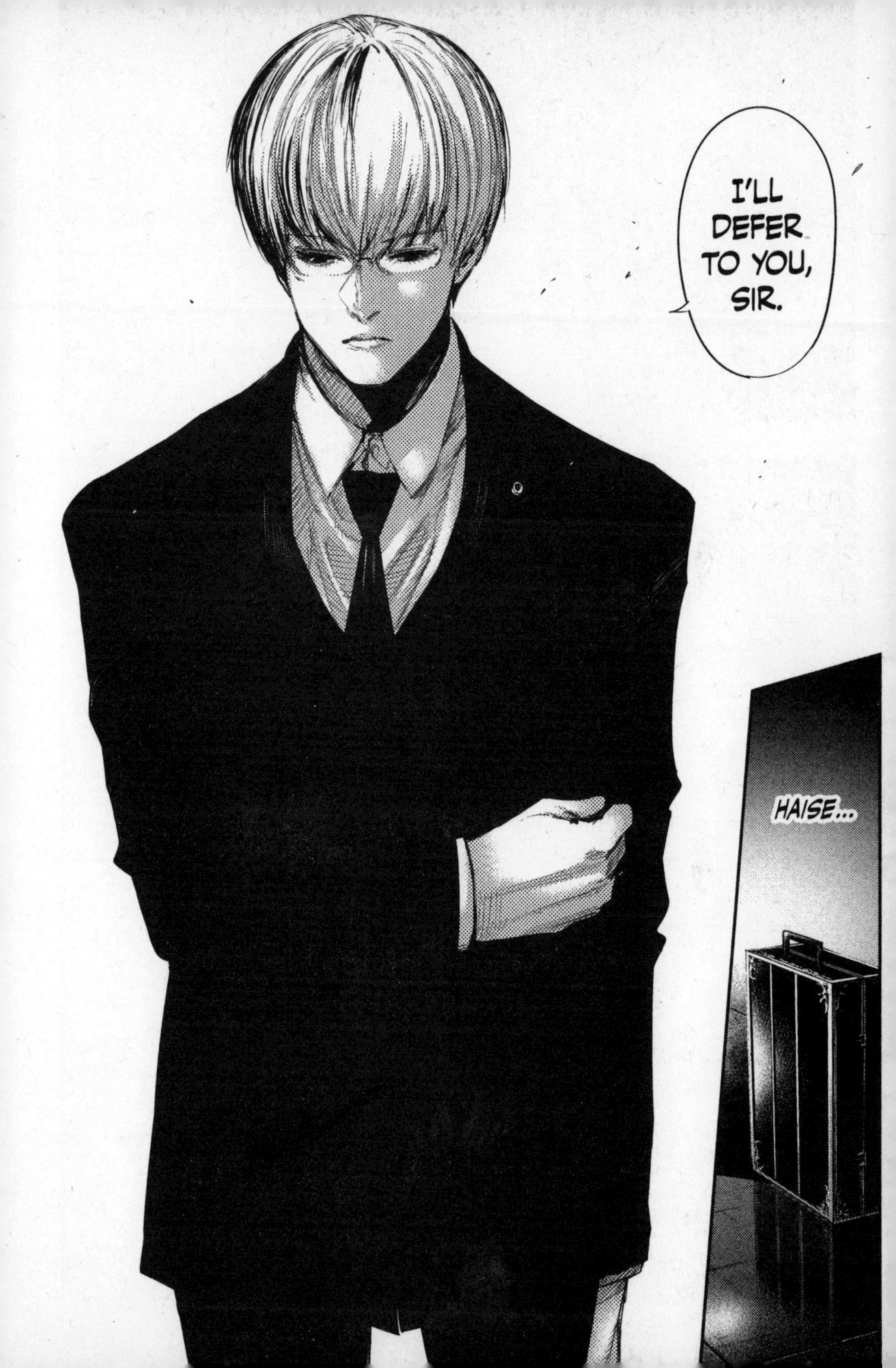
I'LL DEFER TO YOU, SIR.
HAISE...

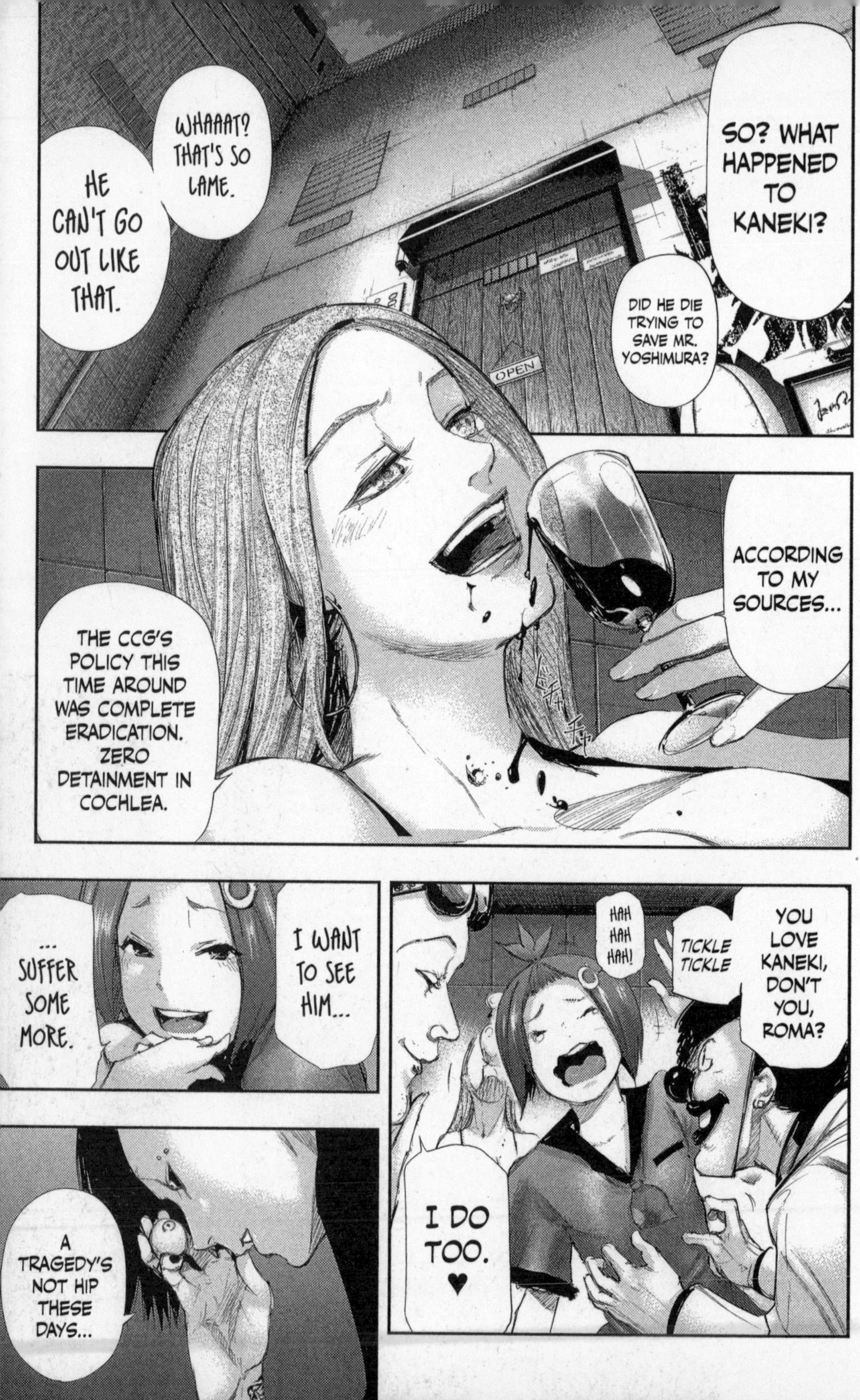
SO? WHAT HAPPENED TO KANEKI?
DID HE DIE TRYING TO SAVE MR. YOSHIMURA?
OPEN
WHAAAT? THAT'S SO LAME.
HE CAN'T GO OUT LIKE THAT.
ACCORDING TO MY SOURCES...
THE CCG'S POLICY THIS TIME AROUND WAS COMPLETE ERADICATION. ZERO DETAINMENT IN COCHLEA.
YOU LOVE KANEKI, DON'T YOU, ROMA?
TICKLE TICKLE
HAH HAH HAH!
I DO TOO. ♥
I WANT TO SEE HIM...
... SUFFER SOME MORE.
A TRAGEDY'S NOT HIP THESE DAYS...

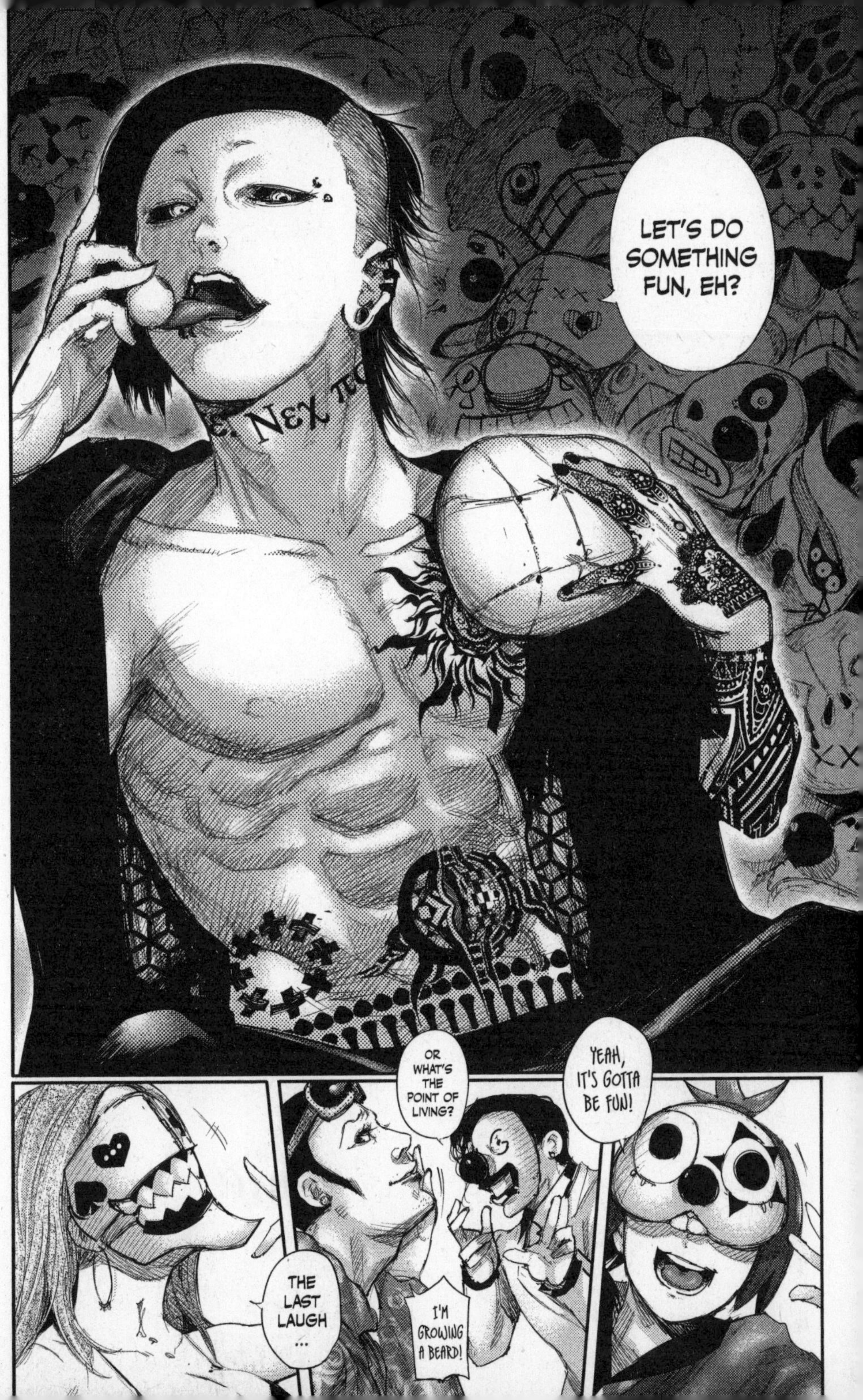
LET'S DO SOMETHING FUN, EH?
YEAH, IT'S GOTTA BE FUN!
OR WHAT'S THE POINT OF LIVING?
THE LAST LAUGH ...
I'M GROWING A BEARD!

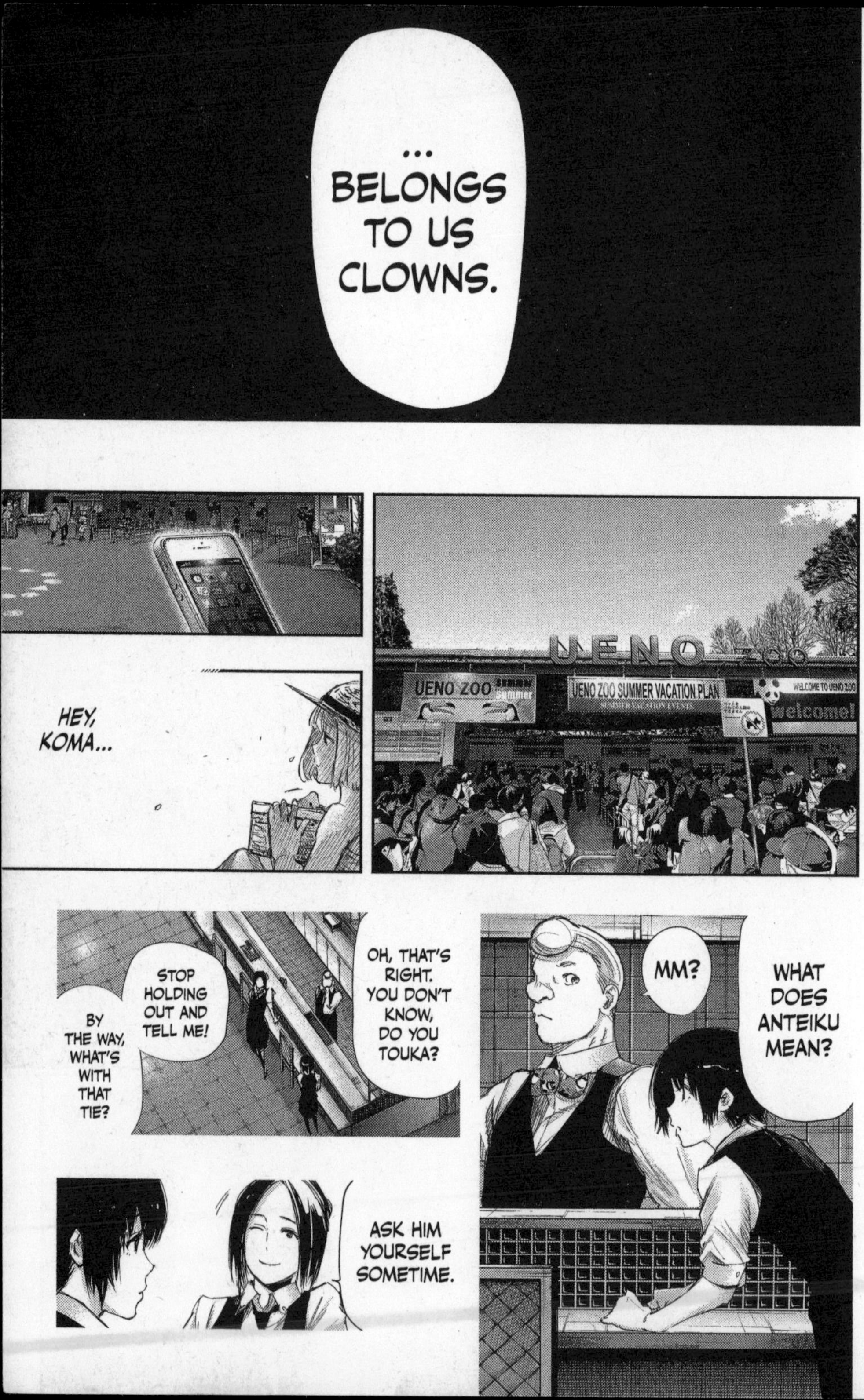
... BELONGS TO US CLOWNS.
UENO ZOO
UENO ZOO
UENO ZOO SUMMER VACATION PLAN
SUMMER VACATION EVENTS
WELCOME TO UENO ZOO
welcome!
HEY, KOMA...
WHAT DOES ANTEIKU MEAN?
MM?
OH, THAT'S RIGHT. YOU DON'T KNOW, DO YOU TOUKA?
STOP HOLDING OUT AND TELL ME!
BY THE WAY, WHAT'S WITH THAT TIE?
ASK HIM YOURSELF SOMETIME.

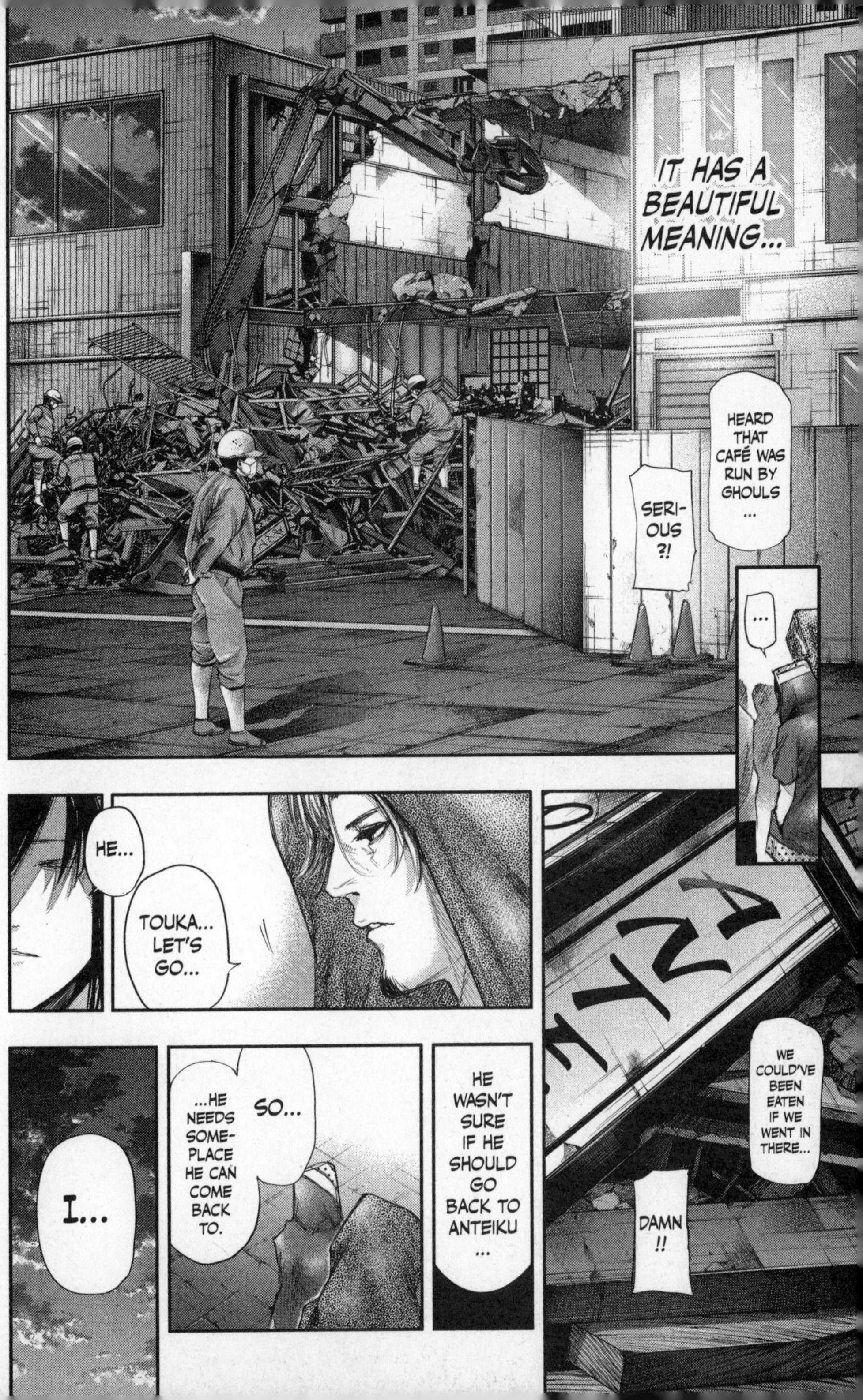
IT HAS A BEAUTIFUL MEANING...
HEARD THAT CAFÉ WAS RUN BY GHOULS...
SERIOUS?!
...
WE COULD'VE BEEN EATEN IF WE WENT IN THERE...
DAMN!!
TOUKA... LET'S GO...
HE...
HE WASN'T SURE IF HE SHOULD GO BACK TO ANTEIKU...
SO...
...HE NEEDS SOMEPLACE HE CAN COME BACK TO.
I...

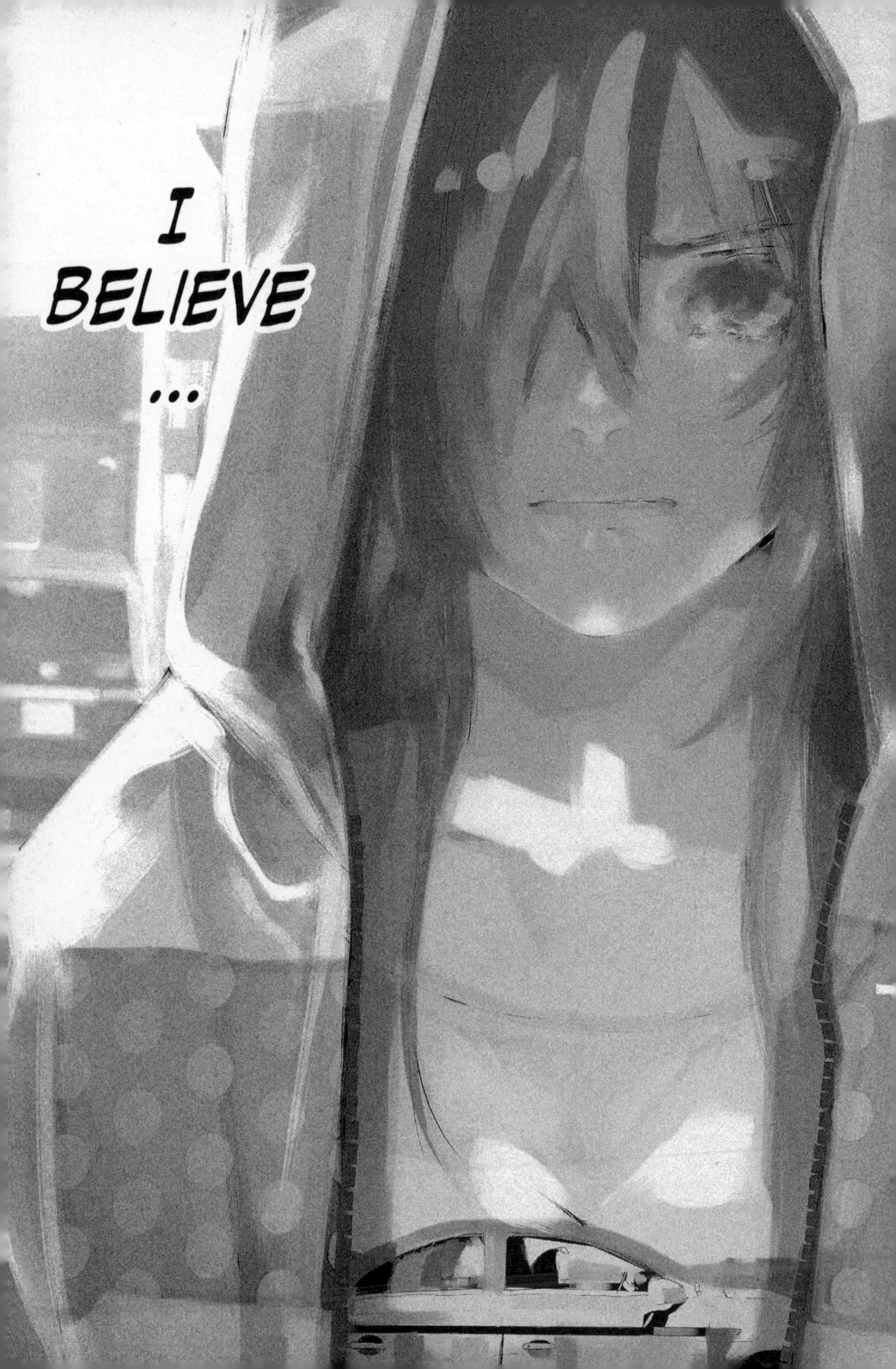
I BELIEVE ...

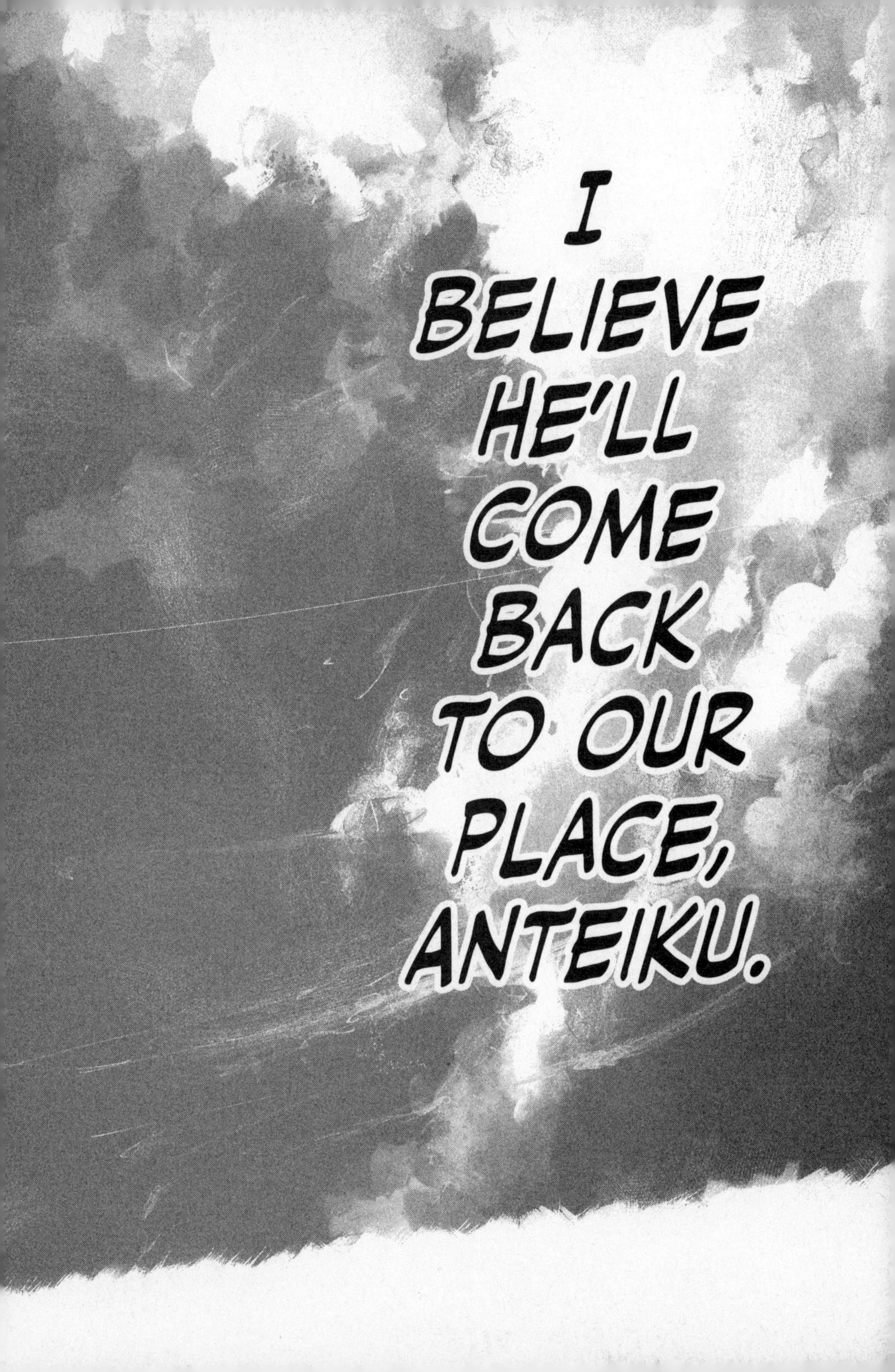
I BELIEVE HE'LL COME BACK TO OUR PLACE, ANTEIKU.

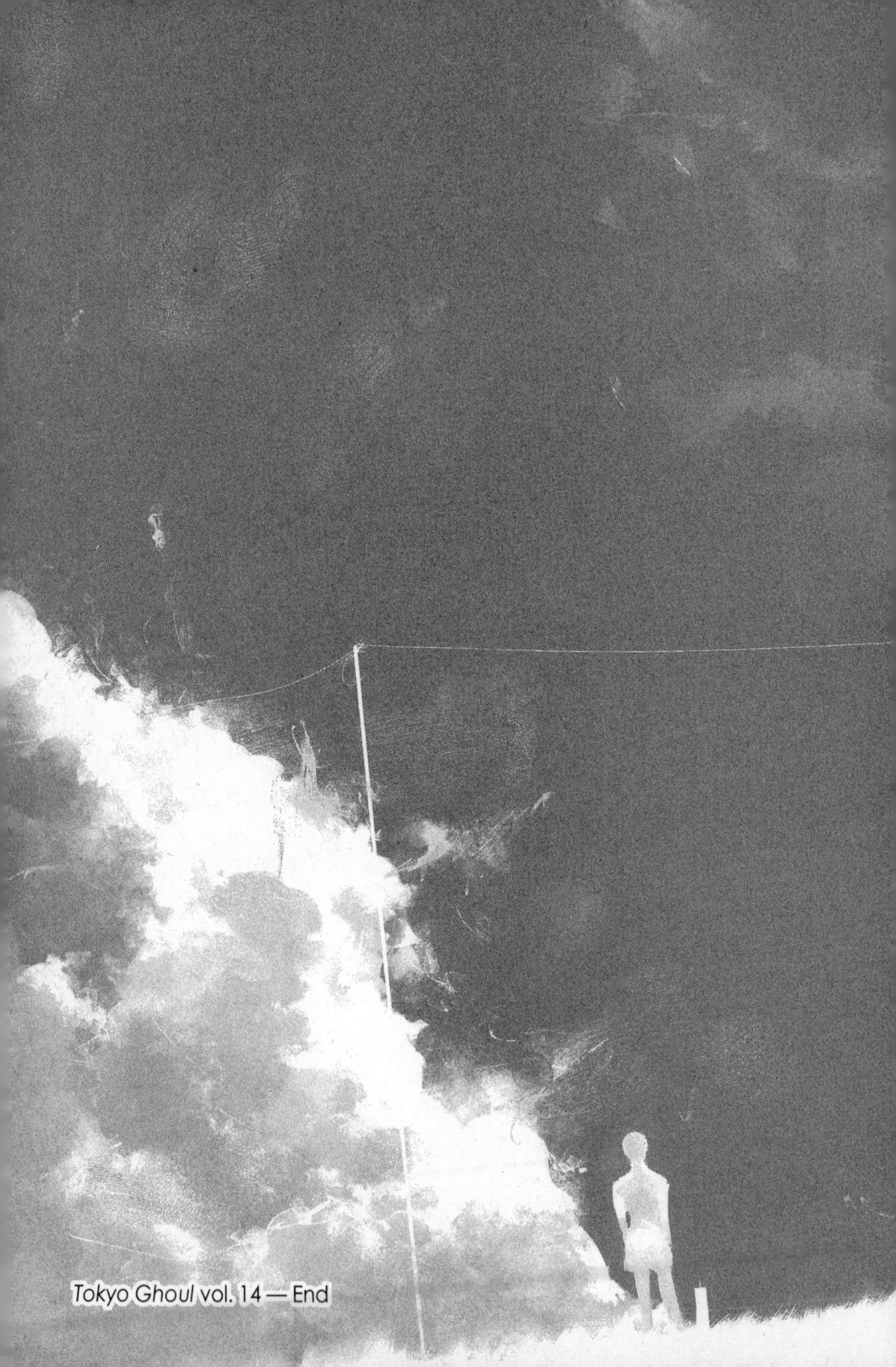
Tokyo Ghoul vol. 14 — End

Tokyo Ghoul

Sui
Ishida

Staff
Mizuki Ide
Matsuzaki
Kota Shugyo
Hashimoto
Haraguchi

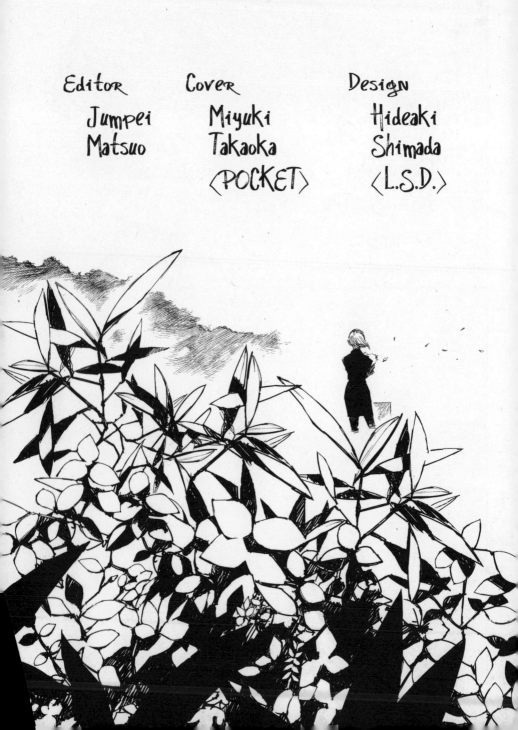

Editor
Jumpei Matsuo

Cover
Miyuki Takaoka
〈POCKET〉

Design
Hideaki Shimada
〈L.S.D.〉

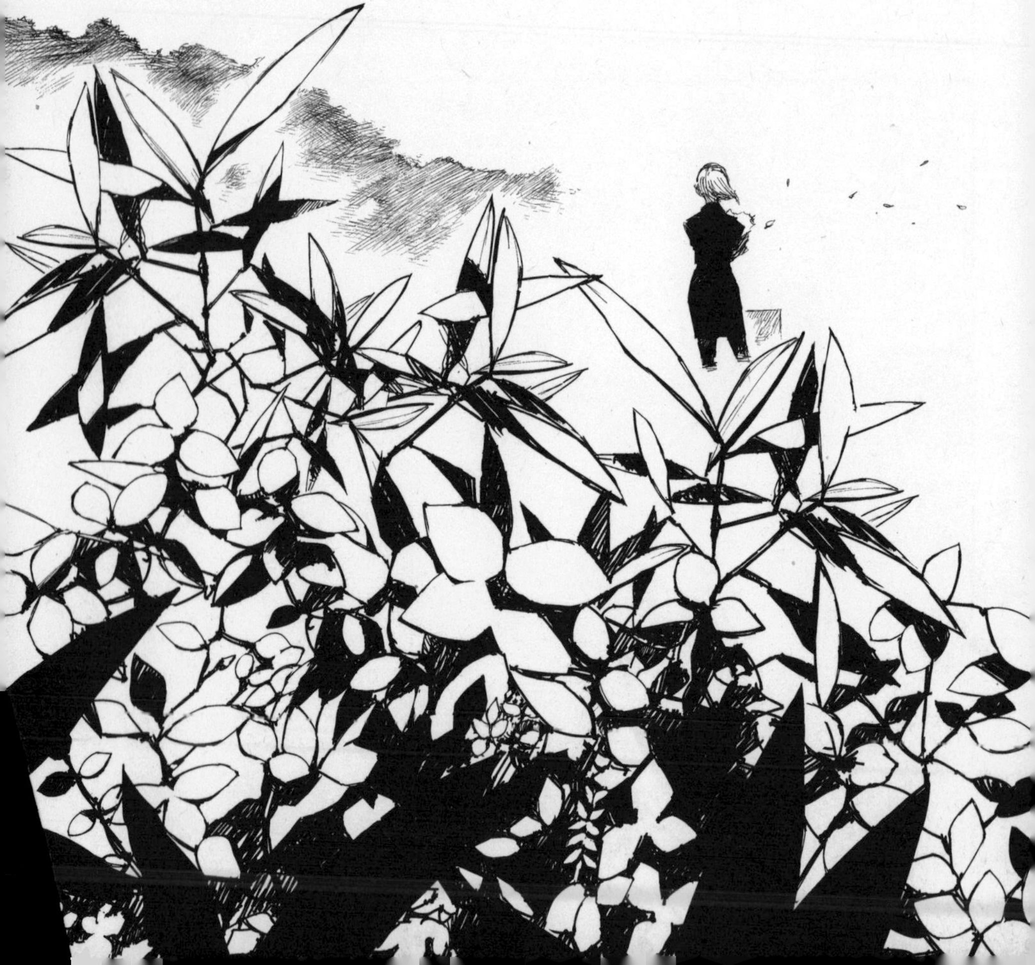

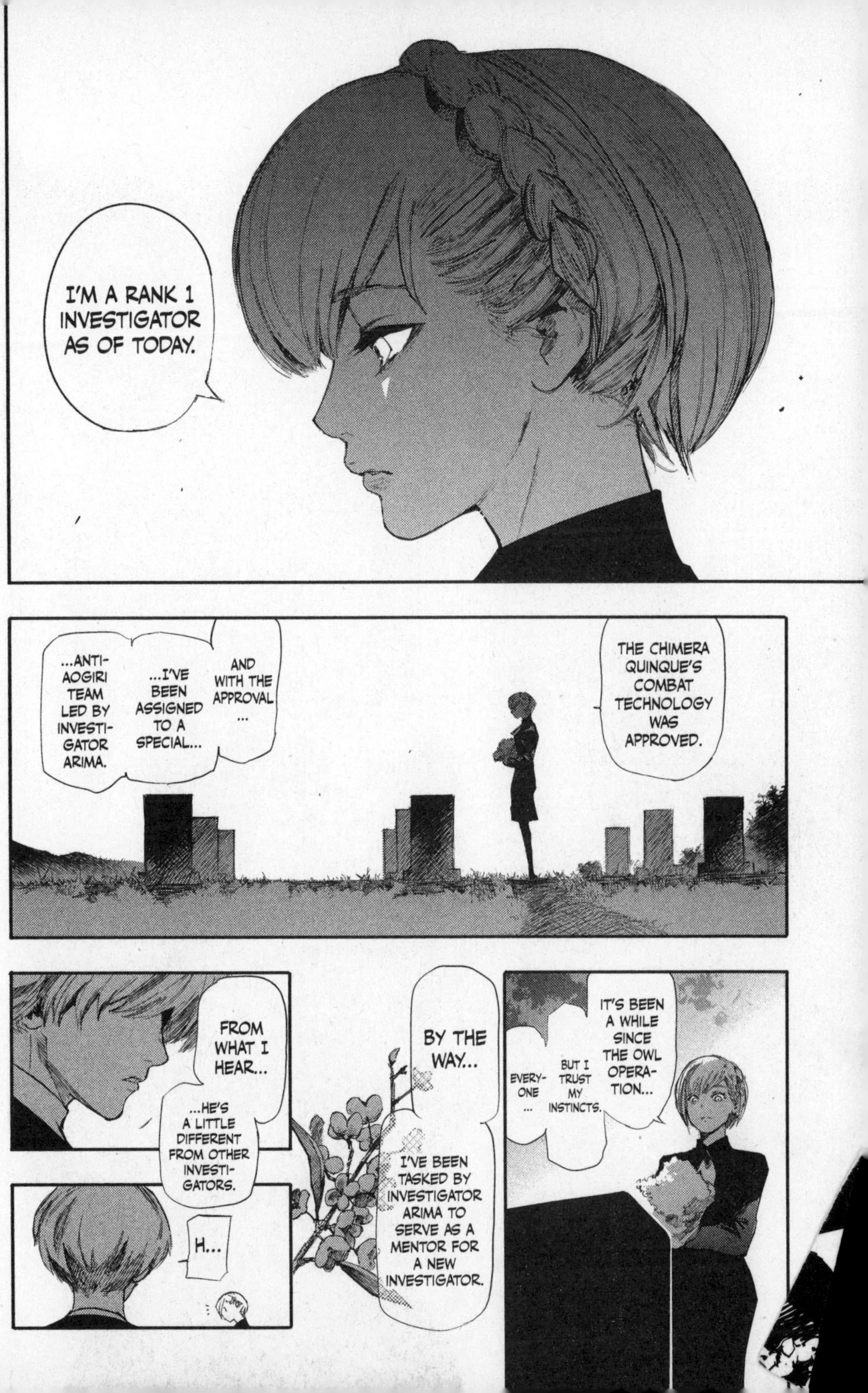
I'M A RANK 1 INVESTIGATOR AS OF TODAY.
THE CHIMERA QUINQUE'S COMBAT TECHNOLOGY WAS APPROVED.
AND WITH THE APPROVAL ...
...I'VE BEEN ASSIGNED TO A SPECIAL...
...ANTI-AOGIRI TEAM LED BY INVESTIGATOR ARIMA.
IT'S BEEN A WHILE SINCE THE OWL OPERATION...
BUT I TRUST MY INSTINCTS.
EVERYONE ...
BY THE WAY...
I'VE BEEN TASKED BY INVESTIGATOR ARIMA TO SERVE AS A MENTOR FOR A NEW INVESTIGATOR.
FROM WHAT I HEAR...
...HE'S A LITTLE DIFFERENT FROM OTHER INVESTIGATORS.
H...

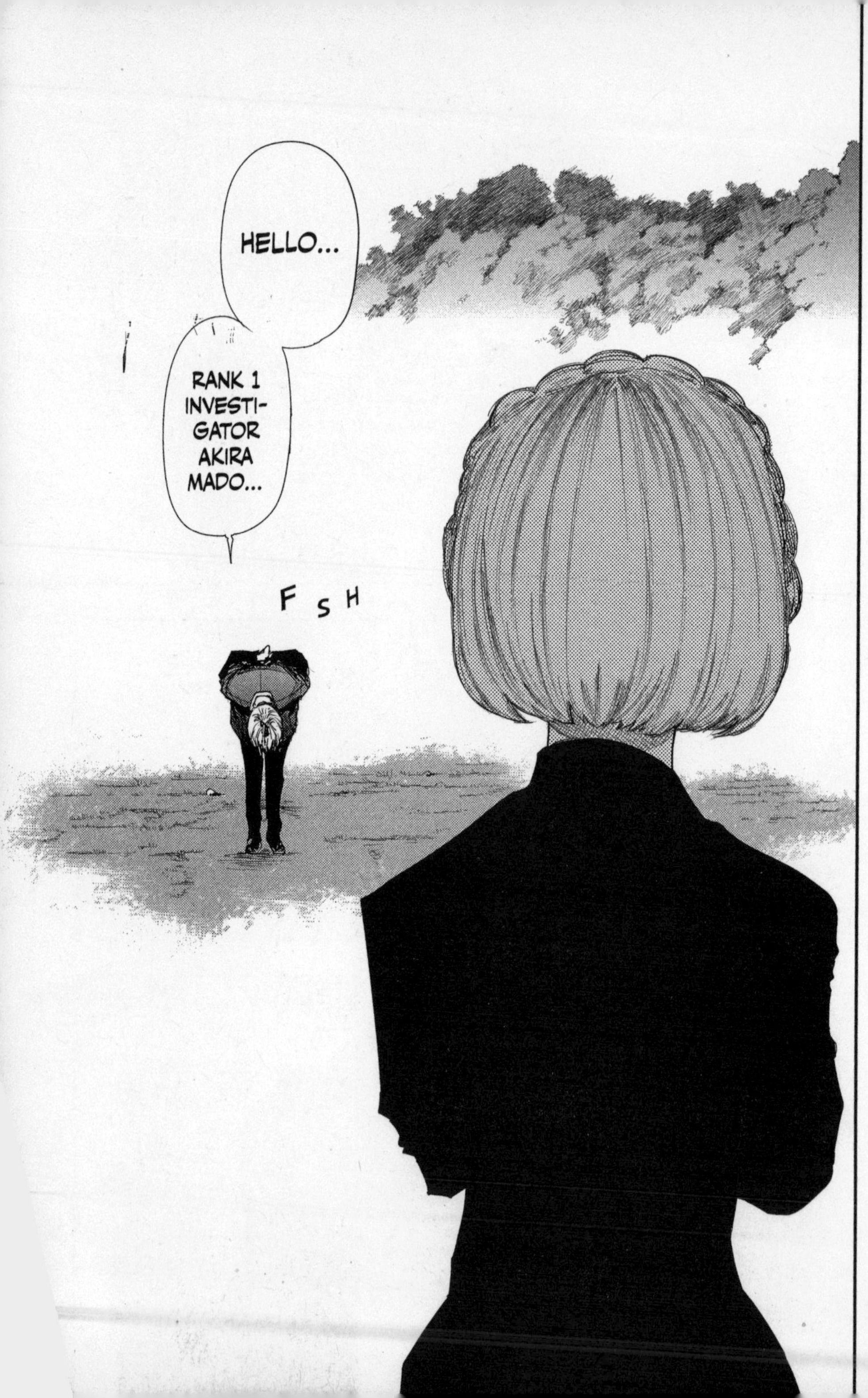
HELLO...
RANK 1 INVESTIGATOR AKIRA MADO...
FSH

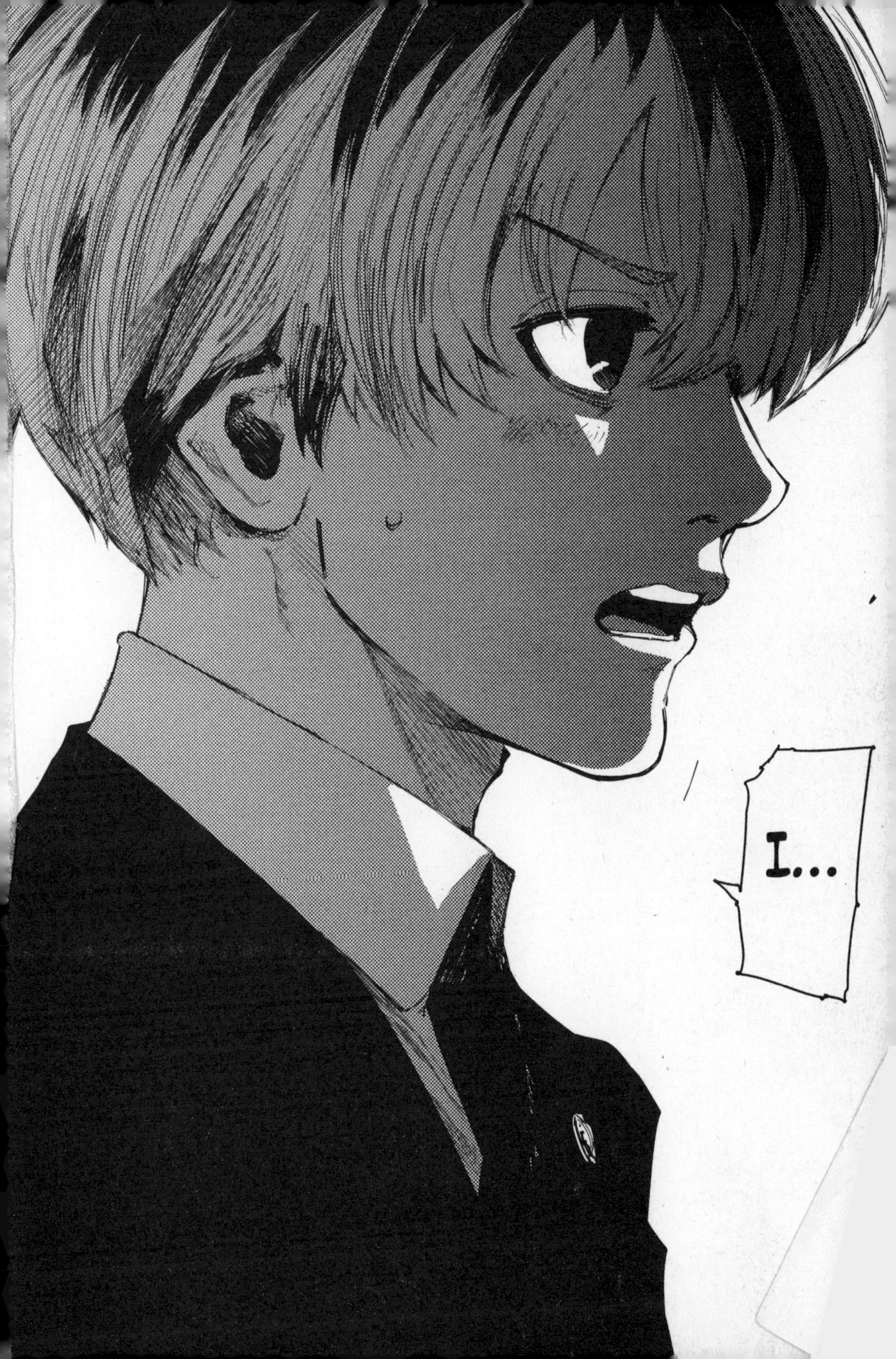
I...

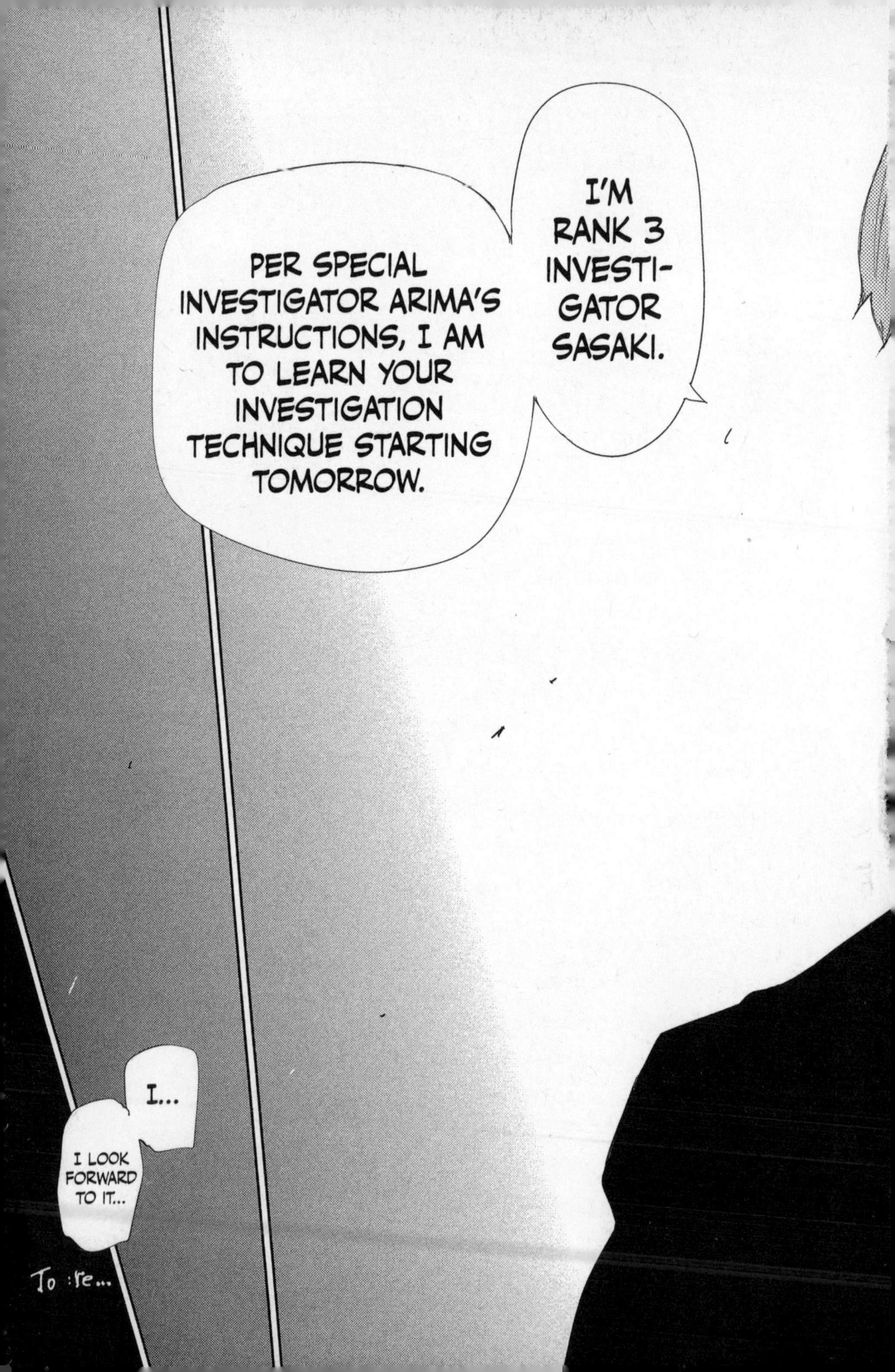
I'M RANK 3 INVESTIGATOR SASAKI.
PER SPECIAL INVESTIGATOR ARIMA'S INSTRUCTIONS, I AM TO LEARN YOUR INVESTIGATION TECHNIQUE STARTING TOMORROW.
I...
I LOOK FORWARD TO IT...
To :re...

TOKYO GHOUL
東 京 喰 種

VOLUME 14
VIZ Signature Edition

Story and art by
SUI ISHIDA

TOKYO GHOUL © 2011 by Sui Ishida
All rights reserved.
First published in Japan in 2011 by
SHUEISHA Inc., Tokyo.
English translation rights arranged by
SHUEISHA Inc.

TRANSLATION. Joe Yamazaki

TOUCH-UP ART AND LETTERING. Vanessa Satone

DESIGN. Shawn Carrico

EDITOR. Joel Enos

Printed in the U.S.A.

Published by VIZ Media, LLC
P.O. Box 77010
San Francisco, CA 94107

10 9 8 7 6 5 4 3 2 1
First printing, August 2017

VIZ
media
www.viz.com

VIZ SIGNATURE